RS   16 Dec. 1991

W9-BCQ-560

Aristotle, *On Rhetoric*

ARISTOTLE
ON RHETORIC
A Theory of Civic Discourse

Newly translated with Introduction,
Notes, and Appendixes by

GEORGE A. KENNEDY

New York   Oxford
OXFORD UNIVERSITY PRESS
1991

Oxford University Press

Oxford   New York   Toronto
Delhi   Bombay   Calcutta   Madras   Karachi
Petaling Jaya   Singapore   Hong Kong   Tokyo
Nairobi   Dar es Salaam   Cape Town
Melbourne   Auckland

and associated companies in
Berlin   Ibadan

Copyright © 1991 by George A. Kennedy

Published by Oxford University Press, Inc.,
200 Madison Avenue, New York, New York 10016

Oxford is a registered trademark of Oxford University Press

All rights reserved. No part of this publication may be reproduced,
stored in a retrieval system, or transmitted, in any form or by any means,
electronic, mechanical, photocopying, recording, or otherwise,
without the prior permission of Oxford University Press.

Library of Congress Cataloging-in-Publication Data
Aristotle.
[Rhetoric. English]
On rhetoric : a theory of civic discourse /
newly translated, with introduction, notes,
and appendices by George A. Kennedy.
p. cm.
Includes bibliographical references and index.
ISBN 0-19-506486-0
ISBN 0-19-506487-9 (pbk.)
1. Rhetoric, Ancient. 2. Aristotle. Rhetoric.
I. Kennedy, George Alexander, 1928–
II. Title. PN173.A7K46 1991 808.5—
dc20   90-20342

2 4 6 8 9 7 5 3 1

Printed in the United States of America
on acid-free paper

To My Grandson,
Alexander Kennedy Morton,
the Original Rhetoric *for a Later Alexander*

Prooemion

The study of rhetoric began in Greece in the fifth century B.C. Democratic government was emerging in Athens and some other cities, based on the assumption that all citizens had an equal right and duty to participate in their own government. To do so effectively, they needed to be able to speak in public. Decisions on public policy under the democracies were made in regularly held assemblies composed of adult male citizens; and, as in New England town meetings, anyone who wished could speak. Not surprisingly, however, the leadership role in debate was played by a small number of ambitious individuals called *rhētores,* who sought to channel the course of events in a direction that they thought was best for the city or for themselves. There were no professional lawyers in Greece; if people wished to seek redress in the courts for some wrong done them—and the Greeks were very fond of going to law—or if people were summoned to court as defendents, they were expected to speak on their own behalf. There were other occasions for public address in connection with public holidays or funerals, as well as more informal discussions at symposia or private meetings.

In modern society, the ability to communicate effectively is at least as important as it was in ancient Greece; and through television and radio a speaker can reach a much larger audience than was possible in the past. Many of us do not aspire to a public career and may never make a speech to a large audience; but almost all of us feel a regular need to persuade someone of something, to defend our actions, and to organize our thoughts so that others will understand our point of view. To do this, we speak personally to individuals or small groups or we write reports or letters. Furthermore, to a greater extent than in the past, we are constantly being addressed by others—politicians, salespeople, preachers, or teachers—and we need to understand the techniques they are using if we are correctly to judge the importance or validity of what they say. Not surprisingly, the study of rhetoric has enjoyed increased popularity in the second half of the twentieth century. With it has arisen a renewed interest in Aristotle's *Rhetoric* as the source of our basic understanding of communication skills.

Today, as in Greece, some people seem to have a natural gift for communication. Others can develop these skills by coming to understand the principles of speech and composition, by observing the method of successful speakers and writers, and by practice. To meet the needs of students in Greece, teachers called "sophists" emerged who took students for pay and taught them how to be effective in public life by marshaling arguments, dividing speeches into logical parts, and carefully choosing and combining words. In the history of rhetoric the most important of these teachers was a man named Gorgias, who came from Sicily to Athens in 427 B.C. and made a great impression on his audiences by his poetic style and paradoxical arguments. Some lesser figures began to publish short handbooks on the *Art of Speech,* concerned primarily with showing how to organize a speech in the law courts in a clear and orderly way, arouse the emotions of an audience, and argue on the basis of the probability of what people might be expected to have done in a given situation. Socrates and his student Plato distrusted the teaching of both the sophists and the handbook writers, and Plato's dialogue *Gorgias* is the earliest example of an attack on rhetoric as essentially a form of flattery—morally irresponsible and not based on knowledge of the truth.

The debate over the role of rhetoric in society has existed ever since; and there are still today people to whom the word *rhetoric* means empty words, misleading arguments, and appeal to base emotions. There are dangers in rhetoric (e.g., political extremism, racism, and unscrupulous sales techniques) but by studying rhetoric we can become alert to its potential for misuse and learn to recognize when a speaker is seeking to manipulate us. There is great positive power in rhetoric, as well, which we can use for valid ends. It was by persuasive preaching—and thus by rhetoric—that Saint Paul, the other apostles, and their successors brought Christianity to the world; and it was by rhetoric that the Founding Fathers organized public opinion in the cause of American independence. Rhetoric also has helped black leaders, women, and minority groups begin to secure their rights in society.

Aristotle was the first person to recognize clearly that rhetoric as an art of communication was morally neutral, that it could be used either for good or ill. Its persuasion, he says, depends on three things: the truth and logical validity of what is being argued; the speaker's success in conveying to the audience the perception that he or she can be trusted; and the emotions that a speaker is able to awaken in an audience to accept the views advanced and act in accordance with them. Modern rhetoricians use terms derived from Aristotle to refer to these three means of persuasion, though they have somewhat broadened his definitions, as the notes to the translation will indicate: logical argument is called *logos;* the projection of the speaker's character is called *ēthos;* awakening the emotions of the audience is called *pathos.*

Aristotle wrote his treatis *On Rhetoric* in the middle of the fourth century B.C., but it has been more studied in modern times than it ever was in antiquity or the Middle Ages. Most teachers of composition, communication, and speech regard it as seminal work that organizes its subject into essential parts, provides insight into the bases of speech acts, creates categories and terminology for discussing discourse, and illustrates and applies its teachings so that they can be used in society. Although Aristotle largely limits the province of rhetoric to public address, he takes a broader view of what that entails than do most modern writers on communication. This often surprises and interests readers today. He addresses issues of philosophy, government, history, ethics, and literature; and in book 2 he includes a comprehensive account of human psychology. In Aristotle's view, speakers need to understand how the minds of their listeners work, and in the process we come to understand something of who we are and why we do what we do. The German philosopher Martin Heidegger has called the second book of the *Rhetoric* "the first systematic hermeneutic of the every-dayness of being with one another."[1]

Modern theorists frequently refer to the *Rhetoric* as a source

---

1. Heidegger 1962, 178.

for ideas about communication and as the basis for rhetorical analysis or criticism of speeches and discursive writing. It also has some application to the analysis of literature and regularly draws examples from poetry and drama. There are, of course, other ways of approaching rhetoric today, some of them consciously anti-Aristotelian; but the distinctive contribution of these other approaches can often be better understood when compared with Aristotle's. Among major modern theorists of rhetoric, Chaim Perelman is perhaps the one most indebted to the ancient Greek philosopher. Like Aristotle, Perelman regarded argumentation as the most important element in rhetoric. He remarks, "It is sufficient to cite the *Rhetoric* of Aristotle to show that our way of looking at rhetoric can take pride in illustrious examples."[2] A widely read book by Stephen Toulmin, *Uses of Argument*[3] is also strongly Aristotelian. Kenneth Burke's very different approach to rhetoric reorganizes the subject. But he probably could not have written his books had not Aristotle gone first; and understanding Burke often requires an understanding of Aristotle, to whom he frequently refers. Many textbooks, such as Edward P. J. Corbett's rhetoric for modern students of English composition, base their theories squarely on Aristotle. As Corbett remarks, "With his philosophic treatise, Aristotle became the fountainhead of all later rhetorical theory." And he continues with a quotation from Lane Cooper, one of the founders of the modern study of rhetoric: "The rhetoric not only of Cicero and Quintilian, but of the Middle Ages, of the Renaissance, and of modern times, is, in its best elements, essentially Aristotelian."[4] Even Edwin Black's well-known attack on neo-Aristotelian criticism[5] is not so much an attack on Aristotle as a demonstration that modern critics have failed to understand him.

One reason may be the unsatisfactory editions from which they have worked. The *Rhetoric* is a difficult work, and modern readers need considerable help in reading it. Difficulties result sometimes from uncertainty about what Aristotle wrote, since we are depen-

2. Perelman and Olbrechts-Tyteca 1969, 6.
3. Toulmin 1958.
4. Corbett 1990, 543–44.
5. *Rhetorical Criticism* (New York: Macmillan, 1965).

dent for the text on handwritten copies made in the Middle Ages, which do not always agree. More often the difficulty comes from Aristotle's style, which is compressed in the extreme: words, thoughts, or transitions need to be supplied to make the argument clear. Another problem results from the fact that he wrote different parts of the work at different times and his ideas or point of view changed as he taught different groups of students. Although he completed some revisions to bring parts of the work written earlier into agreement, there remain inconsistencies in what he says and in the terms he uses. There is thus present in the text as a whole a kind of dialogue in Aristotle's mind between two views of rhetoric, one making strong moral and logical demands on a speaker, one looking more toward success in debate. This can be confusing to a reader, but exploring the issues also can be a positive feature of studying Aristotle. The differing views found in the text, especially when taken in conjunction with Plato's criticism or Isocrates' celebration of rhetoric, can provide a good starting point for discussions by modern students about the nature and functions of rhetoric in society.

This new translation attempts both to convey something of Aristotle's distinctively compressed style and his thinking and to render the work more accessible to modern readers by introductory comments, supplemental phrases in the text, and notes. Our understanding of Aristotle has significantly increased in recent years through scholars' textual and interpretative studies, and this version tries to take advantage of the best of this work. Until now, there have been only three English translations of Aristotle's *Rhetoric* readily available to students and general readers, each often reprinted; they were published by W. Rhys Roberts (1924), Lane Cooper (1932), and J. H. Freese (1926). All three were made at a time when the subject of rhetoric was distrusted in academic circles and readers were unfamiliar with its technical vocabulary. The translators thus sometimes paraphrased or avoided technicalities to make the text more acceptable. But in our generation one reason for reading Aristotle is to understand his technical language. I have kept this and offered explanations of it. At times the earlier translators worked from what is now regarded as a faulty version of the Greek original; at times they do not seem to have understood what Aristotle is saying. Though they provide some introductory material or notes (Cooper especially), these are often inadequate to enable the average reader to understand the text; and of course, they could not take advantage of the scholarship of the last sixty years. I have tried to meet these needs.

Since no single version of the Greek text is entirely satisfactory, I have worked from those of Kassel (1976), Dufour and Wartelle (1960–73), and Ross (1950) but have also adopted some textual suggestions made by Grimaldi in his commentary (1980–88) on books 1 and 2 and by others in recent articles. Many textual variants are not significant for the thought; those that seem so are identified in the notes. At book 1, chapter 13, section 2 (1.13.2) I have ventured one conjectural emendation of my own.

Two features of my translation may be worth pointing out in advance. A major doctrine of the *Rhetoric* is the use of the enthymeme, or rhetorical syllogism. In Aristotle's own writing enthymemes often take the form of a statement followed by a clause introduced by the Greek particle *gar,* which gives a supporting reason or sometimes a corollary. These occur on every page but are often obscured by other translators. I have kept them, using a semicolon and the English particle *for* as a way of drawing them to the attention of the reader and making the device familiar. A second feature is avoidance of some of the sexist language seen in older translations, which often speak of "men" when Aristotle uses a more general plural. I have used *man* or *men* only in those few instances in which the word appears in the Greek; otherwise I use *someone, people,* or *they.* On the other hand, to alter Aristotle's many uses of *he, his,* or *him* in reference to speakers or members of a Greek assembly or jury would be unhistorical and involve an actual change in the text. Aristotle usually envisions only males as speaking in public; but he clearly did not think that rhetoric was a phenomenon limited to males, for he draws examples of rhetoric from Sappho (a woman poet in the early sixth century), from a few other women, and from female characters in epic and drama. In 1.5.6 he remarks that "happiness" is only half present in states where the condition of women is poor.[6]

---

6. Greek nouns have grammatical gender and as a result of the conventions of Greek word formation, most rhetorical terms in Greek are feminine, as the Glossary at the end of this volume reveals. It is not clear, however, whether the ancient Greeks were conscious of rhetoric as operating in feminine space.

In preparing this translation, I am indebted to the students with whom I have read the *Rhetoric* over many years and to several scholars who have given me advice—although I have not always followed it. I particularly want to thank Thomas Conley, William Fortenbaugh, Michael Leff, Erika Lindemann, Eckhardt Schütrumpf, Jacob Wisse, and David Mirhady (the latter for important contributions to understanding 1.15). It should be clear from the notes that I am also deeply indebted to Grimaldi's fine commentary, even though I differ from his conclusions repeatedly. Through the kindness of David Furley I was able to participate in an international Symposium Aristotelicum held at Princeton University in August 1990, which was devoted to a consideration of the *Rhetoric*. From this experience I derived a number of insights into the text. For their good work in seeing the book through various stages to publication at Oxford University Press, I want to thank Rachel Toor, Henry Krawitz, and Michael Lane.

Chapel Hill, N.C. G.A.K.
August 1990

Contents

Appendix II: Supplementary Essays

Aristotle, *On Rhetoric*

Introduction

A. ARISTOTLE'S LIFE AND WORKS

Aristotle tells us almost nothing about the events of his life, though he reveals his mind and values fully, especially in *Nicomachean Ethics*. What we know (or think probable) about the sequence of his activities and relationships with others derives from later sources, including a biography and list of works in *Lives of the Philosophers* by Diogenes Laertius, probably written in the third century C.E. The most important facts that contribute to an understanding of Aristotle's writings are his close ties with the kings of Macedon and his association with Plato as a student and colleague for twenty years.[1]

Aristotle was born in Stagiros (later called Stagira) in Northern Greece in 384 B.C. This was a thoroughly Greek city but near the Macedonian kingdom, which was then only partially Hellenized. Aristotle's father was a friend of, and personal physician to, the king of Macedon. Aristotle probably spent some of his youth in Macedon; and he continued to have ties with the court, culminating in his being given responsibility for directing the education of the young prince who became Alexander the Great. His Macedonian connections rendered him somewhat suspect to Athenians in later life. Aristotle's education probably included the usual study of language, poetry, music, and geometry, as well as athletic training in the gymnasium. Doubtless he learned something about medicine from his father, and this may have been the source of his

1. For further information see Düring 1957 and Rist 1989.

unusual interest in biology and his inclination to see change in terms of organic development.

In 367 B.C., at age seventeen, Aristotle went to Athens to become a student in Plato's Academy, a clear sign of an early, serious interest in philosophy. He retained throughout his life personal affection for Plato and learned much from him. But his instinctive feeling for philosophy was far more pragmatic than Plato's; and whatever his initial attitude, he eventually rejected fundamental Platonic concepts, such as the reality of transcendent ideas. In particular, the Forms of the Good, the Beautiful, and the True—which Plato accorded the status of the only absolute reality—were to Aristotle not independent entities but abstractions created by the human mind.[2] From an early time Aristotle seems to have been interested in logic, very likely with Plato's encouragement; and he is the inventor of formal logic, set forth in detail in a series of treatises known as the *Organon*. His interest in political theory clearly developed out of Plato's work but again was more pragmatic, based on a study of existing constitutions in their historical development and defining the checks and balances that might create stability in a mixed constitution rather than in imagining an ideal state, as Plato did in the *Republic* and *Laws*. Though conventionally pious, Aristotle preferred to live in the real world; his theory of ethics is not based on religious belief or reward and punishment in the afterlife (as is Plato's) but on how to achieve happiness in a secular society by rational control of the emotions. Rhetoric came to interest him as a practical aspect of society, an interest probably sharpened by seeing political rhetoric in action in Athens, as well as by debates about it in Plato's Academy.

The writings of Aristotle that survive in complete form, transmitted through manuscripts copied in the Middle Ages, are treatises—systematic expositions of subjects on which he probably lectured at different times during his career. They were not published (i.e., copied by scribes and sold in bookstores) but were available in his own library for study by others. They are therefore known as his "esoteric" works. This status is the explanation for their highly compressed style.

Aristotle also published some works, mostly in the form of

2. See esp. his discussion in *Nicomachean Ethics* 1.6.

dialogues, especially during the early phase of his career, when he was associated with Plato. These were read in antiquity and admired for their style as well as their contents. They did not survive the devastations of late antiquity; and we know them today only from quotations, abstracts, and allusions by others. The dialogues included *On the Poets,* which probably anticipated some of the ideas found in the *Poetics,* and a dialogue on rhetoric, entitled *Gryllus. Gryllus* was named in memory of the son of the historian Xenophon (d. 362 B.C.) and was probably published within the next two or three years. According to the Roman rhetorician Quintilian (2.17.14), it contained an argument that rhetoric is not an "art." This seems reminiscent of Plato's *Gorgias;* but since the work was in dialogue form, it is apt to have argued both sides of the question and thus may have anticipated some of the ideas in the *Rhetoric.*[3]

Sometime in the 350s, while still a member of the Academy, Aristotle is said by later sources to have begun to offer a course on rhetoric.[4] Our information is not entirely reliable; but the course seems to have been open to the general public—offered in the afternoons as a kind of extension division of the Academy and accompanied by practical exercises in speaking. Our sources say that one reason for offering the course was a desire to counteract the influence of Isocrates, who was teaching his own form of sophistic rhetoric (with little emphasis on logical argument) to large numbers of students from Athens and abroad. Isocrates' defense of his teachings in the *Antidosis* dates from about this same time and may possibly represent, at least in part, his own response to Aristotle. Some parts of the *Rhetoric* (esp. 1.5–15 and parts of book 3) were probably written at this time and were only slightly revised later. The reasons for believing that these chapters date from an early period include the presence of some philosophical views known to have been discussed in the Academy but inconsistent with those Aristotle held later, the absence of cross-references (except for a few that could have been added later) to other treatises of Aristotle, and numerous historical references to events and people of the 350s. Perhaps in preparing to teach rhetoric, Aristotle com-

---

3. See Lossau 1974.
4. For the sources see Appendix II.A.

piled a survey of the rhetorical doctrines found in handbooks of the fifth and fourth centuries.[5]

In 347 B.C., in anticipation of or soon after the death of Plato, Aristotle left Athens and went first to Assos in Asia Minor and then to the island of Lesbos, where he did much of his biological research and where his most famous student, Theophrastus, joined him. In 343 or 342 King Philip persuaded him to come to Macedon as tutor to Alexander, then about thirteen years old. Aristotle probably offered him instruction in logic, literature, rhetoric, political theory, and ethics. A letter from Isocrates to Alexander that was enclosed in a letter to Philip praises Alexander for studying rhetoric but seems to imply criticism of the approach used by Aristotle.[6]

Aristotle's work with Alexander ended about 340 B.C. From 340 until 335 he was probably living in Macedon or Stagiros and continuing his studies with a few private students of philosophy. He apparently worked on the *Politics* and substantially completed the *Rhetoric,* which contains references to historical events of this time but not to later ones.[7] In 338 Philip defeated Athens and the other Greek city states at the Battle of Chaeronea, ending their political significance in the ancient world (though Athens remained a cultural center—a kind of university town—for centuries). In 336 Philip was assassinated, and Alexander succeeded to the throne. In 335 Aristotle returned to Athens and opened his own school there in the *peripatos* ("colonnade"; thus the name Peripatetic School) of the gymnasium of the Lyceum, not far from the Hilton Hotel today. In the gymnasium or nearby were a library, study rooms, and a dining room where he could meet with his students. It seems possible that on first returning to Athens he chose to teach rather popular subjects, including poetics, rhetoric, politics, and ethics,[8] but later devoted his attention to metaphysics. On the death of Alexander in 323, when anti-Macedonian sentiment was strong in Athens, Aristotle turned his school over to

5. Called the *Synagōgē Tekhnōn;* see Appendix I.D and Douglas 1955.

6. See Merlan 1954.

7. For more detailed consideration of the date of composition of the *Rhetoric,* see Appendix II.A.

8. See Rist 1989, 23–24.

Theophrastus and went to live in Chalcis on the island of Euboea, where he died in 322.[9] Later biographers say that he had thin legs, was partially bald, liked to wear rings, and spoke with a lisp. He was married, had one daughter, and after his wife's death fathered a son by a concubine.

B. RHETORIC BEFORE ARISTOTLE

Both animals and human beings have a natural instinct to preserve and defend themselves, their territory, and their group and families. They do this by physical acts and by the use of signs, including utterances such as howls, cries, and human speech. *Rhetoric,* in the most general sense, is the energy inherent in emotion and thought, transmitted through a system of signs, including language, to others to influence their decisions or actions. In developed human societies, such as ancient Greece, social and political contexts emerge that mold speech into certain conventional forms shaped by the psychology and expectation of audiences. Both literature and public address develop in this way. Aristotle was primarily concerned with public address on the occasions offered by civic life in Greece, though he notes the presence of rhetoric in literature and in private communications. In *Rhetoric* 1.3 he identifies three occasions, or species, of civic rhetoric: (1) deliberation about the future action in the best interests of a state; (2) speeches of prosecution or defense in a court of law seeking to determine the just resolution of actions alleged to have been taken in the past; and (3) what he calls *epideictic,* or speeches that do not call for any immediate action by the audience but that characteristically praise or blame some person or thing, often on a ceremonial occasion such as a public funeral or holiday. In all three settings speakers seek to persuade or influence action or belief and thus to impose their own ideas or values on others.

The three settings in which Aristotle envisioned rhetoric as operating existed in Greece—and elsewhere—long before his

9. For the subsequent history of Aristotle's personal library, including the text of the *Rhetoric,* see Appendix II.B.

time. A unique contribution of the Greeks, however, was their interest in describing this phenomenon, dividing it into categories, and giving names to the various techniques observed so that they could be taught to others. This conceptualization of rhetoric is parallel to the conceptualization of philosophy, political theory, grammar, and other subjects in Greece. That the Greeks could do this resulted in large part from the nature of the Greek language, which has a capability of coining abstract terms not found in most other ancient languages. That the Greeks needed to conceptualize these disciplines resulted in large part from the development, also unique to Greece, of constitutional governments. In the orderly administration of policy making and adjudication, an individual could hope to influence decision making by appeal to reason.

Handbooks of rhetoric were published, beginning with Corax and Tisias in Sicily in the second quarter of the fifth century B.C. and continuing with others in Athens down through Aristotle's time. They outlined techniques for effective public speaking, especially in the law courts. Not only were there no professional lawyers in Greece, there were no professional judges. Cases were decided by juries (in Athens made up of 201 or more citizens) chosen by lot. Litigants had a limited time to make their cases in formal speeches, convincing the jury that they were trustworthy persons, persuading them of the truth of what they were saying, and arousing in them the motivation to share their views and take the decisions they wanted. In *Rhetoric* 1.2 Aristotle identifies these three things as the three basic *pisteis,* or means of persuasion, available to a speaker.[10]

Plato gives a brief summary of the rhetorical handbooks in the *Phaedrus* (266–67), and Aristotle criticizes them in the *Rhetoric* 1.1. These handbooks seem to have outlined the logical parts into which a speech in a court of law should be divided. The basic parts, which are also seen in surviving judicial speeches written by Lysias and others, are first a *prooimion,* or introduction, designed to get

10. Modern rhetoricians often refer to these means of persuasion as *ēthos, logos,* and *pathos,* respectively. This is a convenient extension of Aristotle's own usage. In his writings, *ēthos* means the character of a person, not the rhetorical presentation of that character; and *pathos* means an emotion felt by someone, not the awakening of emotion by a speaker. *Logos,* however, does mean "argument," or what is said in a speech; and a speech as a whole is also called a *logos.*

the good will and attention of the jury, then a *diēgēsis,* or narration, of the facts of the case from the point of view of the speaker. There followed a *pistis,* or proof. Here the handbooks concentrated on what was called "argument from probability" to the neglect of using direct evidence. Greek juries distrusted direct evidence such as witnesses or documents because they thought these might be bribed or faked. They put more confidence in what those involved would have been likely to do in terms of the circumstances or their character. Thus, a male defendant accused of assaulting someone might argue that it was unlikely he had started the fight despite what witnesses might say to the contrary, for he was much weaker than his opponent (cf. *Rhetoric* 2.24.11, where this argument is criticized as fallacious); or that given his past record of honorable dealing, it was improbable that he would have tried to defraud someone of a small sum. Conversely, the other speaker might argue that though the defendant was weaker, he took advantage of that fact, knowing that people would not think him a likely aggressor; or that it is likely that most anyone would be tempted by an opportunity to get some money, especially if he thought he would be able to get away with it by pleading good character. The final part of a speech was the *epilogos,* or conclusion. The handbooks recommended that the speaker recapitulate the argument and seek to arouse the emotions of the jury— perhaps their pity for the victim or their outrage at what had been done by the opponent. Some handbooks added additional parts to an oration, and a few seem to have had something to say about diction and style.

Aristotle's criticisms of the handbooks are that they concentrated on judicial situations to the neglect of the other species of rhetoric, that they gave attention to arousing emotions to the neglect of showing how to use logical argument, and that dividing speeches into the parts named in the handbooks was not a very important aspect of rhetoric. Despite these criticisms, he devotes part of the *Rhetoric* (2.2–11) to a discussion of emotion and how it is aroused and another section (3.13–19) to the division of a speech into parts. His primary interest, however, is in the logical side of persuasion, which includes—but is by no means limited to— argument from probability. Aristotle's view of rhetoric was influenced by the speeches he heard or read, by his feeling that the existing handbooks were unsatisfactory and by the thinking of two individuals: Plato and Isocrates.

Plato (429–347 B.C.) had been embittered against contemporary rhetoric by his own frustrated attempts to participate in politics and by the trial and execution of his master, Socrates, at the hands of the Athenian democracy in 399 B.C.[11] Plato's criticism of rhetoric is most shrill in the dialogue *Gorgias,* completed about the time Aristotle was born. Gorgias was a teacher of rhetoric who had come to Athens from Sicily and who introduced a flamboyant, poetic style (criticized by Aristotle in *Rhetoric* 3.1.9). We know his work principally from two rhetorical exercises, the *Defense of Palamedes* and the *Encomium of Helen.*[12] According to Aristotle, Gorgias taught by example, which his students then tried to imitate, rather than by theory and precept.[13] In the first two parts of Plato's dialogue—the conversations of Socrates with Gorgias and his pupil Polus—the existence of any valid art of rhetoric is called into question, though some of the dialogue is ironic or deliberately provocative on Socrates' part. This is especially true of his analogy between rhetoric and cookery as sham arts of flattery. Socrates demands that rhetoric have some subject matter particular to itself; but none of the possibilities (e.g., politics or justice) satisfy him. Aristotle will provide an eventual—and valid—answer to Socrates' demand in the opening chapters of the *Rhetoric.* Rhetoric, Aristotle insists, is, like dialectic, a verbal, intellectual tool; though it has artistic techniques and a method special to itself, it borrows the ideas and premises it uses from popular forms of other disciplines, especially politics and ethics.

In Plato's dialogue *Phaedrus,* written about ten years later, Socrates is made to sketch out the possibility of an ideal, philosophical rhetoric—quite different from that flourishing in Greece—in which the speaker would be a virtuous person with a firm knowledge of the subject under discussion, would know the logical techniques of definition and division of a question, and would understand the "souls" of an audience, adapting a speech

---

11. See the autobiographical account in Plato's *Seventh Epistle* 324–26.

12. See Appendix I.A.

13. See *Sophistical Refutations* 34; Plato also represents Gorgias as inept at conceptualized discussion of rhetoric.

to their understanding and moving them to accept and experience "the truth." In Aristotle's system, Socrates' requirements are adapted to realistic situations. A speaker should not seek to persuade the audience of what is "debased" (1.1.12). Aristotle provides a speaker with knowledge of the propositions of politics and ethics and of how to use this knowledge to construct inductive or deductive arguments (1.5–14, 2.18–26). He also supplies an understanding of psychology (2.1–11) and advice about adapting a speech to the character of an audience, viewed as types (2.12–17). His response to Plato on the subject of rhetoric, (though without naming him) is analogous to his responses on the subject of the value of poetry, the nature of politics, ethics, and other subjects—less idealistic and more pragmatic, but based on philosophical method.

Isocrates (436–338 B.C.) was the most influential teacher of rhetoric in Aristotle's time. Around 390 B.C., before Plato created the Academy, Isocrates opened a school in Athens to train future leaders of Greek society in the skills of civic life, especially speech. He had probably been a student of Gorgias. The method of his school resembles the teaching of Gorgias and other sophists in that the teacher composed speeches for students to imitate. But Isocrates probably also lectured on rhetorical theory; and since he had apparently come under some influence from Socrates, he presents his teaching as "philosophy." In his own way, Isocrates sought to answer the kind of criticism of rhetoric found in the *Gorgias* by proposing a subject matter for rhetoric: his main themes are the great issues of Greek society and its historical tradition, especially the need for the union of the Greek states against threats from Persia. By composing speeches on such themes (as described in his *Antidosis* and elsewhere), he sought to condition students' behavior so that they would think and speak noble, virtuous ideas and implement them in civic policy. His own speeches were not delivered in public but published as pamphlets. Aristotle had clearly read them, often quotes examples of rhetorical technique from them, and refrains from explicit criticism of Isocrates in the *Rhetoric*. Later sources, however, record a tradition of hostility between the two men;[14] and it has become a commonplace to regard the

14. See, e.g., Cicero, *On the Orator* 3.141.

subsequent history of rhetoric as falling into two traditions: the
Aristotelian, which stresses logical reasoning, and the Isocratean,
which puts emphasis on elegance of style and literary structure.
Aristotle doubtless thought that Isocrates was at heart a sophist,
that his philosophy was shallow, and that as a teacher of rhetoric he
failed to give his students an adequate understanding of logical
argument—which Isocrates, for his part, seems to have regarded
as largely eristic (verbal wrangling).[15]

C. ARISTOTLE'S VIEW OF RHETORIC

Aristotle was the first person to give serious consideration to drawing a map of learning and to defining the relationship between the
various disciplines of the arts and sciences, which were emerging as
separate studies for the first time in the fourth century B.C. Aristotle's map of learning is the ultimate ancestor for library cata-
logues and the curriculum of the modern university. His own
scheme can be found in book 6 of the *Metaphysics,* in book 6 of the
Nicomachean Ethics, and in passing references elsewhere.

Aristotle divided intellectual activity into (1) theoretical sciences, which include mathematics, physics, and theology; (2) practical arts, including politics and ethics; and (3) productive arts,
including the fine arts, the crafts, and also medicine. In addition,
there are (4) methods or tools (*organa*), applicable to all study but
with no distinct subject matter of their own. Logic and dialectic
belong in that class. Aristotelian scholars of late antiquity and the
Middle Ages regarded rhetoric as one of these methods or tools,
largely on the basis of *Rhetoric.* 1.1. Modern scholars have tended
to attribute to Aristotle the view that rhetoric is a productive art,
like poetics. What he actually says in 1.2.7, however, is that rhetoric is a mixture. It is partly a method (like dialectic) with no necessary subject of its own but partly a practical art derived from ethics
and politics on the basis of its conventional uses. In *Nicomachean
Ethics* 1.2.4–6 he calls rhetoric a part of the architectonic subject

---

15. See Isocrates' remarks in *Against the Sophists* and the *Letter to Alexander.*

of politics. In defining rhetoric in 1.2.1, however, he says that it is the ability of "seeing" the available means of persuasion (thus not necessarily of using them) and employs a verb related to the word *theory.* Thus, rhetoric in Aristotle's view has a theoretical element and in addition clearly does often "produce" persuasion, speeches, and texts. In reading the *Rhetoric* we perceive a gradual shift of focus, moving from the use of rhetoric as a tool (like dialectic) in 1.1 to its theoretical aspects in 1.2, its political and ethical content in the rest of books 1 and 2, and its productive aspects in book 3. There are some excellent comments on the classification of rhetoric, showing Aristotle's influence, in Quintilian 2.18.2–5, leading to the conclusion that its primary role is that of a "practical" art.

D. A CHAPTER-BY-CHAPTER OUTLINE OF THE *RHETORIC*

In order to clarify the overall structure of the *Rhetoric* and to give readers an initial understanding of its coverage, a chapter-by-chapter outline of the work follows. The book divisions originated with Aristotle (book 3 was in fact probably originally a separate work) and represent convenient lengths for a payprus scroll in Aristotle's time. The chapter divisions were first made by George of Trebizond in the fifteenth century and in most cases represent logical units. This outline does not comment on inconsistencies between various parts of the work written at various times or on problems in terminology or interpretation, which are discussed in the notes to the translation. The outline is only a general guide to content.

Books 1–2: *Pisteis,* or the Means of Persuasion in Public Address

Book 1: Introduction; Definition and Divisions of the Subject To Be Discussed; Special Topics Useful for Logical Argument in Deliberative, Epideictic, and Judicial Rhetoric

Introduction (Chapters 1–3)

1.1 Introduction to Rhetoric for Students of Dialectic. The art of rhetoric is an *antistrophos,* or counterpart, to the art of dialectic (formal logical debate on general issues as taught in Aristotle's school); both dialectic and rhetoric are concerned with subjects within the knowledge of anyone, not with special sciences; both are methods of discourse and arts in which the cause of success can be observed.

Existing handbooks of rhetoric neglect logical argument, the most important part of the subject, and concern themselves with external matters, including appeals to the emotions of an audience and the parts of an oration. Also, they only discuss judicial oratory, whereas deliberative oratory is a finer form. A student of rhetoric needs especially to understand the use of an enthymeme. This is a rhetorical syllogism, or probable argument in a form suited to a popular audience.

Rhetoric is useful, since without it the truth can be defeated in debate. Rhetoric also allows one to debate both sides of an issue, *not* to persuade an audience of what is untrue or wicked but to help the speaker understand the real state of the case and be able to refute an opponent. It would be strange if we could not use words to defend ourselves when it is acceptable to use physical force in self-defense.

1.2 The Definition of Rhetoric. Rhetoric is an ability, in each particular case, to see the available means of persuasion. Means of persuasion (*pisteis*) fall into two groups: one, such as the evidence of witnesses or written contracts, is not invented by the speaker and is thus nonartistic. Artistic means of persuasion are three in number: those derived from the character (*ēthos*) of the speaker, when in a speech he shows himself fair-minded and trustworthy; those derived from the emotion (*pathos*) awakened by a speaker in an audience; and those derived from true or probable argument (*logos*). Rhetoric is a kind of offshoot of dialectic and of political and ethical studies.

Logical arguments take one of two forms: they are either inductions (which in rhetoric is the use of examples) or deductions (called in rhetoric enthymemes). The function of rhetoric is to debate about doubtful matters before a general audience, which may not be able to follow a complex chain of arguments and will not be persuaded unless the premises of arguments are agreed to. If a premise of an enthymeme is well known, it need not be stated. Enthymemes are derived from probabilities and signs. A probability is what happens for the most part. Signs are of two sorts: some point to a necessary conclusion, as when we say it is a sign of sickness if someone has a fever; some are refutable, as if we were to say it is a sign of fever that someone breathes rapidly. The premises of ethymemes are derived from the propositions of specific bodies of knowledge, such as physics, politics, and ethics; but enthymemes also make use of topics applicable to any subject, such as argument from the "more and the less." The more an argument is based on the propositions of some other science or art, the less rhetorical it becomes. (Premises, or specific topics, drawn from politics and ethics will be discussed in 1.5–15; common topics in 2.23–24.)

1.3 The Three Species of Rhetoric. A speech situation consists of a speaker, a subject, and an audience. The audience is either judge or spectator. If the audience is asked to judge an action in the future, the speech is *deliberative;* if an action in the past, *judicial.* If the audience is not asked to make a judgment about a past or future action, the speech is *epideictic.* Deliberative speeches are either exhortations or dissuasions to action and aim at showing the potential advantage or harm of the action. Judicial speeches are either accusations or defenses about things done in the past and aim at showing the justice or injustice of what has been done. Epideictic speeches either praise or blame and aim at showing that a person is honorable or shameful; however, they often remind the audience of events of the past and project the course of the future.

Some kinds of propositions are common to all three species of rhetoric: whether something is possible, whether it is a fact in past time, whether it will be a future fact, and whether it is greater or smaller in degree. Others are specific to one of the three species of rhetoric. (In the rest of Book 1 Aristotle takes up separately each of the species of rhetoric—deliberative, epideictic and judicial—to provide an understanding of the subjects with which it deals and propositions or topics specific to it that may be used by a speaker in developing an argument.)

Deliberative Rhetoric (Chapters 4–8)

1.4 Political Topics. The most important subjects on which people deliberate are finances, war and peace, national defense, imports and exports, and the framing of laws. Topics useful for each of these subjects are listed.

1.5 Ethical Topics. The goal of action is happiness, of which some definitions are offered. The constituent parts of happiness are good birth, numerous and good friendships, good children, a good old age, the virtues of the body (health, beauty, strength, stature, athletic prowess), reputation, honor, good luck, and virtue. Each is explained and topics listed (except for virtue, which is deferred for later discussion in 1.6 and 1.9).

1.6 Ethical Topics (continued). Since deliberative rhetoric aims at what is beneficial and since the beneficial is "good," a speaker needs to grasp the topics of the good, which is whatever is chosen for its own sake. Good things include happiness, virtues of the soul, virtues of the body, wealth, friends, honor, the ability to speak and act, natural talent, knowledge, and the like, including life itself. Some topics for argument on these subjects are listed.

1.7 How to Argue That Something Is a Greater Good. This chapter resumes discussion of one of the propositions mentioned at the end of chapter 3 as common to all species of rhetoric. Aristotle now considers its application in deliberative oratory. Arguments are suggested to show that something is "greater" than something else.

1.8 Topics About Political Constitutions. There are four forms of constitution: democracy, oligarchy, aristocracy, and monarchy. A speaker needs to understand their differences and be acquainted with the presentation of character that will be most effective in each context.

Epideictic Rhetoric (Chapter 9)

1.9 Topics Useful in Epideictic Rhetoric; Discussion of Amplification. Epideictic rhetoric seeks to demonstrate the excellence of a person or thing. In the case of a person this is identified with what is honorable. Virtue is honorable; and its parts are justice, courage, self-control, magnificence, liberality, gentleness, prudence, and wisdom. Each is defined, and topics are suggested for an epideictic speaker to use. Specific advice is offered about how to praise or blame someone and about how to amplify praise, which is characteristic of epideictic.

Judicial Rhetoric (Chapters 10–15)

1.10 Topics About Wrongdoing. Wrongdoing is doing harm willingly in contravention of the law. There follows discussion of seven causes of wrongdoing: chance, nature, compulsion, habit, reason, anger, and longing. Topics for arguments relating to each are suggested.

1.11 Topics About Pleasure. Pleasure is defined as a movement of the soul and topics for arguments about the pleasurable are suggested.

1.12 Topics About Wrongdoers and Those Who Are Wronged. Topics for arguments about such persons are listed.

1.13 Topics About Justice and Injustice. Action may violate specific, written law or unwritten law based on natural principles. Some unjust actions are against the community, some against individuals. Crimes need to be defined, since people often admit to an action but deny that it constitutes a crime in the legal sense. Fairness goes beyond the written law. Topics for argument about what is fair are suggested.

1.14 How to Argue That Something Is a Greater Wrong. This chapter parallels chapter 7, exploring propositions of greater and lesser degree as applicable to judicial rhetoric.

1.15 Nonartistic Means of Persuasion. This chapter resumes discussion of the use of documentary eivdence, which was one of the forms of *pistis* identified in 1.2.2. Advance is given about how to deal with laws, witnesses, contracts, the evidence of slaves, and oaths when they favor and when they are opposed to, a speaker's case in court.

Book 2: Persuasion Derived from the Character of the Speaker and from Appeal to the Emotions of the Audience; Further Discussion of Logical Argument

Introduction (Chapter 1)

2.1 The Need for an Understanding of the Role of Character and Emotion in Persuasion. This chapter resumes the discussion in 1.2.3–5. A speaker presents a trustworthy character by showing practical wisdom, virtue, and good will. Emotions should be considered in terms of what the state of mind is of the person who feels a particular emotion, in regard to whom the emotion is felt, and for what reason. Propositions for creating or modifying each emotion will be supplied.

How to Arouse Emotion in an Audience (Chapters 2–11)

2.2–3 Anger and Calmness.

2.4 Friendly Feeling and Enmity.

How to Adapt the Character of a Speaker to the Character of the
Audience (Chapters 12–17)

Further Discussion of the Forms of Logical Argument
(Chapters 18–26)

2.18 Brief Introduction.

2.19 Propositions Common to All Species of Rhetoric. This chapter resumes discussion of possible and impossible, past and future fact, and
degree of magnitude or importance spoken of earlier in 1.2.7, 1.7, and
1.14. Additional propositions on these subjects are provided.

2.20 Argument from Example. This chapter resumes discussion of the use
of examples, identified in 1.2 as one of the two forms of logical argument.
Examples may be historical or made up, the latter including comparisons
and fables.

2.21 The Use of Maxims in Argument. A maxim is the conclusion of an enthymeme. A supporting reason is sometimes expressed, sometimes omitted. Examples are given.

2.22 The Use of Enthymemes. This chapter resumes discussion of enthymemes from 1.2, amplifying some of what is said there. An enthymeme need not express all its premises, and these should be based on opinions already held by the audience. A knowledge of the facts is needed. These are the "specific" topics of 1.4–15. "Common" topics are yet to be discussed. Enthymemes are either demonstrative or refutative, and there are statements that appear to be enthymemes but are not logically cogent.

2.23 Common Topics. This chapters lists and illustrates twenty-eight strategies of argument that can be used in any of the three species of rhetoric.

2.24 Fallacious Enthymemes. A statement may appear to be an enthymeme and not really be one—for example, if it is compact and antithetical but lacks logical cogency. Nine fallacious topics are described.

2.25 Refutation of Enthymemes. The enthymemes of an opponent can be refuted by stating an opposite enthymeme or by bring an objection to its assumptions. Objections are derived from the original statement, something smiilar to it, the opposite of it, or something otherwise judged true. Advice is given for refuting probabilities, examples, and signs.

2.26 Amplification, Refutation, and Objection Are Not Topics; Conclusion of Books 1–2. Amplification and so forth are not distinct lines of argument. This concludes discussion of the thought of a speech and the sources of argument; it remains to discuss style and arrangement.

Book 3: Style and Arrangement

Introduction (Chapter 1)

3.1. Summary of Books 1–2; Remarks on Delivery; the Origins of Artistic Prose. Although previous writers have had something to say about delivery in drama, the subject has not been explored in regard to oratory. This is, however, a rather minor matter. Early efforts to create an artistic prose style, such as those of the sophist Gorgias, were based on imitation of poetry; but prose style should differ from that of poetry.

The Diction and Composition Appropriate to Prose and Speech
(Chapters 2–12)

(Chapters 2–4 relate primarily to word choice, whereas chapters 5–12 relate to the composition of sentences.)

3.2 The Qualities of Good Prose Style. The "virtue" of style is to be clear and neither flat nor above the dignity of the subject but appropriate to it. The art of the speaker or writer should escape notice. Of the various kinds of words discussed in the *Poetics,* only those in their prevailing native meaning and metaphors are useful in prose. Metaphor has clarity and sweetness and makes what is said seem unusual, thus striking. Examples of epithets and metaphors appropriate and inappropriate in prose are given.

3.3 Frigidity, or Faults in Diction. This results from the use of poetic and compound words, strange or foreign words, inappropriate or crowded epithets, and metaphors that are ludicrous or too elevated.

3.4 The Use of Similes. Similes are metaphors needing an explanatory word. Examples are given.

3.5 Grammatical Correctness. Care is needed in the coordination of connectives. Circumlocutions and ambiguities should be avoided. Grammatical gender and number should be observed.

3.6 Onkos *in Composition.* An expansiveness or swelling can be imparted to the composition by such techniques as substituting the definition of a word for the word itself, using the plural for the singular, and describing something by listing qualities it lacks.

3.7 Appropriateness. Style in speech will be appropriate if it expresses emotion and character and is proportional to the subject.

3.8 Prose Rhythm. The language should be neither metrical nor unrhythmical. Avoid metrical feet commonly used in poetry, such as the dactyl or trochee, and cultivate use of the two forms of the paean.

3.9 The Periodic Style. Sentences can be "strung-on" or periodic. A period is an expression (not necessarily a complete sentence) having a beginning and ending and a magnitude easily taken in at a glance. It may be simple or divided into two parts, called *kola,* which may be parallel or in contrast to each other. Antithesis is an example of the latter. If two cola have an equal number of syllables, it is called *parison* or *parisōsis;* if their beginnings or endings are similar in sound, it is called *paromoiōsis.* Examples are given.

3.10 Urbanities and Visualization. Elegance, wit, and good taste can be given to language by the use of metaphor from analogy and by visual imagery that allows the audience to see things as actually being done. The appeal of metaphor is that it brings about learning. Examples are cited.

3.11 Continued Discussion of Visualization, Metaphor, and Other Devices of Style. Language brings ideas before the eyes or makes them vivid when things are described as engaged in activity (*energeia*). Good metaphors are the transference of words from things that are related (but not obviously so) and have an element of surprise. It becomes clear to hearers that they have learned something different from what they believe. Similes, as has been said in 3.4, are a form of metaphor, as are proverbs and hyperboles.

3.12 Oral and Written Styles; Deliberative, Judicial, and Epideictic Styles. Written compositions use a precise style that seems thin when delivered orally; asyndeton and constant repetition are needed in oral delivery but not in writing. In deliberative rhetoric the style is like that of an outline sketch in painting; the lawcourts require more exactness of detail; the epideictic style is most like writing, for its objective is to be read.

Arrangement of the Parts of a Speech (Chapters 13–19)

3.13 The Necessary Parts of a Speech. The only necessary parts are a statement of the proposition and proof, or at the most prooemium, statement, proof, and epilogue.

3.14 The Prooemion. The function of the introduction to a speech is to make clear its purpose. Thus, if the subject is short and clear, there is no need for a prooemion. Beyond that, the introduction is used to counteract prejudice or create it against the opponent. The speaker seeks to make the hearers well disposed and sometimes to make them attentive or the opposite. Prooemia as used in epideictic, judicial, and deliberative rhetoric are discussed.

3.15 Ways of Meeting a Prejudicial Attack. This chapter continues with a list of topics that can be used by a speaker to counteract prejudice.

3.16 The Narration. The use of narrative passages in epideictic, judicial, and deliberative speeches is discussed.

3.17 The Proof as a Part of an Oration. This somewhat rambling chapter offers advice about possible topics for argument in each of the three species of rhetoric and also comments on ways of presenting the speaker's character and on arousing the emotions of the audience.

3.18 Interrogation. This chapter discusses the use and potential danger of questions by a speaker to an opponent in a lawsuit.

3.19 The Epilogue. The conclusion of a speech should dispose the audience favorably toward the speaker and unfavorably toward the opponent, amplify the subject, and remind the audience of the chief points made earlier.

ARISTOTLE, *ON RHETORIC:* TRANSLATION AND NOTES

The title of the work in the manuscripts is *Tekhnē rhētorikē,* (*Art Rhetorical,* or *Art of Rhetoric*). When Aristotle himself refers to the treatise in *Poetics* 19.2 he calls it *Peri rhētorikēs* (*On Rhetoric*).

On the origin of the traditional division into books, chapters, and sections, see the end of Appendix II.B. The numbers and letters in boldface type indicate pages and columns in the Berlin edition (1831) of the complete works of Aristotle. These numbers are used by scholars to refer to passages in the Greek text. In a translation their location is necessarily only approximate.

[. . .] within the translated text supplies the Greek term used by Aristotle or words and phrases implied but not stated in the text that may elucidate meaning.

(. . .) indicates what appear to be parenthetical remarks by Aristotle.

A macron over vowels (ē and ō) in transliterations of Greek words indicates Greek eta and omega.

BOOK 1:
Pisteis, or the Means of Persuasion in Public Address

■ Books 1–2 discuss the means of persuasion available to a public speaker from logical argument, the presentation of the speaker's character, and moving the emotions of the audience. Although this part of rhetoric has come to be known as "invention," Aristotle himself offers no general term for it until the transition section at the end of book 2, where he refers to it as *dianoia,* "thought." Throughout books 1 and 2, understanding the available means of persuasion is treated as constituting the whole of rhetoric, properly understood; and until the last sentence of 2.26 there is no anticipation of discussion of style and arrangement in book 3. Books 1–2 are a unit and probably made up the whole of the *Rhetoric* as it once existed.

Chapters 1–3: Introduction

Chapter 1: Introduction to Rhetoric for Students of Dialectic

■ The *Rhetoric* shows signs of being addressed to different audiences, probably reflecting differing contexts in which Aristotle lectured on rhetoric at different times in his career. Though much of the work provides practical instruction on how to compose a speech, useful to any citizen, some parts seem to be addressed primarily to students of philosophy. What is now regarded as the first chapter of Book 1 was apparently originally addressed to students who had completed a study of dialectic (such as is found in the *Topics*) and who had little knowledge of rhetoric, though they may have been aware of the existence of handbooks on the subject. For them Aristotle explains the similarities between dialectic as they know it and rhetoric as he understands it but does not comment on the differences. The chapter as a whole is very Platonic and contains echoes of several of Plato's dialogues.

Dialectic, as understood by Aristotle, was the art of philosophical disputation. Practice in it was regularly provided in his philosophical school, and his treatise known as *Topics* is a textbook of dialectic. The opening chapters of the *Topics* may be found in Appendix I.C. The procedure in dialectic was for one student to state a thesis (e.g., "Pleasure is the only good") and for a second student to try to refute the thesis by asking a series of questions that could be answered by *yes* or *no*. If successful, the interlocutor led the respondent into a contradiction or logically undefensible position by means of definition and division of the question or by drawing analogies; however, the respondent might be able to defend his position and win the argument. Dialectic proceeds by question and answer, not, as rhetoric does, by continuous exposition. A dialectical argument does not contain the parts of a public address; there is no introduction, narration, or epilogue, as in a speech—only proof. In dialectic only logical argument is acceptable, whereas in rhetoric (as Aristotle will explain in chapter 2), the impression of character conveyed by the speaker and the emotions awakened in the audience contribute to persuasion. While both dialectic and rhetoric build their arguments on commonly held opinions (*endoxa*) and deal only with the probable (not with scientific certainty), dialectic examines general issues (such as the nature of justice) whereas rhetoric usually seeks a specific judgment, (e.g., whether or not some specific action was just or whether or not some specific policy will be beneficial). Epideictic is a partial exception to this. Platonic dialogues make extensive use of dialectic as Socrates seeks to refute the position of an opponent—for example Gorgias, Polus, and Callicles in the *Gorgias*. Platonic dialogues also contain rhetorical passages expressive of Socrates' character and appeals to the emotions of the hearer, as in his second speech in the *Phaedrus*.

After discussing the similarities between dialectic and rhetoric, Aristotle criticizes (sections 3–11) the *arts,* or handbooks, of previous writers, which he finds unsatisfactory in several ways. These handbooks are now lost; and the only surviving treatise on rhetoric from the classical period other than Aristotle's is a slightly later work known as the *Rhetoric to Alexander.* Into this discussion are inserted parenthetical remarks (sections 7–9) on the specificity desirable in framing good laws, a subject of interest to students of political philosophy but of limited relevance to rhetorical theory. The chapter concludes (sections 12–14) with a discussion of why rhetoric is useful—remarks that can be thought of as addressed primarily to students of philosophy who, under the influence of Plato, may regard the subject of rhetoric as trivial. A general Greek audience would probably have assumed that rhetoric was useful and been more dubious about dialectic, which could easily seem pedantic hairsplitting, as it did to Isocrates (see, e.g., *Against the Sophists* and the prooemion to the *Encomium of Helen*).

Chapter 1 creates acute problems for the unity of the treatise. Aristotle here seems firmly to reject using the emotions, identifies rhetoric with logical argument, and gives no hint that style and arrangement may be important in rhetoric (as will emerge in book 3). In section 6 he even seems to say that the importance and the justice of a case are not appropriate issues for a speaker to discuss; they should be left for the audience to judge. But the justice of a speaker's case, its importance, and its amplification subsequently will be given extended treatment. Some interpreters seek to force the point of view of chapter 1 into conformity with what follows by making very careful distinctions about what Aristotle is saying. This involves claiming, for example, that *pisteis,* "proofs," in section 3 already includes the use of character and emotion as means of persuasion, that *verbal attack, pity,* and *anger* in section 4 refer to *expressions* of emotion rather than to the reasoned use of an understanding of psychology and motivation. Section 6 can be made consistent with later parts of the work if Aristotle is regarded as saying that the speaker's interpretation of what is just or important should not be allowed to color the audience's judgment. It can be stressed that a speaker needs to understand tricks that may be used by an opponent but should not employ them himself. Despite other possible interpretations, it is probably better to acknowledge frankly that chapter 1 is inconsistent with what follows, that it is far more austere in tone than Aristotle's general view of rhetoric, and that the difference results from addressing different audiences and from the attempt to link the study of dialectic with that of rhetoric. Aristotle either failed to revise the chapter or has let stand a deliberately provocative critique of the teaching of rhetoric in his own time as a way of emphasizing the needs for greater attention to logic, thus justifying the writing of a rhetoric handbook by a philosopher. The chapter might even be compared to Socrates' provocative description in the *Gorgias* of contemporary rhetoric as a form of flattery, a view that Socrates, too, subsequently modifies. The result is to encourage a dialogue between the reader and the text of the *Rhetoric* about the moral purpose and valid uses of rhetoric.

The first chapter is one of the earliest examples of an introduction to the study of a discipline (the beginning of the *Topics* is another) and is thus an antecedent of the Greek *prolegomenon* or Latin *accessus* commonly found at the beginning of technical works in later antiquity and the Middle Ages.

[1354a] 1. Rhetoric[1] is an *antistrophos*[2] to dialectic; for both are concerned with such things as are, to a certain extent, within the

---

1. *Hē rhētorikē* (the rhetorical), a feminine singular adjective used as an abstract noun; cf. *dialektikē, poiētikē.* Neither dialectic nor rhetoric assume knowledge of any technical subject, and both build a case on the basis of what any reasonable person would believe. Aristotle takes the term *rhetoric* from Plato; others usually spoke of the "art of speech"; see Schiappa 1990.

2. *Antistrophos* is commonly translated "counterpart." Other possibilities include "correlative" and "coordinate." The word can mean "converse." In Greek choral lyric, the metrical pattern of a *strophē*, or stanza, is repeated with different words in

knowledge of all people and belong to no separately defined science.[3] A result is that all people, in some way, share in both; for all, to some extent, try both to test and maintain an argument [as in dialectic] and to defend themselves and attack [others, as in rhetoric]. 2. Now among the general public, some do these things randomly and others through an ability acquired by habit,[4] but since both ways are possible, it is clear that it would also be possible to do the same by [following] a path; for it is possible to observe[5] the cause why some succeed by habit and others accidentally,[6] and all would at once agree that such observation is the activity of an art [*tekhnē*].[7]

3. As things are now,[8] those who have composed *Arts of Speech*

---

the *antistrophē*. Aristotle is, however, probably thinking of, and rejecting, the analogy of the true and false arts elaborated by Socrates in the *Gorgias,* where justice is said to be an *antistrophos* to medicine (464b8) and rhetoric, the false form of justice, is compared to cookery, the false form of medicine (465c1–3). Isocrates (*Antidosis* 182) speaks of the arts of the soul (called philosophy, but essentially political rhetoric) and the arts of the body (gymnastic) as *antistrophoi.* This view is equally unacceptable to Aristotle, for whom rhetoric is a tool, like dialectic, though its subject matter is derived from some other discipline, such as ethics or politics; see *Rhetoric* 1.2.7. Aristotle thus avoids the fallacy of Plato's *Gorgias* where Socrates is obsessed with finding some kind of knowledge specific to rhetoric. On later interpretations of *antistrophos* see Green 1990.

3. The first sentence of the treatise, with its proposition and supporting reason, is an example of what Aristotle will call an enthymeme. The reader should become sensitive to the constant use of enthymemes throughout the text, often introduced by the particle *gar* (for).

4. The former hardly know what they are doing; but the latter, by trial and error, have gained a practical sense of what is effective.

5. *Theorein,* lit. "see" but with the implication "theorize." This is an instance of the visual imagery common in the *Rhetoric.*

6. Here, as often, Aristotle reverses the order of reference: *accidentally* refers back to *randomly.* Such *chiasmus* is a common feature of Greek.

7. In contrast to Socrates in the *Gorgias,* Aristotle has no doubt that rhetoric is an art. Awareness of the cause of success allows technique to be conceptualized and taught systematically. On Aristotle's understanding of an "art," see the passage from *Nicomachean Ethics* 6.4 in Appendix I.B.

8. In 1.2.4 Aristotle again criticizes contemporary technical writers. He thus appears to be thinking primarily of the handbooks of the mid–fourth century, such as those by Pamphilus and Callippus cited in 2.23.21. Aristotle collected the doctrines of some handbooks in a lost work, *Synagōgē tekhnōn;* see Appendix I.D. Plato provides a brief summary of the earlier ones in *Phaedrus* 266d–67d.

have worked on a small part of the subject; for only *pisteis*[9] are
artistic (other things are supplementary), and these writers say
nothing about enthymemes, which is the "body" of persuasion,[10]
while they give most of their attention to matters external to the
subject; 4. for verbal attack and pity and anger and such emotions
of the soul do not relate to fact but are appeals to the juryman.[11]
As a result, if all trials were conducted as they are in some present-
day states and especially in those well governed, [the handbook
writers] would have nothing to say; 5. for everyone thinks the laws
ought to require this, and some even adopt the practice and forbid
speaking outside the subject, as in the Areopagus too,[12] rightly so
providing; for it is wrong to warp the jury by leading them into
anger or envy or pity: that is the same as if someone made a
straightedge rule crooked before using it. 6. And further, it is clear
that the opponents have no function except to show that something
is or is not true or has happened or has not happened;[13] whether it
is important or trivial or just or unjust, in so far as the lawmaker

9. *Pistis* (pl. *pisteis*) has a number of different meanings in different contexts:
"proof, means of persuasion, belief," etc. In 1.2.2–3 Aristotle distinguishes between artistic and nonartistic *pisteis,* and divides the former into three means of
persuasion based on character, logical argument, and arousing emotion. Here in
chap. 1 readers familiar with dialectic have no knowledge yet of persuasion by
character or emotion and will assume that *pistis* means "logical proof." In 3.17.15
pistis means "logical argument" in contrast to character presentation.

10. *Body* is here contrasted with "matters external" in the next clause. Though
Aristotle does not say so, one might speculate that the soul, or life, of persuasion
comes from ethical and emotional qualities.

11. The handbooks offered examples of argument from probability, but they did
not recognize its logical structure. The concept of the logical syllogism and its
rhetorical counterpart, the enthymeme (to be discussed in chap. 2), are Aristotelian
contributions. The handbooks probably treated the emotions in discussing the
prooemium and epilogue (on which see Aristotle's account in 3.13,19) and in
separate collections or discussions such as the *Eleoi* of Thrasymachus (see *Rhetoric*
3.1.7).

12. In Aristotle's time the jurisdiction of the Athenian court of the Areopagus was
chiefly limited to homicide cases. That its rules of relevance were strict is also
attested in Lycurgus' speech *Against Leocrites* 12.

13. On the possible implications of this statement for Aristotle's view of a "general
rhetoric," see Wieland 1968; but there is no other passage in Aristotle expressly
supporting the view Wieland advances.

has not provided a definition, the juryman should somehow decide
himself and not learn from the opponents.[14]

■ The following passage on framing laws resembles some of
what Plato says in *Laws* 9.875–76[15] and is apparently a parenthetical remark of Aristotle to students of political philosophy; he may well have said something of this sort to young
Alexander. Section 9 will take up where section 6 leaves off.

(7. It is highly appropriate for well-enacted laws to define everything as exactly as possible and for as little as possible to be left to
the judges:[16] first because it is easier to find one or a few than [to
find] many who are prudent and capable of framing laws and judging; [1354b] second, legislation results from consideration over
much time, while judgments are made at the moment [of a trial or
debate], so it is difficult for the judges to determine justice and
benefits fairly; but most important of all, because the judgment of
a lawmaker is not about a particular case but about what lies in the
future and in general, while the assemblyman and the juryman are
actually judging present and specific cases. For them, friendliness
and hostility and individual self-interest are often involved, with
the result that they are no longer able to see the truth adequately,
but their private pleasure or grief casts a shadow on their judgment. 8. In other matters, then, as we have been saying, the judge
should have authority to determine as little as possible; but it is
necessary to leave to the judges the question of whether something
has happened or has not happened, will or will not be, is or is not
the case; for the lawmaker cannot forsee these things.)

9. If this is so, it is clear that matters external to the subject are
described as an art by those who define other things: for example,
what the introduction [*prooimion*] or the narration [*diēgēsis*][17]

14. On the problems created by this statement, see the introductory comment to
this chapter.

15. A suggestion made to the translator by Eckhardt Schütrumpf.

16. This "philosophical" position is somewhat modified in 1.13.13, when Aristotle
considers the practical problems involved.

17. The *Arts,* or handbooks of rhetoric, were organized around discussion of what

should contain, and each of the other parts; for [in treating these matters] they concern themselves only with how they may put the judge in a certain frame of mind,[18] while they explain nothing about artistic proofs; and that is the question of how one may become *enthymematic*.[19] 10. It is for this reason that although the method of deliberative and judicial speaking is the same and though deliberative subjects are finer and more important to the state than private transactions, [the handbook writers] have nothing to say about the former, and all try to describe the art of speaking in a lawcourt, because it is less serviceable to speak things outside the subject in deliberative situations;[20] for there the judge judges about matters that affect himself, so that nothing is needed except to show that circumstances are as the speaker says.[21] But in judicial speeches this is not enough; rather, it is serviceable to gain over the hearer; for the judgment is about other people's business and the judges, considering the matter in relation to their own affairs and listening with partiality, lend themselves to [the needs of] the litigants but do not judge [objectively]. **[1355a]** Thus, as we said earlier, in many places the law prohibits speaking outside the subject [in court cases]; in deliberative assemblies the judges themselves adequately guard against this.

11. Since it is evident that artistic method is concerned with

---

should be said in each of the separate parts usually found in a judicial speech. These included *prooimion* (introduction), *diēgēsis* (narration), *pistis* (proof), and *epilogos* (conclusion) and sometimes additional parts. See 3.13–19.

18. This was regarded as a major function of the prooemium (cf. 3.14.9–11) and epilogue (3.19.1).

19. The meaning of this term will be explained in the next paragraph.

20. The *Arts* of rhetoric to which Aristotle refers were certainly largely concerned with techniques useful in the law courts; but speeches like Demosthenes' *On the Crown* show that these could be as fine and as politically significant as speeches in the democratic assembly and were by no means limited to "private transactions," or contracts, as Aristotle insinuates. In the manuscripts the sentence continues, "and deliberative oratory is less mischievous than judicial, but of more general interest." This is probably an addition by a later writer.

21. In deliberative rhetoric the "judges" are members of a council or assembly making decisions about public matters that affect themselves.

pisteis and since *pistis* is a sort of demonstration [*apodeixis*]²² (for we most believe when we suppose something to have been demonstrated) and since rhetorical *apodeixis* is enthymeme (and this is, generally speaking, the strongest of the *pisteis*) and the enthymeme is a sort of syllogism [or reasoning] (and it is a function of dialectic, either as a whole or one of its parts, to see about every syllogism equally), it is clear that he who is best able to see from what materials, and how, a syllogism arises would also be most enthymematic— if he grasps also what sort of things an enthymeme is concerned with and what differences it has from a logical syllogism; for it belongs to the same capacity both to see the true and [to see] what resembles the true, and at the same time humans have a natural disposition for the true and to a large extent hit on the truth; thus an ability to aim at commonly held opinions [*endoxa*] is a characteristic of one who also has a similar ability to regard to the truth.²³

22. *Apodeixis* = "demonstration," usu. with logical validity (as in scientific reasoning) but occasionally more generally, including probable argument (as here).

23. On *endoxa* see *Topics* 1.1 in Appendix I.C. The student is assumed already to understand, from earlier study of logic and dialectic, the concepts of *pistis*, *apodeixis*, and *enthymēma*. Enthymeme literally means "something in the mind" and had been used by Alcidamas and Isocrates to mean an "idea" expressed in a speech. In *Prior Analytics* 2.27 an enthymeme is defined as "a syllogism from probabilities or signs." Aristotle sometimes uses *syllogismos* loosely to meaning "reasoning," *enthymēma* to mean a consideration in whatever form it is put. A valid syllogism in the technical sense is a logical certainty, "true," and most perfectly seen only when expressed symbolically, e.g., "If all A is B, and some A is C, then all C is B." The traditional example in post-Aristotelian logic is, "If all men are mortal, and Socrates is a man, then Socrates is mortal." In 1.2.14 Aristotle says that "few" of the premises of enthymemes are necessarily true, thus slightly modifying the definition in the *Analytics*. In 1.2.13 and 2.22.3 he says that an enthymeme need not express all its premises. The Aristotelian distinction between a syllogism and an enthymeme thus seems largely one of context—tightly reasoned philosophical discourse in the case of the syllogism versus popular speech or writing with resulting informality in the expression of the argument in an enthymeme. In public address an argument may be a worthwhile consideration even if it is not absolutely valid. An example of a typical enthymeme might be "Socrates is virtuous; for he is wise" or "Since/If Socrates is wise, he is virtuous." Here the premises are only probable and a universal major premise, "All the wise are virtuous" is assumed. For Aristotle's own examples of enthymemes, see 2.21.2 and the end of 3.17.17.

THE USEFULNESS OF RHETORIC

That other writers describe as an art things outside the subject [of a speech] and that they have rather too much inclined toward judicial oratory is clear; 12. but rhetoric is useful [first] because the true and the just are by nature[24] stronger than their opposites, so that if judgments are not made in the right way [the true and the just] are necessarily defeated [by their opposites]. And this is worthy of censure.[25] Further, even if we were to have the most exact knowledge, it would not be very easy for us in speaking to use it to persuade some audiences. Speech based on knowledge is teaching, but teaching is impossible [with some audiences]; rather, it is necessary for *pisteis* and speeches [as a whole] to be formed on the basis of common [beliefs], as we said in the *Topics*[26] about communication with a crowd. Further, one should be able to argue persuasively on either side of a question, just as in the use of syllogisms, not that we may actually do both (for one should not persuade what is debased)[27] but in order that it may not escape our notice what the real state of the case is and that we ourselves may be able to refute if another person uses speech unjustly. None of the other arts reasons in opposite directions; dialectic and rhetoric alone do this, for both are equally concerned with opposites.[28] Of course the underlying

24. Aristotle believed that truth was grounded in nature (*physis*) and capable of apprehension by reason. In this he differs both from Plato (for whom truth is grounded in the divine origin of the soul) and from the sophists (for whom judgments were based on *nomos* [convention], which in turn results from the ambivalent nature of language as the basis of human society).

25. On the text and interpretation of this sentence, see Grimaldi, 1980–88, 1:25–28. Judgments will not be made in the right way if the facts and reasons are not brought out persuasively. To do this, the speaker needs a knowledge of rhetoric.

26. *Topics* 1.1.2; see Appendix I.C.

27. *What is debased* (*ta phaula*) refers to whatever is bad, cheap, or morally and socially useless. This principle, important as a response to the criticisms of Plato, appears only in a parenthetical remark and is not repeated in the prescriptive parts of the treatise.

28. There is, however, the difference that in dialectic, opposite trains of argument are actually expressed in the dialectical situation, whereas in rhetoric the speaker has usually tried to think out the opposing arguments before speaking to be able to answer them if need arises. But occasionally, an orator will both express and refute an opposing argument in the course of a speech or even be seen debating with himself about what is right.

facts are not equally good in each case; but true and better ones are by nature always more productive of good syllogisms and, in a word, more persuasive. In addition, it would be strange if an inability to defend oneself by means of the body is shameful, while there is no shame in an inability to use speech; **[1355a]** the latter is more characteristic of humans than is use of the body. 13. And if it is argued that great harm can be done by unjustly using such power of words, this objection applies to all good things except for virtue, and most of all to the most useful things, like strength, health, wealth, and military strategy; for by using these justly one would do the greatest good and unjustly, the greatest harm.[29]

14. That rhetoric, therefore, does not belong to a single defined genus of subject but is like dialectic and that it is useful is clear— and that its function is not to persuade but to see the available means of persuasion in each case, as is true also in all the other arts; for neither is it the function of medicine to create health but to promote this as much as possible; for it is nevertheless possible to treat well those who cannot recover health. In addition, [it is clear] that it is a function of one and the same art to see the persuasive and [to see] the apparently persuasive, just as [it is] in dialectic [to recognize] a syllogism and [to recognize] an apparent syllogism;[30] for sophistry is not a matter of ability but of deliberate choice [*proairesis*] [of specious arguments].[31] In the case of rhetoric, however, there is the difference that one person will be [called] *rhētōr*[32] on the basis of his knowledge and another on the basis of

29. Another possible echo of instruction to Alexander.

30. Rhetoric uses both logically valid arguments and probabilities. The jump to sophistry in the next sentence perhaps implies a recognition that "the apparently persuasive" and "an apparent syllogism" include fallacious arguments that initially sound valid in an oral situation but will not hold up under scrutiny. Both the orator and the dialectician need to be able to recognize these.

31. In modern linguistic terminology, *sophist* is the "marked" member of the pair *dialectician/sophist* in that the first includes the second; but *rhētōr* is "unmarked" and may be interpreted either as any effective speaker or as a speaker who uses tricky arguments.

32. In classical Greek, *rhētōr* means any public speaker, though often referring to a person who plays a leadership role in public debate or is active in the law courts. In the Roman period, *rhētōr* frequently means "rhetorician, "teacher of rhetoric." Latin *orator* (orig. "envoy") and thus English "orator," are translations of *rhētōr* but take on an implication of eloquence not necessarily present in the Greek word.

his deliberate choice, while in dialectic *sophist* refers to deliberate choice [of specious arguments], *dialectician* not to deliberate choice, but to ability [at argument generally]. Let us now try to discuss the method itself: how and from what sources we may reach our objectives.[33] Starting again, therefore, as it were from the beginning, after defining what rhetoric is, let us say all that remains [to be said about the whole subject].

Chapter 2: *Definition of Rhetoric;* Pisteis, *or the Means of Persuasion in Public Address; Paradigms, Enthymemes, and Their Sources; Common Topics;* Eidē *and* Idia

1. Let rhetoric be [defined as] an ability, in each [particular] case, to see the available means of persuasion.[34] This is the func-

33. For some speculations on Aristotle's objectives, see Lord 1981. Aristotle's own objective is clearly an understanding of the nature, materials, and uses of rhetoric; but he has pointed out that the art is useful, and as the treatise unrolls it will often take on the tone of a prescriptive handbook on how to compose a persuasive speech.

34. Aristotle uses the phrase *estō dē,* "Let X be . . ." commonly of a working hypothesis rather than a final definition and occasionally to resume a definition made earlier. The definition here is anticipated in 1.1.14 on the *ergon* of rhetoric. He identifies the genus to which rhetoric belongs as *dynamis:* "ability, capacity, faculty." In his philosophical writing *dynamis* is the regular word for "potentiality" in matter or form that is "actualized" by an efficient cause. The actuality produced by the potentiality of rhetoric is not the written or oral text of a speech, or even persuasion but the art of "seeing" how persuasion may be effected. In *Nicomachean Ethics* 6.4 (see Appendix I.B) he defines all art as a reasoned capacity to make something and says that it is concerned with the coming-into-being of something that is capable of either being or not being. Art is thus for him not the product of artistic skill, but the skill itself. Later rhetoricians often amplify Aristotle's definition by adding *through speech;* the root of the word *rhetoric, rhē–,* refers specifically to speech. Though he uses *poetics* to refer to arts other than poetry (dance, painting, sculpture), he never uses *rhetoric* to refer to any art except that of speech. As is clear from chap. 3, Aristotle primarily thinks of rhetoric as manifested in the civic context of public address; but he often draws examples of rhetoric from poetry or historical writing, and in the *Poetics* (19.1456a–b) the "thought" of a speaker in tragedy is said to be a matter of rhetoric. *In each case (peri hekaston)* refers to the fact that rhetoric deals with specific circumstances (particular individuals and their

tion of no other art;[35] for each of the others[36] is instructive and persuasive about its own subject: for example, medicine about health and disease and geometry about the properties of magnitudes and arithmetic about numbers and similarly in the case of the other arts and sciences. But rhetoric seems to be able to observe the persuasive about "the given," so to speak. That, too, is why we say it does not include technical knowledge of any particular, defined genus [of subjects].

2. Of the *pisteis*, some are atechnic ["nonartistic"], some entechnic ["embodied in art, artistic"].[37] I call atechnic those that are not provided by "us" [i.e., the potential speaker] but are preexisting: for example, witnesses, testimony of slaves taken under torture,[38] contracts, and such like; and artistic whatever can be prepared by method and by "us"; thus, one must *use* the former and *invent*[39] the latter. **[1356a]** 3. Of the *pisteis* provided through speech there are three species: for some are in the character [*ēthos*] of the speaker, and some in disposing the listener in some way, and some in the argument [*logos*] itself, by showing or seeming to show something.[40]

---

actions). *To see* translates *theorēsai*, "to be an observer of and to grasp the meaning or utility of." English *theory* comes from the related noun *theoria. The available means of persuasion* renders *to endekhomenon pithanon*, "what is inherently and potentially persuasive" in the facts, circumstances, character of the speaker, attitude of the audience, etc. *Endekhomenon* often means "possible."

35. Dialectic comes closest but deals with general questions, not specific cases; and for dialectic the final term, *means of persuasion (pithanon)*, would presumably become *means of reasoning (syllogismos)*; see *Topics* 1.1 in Appendix I.C.

36. Except, of course, dialectic.

37. Later writers sometimes call these *extrinsic* and *intrinsic*, respectively. Aristotle discusses atechnic proof in 1.15. In 3.16.1 he also refers to the "facts" in a epideictic speech as atechnic.

38. In Greek law, the evidence of slaves was only admissable in court if taken under torture. There was much debate about its reliability; see 1.15.26.

39. *Heurein*, "to find out"; *heuresis* becomes the regular word for rhetorical invention.

40. *Ēthos* in Aristotle means "character," esp. "moral character," and except in 2.21.16 is regarded as an attribute of a person, not of a speech. Aristotle does not use the term in the technical sense of "rhetorical ethos," the technique or effect of the presentation of character in a discourse. "Disposing the listener in some way" is defined in sec. 5 below as leading the hearers to feel emotion (*pathos*). Again, *pathos* is an attribute of persons, not of a speech. The shorthand ethos–pathos–

4. [There is persuasion] through character whenever the speech is spoken[41] in such a way as to make the speaker worthy of credence; for we believe fair-minded people to a greater extent and more quickly [than we do others] on all subjects in general and completely so in cases where there is not exact knowledge but room for doubt.[42] And this should result from the speech, not from a previous opinion that the speaker is a certain kind of person;[43] for it is not the case, as some of the technical writers propose in their treatment of the art, that fair-mindedness [*epieikeia*] on the part of the speaker makes no contribution to persuasiveness;[44] rather, character is almost, so to speak, the controlling factor in persuasion.

5. [There is persuasion] through the hearers when they are led to feel emotion [*pathos*] by the speech; for we do not give the same judgment when grieved and rejoicing or when being friendly and hostile. To this and only this we said contemporary technical writ-

---

logos to describe the modes of persuasion is a convenience but does not represent Aristotle's own usage.

41. Aristotle is not thinking of style and delivery but of the thought and contents.

42. Here and in 1.9.1 and 2.1.5–7 the role of character in a speech is regarded as making the speaker seem trustworthy. The extended discussion of types of character in 2.12–17 relates to the somewhat different matter of the adaptation of the character of a speaker to the character of an audience. Aristotle's later treatment of character in rhetoric is in fact somewhat wider than in this initial definition.

43. Aristotle thus does not include in rhetorical ethos the authority that a speaker may possess due to his position in government or society, previous actions, reputation for wisdom, or anything except what is actually contained in the speech and the character it reveals. Presumably, he would regard all other factors, sometimes highly important in the success of rhetoric, as inartistic; but he never says so. One practical reason for stressing character as revealed within the speech was that Greek law required defendants to speak on their own behalf, and they were often lacking in external authority. They could commission a speech from a professional speechwriter (logographer) and then memorize it for delivery in court. Lysias, in particular, had great success in conveying a favorable impression or moral character (*ēthopoiia*) in the many speeches he wrote for defendants.

44. Some handbook writers perhaps rejected an appearance of fair-mindedness as too mild and favored an uncompromising attitude. Aristotle's point is that an appearance of fair-mindedness gives the speaker an initial advantage.

ers try to give their attention. The details on this subject will be made clear when we speak about the emotions.[45]

6. Persuasion occurs through the arguments [*logoi*] when we show the truth or the apparent truth from whatever is persuasive in each case.

7. Since *pisteis* come about through these [three means], it is clear that to grasp an understanding of them is the function of one who can form syllogisms and be observant about characters and virtues and, third, about emotions (what each of the emotions is and what are its qualities and from what it comes to be and how). The result is that rhetoric is a certain kind of offshoot [*paraphues*] of dialectic and of ethical studies (which it is just to call politics).[46] (Thus, too, rhetoric dresses itself up[47] in the form of politics, as do those who pretend to a knowledge of it,[48] sometimes through lack of education, sometimes through boastfulness and other human causes.) Rhetoric is partly [*morion ti*] dialectic, and resembles it, as we said at the outset; for neither of them is identifiable with knowledge of any specific subject, but they are distinct abilities of supply-

45. In 2.2–11. Aristotle's inclusion of emotion as a mode of persuasion, despite his objections to the handbooks, is a recognitiion that among human beings judgment is not entirely a rational act. There are morally valid emotions in every situation, and it is part of the orator's duty to clarify these in the minds of the audience. On this question in general, see Johnstone 1980; 1–24.

46. In calling rhetoric an *antistrophos* of dialectic in 1.1.1, and an offshoot of dialectic and ethical studies here, and "partly dialectic" and like it in the next sentence, Aristotle avoids use of the formal categories of genus and species. He cannot very well call rhetoric a species of dialectic, since it contains elements—the persuasive effect of character and emotion in particular—that are not proper to dialectic; but at the same time he stresses the logical side of rhetoric and thus its relationship to dialectic. He does not entertain the possibility that dialectic should be regarded as a species of rhetoric, perhaps because dialectic deals with universals, rhetoric with specifics; dialectic is logically prior. Also, to make rhetoric the more general term would lead to the celebration of it as the most characteristic and worthwhile human activity, as Isocrates regarded it. For Aristotle, that honor belongs to philosophy—hence his attempt to find metaphors to describe rhetoric as a mixture of logical, political, and ethical elements. In *Nicomachean Ethics* 1.2.4–6 he says that politics is an "architectonic" subject, of which generalship, economics, and rhetoric are parts.

47. *Hypoduetai,* an echo of Plato, *Gorgias* 464c.

48. Gorgias, Polus, Isocrates, and their followers.

ing words. Concerning their potentiality and how they relate to each other, almost enough has been said.

8. In the case of persuasion through proving or seeming to prove something, just as in dialectic **[1356b]** there is on the one hand induction [*epagōgē*] and on the other the syllogism and the apparent syllogism, so the situation is similar in rhetoric; for the *paradeigma* ["example"] is an induction, the *enthymēma* a syllogism. I call a rhetorical syllogism an enthymeme, a rhetorical induction a paradigm.[49] And all [speakers] produce logical persuasion by means of paradigms or enthymemes and by nothing other than these. As a result, since it is always necessary to show something either by syllogizing or by inducing (and this is clear to us from the *Analytics*),[50] it is necessary that each of these be the same as each of the others.[51] 9. What the difference is between a paradigm and an enthymeme is clear from the *Topics* (for an account was given there earlier of syllogism and induction):[52] to show on the basis of many similar instances that something is so is in dialectic induction, in rhetoric paradigm; but to show that if some premises are true, something else [the conclusion] beyond them results from these because they are true, either universally or for the most part, in dialectic is called syllogism and in rhetoric enthymeme. 10. And it is also appar-

49. Aristotle will discuss the paradigm at greater length in 2.20 and the enthymeme in 2.22. The first three sentences of this paragraph, found in all manuscripts, are double-bracketed by Rudolf Kassel in his Berlin 1976 edition of the Greek text, which is Kassel's way of indicating passages that he regarded as later additions by Aristotle to the otherwise completed treatise. These are interesting suggestions, but essentially subjective in each case.

50. *Prior Analytics* 2.23; *Posterior Analytics* 1.1.

51. Not identical, in which case there would be no need for two sets of terms, but *essentially* the same in their underlying structure. In formal logic an induction consists of a series of particular observations from which a general conclusion is drawn; in rhetoric it takes the form of a particular statement supported by one or more parallels, with the universal conclusion left unstated. Similarly, an enthymeme rarely takes the full syllogistic form of major premise, minor premise, and conclusion; more often a conclusion is offered and supported by a reason, as in the first sentence of the *Rhetoric*. On the logic of this passage see Schröder 1985. Schröder does not agree with Kassel's view that it is a later addition.

52. There is some discussion of syllogism in *Topics* 1.1, and 1.12 offers a definition of induction with an example: "If the skilled pilot is best, and [similarly] the charioteer, then in general the skilled is the best in each thing,"

ent that either species of rhetoric[53] has merit (what has also been said in the *Methodics*[54] is true in these cases too); for some rhetorical utterances are paradigmatic, some enthymematic; and similarly, some orators are paradigmatic, some enthymematic. Speeches using paradigms are not less persuasive, but those with enthymemes excite more favorable audience reaction. 11. The cause—and how each should be used—we shall explain later;[55] now we shall explain these things themselves more clearly.

Since the persuasive is persuasive to someone (and is either immediately plausible and believable in itself or seems to be shown by statements that are so) and since no art examines the particular—for example, the art of medicine does not specify what is healthful for Socrates or for Callias but for persons of a certain sort (this is artistic, while particulars are limitless and not knowable)—neither does rhetoric theorize about each opinion—what may seem so to Socrates or Hippias—but about what seems true to people of a certain sort, as is also true with dialectic.[56] For the latter does not form syllogisms from things at random (some things seem true even to madmen) but from that [which seems true] to people in need of argument, and rhetoric [forms enthymemes] from things [that seem true] to people already accustomed to deliberate among themselves.[57] **[1357a]** 12. Its function [*ergon*] is concerned with the sort of things we debate and for which we do not have [other] arts and among such listeners as are not able to see many things all together or to reason from a distant starting point. And we debate about things that seem to be capable of admitting two possibilities; for no one debates things incapable of being different either in past or future or present, at least not if they suppose that to be the case; for there is nothing more [to say]. 13. It is possible to form syllogisms and draw inductive conclusions either from previous syllogisms or from statements that are not reasoned out but require a syllogism [if

53. The species using example or that using enthymeme.

54. A lost logical work by Aristotle of which the extant *On Interpretation* may have been a part; see Rist 1989, 84.

55. In 2.20–24.

56. Dialectic builds its proof on the opinions of all, the majority, or the wise; cf. *Topics* 1.1 in Appendix I.C.

57. Translating the text as conjectured by Kassel.

they are to be accepted] because they are not commonly believed
[*endoxa*]; but the former of these [i.e., a chain of syllogisms] is
necessarily not easy to follow because of the length [of the argu-
ment] (the judge is assumed to be a simple person),[58] and the latter
is not persuasive because the premises are not agreed to or commonly believed. Thus, it is necessary for an enthymeme and a paradigm to be concerned with things that are for the most part capable
of being other than they are—the paradigm inductively, the
enthymeme syllogistically—and drawn from few premises and often
less than those of the primary syllogism;[59] for if one of these is
known, it does not have to be stated, since the hearer supplies it: for
example, [to show] that Dorieus has won a contest with a crown it is
enough to have said that he has won the Olympic games, and there is
no need to add that the Olympic games have a crown as the prize; for
everybody knows that.[60]

14. Since few of the premises from which rhetorical syllogisms
are formed are necessarily true (most of the matters with which
judgment and examination are concerned can be other than they
are; for people deliberate and examine what they are doing, and
[human] actions are all of this kind, and none of them [are], so to
speak, necessary) and since things that happen for the most part
and are possible can only be reasoned on the basis of other such
things, and necessary actions [only] from necessities (and this is
clear to us also from the *Analytics*),[61] it is evident that [the prem-
ises] from which enthymemes are spoken are sometimes necessar-

58. By *judge* (*kritēs*) Aristotle means a member of the assembly or of a jury. In
Athenian legal procedure there were no professional judges in the modern sense.
The democratic juries of the Athenian courts ranged in size from 201 to 5,001,
drawn by lot from the male citizen body.

59. The fully expressed syllogism that is logically inherent in the enthymeme.

60. Later writers (see Appendix I.F) often regard an enthymeme as an abbreviated
syllogism in which one premise, usually the major, is not expressed but is assumed,
e.g., "Socrates is mortal, for he is a man," assuming "all men are mortal." Aristotle
notes that this is often the case, but it is not a necessary feature of the enthymeme.
The real determinant of an enthymeme in contrast to a syllogism is what a popular
audience will understand. Aristotle regards rhetoric, and thus the enthymeme, as
addressed to an audience that cannot be assumed to follow intricate logical argument or will be impatient with premises that seem unnecessary steps in the argument. The underlying logical structure should, however be present.

61. *Prior Analytics* 1.8, 1.12–14, 1.27; *Posterior Analytics* 1.6, 1.30, 2.12.

ily true but mostly true [only] for the most part. Moreover, enthymemes are derived from probabilities [*eikota*] and signs [*sēmeia*], so it is necessary that each of these be the same as each [of the truth values mentioned];[62] 15. for a probability [*eikos*] is what happens for the most part, not in a simple sense, as some define it, but whatever, among things that can be other than they are, is so related to that in regard to which it is probable as a universal is related to a particular.[63] **[1357b]** 16. In the case of signs [*sēmeia*], some are related as the particular to the universal, some as the universal to the particular. Of these, a necessary sign is a *tekmērion,* and that which is not necessary has no distinguishing name. 17. Now I call necessary those from which a [logically valid] syllogism can be formed; thus, I call this kind of sign a *tekmērion;* for when people think it is not possible to refute a statement, they think they are offering a *tekmērion,* as though the matter were shown and concluded [*peparasmenon*]. (*Tekmar* and *peras* ["limit, conclusion"] have the same meaning in the ancient form of [our] language.) 18. An example of signs [*sēmeia*]] related as the particular to the universal is if someone were to state that since Socrates was wise and just, it is a sign that the wise are just. This is indeed a sign, but refutable, even if true in this case; for it is not syllogistically valid. But if someone were to state that there is a sign that someone is sick, for he has a fever, or that a woman has given birth, for she has milk, that is a necessary sign. Among signs, this is only true of a *tekmērion;* for only it, if true, is irrefutable. It is an example of the relation of the universal to the particular if someone said that it is a sign of fever that someone breathes rapidly. This, too, is refutable, even if true [in some case]; for it is possible to breathe rapidly and not be feverish. Thus, what probability is and what sign and *tekmērion* are and how they differ has now been

62. I.e., probabilities correspond to things true for the most part, signs to things necessarily true. But Aristotle will modify this in what follows: some signs are necessary, others only probable. Both probabilities and signs are statements about human actions, though they may be based on physical manifestations, as the following examples show.

63. Grimaldi (1980–88, 1:62) instances "Children love their parents": it is a "probability" because a general observation—universal in form, probably, but not necessarily true in particular instances. "Some" may refer to handbook writers who discussed argument from probability.

explained. In the *Analytics*[64] they are defined more clearly, and the cause explained why some are not syllogistic and others are.

19. It has been explained that a paradigm is an induction and with what kinds of things it is concerned. It is reasoning neither from part to whole nor from whole to part but from part to part, like to like, when two things fall under the same genus but one is better known than the other.[65] For example, [when someone claims] that Dionysius is plotting tyranny because he is seeking a bodyguard; for Peisistratus also, when plotting earlier, sought a guard and after receiving it made himself tyrant, and Theagenes [did the same] in Megara, and others, whom the audience knows of, all become examples of Dionysius, of whom they do not yet know whether he makes his demand for this reason. All these actions fall under the same [genus]: that one plotting tyranny seeks a guard.[66]

[1358a] The sources of *pisteis* that seem demonstrative [*apodeiktikai*] have now been explained. 20. But in the case of enthymemes, a very big difference—and one overlooked by almost everybody—is one that is also found in the case of syllogisms in dialectical method; for some [enthymemes] are formed in accord with the method of rhetoric, just as also some syllogisms are formed in accord with the method of dialectic, while others accord with [the content of] other arts and capabilities, either those in existence or those not yet understood.[67] Hence, [the differences] escape notice of the listeners; and the more [speakers] fasten upon [the subject matter] in its proper

64. *Prior Analytics* 2.27.

65. There is an "unmediated inference," or unspoken recognition of the universal proposition. See Hauser 1985, 171–79.

66. It could be argued that seeking a bodyguard is a "sign" of intent to establish a tyranny, and certainly paradigms and signs have some similarity; but Aristotle seems to think of a paradigm as useful in indicating motivation or the probable course of events that the audience might not otherwise anticipate, whereas a sign is usually an existing fact or condition that anyone might recognize. More important to him, however, is the logical difference that the paradigm moves from the particular premises to a particular conclusion, with the universal link not necessarily expressed (just as the universal major premise of an enthymeme need not be expressed), whereas the sign moves either from universal to particular or particular to universal.

67. It is characteristic of Aristotle to feel that there were other subjects not yet systematically studied.

sense, [the more] they depart from rhetoric or dialectic.[68] This statement will be clearer if explained in more detail.

THE "TOPICS" OF SYLLOGISMS AND ENTHYMEMES

■ *Topos* literally means "place," metaphorically that location or space in an art where a speaker can look for "available means of persuasion." Rhetoric itself can be said to operate in civic space. Although the word accords with Aristotle's fondness for visual imagery, he did not originate its use in the sense of "topic"; Isocrates, early in the fourth century, had so used it, and probably others did before him. In Isocrates' *Encomium of Helen* (section 4) *topos* refers to forms of eristical argument, such as fact or possibility—what Aristotle will call *koina*. In the same speech (section 38) *topos* refers to the use of an ancient witness, Theseus' opinion of Helen— what Aristotle regards as "nonartistic" *pistis*. The word may also already have been used in mnemonic theory of the physical setting against which an object or idea could be remembered. Neither in *Topics* nor in *Rhetoric* does Aristotle give a definition of *topos,* another sign that he assumed the word would be easily understood; he does, however, give his own special twist to its meaning, usually distinguishing it from *koina* and *idia* and using it primarily of strategies of argument as discussed in 2.23. See Sprute 1982, 172–82.

68. This passage is regarded as textually corrupt by the editors. Kassel indicates that something has been lost after *listeners;* Ross rejects *the more.* The basic thought is that people do not realize that rhetoric and dialectic, though they have a method, lack content or facts and must borrow these from other disciplines, such as politics or ethics. Enthymemes are rhetorical strategies but also usually substantive arguments; and the more the argument comes from the premises of politics, ethics, or other subjects, the more the enthymeme becomes an argument of that discipline and the less it is purely rhetorical. In practice, the limits are never reached; any argument has some strategy (what Aristotle will call "topics" in 2.23) and some content (what he will call *idia* and discuss in 1.4–14 and 2.1–17). Some possible implications of this passage are discussed by Garver 1988, but he twists the meaning of some of Aristotle's words (*metabainō, tynkhanō,* etc.) to create problems that perhaps do not exist.

21. I am saying that dialectical and rhetorical syllogisms are those in which we state *topoi*, and these are applicable in common [*koinēi*] to questions of justice and physics and politics and many different species [of knowledge]; for example, the *topos* of the more and the less;[69] for to form syllogisms or speak enthymemes from this about justice will be just as possible as about physics or anything else, although these subjects differ in species.[70] But there are "specifics"[71] that come from the premises of each species and genus [of knowledge]; for example, in physics there are premises from which there is neither an enthymeme nor a syllogism applicable to ethics; and in ethics [there are] others not useful in physics. It is the same in all cases. The former [the common *topoi*] will not make one understand any genus; for they are not concerned with any underlying subject. As to the latter [the specifics], to the degree that someone makes better choice of the premises, he will have created knowledge different from dialectic and rhetoric without its being recognized; for if he succeeds in hitting on first principles [*arkhai*], the knowledge will no longer be dialectic or rhetoric but the science of which [the speaker] grasps the first principles.[72] 22. Most enthymemes are derived from these species that are par-

---

69. To be discussed in 2.23.4 (the chapter on topics).

70. The *topos* does not tell one anything about these subjects but can be applied to each; for example, "If it is just to punish offenses, it is more just to punish great offenses," "If a small force will move a body, a larger force will move it as well" and "If public revenues will support a large army, they will support a smaller army."

71. *Idia* (n. pl. of the adj. from *eidos*), "specificities, specific or particular things." The word is chosen to denote things characteristic of the species. Aristotle here does not call these specifics topics, but he does so refer to them in 1.15.19; and in sec. 22, as well as in 1.6.1, he speaks of them as *stoikheia,* which he says later (2.22.13, 2.26.1) are the "same" as topics. Thus, many rhetoricians have found it convenient to speak of "special, specific, particular, material" topics belonging to the separate disciplines, in contrast to "common" or "formal" topics, which are rhetorical or dialectical strategies of argument.

72. For the concept of "first principles" see note on 1.7.12. Part or all of a discourse may be thought of as falling in a spectrum, varying from the most general and popular to the most technical. A speech in a law court, for example, will become less "rhetorical" and more "jurisprudential" as it undertakes detailed discussion of the law. In terms of valid proof it is desirable to do this, but too technical a speech will not be comprehensible to the judges.

ticular and specific, fewer from the common [topics].[73] Just as in the case of *topoi,* so also in the case of enthymemes, a distinction should be made between the species and the *topoi* from which they are to be taken. By "species" I mean the premises specific to each genus [of knowledge], and by *topoi* those common to all. But let us take up first the genera [*genē*] of rhetoric so that having defined how many there are, we may separately take up their elements[74] and premises.[75]

Chapter 3: The Three Species of Rhetoric: Deliberative, Judicial, and Epideictic

1. The species [*eidē*] of rhetoric are three in number; for such is the number [of classes] to which the hearers of speeches belong. A speech [situation] consists of three things: a speaker and a subject on which he speaks and someone addressed,[76] **[1358b]** and the objective [*telos*] of the speech relates to the last (I mean the hearer). 2. Now it is necessary for the hearer to be either a spectator [*theoros*] or a judge [*kritēs*], and [in the latter case] a judge of either past or future happenings. A member of a democratic assembly is an example of one judging about future happenings, a juryman an example of one judging the past. A spectator is concerned

73. This is because of the need for "content": rhetoric constantly employs the special knowledge of other arts, such as politics or ethics.

74. Elements (*stoikheia*) are the same as topics; see 2.22.13, 2.26.1.

75. Aristotle's use of *genos, eidos,* and *idia* in this passage may make it somewhat difficult to follow; but he is probably not seeking to make a logical statement about the relationship of genus and species. In a general way he can be said to view knowledge as a genus of which particular forms, (e.g., physics, politics, and ethics) are species (*eidē*). The premises of the *eidē* are their *idia.* In the concluding sentence he also calls the kinds of rhetoric *genē* (genera), but in the first sentence of the next chapter will call them *eidē* (species) and in 3.3 reverts to *genē.* See n. 78.

76. Eighteenth-century rhetoricians add *the occasion* to Aristotle's three factors in the speech situation, and modern authorities have suggested other approaches, e.g., "addresser, message, addressee, context, common code, and contact" (Roman Jakobson).

with the ability [of the speaker].[77] 3. Thus, there would necessarily be three genera of rhetorics;[78] *symbouleutikon* ["deliberative"], *dikanikon* ["judicial"], *epideiktikon* ["demonstrative"]. Deliberative advice is either protreptic ["exhortation"] or apotreptic ["dissuasion"]; for both those advising in private and those speaking in public always do one or the other of these. In the law court there is either accusation [*katēgoria*] or defense [*apologia*]; for it is necessary for the disputants to offer one or the other of these. In epideictic, there is either praise [*epainos*] or blame [*psogos*]. 4. Each of these has its own "time": for the deliberative speaker, the future (for whether exhorting or dissuading he advises about future events); for the speaker in court, the past (for he always prosecutes or defends concerning what has been done); in epideictic the present is the most important; for all speakers praise or blame in regard to existing qualities, but they often also make use of other things, both reminding [the audience] of the past and projecting the course of the future.[79] 5. The "end"[80] of each of

77. This sentence is rejected by Kassel as an insertion into the text by a later reader, perhaps rightly. The audience in epideictic is not called upon to take a specific action, in the way that an assemblyman or juryman is called upon to vote; but epideictic may be viewed as an oratorical contest, either with other speakers or previous speakers (cf., e.g., Isocrates, *Panegyricus* 1), and in 2.18.1 Aristotle notes that the spectator also is in this sense a judge. The definition of epideictic has remained a problem in rhetorical theory, since it becomes the category for all forms of discourse that are not specifically deliberative or judicial; later ancient rhetoricians regarded it as including poetry and prose literature, and since Renaissance times it has sometimes included other arts like painting, sculpture, and music as well. Aristotle, however, thinks of epideictic only as a species of oratory as he knew its forms in Greece, including funeral orations like that by Pericles in Thucydides' *History of the Peloponnesian War* (2.35–46) and the *Encomia* of Helen by Gorgias and Isocrates. In such speeches, praise corrects, modifies, or strengthens an audience's belief about civic virtue or the reputation of an individual.

78. The appearance here of "rhetorics" in the plural is very unusual in Greek and probably results from the use of *genē* in the plural. Aristotle may use *genē* here of the kinds of rhetorics earlier called *eidē* because in the next sentence he is going to divide them further into species.

79. In practice, as in funeral orations, speakers usually praise past actions but with the intent of celebrating timeless virtues and inculcating them as models for the future.

80. *Telos,* the final objective of the speaker and his art, which is actualized in the persuasion of an audience. Later rhetoricians sometimes call these "final headings."

these is different, and there are three ends for three [species]: for
the deliberative speaker [the end] is the advantageous [*sympheron*][81] and the harmful (for someone urging something advises it as
the better course and one dissuading dissuades on the ground that
it is worse), and he includes other factors as incidental: whether it
is just or unjust, or honorable or disgraceful; for those speaking in
the law courts [the end] is the just [*dikaion*] and the unjust, and
they make other considerations incidental to these; for those praising and blaming [the end] is the honorable [*kalon*] and the shameful, and these speakers bring up other considerations in reference
to these qualities. 6. Here is a sign that the end of each [species of
rhetoric] is what has been said: sometimes one would not dispute
other factors; for example, a judicial speaker [might not deny] that
he has done something or done harm, but he would never agree
that he has [intentionally] done wrong; for [if he admitted that,]
there would be no need of a trial. Similarly, deliberative speakers
often grant other factors, but they would never admit that they are
advising things that are not advantageous [to the audience] or that
they are dissuading [the audience] from what is beneficial; and
often they do not insist that it is not unjust to enslave neighbors or
those who have done no wrong. And similarly, those who praise or
blame do not consider whether someone has done actions that are
advantageous or harmful [to himself] **[1359a]** but often they include it even as a source of praise that he did what was honorable
without regard to the cost to himself; for example, they praise
Achilles because he went to the aid of his companion Patroclus

---

Each *telos* often becomes a specific topic in a speech; see, for example, the discussions of expedience and justice in the speeches of Cleon and Diodotus in the
Mytilenian debate in Thucydides 3.37–48.

81. *Sympheron* is often translated "expedient"; literally, it means whatever "brings
with it" advantage (Lat. *utilitas*). Later rhetoricians were troubled by the moral
implication and sought to modify what they saw as Aristotle's focus on expediency
in political discourse; see esp. Quintilian 3.8.1–3. Since Aristotle has said in 1.1.12
that we must not persuade what is bad, he would presumably recommend that a
speaker seek to identify the enlightened, long-term advantage to the audience.
"Advantageous" or "beneficial" seems the best translation. In sec. 6 Aristotle
recognizes that in practice deliberative speakers are often indifferent to the question of the injustice to others of some action.

knowing that he himself must die, though he could have lived. To him, such a death was more honorable; but life was advantageous.

PROPOSITIONS COMMON TO ALL SPECIES OF RHETORIC

■ No technical term appears in this chapter to denote the four subjects of propositions described here, but in 2.18.2 they are called *koina,* "common things," "commonalties," in contrast to *idia,* "specifics." They are discussed in greater detail in 2.19. Since the *koinon* "greater and smaller" discussed in section 9 seems similar to the topic of "the more and the less" mentioned in 1.2.21, these *koina* have often been called "topics" or "common topics." Grimaldi (1980–88, 1:85–86) objects to this, with some reason, though in 3.19.2 Aristotle speaks of "topics" of amplification and seems to be referring to 2.19. Generally, however, Aristotle keeps them distinct: the topic of "the more and the less," discussed separately in 2.23.4, is a strategy of argument, always involving some contrast, whereas "greater and smaller," discussed in 1.7, 14 and 2.19.26–27, are arguments about the degree of *magnitude* (that term occurs in 2.18.4) or importance of something and are analogous to such questions as whether something is possible or has actually been done. Whether something is possible, actually true, or important are fundamental issues in any speech; and thus Aristotle mentions them immediately after identifying the basic issues of the advantageous, the just, and the honorable.

7. It is evident from what has been said that it is first of all necessary [for a speaker] to have propositions [*protaseis*] on these matters.[82] (*Tekmēria* and probabilities and signs are rhetorical propositions. A syllogism is wholly from propositions, and the enthymeme is a syllogism consisting of propositions expressed.)[83] 8. And since impossibilities cannot be done nor have been done, but

---

82. The advantageous, the just, the honorable, and their opposites.

83. The propositions inherent in the underlying syllogism are not necessarily all expressed in the related enthymeme; some may be assumed.

possibilities [alone can be done or have been done], it is necessary for the deliberative, judicial, and epideictic speaker to have propositions about the possible and the impossible and [about] whether something has happened or not and [about] whether it will or will not come to be. 9. Further, since all speakers, praising and blaming and urging and dissuading and prosecuting and defending, not only try to show what has been mentioned but that the good or the evil or the honorable or the shameful or the just or the unjust is great or small, either speaking of things in themselves or in comparison to each other, it is clear that it would be necessary also to have propositions about the great and the small and the greater and the lesser, both generally and specifically; for example, [about] what is the greater or lesser good or injustice or justice, and similarly about other qualities.[84] The subjects about which it is necessary to frame propositions have [now] been stated. Next we must distinguish between each in specific terms; that is, what deliberation, and what epideictic speeches, and, thirdly, what lawsuits, are concerned with.

Chapters 4–15: Sources of *Idia*, or Specific Topics, in Each of the Three Species of Rhetoric

■ In *Topics* 1.14 Aristotle says there are three classes of propositions: ethical, physical, and logical. *Ethical* includes *political*. Since rhetoric does not ordinarily deal with questions of physics, ethical and logical propositions are those useful to a speaker. In these chapters, and continuing in 2.1–17, Aristotle gives lists of opinions (called *endoxa* in dialectic) on political and ethical matters that are commonly held and thus likely to be useful to a speaker. Logical propositions will be discussed when he returns to the dialectical features of rhetoric in 2.18–26.

84. The subjects of propositions common to all species of rhetoric are thus the possible and impossible, past fact (or its nonexistence), future fact (or its nonexistence), and degree of magnitude or importance. These are discussed further in 2.19.

Chapters 4–8: Deliberative Rhetoric

Chapter 4: Political Topics Useful in Deliberative Rhetoric

■ As noted on 1.2.21–22 above, Aristotle's term for the propositions discussed here is *idia,* "specifics," or in 1.6.1 *stoikheia,* "elements"—later (2.22.13 and 2.26.1) equated with "topics," but meaning those derived from some specific body of knowledge. His discussion of the specifics of each species of rhetoric may be viewed as a partial response to Plato's complaints (especially in *Gorgias*) that civic orators lack knowledge of the subjects they discuss. Although Aristotle views rhetoric as a *tool subject*—like dialectic and in contrast to politics, ethics, and other disciplines—he recognizes that an effective civic orator needs to acquire practical knowledge, at least at a popular level, of the subjects under discussion; and he presents this knowledge as familiarity with the sources of propositions. Those discussed in this chapter all relate to the subjects of deliberation[85] in councils and assemblies in Greek cities and fall into the area of "political" thought; this subject is continued in chapter 8 with a discussion of constitutions. The intervening chapters (5–7) deal with ethical thought and the propositions it provides.

1. First, then, one must grasp what kinds of good or evil the deliberative speaker advises about, since [he will be concerned] not with all, but [only] those which can both possibly come to pass and [possibly] not. 2. As to whatever necessarily exists or will exist or is impossible to be or to have come about, on these matters there is no deliberation. 3. Nor is there deliberation about all contingent matters; for some benefits among those that can come to pass or not are the work of nature or happen by chance, and on some subjects deliberation is not worthwhile. But the subjects of deliberation are clear; and these are whatever, by their nature, are within our power

---

85. In 1.1.10 Aristotle indicated that deliberative rhetoric was the finest form. He thus discusses it first and demotes judicial rhetoric (with which the handbooks were most concerned) to last.

and of which the inception lies with us. **[1359b]** [As judges,] we limit our consideration to the point of discovering what is possible or impossible for us to do. 4. It is not necessary at the present moment to enumerate these subjects accurately, particular by particular, and to divide them into species on the basis of what is customary in deliberation or to say what would be a true definition of them, since that is not a matter for the rhetorical art but for a more profound and true [discipline]—and much more than its proper area of consideration has currently been assigned to rhetoric;[86] 5. for what we said earlier[87] is true, that rhetoric is a combination of analytical knowledge[88] and knowledge of characters and that on the one hand it is like dialectic, on the other like sophistic discourses. 6. In so far as someone tries to make dialectic or rhetoric not just mental faculties but sciences, he unwittingly obscures their nature by the change, reconstructing them as forms of knowledge of certain underlying facts, rather than only of speech. 7. Nevertheless, let us now say what it is worthwhile to analyze, while leaving the full examination to political science.

The important subjects on which people deliberate and on which deliberative orators give advice in public are mostly five in number, and these are finances, war and peace, national defense, imports and exports, and the framing of laws.[89]

8. Thus, one who is going to give advice on finances should know what and how extensive are the revenues of the city, so that if any have been left out they may be added and if any are rather small they may be increased; and all the expenses of the city as well, so that if any is not worthwhile it may be eliminated and if any is too great it may be reduced; for people become richer not only by adding to what they have but by cutting down expenses. It is not only possible to get an overall view of these matters from experience in the affairs of one's own city, but it is necessary also to

---

86. E.g., by sophists and Isocrates.

87. In 1.2.7.

88. By *analytical knowledge* Aristotle clearly means the "dialectical," and that correction is found in manuscript Parisinus 1741.

89. The list, except for framing laws, is mentioned by Socrates in Xenophon, *Memorabilia* 3.6.4–13. Possibly it derives from a lost handbook of politics.

be willing to do research about what has been discovered else-where in regard to deliberation about these things.

9. On war and peace, [it is necessary] to know the power of the city, both how great it is already and how great it is capable of becoming, and what form the existing power takes and what else might be added and, further, what wars it has waged and how (it is necessary to know these things not only about one's native city but about neighboring cities) and with whom there is probability of war, in order that there may be a policy of peace toward the stronger and that the decision of war with the weaker may be one's own. **[1360a]** [It is necessary to know] their forces also, whether they are like or unlike [those of one's own city]; for it is possible in this respect as well to be superior or inferior. Additionally, it is necessary to have observed not only the wars of one's own city but those of others, in terms of their results; for like results naturally follow from like causes. 10. Furthermore, in regard to national defense [it is necessary] not to overlook how it is carried out and to know both the size of the defense force and its character and the location of fortifications (this knowledge is impossible without familarity with the countryside), in order that it may be increased if it is rather small and may be removed if unneeded and suitable places may be guarded instead.

11. Further, in regard to food [it is necessary to know] what expenditure is adequate for the city and what kinds are on hand and what can be imported, and what items need to be exported and what imported, in order that contracts and treaties may be made with appropriate parties. (It is necessary to keep the citizens constantly free from complaints from two [foreign] groups: those that are stronger and those that are useful for commerce.)

12. For the security of the state it is necessary to observe all these things but not least to be knowledgable about legislation;[90] for the safety of the city is in its laws, so it is necessary to know how many forms of constitution there are and what is conducive to each and by what each is naturally prone to be corrupted, both forces

90. Greek cities did not usually have written constitutions, and what are described as laws approximated what we would call constitutional provisions. Change in them was deliberately made difficult. "Decrees" on specific subjects performed the function of what we would think of as ordinary legislation.

characteristic of that constitution and those that are opposed to it. By *characteristic forces of corruption* I mean that except for the best constitution,[91] all the others are destroyed by loosening or tightening [their basic principles of governance]; for example, democracy not only becomes weaker when [its principle of equality is] relaxed so that finally it leads to oligarchy but also if the principle is too rigidly applied.[92] Like a hook nose and a snub nose, not only do they reach a mean [i.e., look like a straight nose] if their characteristic features are relaxed, but if they become very hooked or snub the result is that they do not look like noses at all! 13. In legislation [i.e., constitutional revision] it is useful to an investigator not only to know what constitution is advantageous on the basis of past history but also to know the constitutions in effect in other states, observing what constitutions are suitable to what sort of people.[93] Thus, it is clear that in constitutional revision the reports of travelers are useful (for there one can learn the laws of foreign nations) and [that] for debates about going to war the research of those writing about history [is useful].[94] But all these subjects belong to politics, not to rhetoric.

These are the most important subjects on which someone who is going to give counsel ought to have [propositions]. **[1360b]** Let us return to the sources from which arguments of exhortation or dissuasion about these and other matters should be derived.

91. That based on the mean, or rule by the middle class, described in *Politics* 4.11. The forces leading to corruption of constitutions are discussed in *Politics* 5.

92. "Relaxing" the principle of equality of all citizens means that the superiority (whether by birth, by wealth, or by knowledge) of some is recognized, which is a step toward oligarchy, or government by the few; "tightening" the principle means a doctrinaire insistence that all citizens are equal, depriving the city of needed leadership and moving to choice of officials by lot and potential anarchy.

93. Aristotle made a study of many different constitutions as part of his research into politics, but only his account of the *Constitution of the Athenians* has survived.

94. A number of geographical and ethnographical works had been published by travelers before Aristotle's time, describing different parts of the world and the customs of different people. Among those Aristotle may have in mind are the now lost work of Hecataeus and the surviving *Histories* of Herodotus, which includes description of Persians, Egyptians, Scythian, and other nations as well as the history of the wars between Greece and Persia. *About going to war* is Kassel's emendation of the manuscripts (which read *political*) on the basis of the Latin of Hermannus Alemannus.

Chapter 5: Ethical Topics Useful in Deliberative Rhetoric

■ Chapters 5–15 are perhaps the "early core" of the *Rhetoric,* largely written in the mid-350s B.C.; this at least is the conclusion of Rist (1989, 84–85). Chapter 8, however, is probably a later addition; see introductory note thereto. The evidence for early composition of the chapters are some differences (e.g., 1.11.1 on pleasure) between the ethical thought set forth here and Aristotle's developed views on the subject, even allowing for the fact that Aristotle here gives a popular account of ethical views, as well as the relative lack of cross-references to other treatises, the citation of examples that are not later in origin than about 350 B.C., and the absence of some of the terminology (e.g., "topics") on which Aristotle later settled. But portions of these chapters have been touched up in the later revision of the work as a whole, for example, the reference to the *Poetics* in 1.11.29.

In addition to specifically political propositions as discussed in chapter 4, the deliberative orator, in his effort to demonstrate that a course of action is in the best interest of the audience, needs an understanding of the objectives and values of human life, which may provide additional premises for argument. In chapter 5 Aristotle identifies the goal of human action with "happiness" and describes the factors contributing to it. The chapter is a more popular, and probably earlier, version of philosophical discussions of happiness and virtue found in his ethical treatises and again helps to answer some of the objections to rhetoric when not based on knowledge, as voiced by Plato. In contrast to the political issues of the previous chapter, the ethical ones outlined here have less application in Greek deliberative oratory than in epideictic; but Cicero's speech for Pompey, *On the Manilian Law* (sections 27–55), illustrates how some topics can be utilized in deliberation when an epideictic element is present, and some are relevant for modern debates on social issues. A few premises (e.g., those relating to wealth) are applied in judicial oratory on matters of property, contracts, or inheritance. Justification for Aristotle's discussion here lies partly in the fact

that these were probably frequent matters for private deliberation (which he included under deliberative rhetoric in 3.3)
and more importantly that awareness of them on the part of a
deliberative speaker contributes to an overall understanding
of what is best for the state. On Aristotle's ethical thought,
see Hardy 1980 and Nussbaum 1986.

1. Both to an individual privately and to all people generally
there is one goal [*skopos*] at which they aim in what they choose to
do and in what they avoid. Summarily stated, this is happiness
[*eudaimonia*] and its parts. 2. Let us, then, for the sake of giving an
example [of what might be more fully explored], grasp what happiness is, simply stated, and the sources of its parts; for all forms of
exhortation and dissuasion are concerned with this and with the
things that contribute, or are opposed, to it; for one should do
things that provide happiness or one of its parts or that make it
greater rather than less, and not do things that destroy it or impede
it or effect its opposites.

3. Let happiness be [defined as] success [*eupraxia*] combined
with virtue or as self-sufficiency [*autarkeia*] in life or as the pleasantest life accompanied with security or as abundance of possessions and live bodies,[95] with the ability to defend and use these
things; for all people agree that happiness is pretty much one or
more of these.[96]

4. If happiness is something of this sort, it is necessary for its
"parts" to be good birth, numerous friendships, worthy friendships, wealth, good children, numerous children, a good old age,
as well as the virtues of the body (such as health, beauty, strength,
physical stature, athletic prowess), reputation, honor, good luck
[*eutykhia*], virtue;[97] for a person would be most self-sufficient if he

95. *Sōmatōn,* probably meaning both slaves and free men and women in a house or
on an estate.

96. These are thus popular definitions of happiness, appropriate to rhetoric. Aristotle makes some use of all but the last in his dialectical discussion of happiness in
Nicomachean Ethics 1.7–10; but his preferred definition there is "activity [*energeia*]
in accordance with virtue," and the highest virtue is found only in the contemplative
life.

97. Some manuscripts add "or also its parts: practical wisdom, courage, temperance, justice"; but editors generally regard this as an addition to the text by a later

had these goods both internal and external; for there are no others beyond these. Internal goods are those relating to the mind and the body, while good birth and friends and wealth and honor are external. And further, we [all] believe that the power to take actions and good luck should be present; for thus life would be most secure. Let us now, in a similar way,[98] grasp what each of these is.

5. *Good birth,* in the case of a nation or city, is to be autochthonous[99] or ancient and for its first inhabitants to have been leaders and their descendants distinguished in estimable qualities. For an individual, good birth may be traced either on the father's or mother's side and includes legitimacy on both lines, and, as in the case of a city, [implies that] the earliest ancestors were known for virtue or wealth or another of the things that are honored and [that] there have been many outstanding men and women in the family, both among the young and the older.[100]

[1361a] 6. *Good children* and *numerous children* are not unclear. As applied to the community this means a young generation that is numerous and good—and good in excellence of body, for example, in stature, beauty, strength, athletic prowess. Excellences of mind are temperance and courage. In the individual case, being blessed with good and numerous children means having many of one's own and of the quality described, both female and male. In the case of female children, excellence of body means beauty and stature, [excellence] of mind [means] temperance and industry, without servility. Equally in private life and in the community, both among men and among women, there is need to seek the existence of these qualities. Among those like

---

reader. These are the four cardinal virtues of the common philosophical tradition of antiquity and the Middle Ages and constitute the "virtues of the mind," complementing the virtues of "body" and "estate" that Aristotle has listed above.

98. I.e., in accord with popular definition, since this is what is useful in public address.

99. Lit., "sprung from the soil," as claimed in myth—or at least not immigrant within historical times. This is a topic in Greek oratory, though perhaps more useful in epideictic than in deliberative rhetoric, as in Isocrates, *Panegyricus* 24 and *Panathenaicus* 124.

100. Good birth is also a topic more characteristic of epideictic; cf. Isocrates, *Helen* 43, *Evagoras* 13–19, 71–72.

the Lacedaimonians where the condition of women is poor, happiness is only half present.

7. The parts of *wealth* are abundance of cash, land, possession of tracts distinguished by number and size and beauty and also possession of implements and slaves and cattle distinguished by number and beauty; and all these things [should be] privately owned[101] and securely held and freely employed and useful. Things that are productive are more useful, but things used for enjoyment are being freely employed; and by *productive* I mean what produces income, by *enjoyable* that from which there is no gain worth mentioning beyond the use of it. The definition of *securely held* is that which is possessed in such a place and in such a way that use of it lies with the owner; and whether things are "privately owned" or not depends on who has the right of alienation, and by alienation I mean gift and sale. All in all, wealth consists more in use than in possession; for the actualization of the potentialities of such things and their use is wealth.

8. Good reputation [*eudoxia*] is a matter of achieving the respect of all people, or of having something of the sort that all or the general public or the good or the prudent desire.

9. Honor is a sign of a reputation for doing good, and benefactors, above all, are justly honored, although one with the potentiality of doing good is also honored. Benefaction confers safety (and the things that cause it) or wealth or some other good of which the possession is not easily come by or not completely or not in a particular situation or moment; for many people obtain honor through things that [in other situations would] seem trifles, but the place and occasion make the difference. The components of honor are sacrifices [made to the benefactor after death], memorial inscriptions in verse or prose, receipt of special awards, grants of land, front seats at festivals, burial at the public expense, statues, free food in the state dining room, among barbarians such things as *proskynesis*[102] and rights of precedence, and gifts that are held in

101. *Oikeia,* not in the manuscripts but added by recent editors on the basis of the following discussion.

102. The requirement in Near Eastern states that those approaching an important person prostrate themselves on the ground before him, which was offensive to Greek feelings.

honor in each society; for a gift is a grant of a possession and sign of honor, and thus those ambitious for money or honor desire them. Both get what they want: **[1361b]** those ambitious for money get a possession, those for honor an honor.

10. In the case of the body, excellence is health, in the form of making use of the body without illness; for many are healthy in the way said of Herodicus, whom no one would envy for his health since [to keep it] he had to refrain from all, or nearly all, human enjoyments.[103]

11. Beauty is different at each stage of life. In the case of a youth it is a matter of having a body fit for the race course and ordeals of strength, pleasant to look at for sheer delight; thus pentathletes are most beautiful because they are equipped by nature at one and the same time for brawn and for speed.[104] When someone is in his prime, he should be adapted to the toils of war and be thought attractive as well as fear-inspiring. An old man should have adequate strength for necessary exertions and not be painful to look at, lacking any of the characteristic disfigurements of old age.

12. Strength is the ability to move another person physically as one wills; and it is necessary to move another by dragging or shoving or raising or squeezing or crushing, so strength is strength in all or some of these things.[105]

13. Excellence of stature consists in surpassing many others in height [of the body], length [of the limbs], and breadth [of the torso] but in such a way that motions are not too slow as a result of great size.

14. Bodily excellence in competitive athletics is a combination of size and strength and swiftness (and swiftness is actually a form of strength); for one who can throw his legs in the right way and move quickly and for a distance is a runner, and one who can squeeze and hold down is a wrestler, and one who can thrust with

103. See Plato, *Republic* 406a–c; Herodicus was a gymnastics teacher of poor health who wore himself and others out by constant exercise.

104. The Greek pentathlon was an athletic event consisting of running, jumping, discus, javeling, and wrestling, and thus required grace and coordination as well as stamina and brawn.

105. Aristotle continues to think chiefly about athletics, here wrestling.

the fist is a boxer, and one who can do both of the latter two has the skills needed for the *pankration,* and one who can do them all [has the skills] for the pentathlon.

15. *A good old age* is to age slowly without pain; for no one is enjoying a happy old age if he ages quickly or if gradually but with pain. A good old age is a matter of bodily excellences and luck; for unless one is without disease and is strong, he will not lack suffering, and he will not continue without hardship to advanced old age unless he is lucky.[106] Apart from strength and health there is another faculty of longevity; for many are long-lived without the excellences of the body, but detailed discussion of this is not useful for present purposes.[107]

16. The meaning of many friendships and good friendships is not unclear if *friend* is defined: a friend is one who is active in providing another with the things that he thinks are benefits to him. One who has many friends of this sort is a person of many friends; if they are worthy men,[108] he is a person of good friends **[1362a].**

17. *Good luck* [*eutykhia*] means to get and keep those good things of which chance [*tykhē*] is the cause, either all or most or the most important.[109] Chance is the cause of some things that can also be created by the arts and of many things unrelated to art, for example things caused by nature (but it is possible for chance to be contrary to nature): art is the cause of health, nature the cause of

---

106. On the text here, see Grimaldi 1980–88, 1:117–18.

107. This is perhaps a late addition. The other faculty is a certain "natural vitality," or capacity for self-renewal among living things; see Aristotle's discussion "On Length and Shortness of Life" in *Parva Naturalia* 464b–67b.

108. *Andres.* One of the rare specifications of maleness in the *Rhetoric.*

109. In Greece, as elsewhere there was a strong popular belief in *Tykhē* (Fate or Fortune) as a supernatural force that might possibly be appeased and could be worshiped as a goddess. To Aristotle this was superstition; his consistent view throughout his writings is that there is always an element of chance, accident, or contingency both in the physical world and in human affairs. But he does allow that some people are luckier than others; often he uses the word *eudaimonia* (happiness, blessedness) to describe good fortune that is at least partially the result of human intelligence and control, as in the first paragraph of this chapter; but one factor in *eudaimonia* as there listed is *eutykhia* (good luck), which is discussed here and at greater length in *Eudemian Ethics* 8.2. In the ancient world, a reputation for good luck could be a factor in deliberation about the choice of someone to take charge of an operation; see esp. Cicero, *On the Manilian Law* 47–48.

beauty and stature.[110] In general, the kinds of good things that come by chance are those which incur envy. Chance is also the cause of good things that are unaccountable, as when brothers are all ugly except one who is handsome; or when others do not see a lost treasure, but one person finds it; or when a missile hits a bystander rather than the person aimed at; or if a person who always frequents some place was [on one occasion] the only one not to come, and others, going there for the first time, were killed. All such things seem to be matters of good luck.

18. Virtue, since it is a topic most closely connected with forms of praise, must be left for definition when we give an account of praise.[111]

Chapter 6: Ethical Topics Useful in Deliberative Rhetoric (continued): Definitions of a "Good"

■ Since public address necessarily builds persuasion on popularly held assumptions, the ethical values discussed in this chapter are of a rather conventional sort; see Pearson 1962 and Dover 1974. In his ethical treatises, and especially in *Nicomachean Ethics,* Aristotle shows a greater sense of urgency toward knowing and doing what is morally right and gives higher priority to the contemplative life than to active political life.

1. Now it is clear what future or existing things should be aimed at in exhortation and dissuasion; for the latter are the opposite of the former. But since the objective of the deliberative speaker is the advantageous[112] and since [people] do not deliberate about this

110. Health can result from the art of the physician, but there are those lucky enough to be able to abuse their bodies and remain healthy. Beauty and stature are aspects of natural growth from heredity, but then there are the chance cases of the handsome child among ugly siblings or the tall child of short parents, which are, in a sense, contrary to nature.

111. In 1.9.4; but the next chapter contains some remarks on the virtues.

112. *Sympheron;* see n. 81.

objective but about means that contribute to it and these [means] are things advantages in terms of actions and since the advantageous is a good, one should grasp the elements [*stoikheia*][113] of good and advantageous in the abstract.

2. Let a good [*agathon*] be [defined as] whatever is chosen for itself and that for the sake of which we choose something else and what everything having perception or intelligence aims at or what everything would [aim at] if it could acquire intelligence.[114] Both what intelligence would give to each and what intelligence does give to each in individual cases is the good for each; and whatever by its presence causes one to be well off and independent; and independence itself; and what is productive or preservative of such things; and what such things follow upon; and what is preventative and destructive of the opposites.

3. Things "follow upon" another in two senses: either simultaneously or subsequently; for example, knowledge is subsequent to learning, but living is simultaneous with health. Things are "productive" in three senses; some as being healthy is productive of health; some as food is productive of health; some as exercise is, in that it usually produces health. 4. On these premises it necessarily follows that both the acquisition of good things and the elimination of evil things are goods; for in the latter case not having the evil follows simultaneously [with the action and] in the former having the good is subsequent. 5. [And it necessarily follows] that acquisition of a greater good than a lesser one and of a lesser evil than a greater one [are goods]; **[1362b]** for when the greater thing exceeds the lesser there is acquisition of one and elimination of the other. 6. And the virtues are necessarily a good; for those having them are well-off in regard to them, and virtues are productive of good things and matters of action. Something must be said about each [virtue] separately, both what it is and what quality it has. 7. Pleasure, too, is a good;[115] for all living things by nature desire it. Thus, both pleasant things and fine things [*kala*] are necessarily goods [*agatha*]; for some

---

113. Elements are the same as topics; see nn. 71, 74, but the word may be used here in a nontechnical sense.

114. The last clause allows for something to be said to be "good" for a plant or animal.

115. Aristotle gives a critical assessment of this in *Nicomachean Ethics* 10.2.

are productive of pleasure; and in the case of fine things some are pleasant, others desirable in themselves.[116]

8. To speak of these one by one, the following are necessarily good: happiness (it is both desirable in itself and self-sufficient, and we choose other things to obtain it), 9. justice, courage, temperance, magnanimity, magnificence, and other similar dispositions (for they are virtues of the soul); 10. and health and beauty and such things (for they are virtues of the body and productive of many things, for example, health of pleasure and life, so health seems to be the best because it is the cause of the two things most honored by most people—pleasure and life); 11. wealth (for it is the virtue of possession and productive of many things); 12. a friend and friendship (for a friend is desirable in himself and productive of many things); 13. honor, reputation (for they too are pleasant and productive of many things, and the possession of things for which people are honored usually follows with them); 14. the ability to speak, to act (for all such things are productive of goods). 15. in addition, natural talent, memory, ease in learning, quickwittedness, all such things (for these abilities are productive of goods); similarly, all forms of knowledge and art; and life 16. (for even if no other good should follow, it is desirable in itself); 17. and justice (for it is a thing advantageous to society).

These, then, are what are more or less agreed upon as goods; 18. and syllogisms are drawn from [premises about] them in discussions of debatable goods. 19. [Thus, it can be argued that] a thing is good if its opposite is bad and if its opposite is advantageous to one's enemies;[117] for example, if it is especially advantageous to our enemies for us to be cowardly, it is clear that courage is especially advantageous to our citizens. 20. And in general, the opposite of what enemies want or [of] what makes them happy seems advantageous; thus, it was well said, "Yea, Priam would rejoice. . . ."[118] But this is not always the case, only generally true; there is no reason

116. *Kala,* here translated "fine," can mean both things that are beautiful (and thus sources of pleasure) and things that are morally good (thus good in themselves).

117. Variations on this topic are found in the *Olynthiacs* and *Phillipics* of Demosthenes.

118. *Iliad* 1.255, said by Nestor of the advantage to the Trojans from the quarrel of Achilles and Agamemnon.

why the same thing may not sometimes be an advantage to both sides. As a result, it is said that evils bring men together when the same thing is harmful to both groups **[1363a]** 21. And a thing is good when it is not in excess, but whatever is greater than it should be is bad.[119] 22. And what has cost much labor and expense [is good]; for it is an apparent good already, and such a thing is regarded as an "end" and an end of many [efforts]; and the "end" is a good. This is the source of the following: "And it would be a boast left to Priam . . ."[120] and "It is a disgrace for you to have stayed long . . ."[121] and the proverb "[to break] the pitcher at the door."[122] And what many desire and what seems an object of contention [is good]; for the good was [earlier defined as] what all desire and *the many* resembles *all*. 24. And what is praised [is good]; for no one praises what is not good. And what the enemy and the evil praise [is good]; for like all others, they already acknowledge [its goodness]. And what those who have suffered from [praise is good]; for they would agree because it was self-evident, just as those are unworthy whom their friends blame and their enemies do not.[123] Thus, the Corinthians thought they had been slandered when Simonides wrote the verse "Ilium blames not the Corinthians."[124] 25. And what any of the wise or good men or women has shown preference for, as Athena [preferred] Odysseus and Theseus Helen[125] and the goddesses Paris and Homer Achilles. 26. And in general, things that are deliberately chosen [are good]; people prefer to do the things that have been mentioned, both evil things to their enemies and good things to their friends, and things that are possible. 27. But the latter

119. The basic Aristotelian doctrine of virtue and other goods as a mean between extremes.

120. *Iliad* 2.160. It would be something for Priam to boast of if the Greeks left Troy without securing Helen, the "end" for which they had suffered much toil.

121. *Iliad* 2.298. It would be a disgrace for the Greeks to have spent ten years fighting at Troy and return home empty-handed.

122. Presumably when carrying water from a well. But the proverb is not otherwise known in Greek, and whether it is right to understand *to break* is uncertain.

123. Translating Kassel's text in this sentence.

124. Simonides of Ceos, fr. 572, ed. Page. But Aristotle has somewhat misremembered the line.

125. Aristotle is probably thinking of the discussion in Isocrates' *Encomium of Helen* 18–22.

has two senses: things that might be brought about and things that are brought about easily. Easy things are done either without trouble or in a short time; for the difficult is defined either by trouble or length of time. And [things are good if they turn out] as people want; but they want either nothing bad or [an evil] less than [the accompanying] good; the latter will be the case if the cost is either unnoticed or slight. 28. And [people value] things that are peculiarly their own and that no one else [has or does] and that are exceptional; for thus there is more honor. And [people value] things that are suited to them and such things as are befitting their family and power. And [people value] things they think they are lacking in, even if small; for nonetheless, they chose to get these things. 29. And [people value] things easily done; for since easy, they are possible. (The most easily done are things in which all people or most or those like themselves or those [they regard as] inferior have been successful.) And [people value] things that delight their friends or that annoy their enemies. And [people value] anything that those do whom they admire. And [people value] what they are naturally good at and experienced in; for they think to succeed rather easily. And [people value] what no ordinary person does; for these deeds are more praiseworthy. And [people value] things they happen to long for; for this seems not only pleasant but also rather good. 30. And most of all, each category of people [values as a good] that to which their character is disposed, **[1363b]** for example, those fond of victory [value something] if it will be a victory, those fond of honor if it will be an honor, those fond of money if there will be money, and others similarly. Persuasive arguments [*pisteis*] on the subject of a good and the advantageous should be taken from these [elements or topics].

Chapter 7: The Koinon *of Degree of Magnitude—Greater or Smaller—as Applicable to Questions of the Advantageous and the Good in Deliberative Rhetoric*

■ In 1.3.9 Aristotle identified *greater and smaller,* the degree of magnitude or importance, as an argument common to all species of rhetoric, analogous to questions of possibility or fact. In 2.18.2 these types of argument are called *koina* and apparently are to be distinguished from topics. The topic of "the more and the less," mentioned in 1.2.21, is a logical strategy applied to a particular argument, whereas the *koinon* of degree, although sounding much the same, is an aspect of the subject being discussed. A speaker needs to show that something is important or not important much as he needs to show that it is possible or impossible. This chapter resumes the discussion as applied to deliberative rhetoric, the "end" of which is the advantageous; but as in the case of ethical knowledge discussed in the two previous chapters, the question of the degree of good is applicable to all species of rhetoric.

1. Since both sides in a debate often agree about what is advantageous but disagree about which is more advantageous [among possible courses of action], something should next be said about greater good and the more advantageous. 2. Let *exceeding* mean being as great and greater in quantity [than something else] and *exceeded* mean [having a quantity that can be] contained [by something else]; and let *greater* and *more* always be in comparison with *less*, but *great* and *small* and *much* and *little* be in comparison to the magnitude of most things (the great exceeding, while that falling short is small), and similarly *much* and *little*.
3. Since, then, we call something good that is chosen for itself and not for the sake of something else and what all things aim at and what something that has mind and practical wisdom would choose and the productive and the protective (or what follows on such things)[126] and since what exists for itself is an "end" (and the "end" is that for the sake of which other things exist) and since to an individual the good is what has these attributes in relation to him, it necessarily follows that more things are a greater good than one or few, provided that the one or the few are counted within the many; for it exceeds and what is contained is exceeded.[127] 4. And if

126. Cf. 1.6.2.

127. Aristotle's effort to be precise about what might otherwise seem self-evident leads him to compose a complicated sentence that has confused editors and commentators, resulting in efforts at textual emendation. See Grimaldi 1980–88 1:145

the greatest [in one class of things] exceeds the greatest [in another], the former [class] exceeds the latter; and [conversely] when the former [class] exceeds the latter, the greatest [individual item in one class] also exceeds the greatest [individual item in the other].[128] For example, if the largest man is larger than the largest woman, then as a group men are larger than women; and if men are as a group larger than women, [conversely] the largest man is larger than the largest woman; for the superiority [in size] of classes and of the greatest within them are analogous.

5. And [what precedes is the greater] when one thing follows from another but the relationship is not reciprocal (using *follows* in the sense of resulting simultaneously or successively or potentially); for the use of what follows is already inherent in what precedes. Life follows from health simultaneously, but not health from life; knowledge is subsequent to learning; and theft is the potential result of sacrilege; for one violating a holy place might also steal from it.[129]

6. And things exceeding something equal to a greater entity are greater than it; for they necessarily also exceed the greater.[130] And

---

for details. As to the last point in the sentence, five dollars can be said to be a greater good than two dollars, but not a greater good than two quarts; comparison must be within the same category of measure.

128. A difficult passage, but clarified by the followiing example. Aristotle is speaking in universal terms; it is perhaps conceivable that the largest person alive in Athens at some time might be a woman, but taking the human race as a whole over all time it seems a principle of nature that the largest man has been larger than the largest woman; and the largest mouse could never exceeed the size of the largest elephant.

129. Thus, health can be said to be better than mere living, and active learning more valuable than passive knowledge, and unwarranted entry into a sacred place a more heinous act than the potential theft that may follow. This is the interpretation of Cope and Grimaldi, which is probably right. But the crucial clause, "what precedes is the greater" is implied rather than expressed in the Greek, resulting in some possible confusion. Aristotle has said in 1.6.10 that health seems best because it is the source of life. The opposite could, of course, be argued in each case; and despite what Aristotle says, there is some reciprocity inherent in the examples; although health carries the potential for continued life, life itself carries the potential for health and is prior to it, and learning could not exist without knowledge, nor knowledge without learning. Aristotle is, however, here setting out lines of possible rhetorical argument, not making absolute judgments.

130. The interpretation of Grimaldi 1980–88 1:150–51.

things that are productive of greater good are greater; 7. for this was the meaning of *productive of the greater.*[131] And [the good] of which the producer is greater [is greater] in the same way; for if health is preferable to pleasure, it is also a greater good, and health is greater than pleasure. **[1364a]** 8. And what is more preferable in itself [is a greater good] than what is not, for example, strength than what is wholesome; for the latter is not sought for itself, while the former is, which was the meaning of the good. 9. And if one thing is an "end" and another is not, [the "end" is a greater good]; one is sought for its own sake, the other for something else, for example, exercise for the sake of bodily fitness. 10. And what has less need than another for other things [is a greater good than what has more]; for it is more independent, and "to have less need" is to need fewer things or things easily gotten. 11. And when one thing cannot come into being without another but the latter can exist without the former [, the latter is the greater good]; for what does not have this need is more independent, so that it seems a greater good. 12. And if it is a first principle [*archē*] but the other is not, [it is greater]. And if it is a cause and the other is not, [it is greater] for the same reason; for existence or coming to be is impossible without a cause and first principle.[132] And if there are two first principles [of two different things], that from the greater is the greater. And if there are two causes, what comes from the greater cause is greater; and conversely, of two first principles, the first principle of the greater thing is the greater, and of two causes the cause of the greater is the greater cause. 13. It is clear, then, from what has been said that a thing seems greater in two senses; for if one thing is a first principle and another is not, the former seems to be greater, and if one is not a first principle but the other is [what is not a first principle seems greater]; for [in the second sense] the "end" is greater and not the beginning, as Leodamas said in his accusation of Callistratus that the one giving the advice did more wrong than the one who carried it out (for the

131. In 1.7.3.

132. The concept of a first principle (*arkhē*, lit. "beginning") is basic to Aristotle's physical and metaphysical writings. In *Metaphysics* 5.1.1–3 he gives seven meanings of *arkhē* but says all have the common property of being the "starting point" from which something exists or comes into being or becomes known. All causes are *arkhai*, but all *arkhai* are not causes: e.g., the keel of a ship or the foundation of a house.

latter would not have acted if the other had not given the advice),
but against Chabrias he claimed that the one who acted [did
greater wrong] than the one who advised; for there would have
been no effect if there had not been a doer; for this is the purpose
of plots, that people may execute them. [133]

14. And what is scarcer is greater than what is abundant (for
example, gold than iron), though less useful; for possession of it is a
greater thing through being more difficult. But in another way the
abundant [is greater] than the scarce, because it exceeds in useful-
ness; for *often* exceeds *seldom;* thus, it is said, "Water is best."[134]
15. And as a whole, the more difficult [is greater] than the easier;
for it is rarer. But in another way the easier [is greater] than the more
difficult; for that is what we want things to be. 16. And something
whose opposite is greater and whose loss is greater [is greater].[135]
And virtue is a greater thing than nonvirtue, and vice a greater thing
than nonvice; for the former are "ends," the latter not.[136] 17. And
those things are greater whose effects are finer or more shameful.
And where the vices and virtues are greater, the actions are greater
too, since these [vices and virtues] are like causes and first principles, and the results [are greater]; and in proportion to the results so
also the causes and the first principles. 18. And things whose superiority is preferable or finer [are greater]; for example, it is preferable
to be keen of sight rather than of smell; for sight is also preferable to
a sense of smell. **[1364b]** And to be fond of friends is a finer thing
than to be fond of money, so love of friends [is greater] than love of
money.[137] And correspondingly, excesses of better things are better

133. The incident involved the betrayal of Oropus to the Thebans and took place in
366 B.C., soon after Aristotle first arrived in Athens as a student. Although a good
example of contrasting argument, the speeches cited appear to have been given in the
law courts (thus drawn from judicial rhetoric), not in deliberation in the assembly.

134. Pindar, *Olympian* 1.1.

135. For example, as Grimaldi notes (1980–88, 157), the opposite (loss) of health is
a greater evil than the opposite (loss) of wealth.

136. This sentence is much discussed by the commentators, some of whom are
troubled by an implied moral ambivalence. Aristotle is, however, talking about the
difference in degree, not in morality, of active versus passive qualities, as is seen in
the next sentence.

137. Kassel double-brackets sec. 18 to this point as a latter addition by Aristotle.
On the superiority of sight to other senses, see the opening lines of *Metaphysics* 1.1.

and of finer things finer. 19. And things of which the desires are finer or better [are greater]; for the stronger emotions are for greater things. And desires are finer or better for finer or better things for the same reason.

20. And things [are greater] of which the forms of knowledge are finer or more serious and the subjects are finer and more serious; for as knowledge prevails, so does truth: each science commands its own subject. The sciences of more serious and finer things are analogous for the same reasons. 21. And what the wise—either all or many or most or the most authoritative—would judge or have judged the greater good are necessarily so regarded, either absolutely or in terms of the practical wisdom [*phronēsis*] by which they made their judgment. This applies in common to other things; for substance and quantity and quality[138] are regarded as whatever science and practical wisdom say. But we have said this in the case of goods;[139] for that has been defined as good which [living] things would choose, in each case, if they had practical wisdom. It is clear, therefore, that what practical wisdom has more to say about is also greater. 22. And what belongs to better people, [is greater] either absolutely or in so far as they are better, as courage belongs to the strong. And what a better person would choose [is greater], either absolutely or in so far as he is better, for example, to be wronged rather than to wrong;[140] for this the juster person would choose. 23. And the more rather than the less pleasant [is greater]; for all things pursue pleasure, and for its sake they long to be pleased; and it is in these terms that the good and the "end" have been defined.[141] And pleasure is sweeter that is less accompanied by pain and longer lasting. 24. And the finer [is] more [great] than the less fine; for the fine is either the pleasant or what is chosen for itself. 25. And things of which people wish to be the cause to a greater extent, themselves to themselves or to their friends, these are greater goods, and of what [they wish to be the

138. The first three of the ten Aristotelian categories of being; see *Categories* 4 and book 2, n. 69.

139. See 1.6.8.

140. The principle repeatedly enunciated by Socrates, as in *Gorgias* 469c2.

141. E.g., by Eudoxus; see *Nicomachean Ethics* 10.2, where Aristotle criticizes the definition.

cause] the least, [these are] greater evils. 26. And things that last a longer time [are great] rather than those that last a shorter time, and more secure things [are greater] than the less secure; for the utility of the former exceeds over time and [the utility] of the latter [exceeds] in voluntary control; for use of something secure is readier when people want it.

27. And just as would result from etymological connections among words and grammatical inflexions [in the use of other arguments],[142] so, too, other conclusions follow [here]; for example, if *courageously* is finer [than] and preferable to *temperately,* courage is preferable to temperance and being courageous to being temperate. 28. And what all people prefer [is preferable] to what all do not. And what more rather than fewer prefer [is preferable]; for *good* was what all desire **[1365a]** so *greater* is what more people [desire]. And what opponents [regard as a greater good] or enemies or judges or those whom judges judge [to be wise is preferable]; for in the former case it is as though all people would say so, in the latter what authorities and experts [more approve]. 29. And sometimes the greater is what all share (for not to share in it is a disgrace); but sometimes [the greater is] what no one else or a few [have] (for it is rarer). 30. And things that are more praiseworthy [are greater]; for they are finer. And similarly, things of which the rewards are greater [are greater], for reward is a kind of evaluation; and [conversely,] that for which the punishments are greater [is greater]. 31. And things that are greater than those agreed [to be] or seeming to be great [are greater]. And the same things when divided into their parts seem greater; for there seems to be an excess of more things present. As a result, the poet[143] also says that [the following words] persuaded Meleager to rise up [and fight]:

> Whatsoever ills are to men whose city is taken:
> Folk perish, and fire levels the city to the dust,
> And others led off children.

---

142. *Etymological connections among words* = *systoikha* (coordinates); *grammatical inflexions* = *homoioi ptōseis* (similar cases); see *Topics* 2.9.114a–b.

143. Homer, in *Iliad* 9.592–94. Aristotle probably quotes from memory and his version does not entirely agree with our texts.

And combination and building up [of phrases or clauses make something seem greater], as Epicharmus does,[144] both because this is the same as division (for combination points to much excess) and because it seems to be the first principle and cause of great things. 32. And since the more difficult and rarer is greater, so opportunities and ages in life and places and times and powers make things great; for if a person [acts] beyond his power and beyond his age and beyond such things and if [the actions are done] in such a way or place or at such a time, he will have greatness of fine and good and just things and their opposites. Thus, too, the epigram on the Olympic victor:

> In the past, having on my shoulders a rough yoke,
> I used to carry fish from Argos to Tegea.

And Iphicrates lauded himself, speaking of his origins[145] 33. And what is self-generated [is greater] than what is acquired. Thus, the poet, too, says, "But I am self-taught."[146] 34. And the greatest part of the great [is greater]; for example, Pericles said in the Funeral Oration that the youth had been taken from the city "as if the spring had been taken from the year."[147]

35. And things that are useful in greater need [are greater], for example, those useful in old age and illnesses. And of two [goods], that which is nearer the "end" [is greater]. And what is useful to a particular person [is] more [great] than what is gener-

144. *Combination* (*syntithenai, synthesis*) is "accumulation," as in the Homeric example; *building up* (*epoikodomein*) is apparently the figure of speech called "climax," exemplified in some lines of the comic poet Epicharmus quoted by Athenaeus 2.36c–d: "After the sacrifice a feast, after the feast, drinking; after the drinks, . . . insult; after the insults, a lawsuit; after the suit a verdict; after the verdict, chains, stocks, and a fine."

145. Cf. 1.9.31. Iphicrates came from a humble background but became the best Athenian general of the period of Aristotle's first residence in Athens. Aristotle quotes his speeches several times, apparently from memory.

146. Said by the bard Phemius in *Odyssey* 22.347; but as in 1.7.31, "the poet" is apparently Homer.

147. This celebrated simile, quote again in slightly different form in 3.10.7, does not appear in the Funeral Oration attributed to Pericles in Thucydides 2.35–46. Memory of it may have been otherwise transmitted from the speech on that occasion (431 B.C.), or Pericles may have given more than one funeral oration.

ally useful.[148] And the possible [is greater] than the impossible; for one is useful in itself, the other not. And those things involved in the "end" of human life; for ends are more [important] than things supplementary to the end.[149] 36. And things related to truth [are greater] than things related to opinion. **[1365b]** The definition of *related to opinion* is what a person would not choose if he were going to escape notice. As a result, to get a benefit would seem to be more [often] chosen than to do good; for a person will chose the former even if it escapes [others'] notice, but it is not the general view that one would choose to do good secretly.[150] 37. And things people wish to exist in reality [are preferable] to their semblance; for they are more related to truth. Thus, people say that even justice is a small thing, because it rather *seems* to be preferable than *is*.[151] But this is not the case with health. 38. And what is useful in many respects [is preferred to what is not], for example, what relates to life and living well and pleasure and doing fine things. Thus, wealth and health seem to be the greatest goods; for they have all these qualities. 39. And what is less painful and what is accompanied by pleasure [is preferred]; [here there is] more than one thing, so that both pleasure and absence of pain are present as a good. 40. And of two goods, that which added to one makes the whole greater [is greater]. And things that do not escape attention when present [are great] rather than what does; for these point to the truth. Thus, being wealthy would appear to be a greater good than seeming to be. 41. And what is cherished, both by some alone and by others together with other things [, is greater than what is not]; thus, the punishment is not the same if one blinds a one-eyed man or one having two eyes;[152] for someone has taken away what is cherished. Now the sources of *pisteis* in exhortation and dissuasion have pretty much been stated.

148. See Grimaldi 1980–88, 1:173–74, on problems in this passage, but the translation follows the text of Ross and Kassel.

149. As Grimaldi (1980–88, 1:175) indicates, "end" is probably to be taken teleologically, not temporarily.

150. Cf. the story of Gyges's ring in Plato, *Republic* 2.359–60.

151. The view of Thrasymachus in Plato, *Republic* 2.358a and of Callicles in the *Gorgias*.

152. An actual law in Locris according to Demothenes, *Against Timocrates* 140–41.

Chapter 8: Topics About Constitutions Useful in Deliberative Rhetoric

■ Aristotle here resumes discussion of the premises of legislation mentioned in 1.4.12–13, where it was pointed out that the deliberative orator must understand the forces that strengthen or weaken an existing form of constitution. The chapter is probably a late addition to the early core of the *Rhetoric;* note that the discussion of deliberative rhetoric seems to end in 1.7.41. The cross-reference to the *Politics* in 1.8.7 suggests that that work had been completed; but Aristotle here speaks of four forms of constitution, as Plato had in *Republic* 8.544c, rather than the three discussed in *Politics* 3.7, where oligarchy is treated as a perversion of aristocracy. The division into four forms is less scientific but a valid practical description of what was known in Greece and thus more appropriate for rhetoric. Although democracies, like that of Athens, provided the most opportunity for public debate, both in Council and Assembly, oligarchic governments like that of Sparta had councils of elder or wealthy citizens that determined policy and thus engaged in debate; and even within a monarchy like Macedon debate took place among advisers of the king. Familiarity with differing constitutions could be especially important when ambassadors from a city living under one form of government were sent to a city living under another form of government to try to persuade it that some course of action was in its own best interests, as is clear from numerous ambassador speeches in the historical writings of Thucydides and others. Rather surprisingly, Aristotle does not specifically mention ambassador speeches; nor do later rhetoricians give them much attention. On this subject see Wooten 1973. In the case of the founding of a new city or after a revolution, such as that of 411 B.C. in Athens, there might be internal discussion of the advantages of a particular form of government. The earliest extant example of deliberation about the advantages of different forms of constitution is found in Herodotus 3.80–87, describing an imaginary debate in Persia in 521 B.C., which was probably in Aristotle's mind as he wrote this chapter. As he pointed out in

1.4.13, and repeats in 1.8.7, detailed study of the subject belongs to the discipline of politics rather than to the art of
rhetoric.

1. The greatest and most important of all things in an ability to
persuade and give good advice is to grasp an understanding of all
forms of constitution [*politeia*] and to distinguish the customs and
legal usages and advantages of each; 2. for all people are persuaded by what is advantageous, and preserving the constitution is
advantageous. Furthermore, the edict of the central authority is
authoritative, and central authorities differ in accordance with constitutions; for there are as many different central authorities as
there are constitutions. 3. There are four forms of constitution:
democracy, oligarchy, aristocracy, monarchy; thus, the central authority and decision-making element would always be some part of
these or the whole.[153]
  4. Democracy is a constitution in which offices are distributed
by lot,[154] and oligarchy one in which this is done on the basis of
ownership of property,[155] and aristocracy one in which it is based
on education [*paideia*].[156] By *education* I mean that laid down by
law [*nomos*];[157] for those who have remained within the legal tradi-

153. That is, it will always be one of the elements (the people, the rich, the educated, or the royal) that predominates in one of these or a combination of them as
in a mixed constitution.

154. This was characteristic of the more radical democracies in Greece, including
that of Athens and represents the view that all citizens were equal and equally
qualified to take their share in government, though some provision was made to
screen out the most unsuited. Women were citizens in the sense of having the full
protection of the law, but they were not eligible to participate in government; and
all Greek cities had a proportionally large number of slaves and (especially at
Athens) resident foreigners, who only rarely were granted citizenship. Democracy
literally means "rule by the *dēmos*," that is, by "the people, the many."

155. That is, only those participated in government who had a certain minimum of
ratable property. The higher the requirement, the smaller the governing elite.

156. Thus effectively on a combination of birth plus some inherited wealth and an
understanding of the culture. Aristocracy is literally "rule by the best," oligarchy
"rule by the few"; and many writers regard aristocracy as a good form of oligarchy,
which degenerates by admitting the newly rich to office.

157. Primarily, "unwritten law, custom," the traditional educational pattern observed by the upper classes and including for the Greeks *gymnastikē* (athletic

tions [of the city] rule in a aristocracy. These people necessarily seem "best," which is also why it has this name. And monarchy is, in accordance with its name, that in which one person is sovereign over all; **[1366a]** of these, some are a kingdom with orderly government, some a tyranny where power is unlimited.[158]

5. [A deliberative speaker] should not forget the "end" of each constitution; for choices are based on the "end." The "end" of democracy is freedom, of oligarchy wealth, of aristocracy things related to education and the traditions of law, of tyranny self-preservation. Clearly, then, one should distinguish customs and legal usages and benefits on the basis of the "end" of each, since choices are made in reference to this. 6. Now, since *pisteis* not only come from logical demonstration but from speech that reveals character (for we believe the speaker through his being a certain kind of person, and this is the case if he seems to be good or well disposed to us or both), we should be acquanted with the kinds of character distinctive of each form of constitution; for the character distinctive of each is necessarily most persuasive to each.[159] What these [kinds of character] are will be grasped from what has been said above; for characters become clear by deliberate choice, and deliberate choice is directed to an "end."

Summary and Conclusion of Topics Useful in Deliberative Rhetoric as Set Out in Chapters 4–8

7. Thus, a statement has been given of what should be sought while advising about future or present circumstances and of the

---

training) and *musikē* (learning to read and write with some instruction in music and poetry and the history and legal customs of the city).

158. Aristotle discusses the forms of constitution at greater length in *Politics* 3–4.

159. Thus, an envoy should exhibit democratic, oligarchic, aristocratic, or monarchical sympathies as appropriate to the audience or at least show an understanding of the political views of the community. This widens the concept of *ēthos* beyond what was described in 1.2.4 and anticipates what will be said about adapting a speech to an audience in 2.13.16 and at the end of 2.18.1.

sources from which one should take *pisteis* about the advantageous, as well as of the means and manner of acquiring knowledge about characters distinctive of constitutions and legal traditions (in so far as was appropriate for the present, for the details about these matters are described in the *Politics*).

[Chapter 9: Epideictic Rhetoric]

Chapter 9: Topics Useful in Epideictic Rhetoric; Definition of the Virtues and the Honorable as Sources of Praise; Amplification as Characteristic of Epideictic Rhetoric

■ This chapter discusses the virtues and the concept of *to kalon,* the "honorable," "fine," or "noble," and to a lesser extent its opposite, the "shameful," which are the bases of praise or blame in epideictic rhetoric. In 3.19.1 what is said here is described as the "topics" from which portrayal of moral character can be derived. As Aristotle indicates in the first section, knowledge of such matters is very useful in a speaker's efforts to secure the trust of the audience so that they will believe what is said. This can thus be important in judicial rhetoric, where a speaker may be personally unknown to the jury or be under some cloud of distrust. Many of the ways to establish a positive *ēthos* can be illustrated from private orations written on behalf of clients by Lysias, Demosthenes, Hyperides, and other logographers. Further, in sections 35–37 Aristotle points out how epideictic premises can be converted into deliberative ones by applying them to advice for future action rather than praise of what has been done in the past. The views Aristotle sets out here provide an interesting sample of the conventional values of Greek society in his time; though often consistent with his discussions of moral virtue in his ethical treatises, they are here couched in a popular form (as more appropriate for rhetoric) and as a whole place somewhat greater emphasis on social and finan-

cial success than on the intellectual and moral values he himself elsewhere stresses as the most worth attaining.

1. After this, let us speak of virtue and vice and honorable and
shameful;[160] for these are the points of reference for one praising
or blaming. Moreoever, as we speak of these, we shall incidentally
also make clear those things from which we [as speakers] shall be
regarded as persons of a certain quality in character, which was the
second form of *pistis;* for from the same sources we shall be able to
make both ourselves and any other person worthy of credence in
regard to virtue. 2. But since it often happens, both seriously and
in jest, that not only a man or a god is praised but inanimate
objects and any random one of the other animals,[161] propositions
on these subjects must be grasped in the same way. Thus, only for
the sake of giving an example [of what might be more thoroughly
explored] let us speak about these propositions also.

3. Now *kalon* describes whatever, through being chosen for
itself, is praiseworthy or whatever, through being good [*agathon*],
is pleasant because it is good [*agathon*]. If this, then, is the *kalon*,
then virtue is necessarily *kalon;* for it is praiseworthy because of
being good [*agathon*]. 4. Now virtue [*aretē*] is an ability [*dynamis*],[162] as it seems, that is productive and preservative of goods,
and an ability for doing good in many and great ways, actually in
all ways in all things. [1366b] 5. The parts [or subdivisions] of

160. *Aretē, kakia, kalon, aiskhron,* respectively. In this chapter the words are used
in a predominantly moral sense, but they all carry an implication of what is or is not
"fine, seemly." *Aretē* is basically any excellence and Aristotle sometimes so uses it:
in 3.2.1 the *lexeōs aretē* is said to be clarity. *Kalon* means "good" in the sense of
having something beautiful about it; in the previous chapters it has often been
translated "fine," but here it seems to mean what is admired as a fine thing, with a
moral connotation, hence "honorable." Some translators prefer "noble." The other
common word for "good" in Greek is *agathon,* more general in meaning, though
often moral and with no necessary aesthetic connotation.

161. Isocrates (*Helen* 12) mentions encomia of salt or bumble bees; from later
antiquity we have Dio Chrysostom's *Encomium of Hair* and Synesius' *Encomium of
Baldness;* and from the Renaissance Erasmus' *Encomium of Folly.* See Pease 1926.

162. In *Nicomachean Ethics* 2.5–6 Aristotle insists that virtue is a state or habit of
character and not a *dynamis* but that probably represents a view he later developed
and in any event such a fine distinction is not relevant to rhetoric. See Grimaldi
1980–88, 1:194–95.

virtue are justice, manly courage, self-control, magnificence, magnanimity, liberality, gentleness, prudence, and wisdom.[163] 6. Since
virtue is defined as an ability for doing good, the greatest virtues
are necessarily those most useful to others. For that reason people
most honor the just and the courageous; for the latter is useful to
others in war, and the former in peace as well. Next is liberality;
for the liberal make contributions freely and do not quarrel about
the money, which others care most about. 7. Justice [*dikaiosynē*] is
a virtue by which all, individually, have what is due to them and as
the law requires; and injustice [is a vice] by which they have what
belongs to others and not as the law requires. 8. Manly courage
[*andreia*] [is a virtue] by which people perform fine actions in times
of danger and as the law orders and obedient to the law, and
cowardice is the opposite. 9. Self-control [*sophrosynē*] is the virtue
through which people behave as the law orders in regard to the
pleasures of the body, and lack of control [is] the opposite.[164]
10. Liberality [*eleutheriotēs*] is the disposition to do good with
money, illiberality [is] the opposite. 11. Magnanimity [*megalo-
psychia*] is a virtue productive of great benefits [for others], 12. and
magnificence [*megaloprepeia*] is a virtue in expenditures, productive of something great, while little-mindedness [*mikropsychia*]
and stinginess [*mikroprepeia*] are the opposites.[165] 13. Prudence

---

163. These and other moral virtues are further defined in *Nicomachean Ethics* 3–4.

164. In most cases this would be unwritten, moral law of the values of the community. Laws of Greek cities did not usually regulate conduct in matters of sexual
actions, drinking, etc. unless violence or an affront to the community was involved,
though some cities had "sumptuary" laws restricting personal ostentation.

165. In *Nicomachean Ethics* 4.1–2 Aristotle explains the differences between liberality (*eleutheriotēs*) and magnificence, or lavishness (*megaloprepeia*) more clearly
and why the latter is a virtue. The "liberal" person is not necessarily wealthy but is
generous and not disposed to bicker about small sums; the "magnificent" person
(one might think of Lorenzo the Magnificent in the Renaissance) is wealthy and
expends large sums in a grand manner and in good taste, as in the performance of
state assignments (liturgies) such as providing a chorus for a festival or building a
warship or temple. Like all virtues, magnificence must be a mean; it lies between
vulgar excess and niggardliness. *Eleutheriotēs* might well be translated "generosity,"
but "liberality" preserves the connection with *eleutheros,* "free." In Plato's writings
"liberality" is the virtue of a "free" man, and *megaloprepeia* is "high-mindedness";
but Aristotle here gives them economic connotations. In 1.9.25–27, however,
eleutheros means a man free of the need to toil for a living.

[*phronēsis*] is a virtue of intelligence whereby people are able to plan well for happiness in regard to the good and bad things that have been mentioned earlier.

14. Now enough has been said about virtue and vice is general and about their parts for the present occasion, and it is not difficult to see the other things [that were proposed for discussion];[166] for it is clear that things productive of virtue are necessarily honorable (for they tend to virtue), as well as things that are brought about by virtue; and both the signs and works of virtue are of such a sort. 15. But since the signs [of virtue] and such things as are the workings or experiencings of a good man are honorable, necessarily whatever are the works of courage or signs of courage or have been done courageously are honorable; also just things and works justly done [are honorable] (but not things justly suffered; for in this alone of the virtues what is justly experienced is not always honorable, but in the case of being punished, to suffer justly is more shameful than to suffer unjustly), and similarly in the case of other virtues. 16. And things for which the rewards are an honor are *kala,* especially those that bring honor rather than money; and whatever someone does, by choice, not for his own sake; 17. and things absolutely good and whatever someone has done for his country, overlooking his own interest; and things good by nature and that are not benefits to him, for such things are done for their own sake; **[1367a]** 18. and whatever can belong to a person when dead more than when alive (for what belongs to a person in his lifetime has more of the quality of being to his own advantage); 19. and whatever works are done for the sake of others (for they have less of the self); and successes gained for others, but not for the self and for those who have conferred benefits (for that is just); and acts of kindness (for they are not directed to oneself); 20. and things that are the opposites of those of which people are ashamed (for they feel shame when speaking and doing and intending shameful things), as also Sappho has written in a poem:

> (Alcaeus speaking) I wish to say something, but shame hinders me.
> [Sappho replying] If you had a longing for noble or honorable things
> And your tongue had not stirred up some evil to speak,

166. In 1.9.1–2, the topics and propositions relating to the "honorable," useful in praise or blame.

Shame would not have filled your eyes,
But you would have been speaking about what is just.[167]

21. [Those things are honorable] also for which people contend without fear; for they put up with suffering in regard to goods that contribute to their reputation. 22. And the virtues and actions of those who are superior by nature are more honorable, for example, those of a man more than those of a woman. 23. And those that give pleasure to others more than to oneself; thus, the just and justice are honorable. 24. And to take just vengence on enemies and not to be reconciled; for to retaliate is just,[168] and the just is honorable, and not to be defeated is characteristic of a brave man. 25. And victory and glory are among honorable things; for they are to be chosen even if they are fruitless, and they make clear a preeminence of virtue. And things that will be remembered [are honorable]; and the more so, the more [honorable]. And what follows a person when no longer alive (and glory does follow) and things extraordinary and things in the power of only one person are more honorable, for [they are] more memorable. And possessions that bring no fruit [are more honorable]; for [they are] more characteristic of a free man.[169] 26. And things peculiar to each nation are honorable [among them]. And whatever are signs of the things praised among them [are honorable]; for example, in Lacedaimon it is honorable to have long hair, for a sign of a free man. (It is not very easy with long hair to do the work of a hired laborer). 27. And not to work at a vulgar trade [is honorable]; for it is characteristic of a free man not to live in dependence on another.

HOW TO EMPLOY TOPICS OF PRAISE AND BLAME

■ At this point Aristotle becomes prescriptive, for the first time seeming to lay down rules that the orator should follow if he is to succeed in persuading an audience. In so doing he may seem to ignore moral considerations; but rhetoric is use-

167. Sappho, fr. 138 Campbell.
168. By the definition of 1.9.7: for each to have what is due to him is just.
169. One who does not need to toil for a living.

ful in arguing on both sides of a question (1.1.12), and what he describes are "available means of persuasion" as included in the definition of rhetoric in 1.2.1. It is clear from book 1 up to this point that a speaker should have a virtuous moral intent and an understanding of the good. That a speaker can be allowed a certain amount of cleverness in obtaining legitimate ends, given the unsophisticated nature of popular audiences, is an assumption of traditional rhetoric; Quintilian, for example, insists (12.1.36–45) that an orator must be a "good man" but allows him to bend the truth when he regards it as necessary.

28. One should assume that qualities that are close to actual ones are much the same as regards both praise and blame: for example, that a cautious person is cold and designing and that a simple person is amiable or that one who does not show anger is calm; 29. and [when praising] one should always take each of the attendant terms in the best sense; for example, [one should call] an irascible and excitable person "straightforward" and an arrogant person "high-minded" and "imposing" **[1367b]** and [speak of] those given to excess as actually in states of virtue, for example the rash one as "courageous," the spendthrift as "liberal"; for this will seem true to most people and at the same time is a fallacious argument drawn from "cause"; for if a person meets danger unnecessarily, he would be much more likely to do so where the danger is honorable, and if he is generous to those he meets, all the more to his friends; for to do good to everyone is overdoing virtue. 30. Consider also the audience before whom the praise [is spoken]; for, as Socrates used to say, it is not difficult to praise Athenians in Athens.[170] And one should speak of whatever is honored among each people as actually existing [in the subject praised], for example, among the Scythians or Laconians or philosophers.[171] And all in all, attribute what is honored to what is honorable, since they seem related. 31. [Do the same with] whatever is appropriate, for example, if deeds are worthy of the subject's ancestors or his earlier

170. Something like this is attributed to him by Plato, *Menexenus* 235d.
171. Aristotle cites extreme cases of different audiences with different values: barbarians, doctrinaire oligarchs, and intellectuals.

actions; for to acquire additional honor is a source of happiness and honorable. Also [do the same] if something goes beyond the norm in the direction of the nobler and more honorable: for example, if someone shows restraint in times of good fortune but is magnanimous in adversity or in becoming greater becomes nobler and more conciliatory. Such were the remarks of Iphicrates about his [humble] origins and success[172] and of the Olympic victor, "In the past having on my shoulders a rough . . ."[173] and of Simonides, "She whose father and husband and brothers were tyrants."[174]

32. Since praise is based on actions and to act in accordance with deliberate purpose is characteristic of a worthy person, one should try to show him acting in accordance with deliberate purpose. It is useful for him to seem to have so acted often. Thus, one should take coincidences and chance happenings as due to deliberate purpose; for if many similar examples are cited, they will seem to be a sign of virtue and purpose.

33. Praise [*epainos*] is speech that makes clear the greatness of virtue [of the subject praised].[175] There is thus need to show that actions have been of that sort. Encomium, in contrast, is con-

---

172. See 1.7.32.

173. In 1.7.32 the quotation continues "yoke, I used to carry fish from Argos to Tegea."

174. In praise of Archedice, daughter of Hippias, tyrant of Athens in the sixth century. The point is that despite these connections, she was a modest woman; cf. Thucydides 6.59.

175. Further explained in *Eudemian Ethics* 2.1.12, where it is said that *epainos* is a matter of the subject's general character, *enkōmion* of particular deeds. In most Greek usage, *epainos* is a general term for praise and is found in many contexts, whereas *enkōmion* is usually a rhetorical genre, such as Gorgias's or Isocrates' *Enkōmia* of Helen. *Epainos* and *psogos* (blame) are the two species of epideictic (demonstrative oratory). The term *panegyric* originally meant a speech at a festival (*panēgyris*) where many people came together; but since the subject was often praise of the festival or city, that word also comes to be used as a term for laudatory oratory (e.g., Pliny's *Panegyric of Trajan*). In Latin, *laus* or *laudatio* corresponds to *epainos* but is occasionally used as a title, as in the anonymous poem *Laus* or *Laudatio Pisonis*. *Eulogia* is another Greek word meaning "praise"; though not commonly employed by ancient rhetoricians of a speech genre, *eulogy* has subsequently acquired that meaning and is now often used of funeral orations, which in Greek are *epitaphioi logoi*.

cerned with deeds.[176] Attendant things contribute to persuasion, for example, good birth and education; for it is probable that good children are born from good parents and that a person who is well brought up has a certain character. Thus, too, we "encomi-ize" those who have accomplished something. The deeds are signs of the person's habitual character, since we would praise even one who had not accomplished anything if we believed him to be of the sort who could. 34. (*Blessing* [*makarismos*] and *felicitation* [*eudaimonismos*] are identical with each other, but not the same as *praise* and *encomium;* but just as happiness embraces virtue, so felicitation embraces these.)[177]

35. Praise and deliberations are part of a common species [*eidos*] in that what one might propose in deliberation becomes encomia when the form of expression is changed. [1368a] 36. When, therefore, we know what should be done and what sort of person someone should be, [to use this in deliberative oratory] we should change the form of expression and convert these points into propositions: for example, that one ought not to think highly of things gained by chance but of things gained through one's efforts. When so spoken, it becomes a proposition; but as praise [of someone] it takes the following form: "He did not think highly of what came by chance but of what he gained by his own efforts." Thus, when you want to praise, see what would be the underlying proposition; and when you want to set out proposals in deliberation, see what you would praise. 37. The form of expression will necessarily be the opposite when negative advice is given instead of positive.

38. [In epideictic] one should also use many kinds of amplification,[178] for example if the subject [of praise] is the only one or the

---

176. Kassel double-brackets sec. 33–37 as a late addition by Aristotle to his text and further brackets the references to encomium, *makarismos,* and *eudaimonismos* as additions by a later student of rhetoric. In the manuscripts the entire passage 33–37 is repeated at the end of 3.16.3, where it seems to have been used to fill a lacuna in the thought. See Grimaldi 1980–88, 1:213.

177. I.e., praise and encomia are forms of felicitation (*eudaimonismos*). This sentence may well be an addition by a later student.

178. *Ta auxētika* = *auxēsis,* Lat. *amplificatio.* Amplification is especially characteristic of epideictic and contributes to its role as the species of rhetoric in which the speaker's skill or cleverness is demonstrated. It is also characteristic of other species when they are given literary revision and development for publication, as in the

first or one of a few or the one who most has done something; for all these things are honorable. And [praise can be taken] from the historical contexts or the opportunities of the moment, especially if the actions surpass expectation; and if the subject has often had success in the same way (for that is a great thing and would seem to result not from chance but from the person himself); and if incitements and honors have been invented and established because of him; and if he was the first one to receive an encomium, as in the case of Hippolochos; and [if for him,] as for Harmodius and Aristogeiton, statues were set up in the marketplace.[179] And similarly in opposite cases. And if you do not have material enough with the man himself, compare him with others, which Isocrates used to do because of his lack of experience in speaking in court.[180] One should make the comparison with famous people; for the subject is amplified and made honorable if he is better than [other] worthy ones.

---

case of Isocrates' *Philippus* or Cicero's *Verrines,* as well as in other literary forms, both prose and poetry, influenced by epideictic.

179. Hippolochus is unknown. Harmodius and Aristogeiton assassinated Hipparchus, brother of the tyrant Hippias, at Athens in 514 B.C. and were subsequently regarded as heros of the democracy. Kassel, consistent with his view of references to encomia in this passage, double-brackets the first half of the sentence as a late addition by Aristotle.

180. *Lack of experience* is the reading of the oldest manuscript, as well as the medieval commentary of Stephanus and the Latin translation of William of Moerbecke; other manuscripts read *because of his experience.* Early in his career Isocrates wrote judicial speeches, of which six survive; but he never delivered any of his speeches in public. Possibly "because of his experience in speaking in court" is an emendation of the text by someone who knew that Isocrates wrote judicial speeches; he himself seems to deny it in *Antidosis* 2–3 and *Panathenaicus* 9–14. Comparison is a striking feature of some of Isocrates' epideictic speeches, e.g., the extended comparison of Theseus and Heracles in his *Encomium of Helen,* as well as the comparison of Athens and Sparta in the *Panegyricus.* The use of the imperfect *used to do* may imply that this passage was added after Isocrates' death in 338 B.C. More likely, the implication is a gradual abandonment of digressive comparison, which seems arguable from the Isocratean corpus. The commentators have differed over whether or not Aristotle is being critical of Isocrates. He often uses examples from Isocrates' writings without any negative judgment, but he also resisted Isocrates' general influence on rhetoric; and there is some evidence that Isocrates returned the animosity without naming Aristotle. The relationship between Isocrates and Plato had also been strained. See the Introduction and Cope [1877] 1970 and Grimaldi 1980–88 on this passage.

39. Amplification [*auxēsis*], with good reason, falls among forms of praise; for it aims to show superiority, and superiority is one of the forms of the honorable. Thus, even if there is no comparison with the famous, one should compare [the person praised] with the many, since superiority [even over them] seems to denote excellence. 40. In general, among the classes of things common to all speeches,[181] amplification is most at home in those that are epideictic; for these take up actions that are agreed upon, so that what remains is to clothe the actions with greatness and beauty. But paradigms are best in deliberative speeches; for we judge future things by predicting them from past ones; and enthymemes are best in judicial speeches, for what has happened in some unclear way is best given a cause and demonstration [by enthymematic argument].

41. These, then, are the things from which speeches of praise and blame are almost all derived, as well as what to look for when praising and blaming; for if we have knowledge of these [sources of praise], their opposites are clear; for blame is derived from the opposites.

Chapters 10–15: Judicial Rhetoric

Chapter 10: Topics About Wrongdoing Useful in Judicial Rhetoric

[**1368b**] 1. Holding to our plan, we should [next] speak of accusation [*katēgoria*] and defense [*apologia*]: from how many and what sort of sources should their syllogisms be derived? 2. One should grasp three things: first, for what, and how many, purposes people do wrong; second, how these persons are [mentally] disposed; third, what kind of persons they wrong and what these persons

---

181. As Aristotle will point out in 2.26.1, amplification is not a *stoikheion* or *topos*. Rather, it is a *koinon* and form of *pistis* (see 2.18.5), a technique of persuasion, analogous to—though logically weaker than—*paradeigma* and *enthymēma*, as discussed immediately below.

are like. 3. Let us discuss these questions in order after defining wrongdoing.[182]

Let wrongdoing [to adikein] be [defined as] doing harm willingly in contravention of the law. Law is either specific [idion] or common [koinon]. I call specific the written law under which people live in a polis and common whatever, though unwritten, seems to be agreed to among all.[183] People "willingly" do whatever they do knowingly and unforced. Now everything they do willingly they do not do by deliberate choice, but whatever they do by deliberate choice they do willingly; for no one is ignorant of what he has chosen. 4. Vice [kakia] and weakness [akrasia] are the reasons why people make the choice of harming and doing bad things; for if certain people have one depravity or more, it is in relation to this that they are in fact wicked and are wrongdoers; for example, one is ungenerous with money, another is indulgent in the pleasures of the body, another is soft in regard to exertions, another cowardly in dangers (they abandon comrades in danger through fear), another ambitious for honor, another short-tempered through anger, another fond of winning by victory, another embittered through vindictiveness, another foolish through misunderstanding of justice and injustice, another shameless through contempt for public opinion, and similarly each of the others in regard to each of their underlying vices.

5. But these things are clear, partly from what has been said about the virtues,[184] partly from what will be said about the emotions.[185] It remains to say for what reason people do wrong and in what state of mind and against whom. 6. First, therefore, let us define what people long for and what they are avoiding when they

---

182. Motives are discussed in chaps. 10–11, the mental disposition of wrongdoers and those wronged in chap. 12.

183. The common law is the traditional understanding of right and wrong shared among all Greek states: standards of civilized behavior including respect for the gods, for suppliants, and for women, and the right of self-defense. Aristotle does not use the term natural law, but in 1.13.2 he does describe common law as based on a natural principle. His usage should not be confused with common law in the Anglo–American tradition, which is the law of precedent and equity as established by judicial decisions.

184. In 1.9.

185. In 2.2–11.

try to do wrong; for it is clear that the prosecutor should consider, as they apply to the opponent, the number and nature of the things that all desire when they do wrong to their neighbors, and the defendant should consider what and how many of these do not apply.

7. All people do all things either not on their own initiative or on their own initiative. Of those things not done on their own initiative they do some by chance, some by necessity; and of those by necessity, some by compulsion, some by nature. So that all the things people do that are not by their own initiative are done some by chance, some by nature, or some by compulsion. **[1369a]** But whatever they do on their own initiative and of which they are the cause, these [things] are done by habit or by desire, sometimes rational desire, sometimes irrational.[186] 8. In one case there is will, desire for some good; for no one wills something except when he thinks it a good; but anger and longings are irrational desires. Thus, necessarily, people do everything they do for seven causes: through chance, through nature, through compulsion, through habit, through reason, through anger, through longing. 9. (To distinguish actions further on the basis of age or habitual character or other things is beyond the present task; for if it incidentally results that the young are prone to anger or longing, they do not act in this way because of their youth but because of anger and longing. Nor [do those disposed to longing feel this desire] because of wealth or poverty, but it incidentally results that the poor long for money because of lack of it and [that] the rich long for unnecessary pleasures because of excess [of money]. But these, too, will act not because of wealth or poverty but because of longing. And similarly, both the just and the unjust (and others said to act by their habitual character) will do things either through reason or through emotion; but the former will do good things by character or emotion, the latter the opposite. 10. Yet there surely are consequences of having specific characters or emotions; for good reputations and sentiments in regard to his pleasures follow immediately and equally for the temperate person from his temperance, and to the intemperate person the opposites [follow] in regard to the same things. 11. As

---

186. What is meant by *irrational* will be explained in 1.11.5.

a result, though careful distinctions should be left aside [here], there should [later] be consideration of what follows what; for if someone is light or dark or large or small, nothing[187] is ordained as a consequent of such qualities; but if [someone is] young or old or just or unjust, it immediately makes a difference. And generally, [there should be consideration of] what attributes make the moral characters of human beings differ; for example, seeming to oneself to be rich or poor will make some difference, and [thinking oneself] to be lucky or unlucky. We shall discuss these later,[188] but now let us speak first about the remaining matters.)

12. Things that happen by chance are those whose cause is undefined and which do not occur for a purpose and not always nor usually nor in some ordained way. All this is clear from the definition of *chance*. 13. [Things that happen] by nature are those whose cause is in themselves and ordained; **[1369b]** for the result is always or for the most part similar. As for things that happen contrary to nature,[189] there is no need to seek exactness as to whether they occur by a natural principle or some other cause [that is not understood]; chance would also seem to be the cause of such things. 14. By compulsion [occur things] that come into being through the actions of the doers themselves [but] contrary to their desire and reasonings. 15. By habit [occurs] what they do because of having often done it. 16. Through reasoning [occur] things that seem to be advantageous on the basis of goods that have been mentioned or as an "end" or as means to an "end," whenever they are done for the sake of the advantage; for the intemperate also do advantageous things, but because of pleasure, not for the advantage. 17. Through anger and desire [come] things that are vengeful. But revenge and punishment differ; for punishment is for the sake of the sufferer,[190] revenge for the sake of the doer, that he may get a sense of fulfillment. What anger is will become clear in the discussion of the emotions,[191] 18. and through longing is done

187. That is, nothing relevant to wrongdoing.

188. In 2.12–17. The parenthetical passage, with its anticipation of book 2, is probably a late addition.

189. For example, the birth of a deformed offspring of healthy parents.

190. To correct the fault, a view also of Plato; see *Gorgias* 507–8.

191. See 2.2. Probably a late addition.

whatever seems pleasurable. The familiar and the habitual are among the pleasurable; for people even do with pleasure many things that are not pleasurable when they have grown accustomed to them. In short, all things that people do of their own volition are either goods or apparent goods or pleasures or apparent pleasures. But since they do willingly whatever they do on their own initiative and not willingly whatever is not at their own initiative, everything that they do willingly would be goods or apparent goods or pleasures or apparent pleasures. (I place removal of evils or apparent evils or exchange of greater for lesser [evil] among the goods; for they are somehow preferable, and [so is] removal of pains or what appears so; and exchange of lesser for greater similarly among pleasures.) 19. Things that are advantageous and pleasurable, their number and nature, should therefore be understood. Since the subject of the advantageous in deliberative oratory has been discussed earlier,[192] let us now speak about the pleasurable. Definitions should be thought sufficient if they are neither unclear nor inexact[193] on each subject.

Chapter 11: Topics About Pleasure Useful in Judicial Rhetoric

1. Let us assume that pleasure [*hēdonē*] is one form of movement [*kinēsis*] of the soul and a collective organization of sensual perception reaching into [an individual's] fundamental nature and that pain is the opposite.[194] 2. If pleasure is something of this

192. In 1.6.

193. I.e., not overly technical, since the point is not to expect precise, philosophical definitions in discussion of rhetoric.

194. Aristotle here adopts the definition of Speusippus, much debated in Plato's Academy; see Fortenbaugh 1970, para. 4. Later, in *Nicomachean Ethics* 10.4.2, he denies that pleasure is a *kinesis*. Rist (1989, 84) regards the statement here as evidence that this section of the *Rhetoric* is one of the earliest parts of the work, written many years before the development of Aristotle's final views of pleasure and the soul. By the soul [*psykhē*] Aristotle, as always, means the vital principle of life found in all living things. Pain, too, might be called a movement of the soul; but instead of collecting and organizing perceptions, thus inducing a feeling of well-

sort, **[1370a]** it is clear that what is productive of the condition mentioned is also pleasurable [*hēdu*] and that what is destructive [of it] or is productive of the opposite organization is painful. 3. Movement into a natural state is thus necessarily pleasurable for the most part, and especially whenever a natural process has recovered its own natural state. And habits [are pleasurable]; for the habitual has already become, as it were, natural; for habit is something like nature. (What happens often is close to what happens always, and nature is a matter of "always," habit of "often.") 4. What is not compulsory also [is pleasurable]; for compulsion is contrary to nature. Thus, constraints are painful, and it has been rightly said, "Every necessary thing is naturally troublesome."[195] Duties and studies and exertions are painful; for these, too, are necessarily compulsions unless they become habitual; then habit makes them pleasurable. And their opposites are pleasurable; thus, ease and freedom from toil and carefreeness and games and recreations and sleep belong among pleasures, for none of these is a matter of necessity. 5. And everything is pleasurable for which there is longing; for longing is a desire for pleasure. (Some longings are irrational, some in accordance with reason. I call irrational those in which people do not long for something on the basis of some opinion in the mind. Those that are said to be natural are of that sort, like those supplied from the body; for example, thirst and hunger for nourishment and longing for a particular kind of food and longing concerned with taste and sex and in general things that can be touched and things concerned with smell and hearing and sight. [I call things] "in accordance with reason" that people long for on the basis of persuasion; for they desire to see and possess many things after hearing about them and being persuaded [that they are pleasurable].)[196]

6. Since to be pleased consists in perceiving a certain emotion

---

being, it disrupts and distracts or focuses all sensation on what is alien to the natural state of the organism.

195. Quoted also in *Eudemian Ethics* 2.7.4, where is it attributed to the fifth-century elegiac poet Evenus of Paros.

196. The parenthetical passage is double-bracketed by Kassel as a later addition by Aristotle.

and since imagination [*phantasia*][197] is a kind of weak perception and since some kind of imagination of what a person remembers or hopes is likely to remain in his memory and hopes—if this is the case, it is clear that pleasures come simultaneously to those who are remembering and hoping, since there is perception there, too. 7. Thus, necessarily, all pleasurable things are either present in perception or past in remembering or future in hoping; for people perceive the present, remember the past, and hope for the future. [**1370b**] 8. Memories are thus pleasurable, not only about things that were pleasant when they were going on but even about some unpleasant things if their consequences are honorable and good. Thus, too, it has been said,

> But sweet it is to remember toils when saved[198]

and

> For when he remembers later, a man rejoices at his pains,
> He who suffers much and does much.[199]

The cause of this is that not having an evil is also pleasurable. 9. And things hoped for [are pleasurable] that, when present, seem to confer great delights or benefits and to benefit without giving pain. Generally, things that give delight when present [are pleasurable], both when we hope for them and (for the most part) when we remember them. Thus, even anger is pleasurable, as Homer also [said in the verse he] composed about anger,

> Which is much sweeter than honey dripping from the comb;[200]

for no one feels anger at someone who apparently can not get revenge, and people are not angry—or are less angry—at those much above them in power.

10. A kind of pleasure also follows most desires; for people enjoy a certain pleasure as they remember how they got something or as they hope they will get it; for example, those afflicted with thirst in a fever take pleasure both in remembering how they drank

197. For Aristotle's theory of the imagination see *On the Soul* 3.3.11.

198. From Euripides' lost *Andromeda,* fr. 131.

199. An approximate quotation of *Odyssey* 15.400–401.

200. *Iliad* 18.109.

and in hoping to drink, 11. and those in love enjoy talking and writing and continually doing something concerned with the beloved; for in all such things they think, as it were, to have sense perception of the beloved. The starting point of love is the same to all: when [people] not only delight in the beloved's presence but delight in remembering one absent; and they are in love also when there is grief at absence.[201] 12. And similarly, a certain pleasure is felt in mourning and lamentation; for the grief applies to what is not there, but pleasure to remembering and, in a way, seeing him and what he used to do and what he was like. Thus, too, it has been reasonably said,

> Thus he spoke, and raised in them the sweet longing of tears.[202]

13. And to be revenged is pleasurable; for if not attaining something is grievous, getting it is pleasurable, and angry people who do not get revenge are exceedingly pained, but while hoping for it, they rejoice. 14. And winning is pleasurable not only to those fond of it but to all; for there is an imagining of superiority for which all have desire either mildly or strongly. 15. Since winning is pleasurable, necessarily, games of physical combat and mental wit are pleasurable (winning often takes place in these) [1371a] and [similarly] games of knucklebone and ball and dice and backgammon. And similarly in the case of serious sports; for pleasure results if one is practiced [in them], and some are pleasurable from the start, such as tracking with dogs and all hunting; for where there is a contest, there is victory. That is also the source of pleasure in lawsuits and contentious debates to those that are practiced and adept.

16. And honor and reputation are among the pleasantest things, through each person's imagining that he has the qualities of an important person; and all the more [so] when others say so who, he thinks, tell the truth. Such ones are neighbors (rather than those living at a distance) and his intimates and fellow citizens (rather than those from afar) and contemporaries (rather than posterity) and the practical (rather than the foolish) and many (rather than few); for those named are more likely to tell the truth

---

201. The Greek text of this sentence is corrupt and variously reconstructed; see Grimaldi 1980–88, 1:255.

202. *Iliad* 23.108, of Patroclus, and *Odyssey* 4.183, of Odysseus.

than their opposites, [who are disregarded,] since no one pays attention to honor or reputation accorded by those he much looks down on, such as babies or small beasts,[203] at least not for the sake of reputation; and if he does, it is for some other reason.[204]

17. A friend is also one of the pleasures; for to be fond of something is pleasurable (no one is fond of wine unless he takes pleasure in wine), and to be liked is pleasurable. There, too, the good is present to someone in his imagination, which all who perceive desire. To be liked is to be cherished for one's own sake. 18. And to be admired is pleasurable because it is the same as being honored. And to be flattered and [to] have a flatterer is pleasurable; for a flatterer is an apparent admirer and apparent friend.

19. Often to do the same things is pleasurable; for it was noted above that the habitual is pleasurable. 20. And change is pleasurable; for change is a return to nature, because doing the same thing all the time creates an excess of the natural condition.[205] This is the origin of the saying "Change in all things is sweet."[206] For this reason things seen only at intervals are also pleasurable, both human beings and objects; for there is a change from what is present, and at the same time what comes at intervals is rare. 21. And to learn and to admire are usually pleasurable; for in admiration there is desire,[207] so the admirable is desirable, and in learning there is the achievement of what is in accordance with nature.[208] 22. And to benefit [others] and to be well treated are among pleasurable things; **[1371b]** for to be well treated is to attain what

---

203. Grimaldi 1980–88, 1:258, thinks this is to be taken as meaning uncivilized people, but probably it refers to animals. *Thērion* is usually a wild animal—but not necessarily so; and it certainly can be a tame one. One thinks of the animals that attended Greek gods or the dolphin that saved Arion, or (later) St Jerome's lion friend. See n. 61, where the crucial fact is clearly that babies and beasts don't "talk."

204. One might be amused or enjoy the company or hope to get something one wants out of it. Note the transition from this sentence to the next, on friendship.

205. E.g., to learn is pleasant, and thus studying is pleasant; but without an occasional respite from the routine the pleasure is diminished.

206. Euripides, *Orestes* 234.

207. The manuscripts read "desire to learn," but this is probably a misunderstanding by a scribe. See Grimaldi 1980–88, 1:261–62.

208. Defined as pleasurable in sec. 3.

people desire, and to confer benefits is to have [the resources to do so] and to surpass [others], both of which people want. Since conferring benefits is pleasurable, it is also pleasant for people to set their neighbors right and to supply their wants.[209] 23. Since to learn and to admire is pleasurable, other things also are necessarily pleasurable, such as, for example, a work of imitation, as in painting and sculpture and poetry, and anything that is well imitated, even if the object of imitation is not in itself pleasant;[210] for the pleasure [of art] does not consist in the object portrayed; rather there is a [pleasurable] reasoning process [in the mind of the spectator] that "this" is "that," so one learns what is involved [in artistic representation].[211] 24. And *peripeteias*[212] and narrow escapes from dangers [are pleasurable]; for all of these cause admiration. 25. And since what accords with nature is pleasurable and things that are related are related in accordance with nature, all things that are related and similar are, for the most part, a source of pleasure: for example, human being to human being, horse to horse, and youth to youth. This is the source of the proverbs "Coeval delights coeval,"[213] "Always like together," "Beast knows beast," "Jackdaw by jackdaw,"[214] and other such things.

26. But since all likeness and relationship is pleasurable to an individual, and each one experiences this [feeling] most in regard to himself, necessarily all are more or less lovers of themselves; for all such things apply most to oneself. And since all are lovers of themselves, necessarily their own things are also pleasurable to all, for example, their deeds and words. Thus, people are for the most part fond of their flatterers and fond of their lovers and fond of honor and fond of their children; for children are their own doing.

---

209. Sec. 22 has been questioned by some editors as interrupting the sequence of thought. Kassel double-brackets it as a later addition by Aristotle.

210. Such as a disgusting animals or corpses; cf. *Poetics* 4.4.1448b10–12.

211. Cf. *Poetics* 4.4.1448b15–17. As seen throughout the *Poetics,* Aristotle's aesthetics are cognitive. The spectator comes to understand cause and effect and the relation of universals to particulars.

212. Sudden changes, as from good fortune to bad in the plots of tragedy. In this passage Aristotle seems to be thinking both of persons directly involved and of spectators.

213. I.e., people take pleasure in those of their own age.

214. "Birds of a feather flock together."

And to supply things that are lacking is pleasurable; for it becomes their own doing. 27. Further, since people are, for the most part, given to rivalry, it necessarily follows that it is pleasurable to criticize one's neighbors; and to be the leader. (And since to be the leader is pleasantest, to seem to be wise is also pleasurable; for to be wise in a practical way is a quality of leadership, and wisdom is a knowledge of many and admirable things.)[215] 28. And to spend time at what one thinks he is best at [is pleasurable], as the poet also says:

> Each one presses on to this,
> Allotting the most part of the day
> To what happens to be his best endeavor.[216]

29. And similarly, since games are among pleasurable things, all relaxation is, too; and since laughter is among pleasurable things, necessarily laughable things (human beings and words and deeds) are also pleasurable. **[1372a]** The laughable has been defined elsewhere in the books *On Poetics*.[217] Let this much, then, be said about pleasurable things; and painful things are clear from their opposites.

Chapter 12: Topics About Wrongdoers and Those Wronged Useful in Judicial Rhetoric

CHARACTERISTICS OF WRONGDOERS

1. The reasons why people do wrong are these [just discussed]. Let us now discuss their dispositions of mind and whom they wrong. Now, then, [people do wrong] whenever they think that something

---

215. In the manuscripts this sentence is found at the beginning of sec. 27, and one good manuscript (F) omits "and to be leader." Kassel regards the parenthesis as a late addition by Aristotle. Possibly, it was inserted at the wrong place.

216. From Euripides' lost *Antiope,* fr. 183.

217. Presumably in the lost second book, though there is a short definition in *Poetics* 5.1–2: "some kind of mistake and ugliness that is not painful or destructive." The cross-reference is probably a late addition by Aristotle.

[wrong] can be done and that it is possible for themselves to do it—
if, having done it, they [think they] will not be detected or if detected, will not be punished or will be punished but [that] the pe-
nality will be less than the proft to themselves or to those for whom
they care. What sort of things seem possible or impossible will be
discussed later (these are common to all speeches);[218] 2. but those
most think they can do wrong without penalty who are skilled at
speaking and disposed to action and experienced in many disputes
and if they have many friends and if they are rich. 3. They most think
they can get away with it if they themselves are among those enumerated; but if [they are] not, [they think so] if they have friends like
that or helpers or accomplices; for through these means they are
able to act and escape detection and not be punished. 4. [They] also
[think so] if they are friends of those being wronged or of the judges;
for friends are not on guard against being wronged and seek reconciliation before undertaking legal procedures, while the judges favor
their friends and either completely acquit them or assign a small
punishment.

    5. [Wrongdoers] are likely to be unsuspected if [their appear-
ance and condition in life is] inconsistent with the charges; for
example, a weak man [is likely to be unsuspected] on a charge of
assault, and a poor and ugly man on a charge of adultery; and
[people are able to get away with] things that are done in the open
and in the public eye (no precaution being taken because no one
would ever have thought of it) and so great and of such a sort that
no one person [would be thought able to do it]; 6. for these things
also are not guarded against: everybody is on guard against usual
diseases and wrongs, but nobody takes precautions about an afflic-
tion that no one has yet suffered. 7. And [people do wrong] who
have either no enemy or many enemies; the former think that they
will escape because no precautions are being taken against them,
the latter do escape because it does not seem likely they would
attack those on their guard and [so] they have the defense that they
would not have tried. 8. And those [do wrong] who have a means
of concealment, either by artifices or hiding places, or abundant
opportunities for disposal [of stolen property].

    8. For those who do not escape detection there is [the possibil-

218. See 2.19.1–15.

ity of] squashing the indictment or postponing the trial or corrupting the judges. And if a penalty is imposed, there is avoidance of full payment or postponement of it for a while, or through lack of means a person will have nothing to pay. 9. Then there are those for whom the profits are clear or great or immediate and the punishments are small or unclear or remote. **[1372b]** And [there are those] for whom the feared punishment is not equal to the benefit, as is thought to be the case with tyranny.[219] 10. And [there are those] for whom the unjust acts bring substantial reward, but the punishments are only disgrace; and conversely, [there are] those whose wrongful acts lead to some praise, for example, if the results include vengence for a father or mother, as in the case of Zeno,[220] while the punishments lead [only] to fines or exile or something of that sort. People do wrong for both reasons and in both states of mind, except that those who do so are opposites in character. 11. And [people do wrong] when they have often been undetected or not punished. Those [do wrong,] too, who have often been unsuccessful; for there are some among these, too, as among the warlike, who are [always] ready to fight again. 12. And those for whom the pleasure is immediate but the pain comes later, or the profit [is] immediate but the punishment [comes] later; for the weak are like that, and their weakness of character applies to everything they desire. 13. And conversely, those [do wrong] for whom the pain or the penalty is immediate but the pleasure and advantage come later and are long-lasting; for the strong and those who are more prudent pursue such things. 14. And those [do wrong] who can seem to have acted by accident or by necessity or by natural instinct or by habit and all in all seem to have made a mistake rather than committed a crime. And those [do wrong] to whom there is a chance of fair consideration. 15. And those in need [do wrong], but need is of two sorts: for either it is a matter of necessities, as in the case of the poor, or a result of excess, as in the case of the rich. 16. And those [do wrong] who are very well thought of, and those with very bad reputations—the former as not being suspected, the latter as being no worse thought of.

---

219. Double-bracketed by Kassel as a later addition by Aristotle.
220. Incident unknown.

CHARACTERISTICS OF THOSE WHO ARE WRONGED

People take in hand a wrongful action when disposed as just described, and they wrong people of the following sort and in the following ways. 17. [They wrong] those having something they lack, either as necessities of life or for surfeit or for enjoyment, both those afar and those near; 18. for in the latter case they get what they want quickly, and in the former retribution is slow, as in the case of those robbing the Carthaginians.[221] 19 And [they wrong] those who do not take precautions and are not on guard, but trusting; for it is rather easy to take all these unawares. And [they wrong] those who are easygoing; for it is characteristic of a careful person to initiate prosecution. And [they wrong] those who are shy; for they are not likely to make a fight about proceeds. 20. And [they wrong] those who have been wronged by many and have not prosecuted, since these are, as the saying goes, "Mysian spoil."[222] 21. And [they wrong] those who have never—and those who have often—[been wronged]; for both are off their guard, the former since it has never happened, the latter on the ground that it will not happen again. 22. And [they wrong] those who have been slandered or are easy to slander; for they do not choose to go to court for fear of the judges, nor could they persuade them. Those who are hated and despised are in this class. [1373a] 23. And [they wrong] those against whom they have the pretext that those persons' ancestors or themselves or their friends either harmed, or were going to harm, them or their ancestors or those for whom they care; for as the proverb has it, "Wickedness only needs an excuse." 24. And [they wrong] both enemies and friends; for the latter is easier, the former sweet. And [they wrong] those who are friendless. And [they wrong] those not good at speaking or taking action; for either they do not undertake prosecution, or they come to an agreement, or accomplish nothing. 25. And [they wrong] those to whom there is nothing to gain in wasting time by attending on the court or the

---

221. Aristotle is probably thinking of attacks by Greek pirates on Carthaginian shipping; Carthage seemed far away, and the pirates would not be soon caught if at all.

222. I.e., "easy prey." For speculation on why the Mysians may have been so called, see Cope's commentary ([1877] 1970) on this passage.

settlement, for example, foreigners and the self-employed; for they are willing to abandon suit cheaply and are easily put down. 26. And [they wrong] those who have done many wrongs to others or the [same] kinds of wrongs [as are] being done to them; for it almost seems to be no wrong when some one is wronged in the way he himself is in the habit of wronging others. I mean, for example, if some one assaults a person who has the habit of flagrantly insulting others. 27. And [they wrong] those who have done bad things [to the person who now reciprocates] or wanted to or want to now or are going to; for this is both pleasurable and honorable and seems almost no wrong. 28. And [they wrong] those whom people wrong as favors to their friends or to those they admire or love or regard as their masters or, generally, depend on in their lives. And [they wrong] those in regard to whom there is a chance of fair consideration.[223] 29. And [they wrong] those against whom they have made complaints and have had previous differences, as Calippus did with Dion;[224] for such things seem almost to be no wrong. 30. And [they wrong] those who are going to be wronged by others if the doers do not act [first] themselves, since it is no longer possible to deliberate, as Aenesidemus is said to have sent the *kottabos* prize to Gelon after the latter had enslaved a city, because Gelon did first what Aenesidemus was planning.[225] 31. And [they wrong] those for whom they can do many just things after they have wronged them, thus easily remedying the wrong, as Jason of Thessaly said he had to do some few unjust things in order to do many just ones.

SOME REMARKS ON THE NATURE OF WRONGS

32. [People do those things] which all or many are in the habit of doing wrongfully; for they think they will get pardon. 33. [They

223. This is the converse of 1.12.15. The context there suggests that Aristotle is thinking of "fair consideration" from a jury, not from the person injured.

224. Calippus had a role in the death of Plato's friend Dion of Syracuse in 354 B.C.

225. *Kottabos* was a game played by tossing disks into a basin, popular at drinking parties in Sicily. The usual prizes were sweets. Aenesidemus apparently cynically complimented Gelon on success at playing the "game" of tyranny. The date was around 485 B.C. See Grimaldi 1980–88, 1:283.

steal] things easy to conceal and the kind that are quickly consumed,
like eatables, or are easily altered in shape or color or by mixing
[them in with other things] or which there is an opportunity to hide
in many places. 34. Such things include those that are easily carried
and can be concealed in small places 35. and those that are indistin-
guishable and similar to many others that the criminal already has.
And [they commit crimes] that those wronged are ashamed to mention; for example, outrages against the women of their household or
against themselves or their sons. And [they commit] actions in regard to which a complainant would seem to be litigious and such as
are small matters for which there is forgiveness.[226]

The characteristics of those whom people wrong and what sort
of wrongs they do and against what sort of people and for what
reason are more or less these.

Chapter 13: Topics About Justice and Injustice Useful in Judicial Rhetoric

[1373b] 1. Let us now classify all unjust and just actions, beginning first with the following points. Just and unjust actions have
been defined in reference to two kinds of law and in reference to
persons spoken of in two senses. 2. I call law on the one hand
specific, on the other common, the latter being unwritten, the
former written,[227] *specific* being what has been defined by each
people in reference to themselves, and *common* that which is
based on nature; for there is in nature a common principle of the
just and unjust that all people in some way divine, even if they
have no association or commerce with each other, for example,
what Antigone in Sophocles' play seems to speak of when she says
that though forbidden, it is just to bury Polyneices, since this is just
by nature:

226. Cf. the legal principle *De minimis non curat lex,* "The law does not care about
trifles."
227. The translation moves this phrase forward from its position in the sentence to
avoid inconsistency with 1.10.3.

> For not now and yesterday, but always, ever
> Lives this rule, and no one knows whence it appeared.[228]

And, as Empedocles says about not killing a living thing,

> 'Tis not just for some and unjust for others,
> But the law for all, it extends without a break
> Through the wide-ruling ether and the boundless light.[229]

And as Alcidamas says in the *Messeniacus*.[230]

3. And law is divided in two ways in regard to persons; for what one ought to do or not do is defined in regard to the community or in regard to individual members of the community.[231] Thus, unjust and just actions are a matter of being unjust and doing justly in two senses, either in respect to one defined individual or in regard to the community. Commiting adultery and beating someone up are wrongs to some defined individual; refusing to serve in the army wrongs the community.

4. Since all kinds of unjust actions have been classified, some being against the community, others against one or another person or persons, let us take up the matter again and say what it means to be wronged. 5. To be wronged is to suffer injustice at the hands of one who acts voluntarily; for to do injustice has earlier been defined as voluntary.[232] 6. Since a person who suffers injustice is necessarily harmed and harmed against his will, the forms of harm are clear from what has been said earlier. (Things good and bad in themselves have been discussed earlier, as have things that are done voluntarily, which is whatever is done knowingly.)[233] 7. Thus,

---

228. Sophocles, *Antigone* 456–57.

229. Fragment 31.B.135, ed. Diels–Kranz *Vorsokratiker.*

230. Alcidamas was a sophist of the generation before Aristotle. The work mentioned was probably an epideictic oration. The manuscripts of Aristotle do not supply a quotation here, but a medieval commentator supplies, "God has left all free; nature has made no one a slave."

231. Greek law distinguished between a public offense (*graphē*) and violation of private rights (*dikē*); the distinction differs from modern understanding of criminal and civil law in that many actions that today would be regarded as crimes, including murder, were regarded as violations of private rights.

232. See 1.10.3.

233. Aristotle refers back to various parts of the discussion in chaps. 6, 7, 9, and 10.

necessarily, all accusations are either in regard to [wrongs done to] the community or to the individual, the accused having acted either in ignorance and involuntarily or voluntarily and knowingly and in the latter case either with deliberate choice or through emotion. 8. Anger [*thymos*] will be discussed in the account of the emotions;[234] and what sort of things are deliberately chosen and in what disposition of character has been said earlier.[235]

[1374a] 9. Since people often admit having done an action and yet do not admit to the specific terms of an indictment or the crime with which it deals—for example, they confess to have "taken" something but not to have "stolen" it or to have struck the first blow but not to have committed "violent assault" or to have had sexual relations but not to have committed "adultery" or to have stolen something but not to have committed "sacrilege" ([claiming] what they took from a temple did not belong to the god) or to have trespassed but not on state property or to have had conversations with the enemy but not to have committed "treason"—for this reason, [in speaking we] should give definitions of these things: what is theft? What [is] violent assault?[236] What [is] adultery?[237] In so doing, if we wish to show that some legal term applies or does not, we will be able to make clear what is a just verdict. 10. In all such cases the question at issue [*amphisbētesis*] relates to whether a person is unjust and wicked or not unjust; for wickedness and being unjust involve deliberate choice, and all such terms as *violent assault* and *theft* signify deliberate choice; for if someone has struck another it does not in all cases mean he has "violently assaulted" him, but [only] if he has done so for a certain reason, such as to dishonor him or to please himself. Nor has he committed "theft" in

---

234. In 2.2 (where, however, the word used is *orgē*). This is probably a late addition by Aristotle.

235. In 1.11–12.

236. The word translated "violent assault" is *hybris,* which in Greek law describes any violent attack on another person, including rape.

237. Aristotle's observations here were further developed by Hermagoras (2d century B.C.) and later rhetoricians into what is called stasis of definition. E.g., a defendant on a murder charge can perhaps deny that he killed anyone (stasis of fact) but, if unable to do that, can plead that his actions were justifiable homicide not fitting the legal definition of murder. See further on 3.15.

all cases if he took something, but [only] if for harm and his own advantage. The situation in other cases is similar to this.

11. Since there were two species of just and unjust actions (some against written, others unwritten laws), our discussion has dealt with those about which the [written] laws speak; and there remain two species of unwritten law. 12. These are, on the one hand, what involves an abundance of virtue and vice, for which there are reproaches and praises and dishonors and honors and rewards—for example, having gratitude to a benefactor and rewarding a benefactor in turn and being helpful to friends and other such things[238]—and on the other hand things omitted by the specific and written law. 13. Fairness,[239] for example, seems to be just; but fairness is justice that goes beyond the written law.[240] This happens sometimes from the intent of the legislators but sometimes without their intent when something escapes their notice; and [it happens] intentionally when they cannot define [illegal actions] accurately but on the one hand must speak in general terms and on the other hand must not but are able to take account only of most possibilities; and in many cases it is not easy to define the limitless possibilities, for example, how long and what sort of weapon has to be used to constitute "wounding";[241] for a lifetime would not suffice to enumerate the possibilities. 14. If, then, the action is undefinable when a law must be framed, it is necessary to speak in general terms, so that if someone wearing a ring raises his hand or strikes, by the written law he is violating the law and does wrong, when in truth he has [perhaps] not done any harm, and this [latter judgment] is fair.

[1374b] 15. If, then, fairness is what has been described, it is

238. The unwritten law, which includes a code of gracious behavior, requires gratitude and generosity, which the written law does not. Conversely, it regards as unacceptable and cause for reproach such things as ingratitude and rudeness.

239. *Epieikes,* often translated "equity"; but *epieikes* is a broader concept and, unlike equity, applies to both criminal and civil law.

240. Rigid application of the written law may sometimes go against its intent and be inequitable, as the following discussion notes.

241. The legislators cannot list all possible weapons, and what about injury from dull instruments or something small like a pin? Does that constitute "wounding"? The court must decide in terms of the intent of the law and fairness to those involved.

clear what kind of actions are fair and what are not fair and what kind of human beings are fair: 16. those actions that [another person] should pardon are fair, and it is fair not to regard personal failings [*hamartēmata*] and mistakes [*atykhēmata*] as of equal seriousness with unjust actions. Mistakes are unexpected actions and do not result from wickedness; personal failings are not unexpected and do not result from wickedness; [and] unjust actions are not unexpected and do result from wickedness. 17. And to be forgiving of human weaknesses is fair. And [it is also fair] to look not to the law but to the legislator and not to the word but to the intent of the legislator, and not to the action but to the deliberate purpose 18. and not to the part but to the whole, not [looking at] what a person is now but what he has been always or for the most part. And [it is fair] to remember the good things one has experienced [because of him] rather than the bad, and good things experienced [because of him] rather than done for him. And [it is fair] to bear up when wronged. And [it is fair] to wish for an issue to be decided by word rather than by deed. 19. And [it is fair] to want to go into arbitration rather than to court; for the arbitrator sees what is fair, but the jury looks to the law, and for this reason arbitrators have been invented, that fairness may prevail.[242] On the subject of things that are fair let definitions be made in this way.

Chapter 14: The Koinon of Degree of Magnitude as Applicable to Questions of Wrongdoing in Judicial Rhetoric

■ This chapter parallels 1.7, where the same *koinon* was applied to deliberative questions. The first sentence is linked grammatically to the last sentence of the previous chapter, indicating no real break in Aristotle's thinking.

1. And a wrong is greater in so far as it is caused by greater injustice. Thus, the least wrong [can sometimes be] the greatest, as

---

242. On the use of arbitrators, see Aristotle's *Constitution of the Athenians* 53.2–4. Official arbiters (*diaitētai*) were appointed from among men fifty-nine years of age.

for example, the accusation of Callistratus against Melanopus, that he defrauded the temple builders of three consecrated half-obols.[243] But in the case of justice it is the opposite.[244] This results from the fact that [injustice] inheres in the potentiality; for he who steals three consecrated half-obols would be capable of doing any wrong. Sometimes the greater is judged this way, sometimes from the harm done. 2. And [a wrong is greater] where there is no equal punishment but all are too little. And [it is greater] where there is no healing the wrong; for it is difficult, even impossible [to undo]. And [it is greater] where the victim cannot have recourse to a trial; for in such cases there is no healing [the wrong]; for a trial and punishment are a form of healing. 3. And [it is greater] if the victim who is wronged has [as a result] inflicted some great punishment on himself; for the doer should justly be punished with the greater [suffering], as Sophocles,[245] speaking on behalf of Euctemon after he had killed himself because of the outrage he had suffered, **[1375a]** would not fix the penalty as less than the victim had assessed it for himself. 4. [A wrong is greater] that only one person has done or has been the first to do or is one among few to have done. And to commit the same fault often is a great thing [against someone]. Also what results in search and discovery of [new] forms of prevention and punishment [is a great wrong], as in Argos a person was punished because a law was passed [as a result of his actions], as were those for whom a prison was built.[246] 5. And the more brutal a crime, the greater [the wrong]. And the more premeditated [the crime, the greater the wrong]. And what hearers fear or pity more [is a greater wrong]. Rhetorical techniques adaptable to this are [to say] that a person has broken many norms of justice and gone beyond [a single crime], for example, [breaking] oaths, handshakes, promises, marriage vows; for this is a heaping up of wrongs. 6. And

243. A paltry sum, as is explained below. The incident is otherwise unknown, but Callistratus and Melanopus were political rivals around 370 B.C.

244. The most insignificant just actions are not the greatest.

245. Possibly the dramatist, but more likely a fifth-century politician of the same name, in which case perhaps the Sophocles also mentioned in 3.18.6.

246. The incident is unknown, and thus the reference somewhat obscure. Prisons were usually used in Greece only for short detention, as in the case of Socrates awaiting execution.

[wrongs are greater when committed] in a place where wrongdoers are being punished, which is what perjurers do; for where would they not do wrong if they do it even in the law court? And things in which there is the greatest disgrace [are greater wrongs]. And [a wrong is greater] if against the very one by whom a person was benefited; for he does more wrong both because he wrongs and because he does not benefit. 7. And what contravenes the unwritten codes of justice [is a greater wrong]; for it is characteristic of a better person to be just without being required to do so; thus, what is written is a matter of necessity, what is unwritten not. In another way [it is a greater wrong] if it contravenes what is written; for one who does wrong despite his fears and despite the existence of punishments would also do wrong that did not incur punishments. Enough, then, has been said about greater and lesser wrong.

Chapter 15: Atechnic (Nonartistic, Extrinsic) Pisteis in Judicial Rhetoric: Laws, Witnesses, Contracts, Tortures, Oaths

■ The arguments that Aristotle briefly summarizes in this chapter are those available to a speaker in dealing with documentary evidence that supports or weakens a case. In democratic lawcourts, such as those at Athens, the evidence of witnesses was usually taken down at a preliminary hearing and then read out by a clerk rather than being given in person by the witnesses. Orators also sometimes called on the clerk to read the texts of laws or contracts that were in dispute; or they quoted poets, oracles, or proverbs as "witnesses." Oaths taken or refused on previous occasions could be introduced as evidence. Resemblances between this chapter and the discussion of "supplementary" *pisteis* in the *Rhetoric to Alexander* (1431b3ff.) suggest that Aristotle is drawing on some earlier handbook on the subject; see Fuhrmann 1960, 138–42; Thür 1977 and Mirhady 1991.

To some readers this chapter has seemed rather too tolerant of sophistry, but Aristotle is again setting out the "available" means of persuasion in accordance with his definition of 1.2.1. As he states in 1.1.12, rhetoric provides arguments on both sides of a case. Under constitutional governments in Greece a defendant was entitled to state a case in the most favorable way. It may be that a defendant is legally guilty but morally justified, hence Aristotle's emphasis on the importance of what he calle *epieikes,* "fairness." His discussion is clearly focused on judicial procedure in Athens. An Athenian jury, made up of 201, 501, or more citizens selected by lot, can be thought of as representative of the democratic assembly of all citizens and could judge what if any laws should apply as well as the facts of the case. Thus, some aspects of deliberation about laws could be introduced into a trial. Though there are separate words for judge (*kritēs*) and juryman (*dikastēs*) in Greek, in democratic states there was no official judge in the modern sense of one who both presided over a trial and instructed the jury about the law; thus, in most legal procedure judge and jury were identical. Aristotle often uses the words interchangeably. There was no appeal from judicial decisions, though cases were sometimes reopened if new evidence became available or the procedure could be faulted. In the translation of this difficult chapter I have taken into account some suggestions by Brandes (1989, 196–200) and am indebted to David Mirhady for many others.

1. Following on what has been said, [the next subject is] to run through what are called "atechnic" *pisteis;* for they are specifics [*idia*] of judicial rhetoric. 2. They are five in number: laws, witnesses, contracts, evidence [of slaves] taken under torture, oaths.[247]

---

247. Aristotle here adds laws and oaths to those mentioned in his definition of nonartistic proof in 1.2.2. His concept of nonartistic proofs is limited to documentary evidence that could be read out and used as a basis of argument in a trial.

TOPICS AGAINST AND IN FAVOR OF WRITTEN LAWS

3. Let us first speak about laws [*nomoi*], [showing] how they can be used in exhorting and dissuading[248] and accusing and defending; 4. for it is evident that if the written law is contrary to the facts, one must use common law and arguments based on fairness as being more just: 5. [say] that to use "best understanding" is not to follow the written laws exclusively;[249] 6. and that fairness[250] always remains and never changes nor does the common law (for it is in accordance with nature) but written laws often change. This is the source of what is said in Sophocles' *Antigone;* for she defends herself as having performed the burial in violation of the law of Creon, but not in violation of what is unwritten:

[1375b]

> For not now and yesterday, but always, ever
>
> . . . .
>
> This I was not likely [to infringe] because of any man.[251]

7. And [say] that the just is something true and advantageous[252] but what seems to be just may not be; thus, the written law may not be; for it does not [always] perform the function of law. And [say] that the judge is like an assayer of silver in that he distinguishes counterfeit and true justice. 8. And [say] that it is characteristic of a better man to use and conform to the unwritten rather than the written [laws]. 9. And if [a law] is contradictory to [another] approved law or even to itself (for example, sometimes one law orders contracts to be binding while another forbids making contracts in violation of the law) 10. and if it is ambiguous, so that

---

248. *Exhorting and dissuading* is deleted by some editors as appropriate only to deliberative rhetoric, but as Mirhady (1991) argues, its presence here probably reflects the introduction of "political" deliberation about the validity and interpretation of law into a trial, as indicated in the next section.

249. Juries swore to decide a case "in accordance with the law" or, if the law was unclear, in accordance with their "best understanding."

250. *Epieikes,* often translated "equity"; but see n. 239.

251. An approximate quotation of *Antigone* 456, 458. Cf. 1.13.2, where line 457 is found instead of 458.

252. *Sympheron,* the characteristic topic of deliberative rhetoric (see 1.2.5), here introduced in deliberation on the law in a trial.

one can turn it around and see to which meaning it fits, whether with justice or the advantageous, one should make use of this interpretation. 11. And if, on the one hand, the situation for which the law was established no longer prevails but the law still exists, one should try to make this clear and fight with this [argument] against the law.

12 But if, on the other hand, the written law is in accordance with the facts, one should say that *in their best understanding* does not mean that the jury is to judge contrary to the law but is there to provide that the jury not violate its oath if it does not understand what the law says. And [one should say] that no one chooses what is good in general but what is good for himself.[253] And [one should say] that it makes no difference whether a law is not passed or is not used.[254] And [one should say] that in the other arts there is no advantage to being smarter than "the doctor";[255] for a mistake by a physician does not do so much harm as becoming accustomed to disobey one who is in charge. And [one should say] that to seek to be wiser than the laws is the very thing that is forbidden in those laws that are praised. And let distinctions be made this way on the subject of the laws.

QUOTATION OF POETS, ORACLES, PROVERBS, AND WELL-KNOWN
PERSONS AS "WITNESSES"

■ Sections 13–17 differ from the rest of the chapter in that they look beyond the specifics of a case and consider how quotations from literature or historical figures may be used. In section 17 Aristotle turns to actual witnesses of the facts of a case.

13. As for witnesses [*martyres*], they are of two sorts, some ancient, some recent; and of the latter [there are] some sharing the

253. This seems to be an answer to an opponent who wants to have the law, passed in the interest of the community, waived to suit a particular situation. The jury can be reminded that to uphold the law is in their interest.

254. I.e., since the law has been passed, it should be enforced.

255. Or in this case the legislators. Probably, Aristotle is quoting a proverb.

risk [of being brought to trial for perjury], some outside it. By *ancient* I mean the poets and other well-known persons whose judgments are clear; for example, the Athenians used Homer as a witness in their claim to Salamis, and the Tenedians recently used Periander of Corinth against the Sigeans.[256] And Cleophon used the elegies of Solon [as a witness] against Critias, saying that the insolence of his family was ancient; otherwise Solon would never have composed the line:

> Tell the fair-haired Critias to listen to his father for me.[257]

Witnesses about past events are of this sort, 14. while expounders of oracles [are witnesses] about future events; **[1376a]** for example, Themistocles [interpreted] the "wooden wall" to mean that a naval battle must be fought.[258] Also proverbs, [where the phrase] *as has been said* is a form of testimony; for example, if someone were to advise against making a friend of an old man, the proverb "Never do good to an old man" bears testimony to it.[259] And [if someone advises] killing sons whose fathers have already been killed, [he may say,] "Foolish he who after killing the father leaves behind the sons."[260]

---

256. Around 600 B.C. Solon had cited *Iliad* 2.557–58 in support of Athenian claims to the island of Salamis against the claims of Megara. The "recent" incident involving the people of Tenedos (an island off the coast of the Troad) and Sigeum (on the coast nearby) is unknown; but Aristotle lived nearby at Assos from 347 to 345 and could most easily have known about this minor incident then or during the next few years, when he was in Mytilene and Macedon. Periander of Corinth had acted as an arbitrator in another dispute between Athens and Mytilene over Sigeum around 600 B.C.

257. Solon, fr. 22a ed. West.

258. In 480 B.C. Themistocles persuaded the Athenians not to rely on the walls of Athens to defend the city against the Persians but to interpret an oracle from Delphi, promising that the "wooden wall" would not fail to provide security, to mean the Athenian fleet. See Herodotus 7.141.

259. This is an actual Greek proverb of a rather cynical cast; on the character of the old (distrustful, small-minded, thinking only of themselves) see 2.13..

260. Attibuted by Clement of Alexandria (*Strommata* 7.2.19) to Stasinus, author of the early epic *Cypria*. Although the Athenians in the fifth century repeatedly put to death all adult males of cities that had revolted, as at Melos in 416, they usually spared children; and the injunction mostly applies to the heroic world as seen in Greek tragedy. Aristotle regarded rhetoric as useful in writing speeches in tragedy; see *Poetics* 19.2.

15. Recent witnesses are well-known persons who have given a judgment about something; for their judgments are also useful in controversies about similar things. For example, Euboulus, attacking Chares in the law courts, made use of what Plato said to Archebius: that "confessions of vice had become common in the city."[261] [Recent witnesses are] also those who share the risk [of being brought to trial] if they seem to commit perjury. 16. Such persons are only witnesses of whether or not something has happened (whether something is or is not the case) but not [competent] witnesses of the quality of the act—of whether, for example, it was just or unjust or conferred an advantage or not. 17. On such matters, outsiders are [objective] witnesses, and ancient ones the most credible; for they are incorruptable.

TOPICS AGAINST AND IN FAVOR OF WITNESSES

One having no witnesses as corroborators of testimony [should say] that judgment must be made on the basis of probabilities and [that] this is what is meant by *in their best understanding*[262] and that probability cannot deceive for bribes and that probabilities are not convicted of false testimony; the one who has [witnesses should say] against the one who does not that probabilities are not subject to trial and that there would be no need of witnesses if it were enough to speculate on the basis of [probable] arguments. 18. Some testimonies are about the speaker, others about the opponent, and some [are] about the facts, others about character, so it is evident that there is never a lack of useful testimony; for if there is no testimony relating to the fact or supporting the speaker or contradicting the opponent, still [there will be abundance of evidence] about his character that points to fair-mindedness or about the opponent that points to badness. 19. Other points about a witness—whether friend or enemy or in between, whether reputable or disreputable or in

261. Euboulus was a well-known politician and a slightly younger contemporary of Plato. The quotation certainly sounds like something Plato might have said but is otherwise unknown. There was also a comic poet named Plato; but this is not a metrical line from a comedy, and the poet lived a generation earlier.
262. See secs. 5, 12.

between, and any other differences of this kind—should be chosen
from the same topics[263] from which we derive enthymemes.

TOPICS FOR AND AGAINST CONTRACTS

20. As regards contracts [*synthēkai*], argument is useful to the
extent of amplifying or minimizing or making them credible or
not, **[1376b]** [making them credible and valid] if they support [the
speaker's] position but the opposite if they help the opponent.
21. As far as rendering them credible or not credible goes, there is
no difference from the treatment of witnesses; for contracts are
credible insofar as the signatories and custodians of them are.

If it is agreed that a contract exists, this should be amplified as
long as it supports the speaker's side: for [he can say] a contract is a
law that applies to individuals and particulars; and contracts do not
make law authoritative, but laws give authority to contracts made
in accordance with law, and in general the law itself is a certain
kind of contract, so that whoever disobeys or abolishes a contract
abolishes the laws. 22. Further, [he can say] most ordinary and
voluntary transactions are done in accordance with contracts, so
that if they lack authority, the commerce of human beings with
each other is abolished. And other suitable things [to say] are self-
evident.

23. If the contract is opposed to the speaker and on the side of
his opponents, then it is suitable [to say] those things that one
might use to fight an opposing law: for [one can say] it is strange if
we think we do not have to obey laws whenever they are not rightly
framed and those who made them erred but necessary to obey
contracts. 24. Secondly, [one can say] that the jury is an umpire of
justice; it is not this [contract] that should be considered but how
more justly [to treat the parties involved]. And that it is not possible to pervert justice by deceit or compulsion (for justice is based

263. This is the first appearance of the word *topoi* since 1.2.22, where it was used of
common topics in contrast with the *eidē*, or species of arguments in particular
disciplines like politics. Since the *topoi* here mentioned seem to be the specific
political and ethical arguments as discussed in chaps. 4–15, we are given some
textual justification for calling these *specific* topics; but the sentence may be a late
addition by Aristotle; see Appendix II.A.

on nature) 25. but [that] contracts are among those things affected by deceit and compulsion. In addition, look to see whether the contract is contrary to any written or common laws and in the case of written laws either those of the city or foreign ones, then [whether it is contrary] to other earlier or later contracts; for later contracts take precedence, or else the earlier ones are authoritative and the later ones fraudulent (whichever argument is useful). Further, look at the matter of what is advantageous, whether perhaps there is something [about the contracts] opposed to the interest of the judges and anything else of this sort; for these things are easy to see in a similar way.[264]

TOPICS FOR AND AGAINST THE EVIDENCE OF SLAVES

26. Tortures [*basanoi*] are a kind of testimony and seem to have credibility because some necessity [to speak] is involved.[265] It is thus not difficult about them either to see the available [means of persuasion] from which it is possible to provide amplification if they are in favor [of the speaker], [saying] that this form of testimony is the only true one. [1377a] But if they are against him and favor his opponent, one could refute them by speaking [first] about the whole concept of torture; for [slaves] do not lie any less when under compulsion, neither [those who] harden themselves not to tell the truth nor [those who] lie easily to stop the pain more quickly. There is [also] need to cite examples that the judges know, which have [actually] happened. (It is necessary to say that tor-

---

264. With the Athenian system of very large juries, to appeal to the interest of the judges is to appeal to the public interest. Thus, they might invalidate a contract that cornered the market on some product.

265. The evidence of slaves was only admissable in a court of law if extracted under torture, the official assumption being that slaves could not be counted on to tell the truth otherwise. Occasionally slaveowners tried to free their slaves to avoid having them tortured. Aristotle regarded slavery as "natural," in the sense that some human beings had irredeemably servile characters (cf. *Politics* 1.5); but, as this chapter shows, he did not believe that evidence extracted under torture was reliable. Most Greek states had large slave populations, used in agriculture, mining, and in private households; and there were also publicly owned slaves. They were acquired from military action and many were themselves Greeks; few if any were racially distinct from their masters.

tures are not reliable; for many slow-witted and thick-skinned persons and those strong in soul nobly hold out under force, while cowards and those who are cautious will denounce someone before seeing the instruments of torture, so that there is nothing credible in tortures.)[266]

TOPICS RELATING TO OATHS TAKEN OR REFUSED BY THE PRINCIPALS IN A TRIAL

27. On the matter of oaths [*horkoi*], there are four distinctions to make; for [before trial] either [a person both] gives and [himself] takes [an oath], or does neither, or does [only] one or the other of these, and in the last case he may give the other [an oath to swear] but not take [an oath] himself or may take [an oath] but not give one [to his opponent].[267] Further, beyond this, [there is the question] whether an oath was sworn [earlier] by one or the other.

28. If a person does not give [his opponent an opportunity to swear], [he can say] that people swear false oaths easily, and that one who has sworn does not [necessarily] allow his opponent to swear in return, but thinks [a jury] will condemn one who has not sworn and that one who has sworn does not [necessarily] allow his opponent to swear and that the risk is greater before a jury; for he trusts jurymen but not himself.[268]

29. If he does not take [an oath himself, he can say] that an oath

266. Most editors regard this passage as an addition to the text by a later scribe. There are also some textual problems within it; the translation follows the version in Kassel's apparatus criticus.

267. In Greek law an attempt to settle a matter before trial could take the form of an "exculpatory oath." One or both of the disputants challenged the other in writing to take an oath (e.g., that the terms of a contract had been fulfilled). If the matter was not settled and went to trial, these challenges then could be used as evidence for or against the litigants; but throughout much of the passage Aristotle uses the present tense, envisioning the situation when the oaths were first under discussion. This passage is difficult to translate because the Greek idiom *to give an oath* means to dictate, or administer, the terms on which another person will swear, while *to take an oath,* as in English, means to swear to the terms given by another.

268. Reading *autōi d'ou,* as conjectured by Mirhady (1991). This seems to be the converse of what is described in sec. 30.

is a substitute for something more tangible;[269] and that if he were a bad man he would have taken the oath; for it is better to be bad for some profit than for nothing, since [the one who] has sworn will win the case but [the one who has] not sworn will not; and thus [a refusal] is because of virtue, not because of a [fear of] perjury. And Xenophanes' maxim applies,[270] that the same challenge to take an oath is not equal for an irreligious man in comparison with a religious one; for it is much as if a strong man called out a weak one to hit or be hit.

30. If he takes an oath, [he can say] that he trusts himself, not the opponent. And by reversing the maxim of Xenophanes, one should say that in this way it is equal if the irreligious man gives an oath and the religious one swears it. And that it would be terrible for him not to want [to decide the case by his oath][271] about matters on which he would think it right for the judges to decide only after being sworn.

31. If he gives an oath, he can say that it is pious to want to entrust the matter to the gods and that there is no need for his opponent to demand any other judges; for he [the speaker] is giving the decision to him [the opponent]. And that it would be out of place not to want to swear on a matter about which he would think it right that others swear.

32. Since it is clear how one should speak in each of these cases, it is also clear how to speak when they are combined, for example if the speaker wishes to take [an oath] but not to give one to his opponent and if he wishes to give an oath to his opponent but does not wish to take one himself, and if he wishes both to take and to give [oaths] or if neither; **[1377b]** for these necessarily are a combination of the positions mentioned, so that the arguments are composed of those described.

And if an oath has been taken by the speaker, and is in conflict

---

269. *Khrēmata,* lit. "things," usually translated as "money" (a common meaning of the word) but here perhaps "hard evidence."

270. Xenophanes of Colophon, philosopher and poet who lived around 500 B.C. The following clause in Greek resembles iambic verse.

271. The verb to be supplied is apparently *dikazein,* as Mirhady has suggested to the translator. Taking an oath effectively settles the case; cf. what is said in the next section and Demosthenes 29.52–53.

[with what he now says, he should say] that there is no perjury; for wrongdoing is voluntary and to commit perjury is wrongdoing, but what is done under force and under deceit is involuntary. 33. Here, then, one should also conclude that committing perjury is with the mind and not with the tongue.[272] If, on the other hand, [the oath] is opposed to the opponent and he is the one who has sworn, [the speaker can say] that he who does not abide by what he has sworn overturns everything; for this is why [juries] administer the laws under oath. And [he can say to the jury], "[My opponents] think it right for you to abide by the oaths by which you swore you would judge, but they themselves do not abide [by their oaths.]" And there are many other things one might say in amplification.

272. Cf. the notorious line from Euripides' *Hippolytus* (612), "It was my tongue that swore; my heart is unsworn." Aristotle cites it in 3.15.8.

BOOK 2:
Pisteis, or the Means of Persuasion in Public Address (continued)

■ In 1.2.3–6 Aristotle identified three artistic modes of persuasion, derived from presenting the character (*ēthos*) of the speaker in a favorable light, awakening emotion (*pathos*) in the audience so as to induce them to make the judgment desired, and showing the probability of what is said by logical argument (*logos*). In 2.1.1–4 he repeats this in the order *logos, ēthos, pathos.* This order is then reversed (chiasmus) in the following discussion: chapters 2–11 explore the emotions; chapters 12–17 the adaptation of the character of the speaker to the character of the audience; and chapters 18–26 return to logical techniques, including paradigms, enthymemes, and topics, concluding the discussion of rhetorical invention or thought.

Chapter 1: Introduction

Chapter 1: The Need for an Understanding of the Role of Character and Emotion in Persuasion

■ Sections 1–4 of this chapter resume the discussion in 1.2.3–5 of the character of the speaker (on which see also 1.9.1) and the emotions of the audience as artistic modes of

persuasion. Sections 5–7 discuss the need for the speaker to
render himself trustworthy to the audience; section 8 turns to
the matter of pathos and outlines the method Aristotle will
follow in discussing the emotions in chapters 2–11.

1. These [specifics, or special topics, set forth in book 1] are the
proper sources of exhortation and dissuasion, praise and blame,
and prosecution and defense, and the kinds of opinions and propositions useful for their persuasive expression; for enthymemes are
concerned with these matters and drawn from these sources, so the
result is speaking in a specific way in each genus of speeches.
2. But since rhetoric is concerned with making a judgment (people
judge what is said in deliberation, and judicial proceedings are also
a judgment), it is necessary not only to look to the argument, that
it may be demonstrative and persuasive but also [for the speaker]
to construct a view of himself as a certain kind of person and to
prepare the judge; 3. for it makes much difference in regard to
persuasion (especially in deliberations but also in trials) that the
speaker seem to be a certain kind of person and that his hearers
suppose him to be disposed toward them in a certain way and in
addition if they, too, happen to be disposed in a certain way [favor-
ably or unfavorably to him]. 4. For the speaker to seem to have
certain qualities is more useful in deliberation; for the audience to
be disposed in a certain way [is more useful] in lawsuits;[1] for things
do not seem the same to those who are friendly and those who are
hostile, nor [the same] to the angry and the calm but either altogether different or different in importance: **[1378a]** to one who is
friendly, the person about whom he passes judgment seems not to
do wrong or only in a small way; to one who is hostile, the opposite; and to a person feeling strong desire and being hopeful, if
something in the future is a source of pleasure, it appears that it
will come to pass and will be good; but to an unemotional person
and one in a disagreeable state of mind, the opposite.
5. There are three reasons why speakers themselves are persuasive; for there are three things we trust other than logical demon-

1. The sentence up to this point is double-bracketed by Kassel as a later addition by
Aristotle.

strations. These are practical wisdom [*phronēsis*] and virtue [*aretē*] and good will [*eunoia*];[2] for speakers make mistakes in what they say or advise through [failure to exhibit] either all or one of these; 6. for either through lack of practical sense they do not form opinions rightly; or though forming opinions rightly they do not say what they think because of a bad character; or they are prudent and fair-minded but lack good will, so that it is possible for people not to give the best advice although they know [what] it [is]. These are the only possibilities. Therefore, a person seeming to have all these qualities is necessarily persuasive to the hearers. 7. The means by which one might appear prudent and good are to be grasped from analysis of the virtues;[3] for a person would present himself as being of a certain sort from the same sources that he would use to present another person; and goodwill and friendliness need to be described in a discussion of the emotions.[4]

8. The emotions [*pathē*] are those things through which, by undergoing change, people come to differ in their judgments and which are accompanied by pain and pleasure, for example, anger, pity, fear, and other such things and their opposites. 9. There is need to divide the discussion of each into three headings. I mean, for example, in speaking of anger, what is their *state of mind* when people are angry and against *whom* are they usually angry, and for what sort of *reasons;* for if we understood one or two of these but not all, it would be impossible to create anger [in someone].[5] And similarly, in speaking of the other emotions. Just as we have drawn up a list of propositions [*protaseis*] on the subjects discussed earlier, let us do so about these and let us analyze them in the way mentioned.[6]

2. Practical wisdom and virtue are aspects of character, good will of *pathos,* as sec. 7 makes clear.

3. Topics useful for this can be found in 1.9.

4. Topics useful for this are found in chap. 4 below.

5. Cf. the division of the question of wrongdoing made in 1.10.2.

6. The word *protaseis* suggests that Aristotle may view topics about the emotions as premises for enthymemes, but he does not make this clear; see introductory note to the next chapter.

Chapters 2–11: Propositions About the Emotions Useful to a Speaker in All Species of Rhetoric

■ These famous chapters on the emotions, the earliest systematic discussion of human psychology, seem to have originated in some other context and have been only partially adapted to the specific needs of a speaker. With a few exceptions (e.g., 2.3.13 and 6.20, 24) the examples given are not drawn from rhetorical situations; and some (e.g., 2.2.10–11) do not at all fit a deliberative, judicial, or epideictic audience. The primary rhetorical functions of the account is apparently to provide a speaker with an ability to arouse these emotions in an audience and thus to facilitate the judgment sought (see 1.2.5, 2.1.4, 2.2.27, 2.3.17, 2.4.32, 2.5.15, 2.9.6, and 2.10.11). But some of the emotions (e.g., shamelessness, unkindliness or envy) are not ones a speaker is likely to want to arouse toward himself, and a secondary purpose emerges in 2.4.32 and 2.7.5–6: how to arouse emotion against an opponent and how to refute an opponent's claims to the sympathy of an audience. All these passages seem to be afterthoughts, tacked on to the discussion to adapt them to their present context; chapters 6, 7, 8, and 11 lack any adaptation. Nevertheless, chapters 2–11, taken as a whole, provide an introduction to psychology (at least to conventional Greek psychology of Aristotle's time) that could give a speaker better insight into human motivation and improve speaking in general.

The discussions come in pairs, arranged chiastically in what might loosely be described as positive/negative, negative/positive sequence (e.g., anger/calmness, friendliness/hostility, fear/confidence, shame rightfully felt/shamelessness). George of Trebizond and subsequent editors of the *Rhetoric* somewhat disguised the pairing by separating the first set (discussed at greater length than others) into two chapters (2–3); but the Greek text is continuous. Chapters 8–9 and 10–11 also seem logical units even though the relationship between pity, indignation, and envy as discussed there is somewhat complex (see 2.9.3–5). In the case of each emotion Aristotle considers the reason for it, the state of mind of the person who feels it, and those toward whom it is directed (although not always in the same sequence and detail). This division of the subject has some resemblence to his theory of "four causes" as seen in *Physics* 2.3 (see Fortenbaugh 1975, esp. 9–18).

In 3.19.3 Aristotle refers to these chapters as setting out the "topics" of the emotions, but the word *topic* does not occur in the chapters. At the end of chapter 1 he has said that he will furnish *protaseis,* or propositions, about the emotions in what follows. This raises the question as to whether what is set out in chapters 2–11 are to be regarded as premises for enthymemes. It is the view of Grimaldi (1975, 147–51), also echoed throughout his *Commentary,* and of Conley (1982) that they are—to which Wisse (1989, 20–29) objects. If this was Aristotle's view, he has done remarkably little to make it clear; and in 3.17.8 he actually advises against using enthymemes when seeking to arouse emotion. It is true that some emotional appeals can take the form of an enthymeme; one example would be 2.5.11: "And among those wronged and enemies or rivals it is not the quick-tempered and outspoken who are to be feared but the calm and those who dissemble and the unscrupulous; for with these it is unclear if they are close to acting, with the result that it is never evident that they are far from doing so." One can imagine a speaker saying this to impart fear in an audience. But much of what Aristotle says would not take enthymematic form in a speech. A good example is the list of qualities that create a friendly feeling, given in 2.4.11–22. The audience will feel friendly to a speaker who is pleasant and good-tempered: he can accomplish this by not criticizing other people's faults, by joking, by praising other people, by being neat in appearance, by refraining from slander, by being serious about serious things, and by showing himself to be like his hearers in interests and desires, and so on.

Aristotle's discussion of the emotions here is the only extensive account of this aspect of psychology in his extant works and as such has been a part of the *Rhetoric* especially interesting to medieval and modern students of his philosophy. Emotions in Aristotle's sense are moods, temporary states of mind—not attributes of character or natural desires—and arise in large part from perception of what is publicly due to or from oneself at a given time. As such, they affect judgments.[7] See Rorty 1984; and Wisse 1989, 65–74.

Chapter 2: Orgē, or Anger

THE DEFINITION AND CAUSES OF ANGER

1. Let anger be [defined as] desire, accompanied by [mental and physical] distress, for conspicuous retaliation because of a conspicuous slight that was directed, without justification, against oneself or those near to one.[8] 2. If this is what anger is, necessarily the angry person always becomes angry at some particular individual (for example, at Cleon but not at an [unidentified] human being)[9] and because he has done or is going to do something to him

7. At the 1990 Symposium Aristotelicum, Pierre Aubenque drew attention to the following passage in Martin Heidegger's *Being and Time* (1962, 178): "The different modes of state-of-mind and the ways in which they are interconnected in their foundations cannot be Interpreted within the problematic of the present investigation. The phenomena have long been well-known ontically under the terms 'affects' and 'feelings' and have always been under consideration in philosophy. It is not an accident that the earliest systematic Interpretation of affects that that has come down to us is not treated in the framework of 'psychology.' Aristotle investigates the *pathē* [affects] in the second book of his *Rhetoric*. Contrary to the traditional orientation, this work of Aristotle must be taken as the first sytematic hermeneutic of the everydayness of Being with one another. Publicness, as the kind of Being which belongs to the 'they' not only has in general its own way of having a mood, but needs moods and 'makes' them for itself. It is into such a mood and out of such a mood that the orator speaks. He must understand the possibilities of moods in order to rouse them and guide them aright."

8. On the text, see Wisse 1989, 69. The word translated "slight" (*oligōria*) literally means a "belittling," and that rendering is more apt in some of what follows. Aristotle does not regard *orgē* as an emotion felt when a person understands he or she has been justly treated, e.g., by a superior who issues a justifiable rebuke; nor is it an emotion felt against oneself.

9. This rules out the situation in which in modern times we say a person is angry when he does not know at whom to direct his anger, e.g., the feeling on discovering

or those near to him; **[1378b]** and a kind of pleasure follows all
experience of anger from the hope of getting retaliation. It is pleasant for him to think he will get what he wants; but no one wants
things that seem impossible for himself to attain, and the angry
person desires what is possible for him. Thus, it has been well said
of rage [*thymos*],

A thing much sweeter than honey in the throat, it grows in the breast of
    men.[10]

A kind of pleasure follows from this and also because people dwell
in their minds on retaliating; then the image [*phantasia*] that occurs
creates pleasure, as in the case of dreams.
    3. Belittling [*oligōria*] is an actualization of opinion about what
seems worthless[11] (we think both good and bad things worth serious
attention, also things that contributed to them; but whatever
amounts to little or nothing we suppose worthless), and there are
three species of belittling: contempt [*kataphronēsis*], spite [*epēreas-
mos*], and insult [*hybris*]; 4. for one who shows contempt belittles
(people have contempt for those things that they think of no account, and they belittle things of no account); so, too, the spiteful
person; for the spiteful person is an impediment to [another's]
wishes, not to get anything himself but so that the other does not.
Since, then, there is no gain for himself, he belittles; for clearly he
does not suppose [the other] will harm him (or he would be afraid
and would not belittle) nor that [the other] might benefit [him] in
any way worth mentioning (for then he would be taking thought so
as to become a friend). 5. The person who gives insult also belittles;
for insult [*hybris*] is doing and speaking[12] in which there is shame to
the sufferer, not that some advantage may accrue to the doer or

---

that some unknown person has run into your parked car. Here there is usually no
personal slight. Aristotle also fails to notice the situation in which one group, say
the Athenians, is angry at another, say the Spartans, but in fact his observations can
apply to the latter situation.

10. *Iliad* 18.109.

11. That is, by word or deed one person "puts down" another as of no account, and
what was only a possible opinion is given actual expression.

12. The reading of Parisinus 1741; but other good manuscripts have *harming and
distressing,* and there is no clear basis of choice between the two versions.

because something has happened but for the pleasure of it; for those reacting to something do not give insult but are retaliating.

6. The cause of pleasure to those who give insult is that they think they themselves become more superior by ill-treating others. That is why the young and the rich are given to insults; for by insulting they think they are superior. Dishonor is a feature of insult, and one who dishonors belittles; for what is worthless has no repute, neither for good nor evil. Thus, Achilles, when angered, says,

[Agamemon] dishonored me; for taking my prize, he keeps it himself.[13]

And, as a reason for his anger,

[He treats me] like a dishonored vagrant.[14]

7. And people think they are entitled to be treated with respect by those inferior in birth, in power, in virtue, and generally in whatever they themselves have much of; [1379a] for example, in regard to money a rich man [thinks himself] superior to a poor man, and in regard to speech an eloquent one to one unable to express himself, and a ruler [feels superior] to one who is ruled, and one thinking himself worthy to rule to one worthy to be ruled. Thus, it has been said,

Great is the rage of Zeus-nurtured kings,[15]

and

But still, even afterward, he has resentment.[16]

For they are vexed by their sense of [ignored] superiority. 8. Furthermore, a person [feels belittled by adverse remarks or actions of those] by whom he thinks he should be well treated. These are

---

13. *Iliad* 1.356.

14. Grimaldi (1980–88, 2: 24) denies that Agamemnon was Achilles' inferior and thus that anger in Aristotle's system is limited to reaction against inferiors. Agamemnon is the commander, but he is Achilles' inferior in fighting, in fame, and in birth. The point is that the angry person regards one who insults him as an inferior and that one who insults is trying to assert superiority.

15. *Iliad* 2.196.

16. *Iliad* 1.82.

those whom he has treated well [in the past] or is [treating well] now (either directly by himself or through some of those near to him) or those whom he wants or has wanted to treat well.

THE STATE OF MIND OF THOSE WHO BECOME ANGRY

9. It is now apparent from this what is the state of mind[17] of those who become angry and at whom and for what sort of reasons [they do so]; for [the answer to the first question is] they become angry whenever they are distressed; for the person who is distressed desires something. If, then, someone directly opposes him in any way, for example, preventing his drinking when he is thirsty—and even if not directly, nevertheless seems to accomplish the same thing—and if someone works against him and does not cooperate with him and annoys him when so disposed, he becomes angry at all these. 10. As a result, those who are ill, in need of money, [in the middle of a battle,][18] in love, thirsty—in general those longing for something and not getting it—are irrascible and easily stirred to anger, especially against those belittling their present condition; for example, one who is ill [is easily stirred to anger] by things related to his sickness, one who is in need by things related to his poverty, one at war by things related to the war, one in love by things related to his love, and similarly also in the other cases; for each has prepared a path for his own anger because of some underlying emotion.[19] 11. Further, [a person is easily stirred to anger] if he happened to be expecting the opposite [treatment]; for the quite unexpected hurts more, just as the quite unexpected also delights if what is desired comes to pass. From this, then, it is evident what seasons and times and dispositions and ages are easily

17. Lit. "how they have," a temporary state. In contrast, a person's character is a *hexis,* a continuing and habitual condition.

18. Not in the manuscripts, but supplied by editors in anticipation of the following examples.

19. This formidable sentence has a number of textual and grammatical problems. I have largely followed Grimaldi's reading of it (1980–88, 34–38). Aristotle clearly realized that outbursts of anger often result from some relatively minor slight that represents that "last straw" to someone already under stress.

moved to anger and where and when and that when people are more in these [conditions], they are also more easily moved.[20]

THOSE AT WHOM PEOPLE BECOME ANGRY

12. People so disposed then are easily moved to anger, and they become angry at those who laugh at them and scoff and mock; for these wantonly insult them. And at those doing such harmful actions as are signs of wanton insult [*hybris*]. Necessarily, these actions are of the sort that are not in response to something [done earlier by the sufferer] and not beneficial to those who do them; for only then does it seem they are done through *hybris*. 13. And [people become angry] at those who speak badly of, and scorn, things they themselves take most seriously, for example, those taking pride in philosophy if someone speaks against philosophy[21] or taking pride in their appearance if someone attacks their appearance and similarly in other cases. 14. They do this much more if they suspect they do not really have [what they take pride in], either not at all or not strongly, or do not seem to have it; **[1379b]** for whenever they confidently think they excel in the matters in which they are scoffed at, they do not care. 15. And [they become angry] at friends more than those who are not friends; for they think it is more appropriate for them to to be well treated by them than not. 16. And [they become angry] at those who have been accustomed to honor or respect them if, instead, they do not associate with them in this way; for they think they are being treated with contempt by these as well; for [otherwise] they would treat them in the same way. And at those not returning favors and those not doing so on an equal basis. 17. And at those opposing them if these are inferiors; for all such evidently show contempt, the latter as though looking down [on someone] as inferior to themselves, the former as having received a benefit from inferiors. 18. And [they become angry] more at those

20. Note that the persons mentioned in secs 10–11 are not likely to constitute the audience for public address. Aristotle has not adapted his examples to the context of rhetoric.

21. Probably an indication that the original context of this discussion was philosophical, not rhetorical.

of no account if they belittle [them] in some way; for anger resulting from being belittled is assumed to be against those who have no right to do it, and inferiors have no right to belittle. 19. And [they become angry] against friends if these do not speak well of, or benefit, them and even more if they do the opposite and if they are insensitive to those in need, as in the case of Plexippus in Antiphon's [tragedy] *Meleager;* for lack of sensitivity is a sign of belittling: what we care about does not escape our notice. 20. And [they become angry] against those rejoicing at misfortunes and generally taking pleasure in others' misfortunes; for it is a sign of being either an enemy or a belittler. And [they become angry] against those who do not care if they are suffering. Thus, people become angry at those announcing bad news. 21. And [they become angry] at those listening to bad things about them or seeing their bad side; for these are similar to belittlers or enemies; for friends share griefs, and all grieve when they see faults of those close to them.

22. Further, [they become angry] at those belittling them before five classes of people: those with whom they are rivals, those they admire, those by whom they wish to be admired, or [those] before whom they are embarrassed or [those] who are embarrassed before them. If someone belittles them among these they become all the more angry. 23. And [they become angry] at those belittling others whom it would be shameful for them not to defend, for example, parents, children, wives, dependants. And [they become angry] at those not returning a favor; for the belittlement is contrary to what is fitting. 24. And [they become angry] at those mocking them when they are being serious; for mockery[22] is contemptuous. 25. And [they become angry] at those who do good to others if they do not do it also to them; for this, too, is contemptuous, not to think them also worthy of what they do for all [others]. 26. And forgetfulness is also productive of anger, for example, forgetfulness of names, being such a little thing; for the forgetfulness seems to be a sign of belittlement; for forgetfulness occurs through lack of concern, and lack of concern is belittlement.

27. At one and the same time, then, the persons at whom anger is directed and the dispositions of those angry and the kinds of

---

22. *Eirōneia,* the source of the English word *irony;* but the Greek term means dissimulation, mockery, or an affectation of ignorance.

causes have been stated; **[1380a]** and it is clear that it might be needful in speech to put [the audience] in the state of mind of those who are inclined to anger and to show one's opponents as responsible for those things that are the causes of anger and that they are the sort of people against whom anger is directed.[23]

Chapter 3: Praotēs, *or Calmness*

■ Aristotle regards *praotēs* as the emotion opposite to anger. It is often translated "mildness," which seems rather a trait of character or absence of emotion, while Aristotle views it as a positive attitude toward others and experience, involving an emotional change toward a tolerant understanding: in colloquial English "calming down" is perhaps the closest translation, but there is no single English word that quite captures the meaning. The appearance of mildness, gentleness, patience, tractability, good temper are all aspects of it. As in the case of anger, though viewed as an emotional state, it has its roots in character. On this chapter see Nikolaides 1982.

THE DEFINITION OF CALMNESS AND THOSE TOWARD WHOM PEOPLE FEEL CALM

1. Since becoming calm is the opposite of becoming angry, and anger the opposite of calmness [*praotēs*], the state of mind of those who are calm should be grasped [by a speaker] and toward whom they are calm and for what reasons. 2. Let calmness [*praünsis*] be

---

23. Because the original context of this discussion was philosophical, Aristotle has given more detail than the prospective speaker needs about the causes and circumstances of anger and virtually nothing about the practical application of this to rhetoric, with some examples. It is clear, however, that a speaker might arouse the anger of an audience against an opponent by showing that the latter had "belittled" them or the state or the laws with contempt, spite, or insult and might transmit to an audience feelings of anger at an opponent. Demosthenes' speech *Against Medias,* who had publicly insulted him, expresses his own anger; and his *Philippics* sought to arouse the anger of the Athenians against Philip of Macedon.

[defined as] a settling down and quieting of anger. 3. If, then, people become angry at those who belittle and belittling is a voluntary thing, evidently they are calm toward those doing none of these things or doing them involuntarily or seemingly so. 4. And [they are calm] toward those intending the opposite of what they have done. And [they are calm toward] all who regard them as they themselves would; for no one is thought to belittle himself.[24] 5. And [they are calm] toward those who admit and repent [having belittled someone]; for regarding [the others'] distress as just retribution, they cease from their anger at those who have provoked it. A sign [of this is seen] in the punishment of slaves; for we punish all the more those who argue and deny, but we cease our wrath toward those who confess themselves justly punished. The reason is that to deny clear evidence is disrespectful, and disrespect is belittling and contempt; at least we do not respect those for whom we have much contempt. 6. [People are also calm] toward those who humble themselves toward them and do not contradict them; for they seem to admit being inferiors, and inferiors are afraid, and no one who is afraid belittles. That anger ceases toward those who humble themselves is evident even in the case of dogs, who do not bite those sitting down.[25] 7. And [they are calm] toward those who are serious with them when they are serious; for they think they are being serious and not showing contempt. And [they are calm] toward those who have done greater kindness in the past [than any passing affront]. 8. And [they are calm] toward those begging a favor and entreating them [not to be angry]; for they are humbler. 9. And [they are calm] toward those who are not insulting or scoffing or belittling against anyone, or not against good people or against such as they are. 10. As a whole, things producing calmness should be looked at on the basis of their opposites.[26] [They are] also [calm] toward those whom they fear and respect; for as long as

---

24. In the view of the general public—but in fact there exists the type of the "ironic" person, of whom Socrates furnishes the most famous example; cf. *Nicomachean Ethics* 4.7.14.

25. In *Odyssey* 14.29–38 Odysseus tries this strategy when attacked by dogs. As in that case, it should probably not be counted on to work unless the dog's master is nearby.

26. Double-bracketed by Kassel as a late addition by Aristotle.

they are so disposed, they do not become angry; for it is impossible
to be afraid and become angry.[27] 11. And toward those who have
acted in anger people are not angry or are less angry; for they do
not seem to have acted by belittling, since no one belittles when
angry; for belittling is painless [to the one doing it], but anger is
accompanied by pain.[28] **[1380b]** And [people are calm] toward
those showing respect to them.

THE STATE OF MIND OF THOSE WHO ARE CALM

12. It is clear also that people are calm when their state of mind is
the opposite of being angry; for example, in play, in laughter, at a
feast, in prosperity, in success, in fulfillment, generally in the absence of pain and in pleasure that does not come from insulting
anybody and in reasonable expectation of the future. Further, [they
are calm if] their anger has cooled with time and is not in its first
stage; for time makes anger cease. 13. Greater anger toward a
different person or vengence already taken on another person earlier also causes anger to cease. Thus, when some one asked
Philocrates, at the time the people [of Athens] were angry with him,
"Why do you not defend yourself?," he wisely said, "Not yet." "But
when then?" "When I see someone else has been slandered."[29] For
people become calm whenever they have spent their anger on some
one else, which happened in the case of Ergophilos; for though [the
Athenians] were more angry at him than at Callisthenes, they let

27. Though someone might "be" angry at another who is feared, it is often best not
to worsen the situation by "becoming" angry, that is, expressing anger and instead
to try to "keep calm." The emotions Aristotle discusses and that the speaker needs
to understand are mostly those that come out in public.

28. This is consistent with Aristotle's definition of the terms; cf. Grimaldi 1980–88,
2: 57–58.

29. Largely through the efforts of Demosthenes, Philocrates was prosecuted for
bribery in the peace negotiations he carried on between Athens and Macedon. He
escaped into exile and was condemned to death in absentia in 343. We do not know
where he went into exile, but Macedon or a state friendly to Macedon is likely.
Thus, Aristotle, living in Macedon from about 343 to 340, is likely to have had first-
hand knowledge of him. The date is consistent with the revision of the *Rhetoric* into
its present form in the immediately following years; see Appendix II.B. Kassel
double-brackets the example as a late addition by Aristotle.

him go because they had condemned Callisthenes to death on the previous day.[30] 14. And [people become calm] if they take pity[31] [on offenders] and if these have suffered greater evils than they would have done to them when angry; for they think they have obtained a kind of retaliation. 15. And [people become calm] if they think they themselves have done wrong and suffered justly; for anger does not arise against justice nor against what people think they have appropriately suffered; that was [implicit in] the definition of anger. Thus, one should first chastize in word; for even slaves are less indignant when [so] punished.[32]

16. Also, [people are calmer] when they think that [their victims] will not perceive who is the cause of their suffering and that it is retribution for what they have suffered; for anger is a personal thing, as is clear from its definition. Thus, the verse "Say it was Odysseus, sacker of cities,"[33] was rightly composed, since [Odysseus] would not have been avenged if [Polyphemus the Cyclops] had not realized both from whom and why revenge came. Thus, people do not vent their anger on others who are not aware of it nor continue it against the dead, since the latter have suffered the ultimate and will not suffer nor will they have perception, which is what angry people want. Thus, in wanting Achilles to cease his anger against Hector once he was dead, the poet spoke well: "For it is unseemly to rage at senseless clay."[34] 17. Clearly, then, those wishing to instill calmness [in an audience] should speak from these topics;[35] they produce such a feeling in them by having made them regard those with whom they are angry as either persons to be

---

30. The date is about 362, when Aristotle was living in Athens. Anger at Ergophilos resulted from his actions as a commander in the Hellespont. He may have been fined but was not condemned to death.

31. The reading of Parisinus 1741; other manuscripts have *if they convict* (someone).

32. The verbal rebuke, coming before physical punishment, gives them an understanding of the wrong they have committed; they are thus more inclined to regard the punishment as just.

33. *Odyssey* 9.504.

34. *Iliad* 24.54. The words are spoken by Apollo at a council of the gods.

35. *Topoi*, the first instance of the term in Book 2. These topics are apparently the *idia* (specifics) of ethical knowledge, which includes study of the emotions.

feared or worthy of respect or benefactors or involuntary actors or
as very grieved by what they have done.

Chapter 4: Philia, *or Friendly Feeling, and* Ekhthra, *or Enmity*

■ From the positive emotion of calmness Aristotle moves to
another positive emotion, a feeling of friendliness toward
someone, and then to its negative, enmity and hate, thus
establishing the chiastic order followed in successive chapters. Friendliness and enmity are longer-lasting emotions
than anger and calmness and thus perhaps more intimately
connected with character; but Aristotle is primarily interested in them as feelings that come out in certain situations,
and, like other feelings, they can be produced in an audience
by a speaker who understands how to awaken them.

THE DEFINITION OF FRIENDLINESS AND THOSE TOWARD WHOM PEOPLE HAVE A FRIENDLY FEELING

1. Let us say whom people like and whom they hate and why
after having defined friendliness and being friendly.[36] 2. Let *being
friendly* [*to philein*] be [defined as] wanting for someone what one
thinks are good things for him, not what one thinks benefits oneself, and wanting what is potentially productive of these good
things. **[1381a]** A friend is one who loves and is loved in return,[37]
and people think they are friends when they think this relationship
exists mutually. 3. On these premises, a friend is necessarily one
who shares pleasure in good things and distress in grievous things,

36. *Philia,* with its related verb *philein,* has a spectrum of meanings ranging from
general friendly feelings toward someone to a special friendship and love; but, as
elsewhere in this book, Aristotle is discussing a particular feeling that arises under
particular circumstances and may thus be useful in making a jury or other audience
sympathetic to a speaker's point of view.

37. This clause is double-bracketed by Kassel as a late addition by Aristotle.

not for some other reason but because of the friend; for all rejoice when the things they want happen and grieve at the opposite, so distresses and pleasures are a sign of their wish. 4. And [friends] are those to whom the same things are good and bad and who have the same friends and the same enemies;[38] for they necessarily wish the same things, so the one who also wishes for another what he wishes for himself is evidently a friend to the former. 5. And people are friendly to those who have benefited them—either to them directly or to those they care for—if they have done them great benefit or done it eagerly or at opportune times and for their sake; also to those whom they think wish to benefit them. 6. [They are] also [friendly] to the friends of their friends and those friendly with those they themselves like and those liked by those they themselves like. 7. And [they are friendly to] those who have the same enemies they have and who hate those they themselves hate and who are hated by those they hate; for the same things seem good to all these as to themselves, so that they wish the same things as they do, which was the characteristic of a friend. 8. Further, [they are friendly to those] who are disposed to do good to others in regard to money and safety; therefore, they honor generous and brave people. 9. [They are] also [friendly to] those who are just. And they suppose those who do not live at the expense of others to be of this sort; such also are those who live by their own efforts and, of these, especially those who live from the land or else are craftsmen.[39] 10. And [they are friendly to] those who are self-controlled, because not unjust and those who mind their own business for the same reason.

11. [We are friendly] also to those with whom we want to be friends if they seem to want it; such are those who are morally good and respected, either among all or among the best people or among those we admire or those who admire us. 12. Further, [we

38. This clause is also double-bracketed by Kassel as a late addition by Aristotle.

39. The key word in this sentence is *they suppose*. Aristotle is setting out the assumptions of a typical Athenian jury, largely made up of small landowners, craftsmen, and the like. As seen in plays of Aristophanes and especially in Xenophon's *Oeconomicus*, there was a strong general prejudice (as there continues to be in parts of the United States) in favor of farmers and the self-employed as the backbone of the state. A jury might be expected to be favorably disposed to someone who had friends in that segment of society.

are friendly to] those who are pleasant to deal with and to pass the day with; such are those who are good-tempered and not critical of people's faults and not contentious or quarrelsome; for all such are pugnacious, and those always fighting clearly want the opposite. 13. And [we are friendly to people like] those who are ready to make or receive a joke; for in both cases they are intent on the same thing as their neighbor, able to be kidded and kidding in good sport. 14. And [we are friendly to] those who praise the presence of good qualities [in others] and especially the qualities that these people fear they do not really have. **[1381b]** 15. And [we are friendly to] those who are neat in appearance and in dress and in all their way of life. 16. And [we are friendly to] those who are not critical of mistakes or of benefactions; for in both cases they are reproachful. 17. And [people are friendly to] those not mindful of wrongs done to them nor inclined to cherish their grievances but who are easily appeased; for people think the attitude they suppose shown to others will also be shown to themselves. 18. And [they are friendly to] those who do not say or want to know bad things about neighbors or friends but [look for] good things; for the good person acts this way. 19. And [they are friendly to] those who do not oppose others when [the latter are] angry or being serious; for such persons are pugnacious. And [they are friendly to] those taking them seriously in some way, for example, admiring them and regarding them as serious people and finding pleasure in them, 20. and especially those feeling this way about what they wish to be admired in themselves or in regard to what they want to seem serious about or what they find pleasure in. 21. And [they are friendly to] those like themselves and having similar interests, provided they do not become annoying or get their livelihood from the same source; for then it becomes the case of "potter against potter."[40] 22. And [they are friendly to] those who long for the same things when it is possible to share them at the same time; but if that is not possible, the same result follows as in the previous case.

23. [People have friendly feelings] also toward those with whom their relationship is such that they are not ashamed [in their

---

40. Cf. Hesiod, *Works and Days* 25, on rivalry among craftsmen.

presence] of things that might be thought unless [the others] show contempt. And [they are friendly] toward those with whom they are ashamed at true faults. 24. And [they are friendly] toward those whose prestige they would like to attain and [those] by whom they wish to be emulated and not envied. 25. And [they are friendly to] those for whom they join in doing good, unless greater evils are going to result for themselves. 26. [They are] also [friendly to] those who show equal affection for their friends both absent and present. Therefore, all [people] like those [people] who are such in regard to the dead. And all in all, [people like those] who are very fond of their friends and not inclined to leave them in the lurch; for among the good they most like those who are good at being friends. 27. And [they like] those who are not deceitful with them; such are those who even tell them their faults. (It was said earlier that we do not feel shame before friends in regard to things that might be thought; if then one who feels shame is not a friend, one who does not is like a friend.) And [we like] those [who are] not intimidating and with whom we feel secure; for no one likes a person he fears.

THE CAUSES OF FRIENDSHIP

28. The species of friendship are companionship, intimacy, kinship, and other such things. 29. [Doing] a favor is productive of friendship and doing it unasked and not advertising what has been done; for in this case it seems to have been done for the sake of the friend and not for some other reason.

ENMITY AND HATE

■ Aristotle regards hostile emotions as awakened by the perception that someone belongs to a detested class of individuals, such as thieves or sycophants. The negative feeling toward the class is a permanent one, but the identification of an individual with the class may be established or disproved in a speech.

30. The nature of enmity [*ekhthra*] and hating [*to misein*] is evident from the opposites [of what has been said about friendliness]. **[1382a]** Anger, spite, and slander are productive of enmity. 31. Now anger comes from things that affect a person directly, but enmity also from what is not directed against himself; for if we suppose someone to be a certain kind of person, we hate him. And anger is always concerned with particulars, directed for example at a Callias or a Socrates, while hate is directed also at types (everyone hates the thief and the sycophant).[41] The former [anger] is curable in time, the latter [hatred of types] not curable; the former is the desire [that the other may feel] pain, the latter [that he may suffer] evil; for one who is angry wants his anger perceived, but to the one who hates it does not matter [whether the object of his hatred knows it]. Painful actions [inflicted by one person on another] are all perceived by the senses, but the greatest evils—injustice and thoughtlessness—are least perceived; for the presence of evil causes no pain. Anger is also accompanied by pain [to the one who feels angry], but hate is not accompanied by pain; for the angry person is himself pained, the one who hates is not. One who is angry might feel pity when much has befallen [the person he is angry at], but one who hates under no circumstance; for the former wants the one he is angry at to suffer in his turn, the latter wants [the detested class of persons] not to exist.

32. From this, then, it is evident that it is possible [for a speaker] both to demonstrate that people are enemies and friends and to make them so when they are not and to refute those claiming to be[42] and to bring those who through anger or enmity are on the other side of the case over to whatever feeling he chooses. But what sort of things people fear and whom and in what state of mind will be evident from what follows.

---

41. *Sykophantes* in Greek means "informer," specifically one who denounces another to the government for trading in contraband (*sykon* = "fig," the trade in figs being controlled). Since such a person often hopes to gain from the action, the word has come to mean "self-server" or "servile flatterer for his own advantage."

42. This introduces a new function: the demonstration or refutation of claims of enmity or friendship by the opponent.

Chapter 5: Phobos, *or Fear, and* Tharsos, *or Confidence*

THE DEFINITION OF FEAR AND ITS CAUSES

1. Let *fear* [*phobos*] be [defined as] a sort of pain or agitation derived from the imagination[43] of a future destructive or painful evil; for all evils are not feared (for example, [a person does not fear] that he will become unjust or slow-witted) but [only] what has the potentially for great pains or destruction, and these [only] if they do not appear far-off but near, so that they are about to happen; for what is far off is not feared: all know that they will die; but because that is not near at hand they take no thought of it. 2. If this is what fear is, such things are necessarily causes of fear as seem to have great potentiality for destruction or for causing harms that lead to great pains. Therefore, even the signs of such things are causes of fear; for that which causes fear seems near at hand. (This is danger: an approach of something that causes fear.) 3. Such [signs] are enmity and anger from those with the power to do something; for it is clear that they wish to, and thus they are near doing it. 4. And injustice [is such a sign] when it has power; for the unjust person is unjust by deliberate choice. 5. And outraged virtue [is such a sign] when it has power; **[1382b]** for it is clear that when a person is outraged, he always chooses to act, and now he can. 6. And [another sign] is fear on the part of those with the power to do something; for necessarily such a person also is in readiness [to act].

THOSE WHO ARE FEARED

7. Since most people are rather bad, slaves of profitmaking, and cowardly in danger,[44] being at the mercy of another is in most

43. *Phantasia,* to be taken literally: there is an "appearance" of something bad as going to happen, which the individual "visualizes."

44. This is more cynical than Aristotle's usual view in his later ethical writings. Probably it again reflects the fact that in the *Rhetoric* he is dealing with attitudes that might be assumed to be found on the part of a jury. Certainly, an experience of the law courts does not encourage an optimistic view of the goodness of human beings.

cases a cause of fear, so that the accomplices of one who has done something dreadful are feared [by him], in that they may inform on him or leave him in the lurch, and those able to do wrong [are a cause of fear] to those able to be wronged; 8. for human beings usually do wrong when they can. And [others who are feared] are those who have been wronged or think they have been wronged; for they are always watching for an opportunity [for revenge]. Also those who have done wrong, if they have power, are feared, being apprehensive of suffering in their turn; for this sort of thing is inherent in what is feared. 9. And those who are rivals for the same things [are feared], in so far as it is not possible for both to share at the same time; for people are always fighting against such rivals. 10. And [people fear] those [that seem a cause of fear] to others who are stronger than they are;[45] for they could harm them more if they could even harm those who are stronger.[46] And for the same reason those [are feared] whom the stronger fear. 11. And people [are feared] who have destroyed those stronger than they are. And people [are feared] who attack those weaker than they are; for they are either cause for fear or [will be] when they have grown stronger. And among those wronged and enemies or rivals it is not the quick-tempered and outspoken [who are to be feared] but the calm and those who dissemble and the unscrupulous; for with these it is unclear if they are close [to acting], with the result that it is never evident that they are far from doing so.

12. All fearful things are more fearful in so far as something cannot be set right by those who have made a mistake and is either wholly irremediable or not in their power but in the power of their opponents. And [they are more fearful] when there are no sources of help or not easy ones. In a word, things are fearful that are pitiable when they happen or are going to happen to others. Fearful things, then, and what people fear are pretty much (so to speak) the greatest things. Let us now speak about the state of mind of those who are afraid.

45. Here and in similar contexts the translators often introduce the first person *stronger than us*. This should be avoided, since it destroys the distance that Aristotle usually maintains in the *Rhetoric* between the observer (Aristotle and the student of philosophy or rhetoric) and the phenomenon observed. When he does use the first person plural (as in 2.4.11), it is so translated.

46. A good example of the *topos* of the more and the less.

THE STATE OF MIND OF THOSE WHO FEAR

13. If fear is accompanied by an expectation of experiencing some destructive misfortune, it is evident that no one is afraid if he is one of those who thinks he will suffer nothing; [people fear] neither things they do not think they will suffer nor other [people] by whom they do not think [they will be harmed] and not at a time when they do not think so. Necessarily, then, people who think they might suffer something are in fear, and those [who think they are going to suffer] at the hands of those [from whom they expect to suffer]; and they fear these things and at this time. 14. Those experiencing, and thinking they experience, great good fortune do not think they might suffer; **[1383a]** therefore, they are insolent and belittlers and rash (wealth, strength, an abundance of friends, power, makes them so); nor [are those afraid] who think they have already suffered all dreadful things possible and have become coldly indifferent to the future, like those who have just been crucified on a plank. [For fear to continue,] there must be some hope of being saved from the cause of agony. And there is a sign of this: fear makes people inclined to deliberation, while no one deliberates about hopeless things. 15. The result is that whenever it is better [for a speaker's case] that they [i.e., the audience] experience fear, he should make them realize that they are liable to suffering; for [he can say that] others even greater [than they] have suffered, and he should show that there are others like them suffering [now] (or who have suffered) and at the hands of those from whom they did not expect it and suffering things [they did not expect] and at a time when they were not thinking of [the possibility].[47]

CONFIDENCE AND THOSE WHO INSPIRE IT

16. Since it is evident what fear and fearful things are and [what is] the state of mind of those that are afraid, it is evident from this also what it is to be confident and what sort of things people are confident about and what their state of mind is when they are

47. Thus, awakening fear is especially useful in deliberative oratory, e.g., in showing the danger from a foreign state.

confident; for confidence [*tharsos*] is opposed [to fear, and what inspires confidence][48] to what is fearful.[49] Thus, hope of safety is accompanied by an imagination that it is near, while fearful things either do not exist or are far away. 17. Dreadful things being far off plus sources of safety being near at hand equal feelings of confidence.[50] And if there are remedies and many sources of aid or great ones or both and if people have not been wronged or done wrong and if antagonists do not exist at all or do not have power or, having power, are friends or have been benefactors or have received benefits, [then people are confident]. Or if those with the same interests are numerous or stronger or both [people are confident].

THE STATE OF MIND OF THOSE WHO FEEL CONFIDENT

18. People are themselves confident when they have the following states of mind: if they think they have often succeeded and not suffered or if they have often come into dangers and have escaped; for human beings become free from emotions [of fear] in two ways: either by not having been put to the test or by having the resources needed, just as in dangers at sea both those who are inexperienced with a storm and those with the resources of experience are confident in the outcome. 19. And [people feel confident] when something is not a source of fear to those like them, nor to those [who are] inferior and whose superiors they think themselves to be; and they so regard those they have defeated, either these themselves or their superiors or their equals. 20. And [people feel confident] if they think they have more and better resources, by which they are rendered especially formidable. [1383b] These are a supply of

---

48. Not in the manuscripts, but added by most editors.

49. *Tharsos* is often translated "courage"; but courage (often *andreia* in Greek) is a virtue, a habitual state of character, just as cowardice is a vice. Fear and confidence, as Aristotle discusses them here, are feelings under certain circumstances, analogous to becoming angry or calm. A speaker might instill fear or confidence in an audience but would not thereby make them cowardly or courageous unless these feelings were habituated into permanent traits.

50. The Greek text is uncertain, but the meaning seems clear.

money and live bodies and friends and territory and preparations for war, either all these or the greatest. And [people feel confident] if they have done no wrong to anybody or not to many or not to those from whom they fear anything. 21. And on the whole, [people are confident] if their relationship to the gods is good, both as known from signs and oracles and in other ways.[51] (Anger is a confident thing, and to be wronged rather than to do wrong is productive of anger; but the divine is supposed to come to the aid of those who are wronged.) 22. And [people feel confident] when, laying their hands to some task, they think they are not likely to suffer [now] or will succeed. So the matters relating to fear and confidence have been discussed.[52]

Chapter 6: Aiskhynē, *or Shame, and* Anaiskhyntia, *or Shamelessness*

■ Shamelessness is explicitly mentioned only at the beginning and end of the chapter, but the many actions listed as shameful can be taken as signs of shamelessness. Though the society of ancient Greece is too complex to be labeled a "shame culture" in the sense used by Ruth Benedict and other anthropologists, it is true that Greek literature, beginning with the *Iliad,* shows a relatively highly developed personal fear of being shamed in the eyes of society—what in the orient is called "loosing face"—and conversely, a relatively undeveloped sense of inner personal guilt, which is found somewhat more among ancient Hebrews and Romans. In 2.2.14 Aristotle noted what might be thought of as an "inferiority complex," but as seen in chapter 6 (esp. section 14) shame only occurs if someone else, or society in general, perceives disgrace to an individual.

51. This sentence is double-bracketed by Kassel as a late addition by Aristotle.

52. These observations easily apply to creating confidence in a deliberative assembly when urged to take some action (e.g., going to war), but Aristotle fails to make the application.

THE DEFINITION AND CAUSES OF SHAME

1. What sort of things people are ashamed of and feel no shame about and toward whom and in what state of mind is clear from the following. 2. Let shame [*aiskhynē*] be [defined as] a sort of pain and agitation concerning the class of evils, whether present or past or future, that seems to bring a person into disrepect and shamelessness [*anaiskhyntia*] a belittling and indifference about these same things. 3. If what has been defined is shame, necessarily being shamed applies to such evils as seem [in the eyes of others] to be disgraceful to a person or one about whom he cares. Such are those actions that result from vice, for example, throwing away a shield or fleeing in battle; for these come from cowardice. And [such is] refusing to pay back a deposit; for this comes from injustice. 4. And [such is] having sexual relations with those with whom one should not or where one should not or when one should not; for this comes from licentiousness. 5. And [such is] making a profit from petty or shameful things or from helpless people, for example, the poor or the dead. So, too, [note] the proverb "He would even rob a corpse"; for this comes from shameful profiteering and stinginess. 6. And [such is] not giving aid with money when one can or giving less aid. And [such is] being aided from those with fewer resources. 7. And [such are] borrowing money when seeming to demand it [as a right?] and demanding it when seeming to demand it back and demanding it back when demanding it and praising [someone] in order to seem to demand and, when unsuccessful, nonetheless [continuing to demand];[53] for all these are signs of stinginess. 8. And [such is] praising those present, [for it is a sign] of flattery.[54] And [such are] overpraising good things and glossing over bad ones and showing excessive distress for one in distress when he is present and all such things; for they are signs of flattery.

53. A difficult sentence, since it is not quite clear what is meant by *aitein* ("demand"? "ask a favor"?). The first clause has been interpreted to mean "borrowing money from another person who seems about to ask for money himself." In the next-to-last clause *in order* not *to seem to ask* was conjectured by Richards (see Kassel's apparatus). The point throughout, however, is shameless deceit of some kind.

54. This sentence is double-bracketed by Kassel as a late addition by Aristotle.

9. And [such is] not standing up under labors that older people bear **[1384a]** or those who are delicate or higher in rank or, on the whole, less able; for all these are signs of softness. 10. And [such are] accepting favors from another, and often, and reproaching someone for a good deed; for all these are signs of smallness of mind and meanness. 11. And [such are] talking about oneself and making pronouncements and claiming the achievements of another for one's own; for [these are signs] of boastfulness. Similarly, too, the deeds and signs and the like that result from other vices of character; for these are disgraceful and things to be ashamed of.

12. And in addition [it is shameful] not to share in the fine things of which all have a share or all those like oneself or most of them. By *those like oneself* I mean those of the same nation, fellow citizens, those of the same age, relatives—generally, one's equals; for in the first place it is shameful not to share to the same extent in education and similarly in other ways, but all these [lacks] are more shameful if they seem to be one's own fault; for thus they now [seem to come] more from vice if one is the cause of [one's own] past, present, or future [deficiencies].

13. People feel shame when they suffer or have suffered or are going to suffer such things as contribute to dishonor and censures, and these are things that include providing the services of the body or engaging in shameful actions, of which being physically violated is one (and though actions voluntary and involuntary are a part of licentiousness, the involuntary are done by force); for submission and lack of resistance comes from effeminacy or cowardice.[55] These then, and things like them, are the things of which people are ashamed.

---

55. Frequenting prostitutes and engaging as an "active" partner in male homosexual activity was in Greece not a source of shame; but to take money for sexual favors was (and in the case of a male could lead to loss of civil rights), and, except for a woman with her husband, it was shameful for anyone to allow a man to insert his sexual organ into any part of the body (cf. English *pathic*). Thus, pederasty, out of respect for the boy, often took the form of intercrural rather than anal or oral intercourse; see Dover 1978, 98–99. There was apparently no shame in homosexual activity among women; but heterosexual activity outside of marriage was shameful for the woman, and a woman who was raped was regarded as shamed.

THOSE BEFORE WHOM PEOPLE FEEL SHAME

14. Since shame is imagination [*phantasia*][56] about a loss of reputation and for its own sake, not for its results, and since no one cares about reputation [in the abstract] but on account of those who hold an opinion of him, necessarily a person feels shame toward those whose opinion he takes account of. 15. He takes account of those who admire him and whom he admires and by whom he wishes to be admired and those to whose rank he aspires and those whose opinion he does not despise. 16. Now people want to be admired by those and admire those who have something good in the way of honors or from whom they happen to be greatly in need of something those people have in their control, as lovers [want love or sexual favors]; 17. but they aspire to the rank of those [they regard as] like themselves, and they take account of prudent people as telling the truth, and their elders and educated people are of such a sort. 18. And they feel more shame at things done before these people's eyes and in the open; hence, too the proverb "Shame is in the eyes."[57] For this reason people feel more shame before those who are going to be with them and those watching them, because in both cases they are "in" their eyes. **[1384b]** 19. And [they feel more shame] before those not liable to the same charge; for it is clear that the opposite values seem right to them. And [they feel more shame] before those not inclined to be forgiving to people who have clearly made a mistake;[58] for it is said that one is not angry at neighbors when they do things one does oneself, so clearly one *is* angry when they do what one does not do. 20. And [they feel more shame] before those inclined to tell about it to many others; for not to tell the tale is no different from not thinking it [a fault].[59] Those inclined

56. As usual, this means a mental "visualization" of the effects, not (as the English word might imply) a false conclusion.

57. Grimaldi 1980–88, 2: 117, cites a number of instances of this proverb in literature and concludes that it means, "Shame stands revealed in the eyes of the guilty person," i.e., he "looks" guilty. But it could also mean that the guilty person sees his guilt written in the eyes of the person he has disappointed, as children first sense guilt from the "look" of a parent—which perhaps better fits the context.

58. This clause is double-bracketed by Kassel as a late addition by Aristotle.

59. This would have been clearer if Aristotle had avoided the triple negative: "For when a gossiper tells a tale, it is a sign that he thinks it casts the doer in a shameful light."

to tell tales are those who have been wronged, because they keep on the watch, and slanderers; for if [they tell something false] about those who have commited no error, they will all the more [tell] about those who have. And [people feel shame before those] whose employment is watching the errors of their neighbors; for example, professional jokers and comic poets; for these are in a way slanderers and talebearers. And among those from whom they have never failed to get what they want; for [among them] they are in the position of those that are admired. Thus, too, they feel shame [in refusing] those who have asked for something for the first time, since they have not yet been held in disrespect among these. Such are those who have recently wanted to become their friends (these have seen their best side, and thus the reply of Euripides to the Syracusans applies)[60] and among old acquaintances those not cognizant of anything wrong.

21. And people are ashamed not only of the shameful things that have been mentioned but of all the signs [of shamefulness], as those who freely indulge their sexuality [are ashamed] not only of it but of the signs of it. And [people feel shame] not only in doing but even in saying disgraceful things. 22. Similarly, people are not only ashamed before those who have been mentioned but also before those who will reveal their faults to them, for example servants and friends of these others. 23. But on the whole they are not ashamed before those whose reputation of telling the truth they much look down on (no one feels shame before babies and small beasts); nor [are they ashamed] of the same things before acquaintances and strangers, but before acquaintances [they are ashamed] of things truly regarded [as wrong and] before those from abroad [they are ashamed] of things conventionally so regarded.[61]

60. According to a medieval commentator, Euripides, as Athenian ambassador to Syracuse in Sicily, said, "You ought, Syracusians, even if for no other reason except that we are just now feeling the need of you, to be ashamed to reject us, your admirers."

61. This sentence rambles a little. The parenthesis really applies to those who cannot speak at all ("babies," *paidia* = Lat. *infantes,* Eng. "infants," those who cannot speak), rather than those who have a reputation for not telling the truth; and the second half of the sentence really deals with a very different matter. As in 1.11.16, Grimaldi does not see how *thēria* can mean "animals"; but clearly it does— and in Aristotle's writings often small animals. The adulterer does not much mind if a field mouse observes his actions but might feel shame in the presence of his horse.

THE STATE OF MIND OF THOSE WHO FEEL SHAME

24. People would feel shamed if they were in the following situation: first, if certain others were in the relationship to them that we said was characteristic of those before whom they feel shame (and these were those who are admired or admirers or those by whom they want to be admired or from whom they have some need that they will not attain if they lose their reputation) and, [second, if] these [were] either seeing [what is going on] (as Cydias said to the people in the debate about the allotment of land in Samos; for he thought the Athenians should imagine [all] the Greeks standing around them in a circle, actually seeing and not only later hearing about what they might vote)[62]—or if such persons are nearby or are going to learn of it.[63] Thus too people fallen into misfortune do not want to be seen by those who have ever been their rivals; for rivals are admirers. **[1385a]** 25. And [people feel shame] whenever they have in their background deeds or facts that they will be [seen to] disgrace, whether these are their own or their ancestors' or those of certain others with whom there exists to them some tie of kinship. And on the whole [they feel shame] on account of those on whom they themselves bring shame. These are the people mentioned and those who have been entrusted to them, either those of whom they have been teachers or advisers or if there are others like themselves to whose rank they aspire; 26. for people do and do not do many things out of a sense of shame because of the existence of such people. 27. And if they are going to be seen and be associated in public with those who know their guilt, they are more embarrassed. Thus, too, Antiphon the poet, when on the point of being crucified on a board and beaten to death on orders of Dionysius, made this remark, seeing that those who were going to die by his side covered their faces as they went through the gate: "Why do you cover your faces?" he said. "You

---

62. The speech was probably given in 365 B.C., just before Aristotle's first arrival in Athens. Athens had captured the island of Samos and debated sending out settlers there. Cydias apparently opposed this as contrary to the intent of the Second Athenian League of 377/376.

63. This cumbersome sentence violates a number of rules of good Greek grammar and style and sounds like something written down from dictation as Aristotle rambled on in the presence of a scribe or student.

don't think, do you, that any of these [bystanders] will see you tomorrow?"[64] Now these things apply to shame. Clearly, we shall find good material on shamelessness from their opposites.[65]

Chapter 7: Kharis, *or Kindliness, and* Akharistia, *or Unkindliness*

■ *Kharis* has a number of meanings in Greek—"kindliness," "benevolence," "good will," "a favor," "gratitude," "grace"—and is also frequently used in the accusative case as a preposition meaning "for the sake of." Aristotle's definition in section 2 makes it clear that he is speaking about an altruistic feeling of kindliness or benevolence that at a particular time gratuitously moves a person to do something for another. This short chapter differs from others on the emotions in that it primarily focuses on what *kharis* is, neglecting the state of mind of those who exhibit it, and in that its concluding paragraph deals with how to make an opponent seem to lack kindliness. The noun *akharistia,* "unkindliness," does not actually occur in the chapter; but Aristotle does use the related negative adjective and verb.

DEFINITION OF KINDLINESS

1. To whom people show kindliness and for what reasons and in what state of mind will be clear [to us] after having defined *kharis.* 2. Let *kharis,* in the sense that one is said to "have *kharis,*" be [defined as] as a service to one in need, not in return for anything

64. Dionysius I, tyrant of Syracuse during the first third of the fourth century, composed tragedies that were ridiculed by others, among whom Antiphon may have been one.

65. Aristotle fails to add here (also at the end of chaps. 7, 8, and 11) any application to public address. The example in sec. 24 shows, however, that inducing shame might occasionally be useful in deliberative oratory. It is difficult to imagine any situation in which an orator would want to create a feeling of shamelessness, though he might want to show that the conduct of others was shameless.

nor that the one rendering the service may get anything but as something for the recipient.[66] [*Kharis*] would be great if [the recipient] is either greatly in need or in need of what is great and difficult [to get] or in times of crisis of this sort or if [the giver] is the only one or the first or the one who most confers it. 3. Needs are desires [*orexeis*] and, among desires, especially those accompanied with pain because of something not present. Longings [*epithymiai*] are such things as love, and those [things] felt in sufferings of the body and in times of danger; for one who is in danger and one who is in pain longs. Thus, those who stand by someone in poverty and those in exile [exhibit *kharis*], even if their services are small, because of the greatness of the need and their having shown kindliness at the opportune time, for example, the person who gave the mat in the Lyceum.[67] 4. Necessarily, then, it is most a matter of offering service in these cases or, if not, in cases of equal or greater need. Thus, since it is evident to whom and for what reasons kindliness is offered and in what state of mind,[68] it is clear that [speakers] should derive it from these sources, showing that some people either were or had been in such pain and need and that others had performed some such service in time of want or were doing so.

HOW TO CREATE AN IMPRESSION OF UNKINDLINESS

5. It is also evident how it is possible to refute claims of kindliness and make people seem unkindly; **[1385b]** for [it might be

66. Thus excluding *kharis* in the sense of gratitude.

67. The incident is unknown, but does not need to imply a time when Aristotle was teaching in the Lyceum. It was in use as a gymnasium before and during Aristotle's first residence in Athens, and one might imagine a scene in which a boy or man was injured and someone gave him a straw mat to lie on. Since it was one of the places frequented by Socrates, the story may have been well known in philosophical circles.

68. The last point, at least, has not been directly treated; the doers are in a kindly state of mind; but one might have expected something about why, or what puts them in that state of mind, as in other chapters. Perhaps Aristotle intended to add this but never got around to it; just possibly, something may have been lost in the text.

shown that] either they were performing or had performed a service for their own advantage (and this [by definition] was not *kharis*) or that it fell out by chance or that they had been acting under constraint or that they gave back rather than freely gave [a favor], either knowingly or not knowingly; for in both cases there is a return for something and thus it would not be *kharis*. 6. And the matter should be considered in terms of all the "categories"; for *kharis* is either [determined by] substance or quantity or quality or time or place.[69] And it is a sign [of unkindliness] if a small service is not rendered and if the same or equal or greater services are rendered to enemies; for it is clear that in neither case do they do these things for "our" sake. Or [it is a sign of unkindliness] if knowingly [someone renders a service] of little value; for no one admits having need of what is of little value. This finishes the discussion of being kindly and being unkindly.

Chapter 8: Eleos, *or Pity*

■ Pity is also an important concept in Aristotle's *Poetics;* see especially the definition of tragedy in *Poetics* 6.2 and the discussion in 14.6–9. But in the *Poetics* pity for another is regularly associated with fear for oneself, whereas in the *Rhetoric* the two emotions are separated, except in section 6, where pity is said to be possible only in an intermediate state between courage or insolence on the one hand and extreme fear on the other. Except for one slip in section 13, Aristotle avoids saying a person pities when he "fears" a similar suffering himself, usually substituting a neutral word meaning "expect." Given the frequent importance of arousing pity for a

69. Aristotle is here using *categories* in the technical sense discussed in the logical treatise of that name; cf. also 1.7.21, where, however, the term *category* is not used. In addition to the five categories mentioned here there are five others that Aristotle apparently regarded as not applicable: relation, condition, position, activity, and receptivity. *Substance* would refer to what was given, (e.g., money or a drink of water) *quantity* to amount (much money or a little), *quality* to something like used clothes compared with a new coat, *time* to how opportune the gift or service was, *place* perhaps to whether it was conferred publicly or privately.

defendent in a trial, it is remarkable that Aristotle has added nothing to adapt this chapter to its place in the *Rhetoric*.

THE DEFINITION OF PITY

1. Let us [now] say what sort of things are pitiable and whom people pity and in what state of mind. 2. Let pity be [defined as] a certain pain at an apparently destructive or painful evil happening to one who does not deserve it and which a person might expect himself or one of his own to suffer, and this when it seems close at hand; for it is clear that a person who is going to feel pity necessarily thinks that some evil is actually present of the sort that he or one of his own might suffer and that this evil is of the sort mentioned in the definition or like it or about equal to it. 3. Therefore, those who are utterly ruined do not feel pity (they think there is nothing left for them to suffer; for they *have suffered*) nor [do] those thinking themselves enormously happy; they demonstrate insolent pride [*hybris*] instead. (If they think all good things are actually present, clearly they also think it is not possible to experience any evil; for this [impossibility of suffering] is one of the good things).

THE STATE OF MIND OF THOSE WHO FEEL PITY

4. The kind of people who think they might suffer are those who have suffered in the past and escaped and older people because of their practical wisdom and experience and the weak and those who are rather cowardly and those who have been educated; for they are discerning. 5. Also those that have parents or children or wives; for these are their "own" and subject to the sufferings that have been mentioned. 6. And those who are not in a courageous emotional state, for example, not in a state of anger or confidence (these feelings do not take account of the future) nor in one of violent insolence (these people, too, take no account of suffering anything) nor, conversely, in a state of extreme fear (those who are scared out of their wits do not feel pity because so taken up with their own suffering) but [only] those who are in

between these states. 7. And [people feel pity] if they think certain individuals are among the good people of the world; for one who thinks no good person exists will think all worthy of suffering. **[1386a]** And on the whole, [a person feels pity] when his state of mind is such that he remembers things like this happening to himself or his own or expects them to happen to himself or his own.

THE CAUSES OF PITY

The state of mind, then, of those who feel pity has been described; and what things they pity is clear from the definition: 8. all things are pitiable that are destructive, consisting of griefs and pains, and things that are ruinous, and whatever evils, having magnitude, are caused by chance. 9. Deaths and torments and diseases of the body and old age and sicknesses and lack of food are painful and destructive; 10. and the evils of which chance is the cause are lack of friends, scarcity of friends (thus, too, it is pitiable to be separated from friends and companions), ugliness, weakness, mutilation. [It is] also [pitiable] for some evil to come from a source that ought to have supplied something good. And [it is pitiable] for this to happen often. 11. And [it is pitiable] for some good to have happened [only] after a person has suffered, as when the presents from the king [of Persia] were sent to Diopeithes after he had died.[70] And [it is pitiable] either for nothing good [ever] to have happened [to some one] or, if it happened, for there to have been no enjoyment of it.

THOSE FOR WHOM PITY IS FELT

Now those for whom people feel pity are the following and those like them. 12. They pity their acquantances, unless they are

---

70. Diopeithes led Athenian settlers to the Chersonese—thus bringing Athens in conflict with Macedon—about 342 B.C. and was subsequently honored by the king of Persia. This is one of the later historical references in the *Rhetoric;* see Appendix II.A.

very closely connected to their household, and in that case they feel for them as they feel about their own future suffering; this is why Amasis, according to reports,[71] did not weep when his son was led off to death but did [weep] for a friend reduced to begging; for the latter was pitiable, the former dreadful; for the dreadful is something different from the pitiable and capable of expelling pity and often useful to the opponent;[72] 13. for people no longer pity when something dreadful is near themselves.[73] And they pity those like themselves in age, in character, in habits, in rank, in birth; for in all these cases something seems more to apply also to the self; for in general, one should grasp here, too, that people pity things happening to others in so far as they fear[74] for themselves. 14. And since sufferings are pitiable when they appear near at hand and since people do not feel pity, or not in the same way, about things ten thousand years in the past or future, neither anticipating nor remembering them, necessarily those are more pitiable who contribute to the effect by gestures and cries and display of feelings and generally in their acting [*hypokrisis*];[75] for they make the evil seem near by making it appear before [our] eyes either as something about to happen or as something that has happened, 15. and things are more pitiable when just having happened or going to happen in a short space of time. **[1386b]** For this reason signs and actions [contribute to pity]; for example, the clothes of those who have suffered[76] and any other such things, and words and any other

71. The story is told in Herodotus 3.14 but of Psammenitus (= Psammetichus III), king of Egypt about 525 B.C. Amasis was his father. Aristotle may have misremembered or be following a different source.

72. Adopting the interpretation of Radt (1979, 297–98).

73. This is the text as conjectured by all modern editors. The manuscripts read, "They still pity when the dreadful is near themselves," which seems inconsistent. Aristotle is making a distinction between the nearness of an evil (which awakens pity) and the nearness of something truly awful (which awakens fear).

74. Since Aristotle views strong fear or dread as inconsistent with pity, he generally avoids using that word of the "expectation" of suffering, but here it inadvertently creeps in.

75. Aristotle will discuss acting as a part of rhetoric in 3.1.

76. This is clearest in epic and drama, where suffering characters sometimes appear in rags (Euripides' portrayal of Telephus was the most notorious example), roll in the dust, etc.; but defendants in Greek courts probably sometimes dressed for the part to awaken sympathy.

such things of those in suffering; for example, of those on their deathbed; for all such things, through their appearing near, make pity greater.[77] And most pitiable is for good people to be in such extremities, since one who is unworthy [is suffering] and the suffering is evident before our eyes.

Chapter 9: To Nemesan, *or Being Indignant*

■ Aristotle uses the verbal noun *to nemesan,* "being indignant," rather than the related noun *nemesis,* throughout this chapter except once, in section 3, perhaps because, as noted in section 2, *nemesis* had often taken on the meaning of "divine retribution."

DEFINITION OF BEING INDIGNANT AND ITS RELATION TO OTHER EMOTIONS

1. On the other hand,[78] what is most opposed to pity is what people call being indignant; for it is in some way opposed to feeling pain at undeserved *mis*fortune and, being pained at undeserved *good* fortune, arises from the same moral character [as does pity], and both emotions are characteristic of a good character; 2. for it is right to sympathize with and pity those who suffer undeservedly and to feel indignation at those who [undeservedly] fare well; for what takes place contrary to deserts is unjust, and thus we attribute being indignant to the gods.

3. But it might seem that envy [*phthonos*] is also opposed to feeling pity in the same way, as being closely related and much the same thing as being indignant; and yet it is different. Envy also is agitated pain and directed at success, but of an equal and a like, not of one who is unworthy. What is similarly present in all cases [of being indignant or envious] is not the feeling that some unpleas-

77. The translation follows Kassel's transposition of this clause from the next sentence.
78. The chapter division here is an arbitrary one; Aristotle directly links the discussion with what preceeds.

ant change will befall a person himself but [a feeling of pain] because of [what good befalls] his neighbor; for it will be neither envy nor indignation [*nemesis*] but fear if the pain and agitation are present because something bad will come to him as a result of the other person's success. 4. It is evident that opposite feelings will also follow these [reactions]; for one who is distressed at undeserved misfortunes will take pleasure or be unmoved by misfortunes of the opposite sort [i.e., deserved]; for example, no good person would be distressed when parricides and bloodthirsty murderers meet punishment; for it is right to rejoice in such cases, as in the case of those who deservedly fare well; for both are just things and cause a fair-minded person to rejoice; for necessarily there would be hope that what has befallen [one] like himself will befall himself. 5. All these feelings come from the same moral character, and opposite feelings from the opposite; for one who is malicious is also envious; **[1387a]** for when someone is distressed at the acquisition or possession of something, necessarily he rejoices at its deprivation or destruction. As a result, all these things are hindrances to pity and differ for the reasons mentioned, so that they are similarly useful [to a speaker] in counteracting feelings of pity.

THOSE TOWARD WHOM INDIGNATION IS FELT AND ITS CAUSES

6. First, then, let us speak about being indignant: at whom people are indignant and for what reasons and in what state of mind, then after this about the other emotions. 7. The former is evident from what has been said; for if being indignant is being distressed at the evidence of unworthy success, it is clear, first of all, that it is not possible to be indignant at all good things [that others acquire or possess]; 8. for if someone is just or brave or if he takes on some virtue of character, no one will feel indignation at him (nor are there feelings of pity at the opposites of these) but at [undeserved] wealth and power and such things as, in general, good people are worthy of, for example, noble birth and beauty and things like that [when the possessor is not a morally respected person].[79] 9. Since what is long established seems close to nature,

---

79. This statement has bothered some editors, who then want to insert a phrase saying that people are *not* indignant at natural advantages. Grimaldi, (1980–88, 2:

necessarily people are indignant at those having the same advantage if they have recently gotten it and do well because of it; for the newly rich cause more annoyance than those wealthy a long time and by inheritance. 10. And similarly when they are in public office and in power and with numerous friends and fine children and anything of that sort. And if some other good comes to them because of these things, similarly; for in this case the newly rich cause more distress when they hold office owing to their wealth than do the old rich, and similarly in other cases. The reason is that the latter seem to have what belongs to them, the former not; for when something [such as inherited wealth] has always been evident in this way it seems truly to belong to those who have it, with the result that others seem to have what is not their own. 11. And since each good thing is not deserved by any chance person, but there is a kind of analogy and propriety [about who has it] (for example, beauty of weapons suits a courageous rather than a just person, and distinguished marriages fit the wellborn, not the newly rich), then it is a source of indignation if someone who is good does not attain what is fitting. [It is] also [a source of indignation] for a lesser person to dispute with a greater one, especially those engaged in the same activity, whence, too, this has been said:

> But he avoided battle with Ajax, son of Telamon;

for Zeus was angry at him when he fought with a better man.[80] **[1387b]** But if [the activity] is not the same, even if a lesser person [disputes] with a greater in any way at all, [there is indignation], for example, if a musician [does so] with a just person; for justice is better than music.

---

158) discusses the pros and cons. Given Greek attitudes toward birth—and in particular beauty, where the common phrase *kalos k'agathos*, (handsome and good) asserted the union of the physical and aesthetic—it seems perfectly possible for Aristotle to mean that in conventional views, as appropriate to rhetoric, indignation is aroused at a perceived inconsistency between natural assets and moral worth. Alcibiades might be an example. See Radt 1979, 299.

80. *Iliad* 11.542, plus a line not found in our texts of the poem but also quoted by Plutarch.

THE STATE OF MIND OF THOSE WHO ARE INDIGNANT

At whom, then, people feel indignant and why is clear from this; for they are these and things like them. 12. People are prone to indignation [first] if they happen to be worthy of great advantages and have acquired them; for [they think] it is not just for those unlike them to think themselves worthy of the advantages they have. 13. Second, [they are prone to indignation] if they happen to be virtuous and serious; for [then] they make sound judgments and hate unjust things. 14. And [they are prone to indignation] if they are ambitious and desirous of certain things and, especially, are ambitious in regard to things that others are really unworthy of. 15. And generally, those who think themselves deserving of things they do not believe others deserve are prone to indignation toward the latter and about these things. Thus, the servile, the worthless, and the unambitious are not given to indignation; for there is nothing of which they regard themselves as worthy. 16. It is evident from this at what sort of people in misfortune and evildoing and lack of success one should rejoice or [at least] not feel distressed; for the opposites are clear from what has been said. And so if the speech puts the judges into this [hostile or indifferent] frame of mind [toward the opponent] and shows that those who think they deserve to be pitied (and to be pitied on certain grounds) are unworthy to attain it and worthy not to attain it, it is impossible for pity to be felt.

Chapter 10: Phthonos, *or Envy*

THE DEFINITION OF ENVY AND THE STATE OF MIND OF THOSE WHO
FEEL ENVY

■ Both indignation and envy are emotions opposed to pity. For the distinction between them see 2.9.3–5.

1. It is clear for what reasons and against whom and in what state of mind people are envious, since envy [*phthonos*] is [defined as] a certain kind of distress at apparent success on the part of

one's peers in attaining the good things that have been mentioned, not that a person may get anything for himself but because of those who have it. The kind of people who feel envy are those who have, or seem to themselves to have, [more fortunate acquaintances among] those like themselves. 2. I mean those like themselves in terms of birth, relationship, age, disposition, reputation, possessions, as well as those who just fall short of having all of these on an equal basis. Therefore, those who do great things and are fortunate are envious; for they think everybody is trying to take what is theirs. 3. And those [are envious] who are exceptionally honored for something, and especially for wisdom or happiness. And the ambitious are more envious than the unambitious. And those [are envious] who are wise in their own conceit; for they are ambitious for wisdom. And on the whole, those fond of fame in some way are envious in that regard. And the small-souled [are envious]; for all things seem great to them.

THE CAUSES OF ENVY AND THE PEOPLE WHO ARE ENVIED

4. The good things that people envy have been mentioned; for almost all things that cause people to love fame and honor, whether deeds or possessions, and make them desire attention [1388a] and whatever things are the gifts of fortune are, almost all of them, objects of envy, and especially those that they themselves desire or think they ought to have or things they possess only slightly more than others or slightly less. 5. It is evident, too, whom people envy; for these have been just now stated; for they envy those near to them in time and place and age and reputation, whence it has been said

Kinship, too, knows how to envy.[81]

And [they envy] those they rival; for they rival those mentioned, [feeling] the same way toward them and on the same grounds,[82] but no one rivals people ten thousand years in the future or dead

---

81. Attributed by a medieval commentator to Aeschylus. Kassel double-brackets this as a late addition by Aristotle.

82. The translation transposes this otherwise troublesome phrase from the end of the section.

nor those who live at the Pillars of Heracles[83] nor those they or others regard as inferior or much superior. 6. But since people seek honor in comparison with antagonists and rivals in love and in general those wanting the same things, necessarily they are most envious of these. This is the source of the saying "Potter [against] potter."[84] 7. And people have envy of those who have acquired something or been successful. These, too, are near and like; for clearly, they do not attain this good because of themselves, so distress at this causes envy. 8. And [they envy] those who have or have acquired whatever naturally belongs to themselves or what they once had. This is why the older [envy] the younger. 9. And those who have spent much money envy those who have spent little for the same object.[85] 10. And those who got something with difficulty or did not get it at all envy those who got it quickly.

THE STATE OF MIND OF THOSE WHO ENVY

11. It is also clear what such people rejoice at and for what causes and in what state of mind; for the state of mind that accompanies distress is also the state of mind in which people take pleasure in the opposite situations. So if [speakers] have created this [envious] state of mind [in the audience] and if persons of the sort described have thought themselves deserving to be pitied or to attain some good, clearly they will not attain pity from those in authority.

Chapter 11: Zēlos, *or Emulation*

■ This chapter belongs with the preceeding in that emulation is regarded as the positive counterpart of envy. Both are feelings that may result from a sense of rivalry with those a

83. Gibraltar, the nominal limit of the known world.

84. Cf. 2.4.21.

85. Some manuscripts and early editors insert this sentence after sec. 6, but it is found here in Parisinus 1741.

person regards as in some sense an equal. In Hellenistic and later rhetoric, *zēlos* becomes an important aspect of literary imitation; for it refers to the zeal on the part of a writer to equal the quality of the greater writers of the past. This chapter concludes the chiastically arranged survey of positive and negative emotions.

THE DEFINITION OF *ZĒLOS*, THE STATE OF MIND OF THOSE WHO FEEL IT, AND ITS CAUSES

1. But the state of mind of those who feel emulation, and at what sort of things and what people [feel it], is clear from what follows; for if emulation [*zēlos*] is [defined as] a kind of distress at the apparent presence among others like him by nature, of things honored and possible for a person to acquire, [with the distress arising] not from the fact that another has them but that the emulator does not (thus emulation is a good thing and characteristic of good people, while envy is bad and characteristic of the bad; for the former [person], through emulation, is making an effort to attain good things for himself, while the latter, through envy, tries to prevent his neighbor from having them)—[if this definition is posited,] then necessarily those are emulous who think themselves deserving of goods they do not have **[1388b]** (for no one thinks himself worthy of things that seem impossible).[86] For this reason the young and the great-souled are emulous. Also those [are emulous] who possess such goods as are worthy of men [*andrōn*] who are honored, and these are wealth and numerous friends and offices and all such things; for since it is right to be good, people zealously seek goods of this sort because they are appropriate attributes of the good. 2. And those are given to emulation whom others think worthy [of such goods] 3. and whose ancestors or relatives or households or nation or city are honored on these grounds; for they think these things properly belong to them and that they are worthy of them. 4. But if honored goods are the

---

86. Another of Aristotle's formidable sentences, though grammatical and clear if the parenthical corollary is set aside. Translators often prefer to move the parenthesis out into a separate sentence but at the cost of not seeing Aristotle's mind at work. Kassel double-brackets it as a late addition by Aristotle.

objects of emulation, necessarily the virtues are such things and whatever is a source of advantage and benefit to others; for people honor benefactors and the good. And goods [are causes of emulation] when their enjoyment can be shared with neighbors, for example, wealth and beauty more than health.

THOSE WHO ARE EMULATED

5. What persons are emulated is also evident; for they are those who have acquired these things and things like them. These things are those mentioned, for example, bravery, wisdom, public office; for public officials, including generals, politicians [*rhētores*], [and] all having this kind of power, can benefit many people. 6. And those [are emulated] whom many want to be like, or many of their acquaintances or many of their friends [are emulated]. Or [those are emulated] whom many admire or whom the emulators admire. 7. And those [are emulated] whose praises and encomia are spoken by poets or prose writers [*logographoi*]. But people feel contempt for the opposite [types]; for contempt [*kataphronēsis*][87] is the opposite of emulation and *to emulate* of *to feel contempt for*. Necessarily, those in a situation to emulate or be emulated are contemptuous of others (and for these reasons) who have the bad attributes that are opposites of the emulated good ones. As a result, they are often contemptuous of those who are fortunate, whenever good fortune comes to the latter without [bringing with it] those things that are really valued.[88] This concludes an account of how the emotions are created and counteracted, from which are derived *pisteis* related to them.[89]

---

87. Cf. 2.2.3–4.

88. Thus, they might feel contempt for a person who was very popular with friends but neither handsome nor rich.

89. Or "and [the topics] from which are derived. . . ." *And* is found only in some late manuscripts and medieval translations. It was restored to the text by Kassel and has been vigorously defended by Conley (1982). The interpretative issue is that mentioned in the introduction to chaps. 2–11: the extent to which topics about the emotions are to be regarded as primarily premises for enthymemes. If *and* is not inserted, the sentence claims only that the creation or counteracting of emotions, as described in these chapters, produces persuasion based on emotional feelings.

Chapters 12–17: Topics About *Ēthos*, Useful in Adapting the Character of the Speaker to the Character of the Audience

■ In Plato's *Phaedrus* (see esp. 271d–272b and 277b–c) Socrates argues that there cannot be a true art of speech without a knowledge of the soul, enabling a speaker to fit the appropriate argument to the soul of the hearer. Although this emphasis on psychology was an important contribution to rhetoric, Socrates does not mention the problem inherent in addressing a mixed group with diverse characters. Aristotle takes up the subject in these chapters and develops it by considering character in terms of groups, classified by age and as affected by birth, wealth, power, and fortune. The picture of youth, prime, and old age that he gives reflects the common stereotypical views of antiquity and can be seen also in the comedy of Menander and his Roman imitators, Plautus and Terence.

The predominant meaning of *ēthos* in Aristotle is "moral character" as reflected in deliberate choice of actions and as developed into a habit of mind. At times, however, the word seems to refer to qualities, such as an innate sense of justice or a quickness of temper, with which individuals may be naturally endowed and which dispose them to certain kinds of action. In 1.2.4 one of the three modes of persuasion was identified as provided by *ēthos*. In that sense the word refers to the trustworthy character of a speaker as artistically created in a speech. Students of the *Rhetoric* have taken differing views as to whether the brief passage in 2.1.5–7 or the longer passage 2.12–17 should be regarded as Aristotle's principal discussion of character presentation as a mode of persuasion. It seems clear that 2.1.5–7 resumes the original statement of 1.2.3–5, noted also in 1.9.1, and that 2.12–17 is aimed at something rather different: the adaptation of a speech to the character of the audience, which was anticipated in 1.8.6. The need to discuss the effect of age, wealth, and fortune on character was pointed out in 1.10.10–11, and these chapters provide that account. In 2.22.16 Aristotle seems to refer to 2.12–17 as listing "topics" relating to *ēthos;* these may include, but are not limited to, topics for enthymemes. At the end of 2.18.1 the preceeding discussion is described as a matter of making speech "ethical," and in 3.17.8 we are told that enthymemes should be avoided when the speech is being "ethical." As Grimaldi says (1980–88, 2: 186), "the actual purpose of chapters 12–17 with its study of the major character types is to show the speaker how his *ēthos* must attend and adjust to the *ēthos* of varied types of auditor if he is to address them successfully." This is similar to what Socrates urges in the *Phaedrus* but more pragmatic and open to possible abuse.

Chapters 2.12–17, like 2.2–11, were almost certainly written in a different—nonrhetorical—context and only added to the *Rhetoric* at a later stage, without adequate revision to integrate them into the objectives of the treatise. Note that the chapters contain no examples from oratory and, beginning with the second sentence, link character and emotion. Wisse (1989, 9–43) concludes that these chapters are an "appendix" to the account of both *ēthos* and *pathos*.

Chapter 12: Introduction; the Character of the Young

■ In this chapter Aristotle gives the stereotypical Greek view of young men as pleasure-loving, impulsive, and optimistic. In 2.13.16 he indicates that awareness of this is useful in addressing the young, but the chapter does not indicate any situations in which that might be done. What is actually found in Greek oratory is the use of some of the topics Aristotle mentions to explain the actions and motivations of a young man when he is accused before a jury of some crime. A good example is the sixteenth speech of Lysias, *For Mantitheus* (esp. sections 11, 15–16). Juries have often been disposed to excuse youthful high jinks (cf. Cicero, *For Caelius,* esp. sections 37–47).

1. Next let us go through the kinds of charcter, considering what they are like in terms of emotions and habits and age of life and fortune [*tychē*]. 2. (By emotions [*pathē*] I mean anger, desire, and

the like, about which we spoke earlier,[90] and by habits virtues and vices; these have also been discussed earlier), including what sort of things each type of person chooses and does.[91] The ages of life are youth, prime, and old age. **[1389a]** By fortune I mean good birth and wealth and power and their opposites and in general good fortune and misfortune.

3. In terms of their character, the young are prone to desires and inclined to do whatever they desire. Of the desires of the body they are most inclined to pursue that relating to sex, and they are powerless against this. 4. They are changeable and fickle in desires, and though they intensely lust, they are quickly satisfied; for their wants, like the thirst and hunger of the sick, are sharp rather than massive. 5. And they are impulsive and quick-tempered and inclined to follow up their anger [by action]. And they are unable to resist their impulses; for through love of honor they cannot put up with being belittled but become indignant if they think they are done a wrong. 6. And though they love honor, they love victory more; for youth longs for superiority, and victory is a kind of superiority. They have both of these characteristics more than a love of money, and [of the age groups] they are least lovers of money because they have not yet experienced want, as the saying of Pittacus about Amphiaraus has it.[92] 7. And they are not cynical but guileless, because of not yet having seen much wickedness. And [they are] trusting, because of not yet having been much deceived. 8. And [they are] filled with good hopes; for like those drinking wine, the young are heated by their nature, and at the same time [they are filled with hopes] because of not yet having experienced much failure. And they live for the most part in hope; for hope is for the future, and memory is of what has gone by, but for the young the future is long and the past short; for in the dawn of life nothing can be remembered, and everything [can be] hoped for. And they are easily deceived for the reason given; for they easily hope for the best. 9. And they are more courageous [than the other age groups]; for they are impulsive and filled with good

90. In 2.2–11.

91. Adopting the punctuation suggested by Wisse 1989, 322.

92. Otherwise unknown. Pittacus was chief of state of Mytilene about 600 B.C., Amphiaraus one of the legendary Seven Against Thebes.

hopes, of which the former quality makes them lack fear, and the latter makes them brave; for no one feels fear when angry, and to expect something good is a source of confidence. 10. And they are sensitive to shame; for they have been educated only by convention and do not yet understand other fine things. 11. And they are magnanimous; for they have not yet been worn down by life but are inexperienced with constraints, and to think oneself worthy of great things is magnanimity; and this is characteristic of a person of good hopes. 12 And they choose to do fine things rather than things advantageous [to themselves]; for they live more by natural character than by calculation, and calculation concerns the advantageous, virtue the honorable. 13. And more than other ages of life they are fond of friends and eager for companions, because they enjoy living with others **[1389b]** and do not yet judge anything on the basis of advantage; thus, they do not judge friends that way. 14. And all the mistakes they make are in the direction of excess and vehemence, contrary to the maxim of Chilon;[93] for they do "everything too much": they love too much and hate too much and all other things similarly. And they think they know everything and strongly insist on it; for this is the cause of their doing everything too much. 15. And the wrongs they commit come from insolence, not maliciousness. And they are inclined to pity, because of supposing [that] everybody is good or better than the average; for they measure their neighbors by their own innocence, with the result that they suppose them to be suffering unworthily. And they are fond of laughter and, as a result, witty; for wit is cultured insolence. Such, then, is the character of the young.

Chapter 13: The Character of the Old

■ Instead of moving through the stages of life chronologically, Aristotle jumps to a description of the old as opposites of the young. In chapter 14 he will then return to describe the prime of life as a mean.

---

93. The Spartan sage to whom was attributed the maxim "Nothing too much."

1. People who are older and more or less past their prime have characters that are for the most part the opposite of these [just described]; for through having lived for many years and having been more often deceived and having made more mistakes themselves and since most things turn out badly, they assert nothing with certainty and all things with less assurance than is needed. 2. And they "think," but do not "know" anything. And being doubtful, they always add *perhaps* and *maybe* and say everything that way, but nothing definitively. 3. And they are cynical; for a cynical disposition supposes everything is for the worse. Further, they are suspicious because of their distrust and distrustful because of experience. 4. And for these reasons they neither love nor hate strongly but, following the advice of Bias,[94] they love as if they would one day hate and hate as if they would one day love. 5. And they are small-minded because of having been worn down by life; for they desire nothing great or unusual but things necessary for life. 6. And they are stingy; for one of the necessities is money, and at the same time they know from experience that it is difficult to acquire and easy to lose. 7. And they are cowardly and fearful ahead of time about everything; for their disposition is the opposite of the young. (They are chilled, but the young are hot, so old age has prepared the way for cowardice; for fear is a kind of chilling.) 8. And they are fond of life and more so in their last day because of the presence of desire for what is gone, and people most desire what they lack. 9. And they are more fond of themselves than is right; for this is also a form of small-mindedness. And they live for what is advantageous [to themselves] (not for what is fine) more than is right, through being fond of themselves. (The advantageous is good for the individual, the fine absolutely.) **[1390a]** 10. And they are more shameless than sensitive to shame; for since they do not care equally about what is fine and what is advantageous, they think little of their reputation. 11. And they expect the worst, through experience—[in their view] the greater part of things that happen are bad; at least most turn out for the worse— and through their cowardice, too. 12. And they live in memory more than in hope; for what is left of life is short, what is past is long, and hope is for the future, memory for what is gone. This is

94. One of the Seven Sages of early Greece.

the cause of their garrulity; for they keep talking about things that have passed; for they take pleasure in reminiscence. 13. Their outbursts of anger are sharp but weak; and some of their desires have failed, others are weak, with the result that they are not spirited and do not act on the basis of desire, but for profit. Thus, those in this age group seem self-controlled; for their desires are gone, and they are slaves to profit. 14. And they live more by calculation than by natural character; and calculation is a matter of what is beneficial, character of virtue.[95] And the wrongs they commit are from malice, not insolence. 15. The old are also inclined to pity but not for the same reason as the young; with the latter it is a matter of human feelings [*philanthropia*], with the former weakness; for they think that all kinds of sufferings are close at hand for themselves, and this was the definition of one who feels pity.[96] As a result, they are querulous and not witty nor fond of laughter; for querulousness is the opposite of love of laughter. 16. Such are the characters of the young and the older; as a result, since all people receive favorably speeches spoken in their own character and by persons like themselves, it is not unclear how both speakers and speeches may seem to be of this sort through use of words.

Chapter 14: The Character of Those in the Prime of Life

1. It is evident that those in the prime of life will be between the young and the old in character, subtracting the excess of either, and neither exceedingly confident (rashness is such) nor too fearful but having the right amount of both, 2. neither trusting nor distrusting everybody but rather making realistic judgments and not directing their lives only to what is fine or what is advantageous but to both **[1390b]** and neither to frugality nor to extravagance but to what is fitting. 3. Similarly in regard to impulse and desire. And they combine prudence with courage and courage with prudence, while among the young and the old these things are separated; for the young are brave and lack self-restraint, the older ones prudent

95. Cf. 1.12.12.
96. See 2.8.2.

and cowardly. To speak in general terms, whatever advantages youth and old age have separately, [those in their prime] combine, and whatever the former have to excess or in deficiency, the latter have in due measure and in a fitting way. 4. The body is in its prime from the age of thirty to thirty-five, the mind about age forty-nine.[97] Let this much be said about the kinds of character of youth and old age and the prime of life.

Chapter 15: The Effect on Character of Eugeneia, *or* Good Birth

■ *Tykhē* can mean "chance," "accident," "fortune," or "luck." To Aristotle it represents unmotivated contingency, not Fate or the predetermined will of some divinity; but he realizes that some people seem consistently luckier than others. Some of the advantages Aristotle describes, for example, good birth, can be said to be a matter of chance; but power combines luck with ability and effort on the part of the person who has it.

1. Let us speak next about goods that come from *tykhē* in so far as some kinds of character also result for human beings from them. 2. The character that comes from good birth is a matter of its possessor being rather ambitious; for all people, when some advantage is theirs, usually add others to it, and good birth is rank in society that derives from ancestors.[98] Also, such persons are contemptuous, even of those [of their contemporaries] equal [in achievement] to their own ancestors, because these things are more honorable and easy to boast about when they came into existence further back in

97. Aristotle first taught rhetoric in Athens about the age of thirty and returned there to open his school at the age of forty-nine. If the chronology outlined in the Appendix II.A is correct, he may have written these words when he was approaching forty-nine years old. It is noteworthy that he does not specify the age limit of youth or the beginning of old age, only maturity. The ages specified here only approximately accord with the common Greek theory that life could be viewed in ten stages of seven years each; see *Politics* 7.16.17.

98. Thus, it gives the possessor an initial advantage.

time than when recent. 3. *Good birth* refers to the excellence of the family, whereas *noble* [*gennaion*] refers to there having been no degeneration from [the earlier] nature [of the line]; for the most part such is not the case among the wellborn, since many of them are worthless; for there is a kind of harvest in the generations of men as in what grows on the land; and sometimes, if the stock is good, outstanding men continue to be born into the family, and then again it falls off. Originally good stock [often] degenerates into rather demented forms of character, as in the case of the children of Alcibiades and Dionysius the Elder, while a previously steadfast stock [often] turns into silliness and stupidity, as in the children of Cimon and Pericles and Socrates.

Chapter 16: Character As Affected by Ploutos, or Wealth

1. The kinds of character that follow from wealth are plain for all to see; for [the wealthy] are insolent and arrogant, being affected somehow by the possession of wealth; for their state of mind is that of those who have all good things; **[1391a]** for wealth is a kind of standard of value of other things, so that all things seem purchasable by it. 2. And they are ostentatious and pretentious: ostentatious because of luxury and the display of their prosperity, pretentious and vulgar because all are used to spending their time doing whatever they like and admire and because they think everybody else has the same values they do. At the same time, this feeling is reasonable; for there are many who need what they have. This is the reason for what Simonides said about the wise and the rich to the wife of Hieron when she asked whether it was better to be rich or wise: [he replied] "To be rich"; for he said one sees the wise waiting at the doors of the rich.[99] 3. [Another result of wealth is that the rich] think they deserve to rule; for they think they have that which makes one worthy to rule [i.e., money]. And in sum, the character that comes from wealth is that of a lucky fool. 4. The

99. Hieron was tyrant of Syracuse in the 470s and visited there by the poet, Simonides of Ceos. To a follow-up question the philosopher Aristippus replied, "Philosophers know what they need, the rich do not" (Diogenes Laertius 2.69).

characters of the newly rich and those with old wealth differ in that the newly rich have all the vices to a greater degree and in a worse form; for to be newly rich is, as it were, to lack education in the use of wealth. And the wrongs that they commit are not malicious but sometimes acts of insolence, sometimes the result of lack of self-control, for example, personal injury and adultery.

Chapter 17: Character As Affected by Dynamis, or Power

1. Similarly with power, most of the ways it influences forms of character are evident; for power has some characteristics that are the same as wealth, some that are better; 2. for those holding power are more ambitious and more manly in character than the rich, because of aiming at deeds that they have the means of doing because of their power. 3. And they are more earnest, because of being in a position of responsibility, forced to keep an eye on everything that relates to their power. 4. And they are rather more reserved in a dignified way than inclined to be servere; for their rank makes them quite conspicuous, so they seek moderation. Their dignity is a mild and graceful severity. And if they commit wrong, they do it on a large, not a small, scale.

CONCLUSION TO THE DISCUSSION OF CHAPTERS 15–17

5. Good fortune in its different forms makes for the kinds of character described above (for the kinds of good fortune that seem greatest tend in these directions), and in addition good fortune offers an opportunity for advantages in regard to the blessings of children and the goods of the body. **[1391b]** 6. Although people are more arrogant and unreasonable because of good fortune, there is one very good characteristic that follows from good fortune, namely, that these people are lovers of the gods and have a special relationship to divinity, having faith in the gods because of the benefits that have come to them from fortune. Enough has now been said about types of character as related to stage in life and fortune; for the opposite kinds of character are evident from the

opposites of what has been said, for example, the character of the poor and the unfortunate and the powerless.

Chapters 18–26: Dialectical Features of Rhetoric Common to All Three Species

Chapter 18: Introduction

■ This chapter provides a transition from the discussion of character to a further consideration of premises, forms of proof, and common topics, concepts laid down in 1.2–3. There are, however, a number of obscurities that have troubled the commentators. Rudolf Kassel, in his edition of the Greek text (1976), marks most of section 1 (up to "and [since] characters") as a later addition by Aristotle to the otherwise completed text of the *Rhetoric,* providing a rather cumbersome transition. If that much is taken as a sentence, as Kassel punctuates it, it is not really grammatically complete, there being no clear apodosis, or main clause, following on the "since" and "if" clauses. Grimaldi (1980–88, 2: 230) regards the last clause of section 1 as the logical apodosis, and the translation below follows that assumption. Perhaps the passage should be regarded as an incomplete draft of a transition that sections 2–5 were intended to replace.

1. Since the use of persuasive speech is directed to a judgment[100] (there is no further need of speech on subjects that we know and have already judged) and since there is judgment even if someone, by using speech to address an individual exhorts or dissuades [him], for example, those giving advice or persuading [someone to do something] (a single individual is no less a judge; for a judge is, so to speak, simply one who must be persuaded) and [since] if someone speaks against an opponent and if against a proposition, the same is true (it is necessary to use speech and to refute opposing arguments

100. Aristotle here resumes the thought of 2.1.2.

at which the speech is directed as at an opponent), and similarly in epideictic (the speech is composed for the spectator as a judge) but [since] nevertheless only that person is purely a judge in the géneral sense of the word who is judging the questions at issue in civic debates (for he inquires into the facts of the dispute [in a law court] and the subject on which counsel is being given [in a deliberative assembly]) and [since] characters as found under [different] constitutions have been discussed earlier[101]—as a result, the definition of how and through what means one ought to make speeches ethical should be complete.

2. Since there was a different end for each genus of speech,[102] and opinions and premises have been collected for all of them, from which [speakers] derive *pisteis* when speaking in deliberation and in demonstrations and contention[103] and from which, moreover, it is possible to make speeches appropriate to character,[104] and since definitions have been given on these matters, it remains to describe the *koina;*[105] 3. for it is necessary for all, in their speeches, in addition [to what has been described] to make use of [premises] concerning the possible and impossible and for some[106] to try to show that something will be the case and others[107] that something has taken place. 4. Further, a common feature of all speeches is the matter of magnitude [*megethos*]; for all use diminution and amplification when deliberating and when praising or blaming and when prosecuting or defending themselves. **[1392a]** 5. Once these have been defined, let us try to speak about enthymemes in general terms, so far as we can, and about paradigms, in order that having added what

---

101. The reference is apparently to 1.8.6.

102. According to the definitions of 1.3.5.

103. I.e., in deliberative, epideictic, and judicial rhetoric.

104. Commentators have been troubled at the absence of reference to *pathos* in this summary. Probably it is to be thought of as included in *ēthikous*, "appropriate to character" (cf. 2.12.1); possibly, Aristotle just overlooked it.

105. *Koina* = "the things that are common to all species (or genera) of rhetoric." These are the forms of argument first mentioned—but given no technical term—in 1.3.7–9.

106. Deliberative speakers.

107. Speakers in the law courts.

remains, we may complete the program originally outlined.[108] Of the *koina*, amplification is most proper to epideictic (as has been said),[109] past fact [is most proper] to judicial (judgment there is about past facts), and possibility and future fact [are most proper] to deliberative speeches.

Chapter 19. The Koina: *The Possible and the Impossible; Past and Future Fact; Degree of Magnitude or Importance*

■ This chapter resumes discussion of three subjects of argument, first mentioned in 1.3.7–9, that are useful in all species of rhetoric. Degree of magnitude has also been discussed in 1.7, 14.

THE POSSIBLE AND THE IMPOSSIBLE

1. First let us speak about possible and impossible. If it is possible for the opposite of something to exist or to have happened, the opposite would also seem to be possible; for example, if it is possible for a human being to be healthy, it is possible also to be ill; for the potentiality of opposites is the same, in so far as they are opposites.[110] 2. And if one of two like things is possible, the other is also. 3. And if the more difficult is possible, so is the easier. 4. And if something can come to be good and beautiful, it can also come to be in general; for it is more difficult for a house to be beautiful than for a house to exist. 5. And where the beginning is possible, so also is the end;[111] for no impossible thing comes to be nor begins to come to

108. In 1.1–3. Note that there is still no hint of book 3.

109. In 1.9.40.

110. In this example, as in the following ones, note that Aristotle is talking about what is logically possible, not what is necessarily true in a particular case. The propositions here laid down are dialectical in that they are based on common assumptions that most people would accept and do not require further demonstration.

111. An axiom important in metaphysics: if the world was created, it is possible for it to have an end; if the soul is immortal, it is possible for it to have existed before birth, etc.

be; for example, the diagonal [of a square] could not begin to be, nor be, commensurate [with the side]. And where there is an end, the beginning is also possible; for all things come from a beginning. 6. And if what is later in existence or birth is possible, so also [is] what is prior; for example, if it is possible for a man to exist, so also for a boy (a boy is prior to a man); [it is possible for] a boy [to exist] so also a man (a boy is also a first principle).[112] 7. And that for which there is natural desire or longing [is possible]; for no one desires or longs for things that are impossible, at least not for the most part. 8. And where sciences or arts exist, it is possible for the subject of those studies both to exist and to have existed.[113] 9. And [things are possible] whose first principle lies in things we can compel or persuade; these are those things than which we are stronger or over which we have authority or [those persons] of whom we are friends.[114] 10. And the whole is possible of which the parts are possible, and for the most part the parts are possible if the whole is;[115] for if the sole and toe and top can be made, shoes can be made too; and if shoes [can be made], then [so can] the sole and the toe.[116] 11. And if the genus as a whole is among possible things, so also [is] the species, **[1392b]** and if the species, [so] also [is] the genus; for example, if a ship can be made, a trireme can be, and if a trireme, also a ship. 12. And if either one of two naturally corresponding things [is possible, so] also [is] the other; for example, if double [is possible, so] also [is] half, and if half, [so] also [is] double. 13. And if something is possible without art or preparation, all the more is it possible with art and care. This is the source of Agathon's saying,

112. Or "beginning" (*archē*); see book 1, n. 132.

113. From the popular point of view it is thus logically possible that the subjects of astrology or magic exist, since a systematic body of thought about them seems to exist.

114. It is possible to make a statue of wood or stone because "we" (some human beings) have the strength to work the material; it is possible to hire or dismiss servants because "we" are the masters; it is possible to invite people to dinner because "we" are their friends.

115. An example of the qualification *for the most part* is the begetting of a child. Parents cannot beget the parts (e.g., limbs) separately.

116. We do not know exactly what parts of the shoe Aristotle refers to by *proskhisma, kephalis,* and *khitōn;* the translation is only an approximation.

And indeed we must do some things by art, and some
Happen to us by necessity and chance.[117]

14. And if something is possible for inferior or weaker or less
intelligent people, then [it is] also more possible for the opposites,
as Isocrates said that it was strange if he himself could not understand a subject that Euthynous had learned. 15. As for the impossible, it is clear from the opposites of what has been said.

PAST AND FUTURE FACT

■ Argument from probability is a major characteristic of
Greek rhetoric, in part because of the distrust of direct evidence. Aristotle here sets out a number of useful forms that
argument from probability can take, though it would have
been clearer if he had furnished examples from legal and
deliberative rhetoric rather than from natural science. The
passage thus seems to have originated in some other context
and been added to a revision of the *Rhetoric*. "Past fact" is a
common subject of judicial rhetoric, and the arguments here
discussed roughly correspond to what is called "circumstantial evidence" in modern law; "future fact" is the subject of
deliberative rhetoric. Behind what is said here lies the assumption that human actions and events follow predictable
natural patterns, except in unusual circumstances.

16. Whether some action has or has not taken place should be
considered on the basis of the following.[118] First, if what is naturally less likely to have happened [happened], what is more so
should also have happened.[119] 17. And if what usually occurs after

117. Agathon was a tragic poet of the fifth century (also a character in Plato's
Symposium). These iambic lines seem to come from one of his lost plays.
118. In judicial rhetoric, the first and sometimes the only consideration is whether
or not the defendant has in fact personally committed the alleged act, such as killing
someone, stealing something, breaking the terms of a contract, etc.
119. E.g., if a defendant has been shown on another occasion to have stolen someone else's property, it is likely that he has attempted to recover his own property
from another person when the need arose.

something else has happened [happened], the previous event has also happened; for example, if someone has forgotten something, he also once learned it. 18. And if a person had the capacity and the will [to do something], he has done it; for all act when ability to do so coincides with desire; for nothing hinders them.[120] Further, if someone had the will to do something and no external agency hindered him, [then he acted], 19. and if he had the ability and was angry, and if he had the ability and longed for something [, then he acted]; for usually people do what they long to do if they can, the bad through lack of self-control, the good because they desire good things. 20. And if something was going to happen and someone was going to do it, [then it occurred]; for it is probable [*eikos*] that one who was going to do something also did it. 21. And if things that are naturally antecedents or causes [happened, the consequences happened]; for example, if it has lightened, it has also thundered, and if he tried, he did it. And if something has occurred that is naturally subsequent or a result, then the antecedent and cause have occurred; for example, if it has thundered, it also lightened, and if he did it, he tried. Of all of these, some are related by necessity, some only for the most part. 22. As for what has not happened, that is clear from the opposites of the things mentioned.

What is going to be in the future is clear from the same arguments;[121] **[1393a]** for that will be for which there is both capacity and motivation, 23. and those things for which there is desire and the impulse of anger and calculation together with capacity to act; those things, too, that are on the verge of being done or going to be done will take place; for things that are going to be done, rather than things that are not, usually take place. 24. And if what usually precedes has preceded [what usually follows will probably happen]; for example, if it is cloudy, there is a probability it will rain.[122] 25 And if something has been done for the sake of something else,

---

120. This of course can be a fallacious argument; but if it can be shown that some action, such as theft, occurred and only one person had the capacity and motivation to commit it, the circumstantial evidence is strong that he is guilty.

121. This is the characteristic subject of deliberative rhetoric, since the speaker gives advice about future actions and projects the probable course of future events.

122. Or, perhaps better, if the enemy is collecting troops on the border, it is probable that they will invade.

it is probable that the latter has resulted; for example, if a foundation [has been laid], a house [has probably been built].

26. The subject of largeness and smallness of things and more and less and, on the whole, large and small is evident to us from what has been said; for an account was given in the discussion of deliberative rhetoric of the magnitude of goods and of the greater and lesser in general terms.[123] As a result, since in each kind of speech the projected "end" [*telos*] is a good—for example the advantageous [in deliberative rhetoric] and the honorable [in epideictic] and the just [in judicial][124]—it is evident that one should seize the opportunities for amplification [*auxēsis*] through [discussion of] these [objectives]. 27. To go into the matter of magnitude in general and the concept of superiority in further detail is wasting words; for the particulars of subjects are controlling factors in the application of universals.[125] Thus, let this be enough on the subject of possibility and impossibility and whether something has or has not happened and will or will not be and about largeness and smallness of things.

Chapters 20–22: *Koinai Pisteis*, or Common Modes of Persuasion

■ These chapters resume discussion of the basic tools of logical persuasion, first defined in 1.2.

123. See 1.7.
124. See 1.3.5.
125. Rhetoric, as a practical skill, does not require the scientific knowledge needed in mathematics or physics about the nature of magnitude.

Chapter 20: Paradigm, or Example

1. It remains to speak about *pisteis* that are common to all [species of rhetoric], since the account of specifics has been completed.[126] These common *pisteis* are two in number: paradigm and enthymeme (maxim [*gnōmē*] is a part of an enthymeme). 2. First, then, let us speak of paradigm; for paradigm is similar to an induction, and induction is a beginning.[127]

There are two species of paradigms; for to speak of things that have happened before is one species of paradigm and to make up [an illustration] is another.[128] Of the latter, comparison [*parabolē*] is one kind, fables [*logoi*] another, for example, the Aesopic and Lybian. 3. An instance of speaking of [historical] facts is if someone were to say that it is necessary to make preparations against the king [of Persia] and not allow Egypt to be subdued; for in the past Darius did not invade [Greece] until he had taken Egypt, **[1393b]** but after taking it, he invaded; and again, Xerxes did not attack [Greece] until he took [Egypt], but having taken it, he invaded; thus if he [the present king] takes [Egypt], he will invade [Greece]; as a result it must not be allowed.[129] 4. Socratic sayings are an instance of comparison, for example, if someone were to say that officials should not be chosen by lot (for that would be as if someone chose athletes

126. This sounds as though it originally followed 1.5–15. The common *pisteis* are those called demonstrative in 1.2.19 and should not be confused with the artistic (*entekhnoi*) *pisteis*, which are the more general modes of logical, "ethical," and emotional persuasion. The term *specifics* (*idia*) is also taken up from 1.2.21, where it referred to the subject matter specific to some discipline like politics and ethics, and in subsequent chapters was considered in terms of the specific subject matter of deliberative, epideictic, and judicial rhetoric. We now return to consider the fundamental logical devices of all rhetoric in greater detail. They are basically the same devices used in dialectic, though there called induction and syllogism.

127. A universal major premise, e.g., "All men are mortal," is, in the first instance, established by induction from particulars.

128. Thus, the species are "historical" and "fictional."

129. The structure of this argument is proposition, two historical examples with implied conclusion (whoever takes Egypt invades Greece), and application to the proposition. The "present king" is Artaxerxes III Ochus, who in 343 sent an embassy to Greece asking for an alliance in his efforts to regain Egypt; the passage was therefore written after that date; see Appendix II.A. The king recovered Egypt but did not invade Greece.

randomly—not those able to contest, but those on whom the lot fell); or [as if] choosing by lot any one of the sailors to act as pilot rather than the one who knew how.[130]

5. An example of a fable is what Stesichorus said about Phalaris and Aesop about the demagogue. When the people of Himera had chosen Phalaris as dictator and were about to give him a body-guard, after saying other things at some length, Stesichorus told them a fable about how a horse had a meadow to himself. When a stag came and quite damaged the pasture, the horse, wanting to avenge himself on the stag, asked a man if he could help him get vengeance on the stag. The man said he could, if the horse were to take a bridle and he himself were to mount on him holding jave-lins. When the horse agreed and the man mounted, instead of getting vengeance the horse found himself a slave to the man. "Thus you too," said Stesichorus, "look out, lest while wishing vengeance on your enemies you suffer the same thing as the horse. You already have the bridle [in your mouth], having appointed a general with absolute power; if you give him a bodyguard and allow him to mount, you will immediately be slaves to Phalaris."[131]

6. Aesop, when speaking on behalf of a demagogue who was on trial for his life in Samos, told how a fox, while crossing a river, was carried into a hole in the bank. Not being able to get out, she was in misery for some time and many dog-ticks attacked her. A hedge-hog came wandering along and, when he saw her, took pity and asked if he could remove the ticks. She would not let him and, when asked why, [said], "These are already full of me and draw little blood, but if you remove these, other hungry ones will come and drink what blood I have left." "In your case too, O Samians,"

---

130. On Socrates' use of this example, see Xenophon, *Memorabilia* 1.2.9. Here we have proposition and then two comparisons, of which the latter contains within it another comparison that makes the point: public officials should be chosen on the basis of their knowledge. Note that Aristotle does not remark on any connection between *parabolē* as a demonstrative tool (treated here) and *eikōn*, or simile (treated as a stylistic device in 3.4 and regarded as basically poetic).

131. The date is the second quarter of the sixth century B.C., in Western Sicily. Stesichorus is the lyric poet, mentioned by Aristotle again in 2.21.8 and 3.11.6. Phalaris became the most notorious of the Greek tyrants, alleged to have roasted his victims alive in a brazen bull.

said [Aesop], "this man will no longer harm you; for he is rich. But if you kill him, other poor ones will come who will steal and spend your public funds."[132] **[1394a]** 7. Fables are suitable in deliberative oratory and have this advantage, that while it is difficult to find similar historical incidents that have actually happened, it is rather easy with fables. They should be made in the same way as comparisons, provided one can see the likenesses, which is rather easy from philosophical studies.[133] 8. Although it is easier to provide illustrations through fables, examples from history are more useful in deliberation; for generally, future events will be like those of the past.

9. If one does not have a supply of enthymemes, one should use paradigms as demonstration; for persuasion [then] depends on them. But if there are enthymemes, paradigms should be used as witnesses, [as] a supplement to the enthymemes. When the paradigms are placed first,[134] there is the appearance of induction, but induction is not suitable to rhetorical discourses except in a few cases; when they are put at the end they become witnesses, and a witness is everywhere persuasive. Thus, too, when they are first, it is necessary to supply many of them [but] when they are mentioned at the end one is sufficient; for even a single trustworthy witness is useful.[135] This concludes the discussion of how many species of paradigms there are and how and when they should be used.

132. Aesop is supposed to have been a slave in Samos in the sixth century B.C.; but very little is known about him, and the collections of fables attributed to him by oral tradition were made in later times.

133. Probably, the meaning is that the dialectical exercises in the philosophical schools, with their frequent use of the Socratic technique of analogy, train a student to see likenesses.

134. That is, before the enthymeme, which then functions as a summary conclusion.

135. As the examples Aristotle has given show, induction is chiefly useful in deliberative oratory, where the future must be projected on the basis of past experiences. But induction can be used to create a picture of the character of a litigant in court by drawing a picture of virtues or vices from past conduct. Aristotle's point, however, is that it is usually more effective to state the conclusion first and then support it with examples. E.g., "The king plans to invade Greece; for he is securing his position in Egypt [enthymeme]. This is what Darius and Xerxes did in the past [example]."

Chapter 21: Gnōmē, or Maxim

■ What Aristotle calls *gnōmē*, or "maxim," is in Latin *sententia* (cf. English "sententious"). Literally, *gnōmē* means "a thought," usually an opinion given as a judgment or advice. Pithy, epigrammatic statements have a long history as a feature of rhetoric from classical Greece to the present. Aristotle's successors, however, (e.g., Quintilian 8.5) treat the gnomic saying (maxim, *sententia*) as a stylistic device used primarily for ornament, while he regards it as a tool of logical argument. There was an ancient gnomic tradition in Greece, seen in the utterances of sages and the elegiac poetry of Theognis; and quotable lines are a regular feature of Greek tragedy, especially the plays of Euripides. Aristotle cites a number of these. See Appendix I.F for Aristotle's "enthymematic maxim" as understood in early modern logic.

1. As for the use of gnomic sayings, once it has been explained what a maxim is, it should be very evident on what subjects and when and by whom it is appropriate to use the expression of maxims in speeches. 2. A maxim is an assertion—not, however, one about particulars, such as what kind of a person Iphicrates is, but of a general sort, and not about everything (for example, not that the straight is the opposite of the crooked) but about things that involve actions and are to be chosen or avoided in regard to action. As a result, since enthymemes are like syllogisms about such things, the conclusions of enthymemes and [either of] the premises (with the [full] syllogism omitted) are maxims; for example,

> It is never right for a man who is shrewd
> To have his children taught to be too wise.[136]

This, then, is a maxim. But if the cause is added and the reason, the whole is an enthymeme; for example,

> For apart from the other idleness they have,
> They incur hostile jealousy from fellow-citizens.[137]

136. Euripides, *Medea* 294–95.
137. Ibid, 296–97.

And this: **[1394b]**

> There is no man who is happy in all ways.[138]

And this is a maxim:

> There is no one of men who is free.

But taken with what follows it is an enthymeme:

> For he is a slave of money or of chance.[139]

3. If a maxim is in fact what has been described, there are necessarily four species of maxim; for either it is with or without a supplement.[140] 4. Now those that need demonstration are those that say something paradoxical or disputable, but those that involve no paradox [can stand] without a supplement. 5. Of the latter, necessarily, some need no supplement because of being already known; for example,

> Best for a man is to be healthy, as it seem to me.[141]

(For so it seems to many.) But others, as soon as spoken, are clear to those who look at them carefully; for example,

> No one is a lover who does not always love.[142]

6. Of those with a supplement, some are part of an enthymeme, as "It is never right for a man who is shrewd . . . ,"[143] others are enthymematic but not part of an enthymeme.[144] These are those in

---

138. Said to be from Euripides' lost *Sthenoboe,* fr. 661 ed. Nauck and Snell.

139. Euripides, *Hecuba* 864–65.

140. The supplement is the supporting reason. The four species are (1) commonly known and requiring no supplement, (2) not commonly known but self-evident when examined, (3) part of an enthymeme, (4) not part of an enthymeme but with an enthymematic character in itself when examined.

141. Source of the quotation uncertain; see Grimaldi 1980–88, 2: 262.

142. Euripides, *Trojan Women* 1051.

143. The example from sec. 2. The two lines there quoted are the conclusion of an enthymeme, of which the second set of two lines is the minor premise. The implied major premise is something like "A sensible man should want his children to be busy and well liked."

144. They are the equivalent of enthymemes (since some reason is given or implied) but do not take the form of enthymemes, which is characteristically a conclu-

which the reason for the saying is inherently clear, for example, in the maxim "Being a mortal, do not cherish immortal anger"; for to say one should not cherish it is a maxim, but adding *being a mortal* gives the reason. Similarly, "A mortal should think mortal, not immortal, thoughts."

7. It is, then, evident from what has been said how many species of maxim there are and for what sort of context each is appropriate; for in disputed or paradoxical matters a supplement should not be lacking[145] but use the maxim as a conclusion after first stating the supplement, for example, if some one should say, "As for me, then, since [a child] should not be an object of jealousy nor idle, I say that it is not necessary for one to be educated"; or putting the latter part first, then add the former. When the statement is not paradoxical but yet not clear, add the reason for it as tersely as possible. 8. In such cases Laconic apothegms[146] and enigmatic sayings are suitable; for example, if some one should say what Stesichorus said among the Locrians, **[1395a]** that they should not be insolent, lest their cicadas chirp from the ground.[147] 9. Speaking in maxims is appropriate to those older in years and on subjects of which one is experienced, since to speak maxims is unseemly for one too young, as is storytelling; and on matters in which one is inexperienced it is silly and shows lack of education. There is an adequate sign of this: country folk are most inclined to strike maxims and readily show themselves off.

10. To speak in universal terms of what is not universal is especially suitable in bitter complaint and great indignation,[148] and in these cases either at the outset or after the demonstration. 11. And

---

sion with a supporting clause given a premise. The source of the two following quotations is not known with certainty; cf. Grimaldi 1980–88, 2: 265.

145. This is true in civic discourse, which is all that concerns Aristotle. In religious discourse unsupported maxims made by an authoritative teacher can be effective, as in the case of many sayings of Jesus.

146. Laconia was the territory of Sparta. Since Spartan culture discouraged verbosity, the term *laconic* has come to mean "terse."

147. That is, if they persist, their city may be leveled to the ground. Demetrius (*On Style* 99, 100, 243) attributes the remark to Dionysius of Syracuse rather than to the poet Stesichorus.

148. For example, to cry, "All great men are envied" when there is really only oneself and a critic.

one should even use trite and common maxims if they are useful; for because they are common, they seem true, as though everyone agreed; for example, [it is useful] for one who is exhorting [troops] to face danger without first sacrificing to the gods [to say,] "One omen is best, to fight for one's country."[149] And if they are outnumbered, [to say,] "The War God is impartial."[150] And [exhorting troops] to destroy the sons of their enemies, even though having done no wrong, [to say,] "Foolish he who after killing the father leaves the sons."[151] 12. Further, some proverbs are also maxims; for example, "an Attic neighbor."[152] 13. One should also speak maxims that are contrary to popular wisdom (by *popular wisdom* I mean such as "Know thyself" and "Nothing too much") whenever [the speaker's] character is going to be made to seem better or the maxim is stated with *pathos*. An example of a maxim with *pathos* is if some one in anger were to say that it is a lie that one should know himself: "At least, this man, if he had known himself, would never have thought himself worthy of command."[153] And his character [would appear] better [if he were to say] that contrary to what people say, it is not right to love as though someday one would hate but better to hate as though later going to love. 14. One should make moral purpose clear by the choice of words [*lexis*], but if not, then add the cause; for example, saying something like, "Love should not take the form people say,[154] but it should be as though one were always going to love; for otherwise it is a form of

149. *Iliad* 12.243, when Hector disregards, as a chance occurrence, what Polydamas regards as an unfavorable omen. Throughout the epic, omens, such as the flight of birds, are only valid if specifically recognized as such by those to whom they might apply. Exhortation to troups about to enter battle is a form of deliberative rhetoric found not only in epic poetry but commonly in the historians. This is another passage in which Aristotle gives advice that might have been useful to Alexander.

150. *Iliad* 18.309.

151. Cited also in 1.15.14 above and thought to be from the *Cypria* of Stasinus.

152. Cf. Thucydides 1.70. A neighbor should be a friend, but the volatile Athenians were often a trial to their neighbors.

153. "This man" is probably the fourth-century general Iphicrates, to whom Aristotle refers in a number of other passages. Probably the statement means something like "No one gets ahead in the world by knowing his own limits." This could be said ironically; but Aristotle seems to imply a straightforward, if bitter, interpretation.

154. With the assumption that it will someday turn to hatred.

treachery"; or thus: "The saying does not please me; for the true lover should love as though he were always going to love"; and "That business about 'Nothing too much' isn't true either; one cannot hate the wicked too much." **[1395b]** 15. Maxims make one great contribution to speeches because of the uncultivated mind of the audience; for people are pleased if someone in a general observation hits upon opinions that they themselves have about a particular instance. What I mean will be clear from the following and, at the same time, how one should hunt for maxims. A maxim, as has been said, is an assertion of a generality, and people enjoy things said in general terms that they happen to assume ahead of time in a partial way; for example, if some one had met up with bad neighbors or children, he would accept a speaker's saying that nothing is worse than having neighbors or that nothing is more foolish than begetting children. Thus, one should guess what sort of assumptions people have and then speak in general terms consistent with these views. 16. This is one useful aspect of employing maxims, and another is greater; for it makes the speech "ethical." Speeches have character[155] insofar as deliberate choice is clear, and all maxims accomplish this because one speaking a maxim makes a general statement about preferences, so that if the maxims are morally good, they make the speaker seem to have a good character. Concerning maxims, then, what they are and how many species there are of them and how they should be used and what advantage they have, let this much be said.

Chapter 22: Enthymemes, or Rhetorical Syllogisms

1. Let us speak about enthymemes in general, [first] in what way one should seek for them, and after that about their topics [*topoi*]; for each of these [processes] is different in kind. 2. That the enthymeme is a sort of syllogism had been said earlier and how it is a syllogism and in what it differs from those in dialectic; 3. for

---

155. An unusual expression for Aristotle; otherwise only persons have *ēthos*, though speeches may be "ethical."

[in rhetoric] the conclusion should not be drawn from far back,[156] nor is it necessary to include everything.[157] The former is unclear because of the length [of the argument], the latter tiresome because of stating what is obvious. This is the reason why the uneducated are more persuasive than the educated before a crowd, just as the poets say the uneducated are more "inspired by the Muses" in a crowd;[158] for [the educated] reason with axioms [*koina*] and universals, [the uneducated] on the basis of what [particulars] they know and instances near their experience. Thus, one should not speak on the basis of all opinions but of those held by an identified group,[159] for example, either the judges or those whom they respect; **[1396a]** and the fact that what is said seems true should be clear to all or most people. And do not draw the conclusion only from what is necessarily valid, but also from what is true for the most part.[160]

SPECIFIC TOPICS OF ENTHYMEMES

4. First, then, one should grasp that on whatever subject there is need to speak or reason, it is necessary to have the facts belonging to that subject,[161] whether [supplied] by political or any other argument, either all or some of them; for if you had none, you would have nothing from which to draw a conclusion. 5. I mean, for example, how could we advise the Athenians whether to go to war or not without knowing what their forces are and how great, whether naval or infantry or both; and what revenues they have or

---

156. That is, not from an extended series of arguments, as it can be in dialectic. In rhetoric, the argument should be clear to an audience not skilled in logical subtlety. See 1.2.12.

157. Some premises can be assumed as obvious.

158. Cf. Euripides, *Hippolytus* 988–89. The point is that those untrained in complex logical argument can have a natural appeal to a similarly untrained mob.

159. Reading *horismenois* as conjectured by Kassel.

160. Enthymemes are forms of probable argument, since they deal with human actions, and in most cases not valid in pure logic as a syllogism should be.

161. *Ta hyparkhonta;* the word recurs throughout the chapter and needs to be translated as the context seems to demand. It refers to what underlies or is inherent in a subject, its natural or logical attributes, relevant facts or information, etc.

friends and enemies; further, what wars they have fought and how; and other such things? 6. Or [how could we] praise [the Athenians] if we did not know about the sea battle at Salamis or the fight at Marathon, or [how could we praise the Spartans without knowing] the things done by the Children of Heracles or something of that sort? All [speakers] base their praise on fine things that are, or seem to be, relevant facts. 7. Similarly, too, [speakers] blame [the Athenians] on the basis of the opposites, looking for something [bad that] applies to them or seems to, for example, that they subjugated the Greeks and enslaved the Aeginetans and Potidaeans who had fought with them against the barbarian and done valorous deeds, and other such things and [looking for] whether some other error in judgment is attributed to them. In the same way, those making an accusation and those making a defense do so by considering the relevant facts. 8. It makes no difference whether the subject is Athenians or Lacedaemonians or man or god; the same thing is done. In advising Achilles, [for example,] and praising or blaming him and attacking or defending him, we should take up the relevant facts—or what seem to be the facts— about him in order to say on the basis of these if there is evidence of something honorable or shameful when we are praising or blaming; and of something just or unjust when we are accusing or defending; and of something advantageous or harmful when we are advising.[162] 9. The same is true about any subject whatever, for example, whether justice is a good or not on the basis of the attributes of justice and the good.

10. As a result, since everyone seems to demonstrate arguments in this way, whether they reason in accordance with strict logic or more loosely **[1396b]** (they do not take propositions from all sources but from those that are relevant to each subject), and since it is impossible through speech to demonstrate anything in any other way, it is evident that it is first necessary, as [described] in the *Topics*,[163] to have selected statements about what is possible and most suited to the subject 11. and, when unexpected problems

162. Although "Achilles" can be said to represent any person who is the subject of a speech (or to whom advice is given), Aristotle seems to be thinking specifically of speeches in drama or rhetorical exercises of the type later known as *suasoriae*.

163. 1.4–15.

occur, to try to follow the same method, looking not to the undefined but to what inherently belongs to the subject of the discourse
and marking off as many [facts] as possible and what are most
closely relevant to the subject; for the more relevant facts [are] at
hand, the easier it is to offer a demonstration; and the more closely
related they are, the more at home [in a particular speech] and less
common. 12. By "common" I mean praising Achilles because he
was a man and one of the demigods and because he went on the
expedition against Ilium; for these facts apply to many others, so
such remarks do not praise Achilles any more than Diomedes.
Specifics [*idia*] are what apply to no one other than Achilles; for
example, his killing of Hector, the best of the Trojans, and of
Cycnus, who prevented all [the Greeks] from disembarking and
was invulnerable, and [praising Achilles] because he was the youn-
gest of those who went on the expedition and the one who had not
sworn [to defend Menelaus' right to Helen], and anything else of
this sort.

Now, one way of selecting [enthymemes, and] this the first [in
importance], is the "topical," 13. so let us discuss these elements
[*stoikheia*] of enthymemes; and by *element* and *topic* of an enthymeme, I mean the same thing.[164] 14. But first, let us say some things
that it are necessary to say first; for there are two species of
enthymemes: some are *demonstrative* [*deiktika*] of the fact that
something is or is not the case, and others are *refutative* [*elentika*],
and the difference is like that in dialectic between refutation and
syllogism. 15. The demonstrative enthymeme draws a conclusion
from what is agreed, the refutative draws conclusions that are not
agreed to [by the opponent]. 16. Now the topics [*topoi*] concerned
with each of the species [of rhetoric] that are useful and necessary
are more or less understood by us;[165] for the propositions concerned

164. This sentence is apparently a transition not to what immediately follows but to
chap. 23. The last clause is repeated in 2.26.1. *Topics* thus refers to the common
topics of chap. 23. What Aristotle has been discussing in chap. 22 up to this point
are *idia* (specifics) or premises relating to specific subjects. Sec. 14–17 are perhaps a
later addition, in which case Aristotle's decision to refer to *idia* as topics is a late
stage in the development of the *Rhetoric*.

165. Here Aristotle uses the word *topics* of the specifics [*idia*] that he discussed in
connection with each of the three species of rhetoric (deliberative, epideictic, and
judicial) in 1: 4–14 and of premises for ethical and pathetical *pisteis* discussed in 2:

with each have been selected and as a result the [specific] topics that are sources of enthymemes about good or evil, or honorable or shameful, or just or unjust [are known], and topics concerned with characters and emotions and moral habits, having been selected in a similar way, are already at hand. **[1397a]** 17. But in what follows let us take up the subject [of topics] as a whole in a different way, considering [those that apply to] all [species of rhetoric], and let us discuss it while taking note of refutative and demonstrative [enthymemes] and those of apparent enthymemes,[166] which are not enthymemes since they are not really syllogisms. When we have made these things clear in a supplementary discussion,[167] we shall offer definitions of the sources from which "undoings" and "objections" should be brought to bear on enthymemes.[168]

Chapter 23: Topoi, *or Common Topics*

■ In this chapter Aristotle lists twenty-eight *topoi* of enthymemes. These are lines, or strategies, of argument, useful in treating many different subject matters in all three species of rhetoric. They thus contrast with the *idia*, "specifics" or "particular topics," discussed beginning in 1.4. On Aristotle's use of the term *topos*, see comments prefixed to 1.2.21 and note thereon. Some topics listed here are also discussed in Aristotle's *Topics*. For examples of their use in Aristotle's time, see Palmer 1934.

1. [Topic 1] One *topos* of demonstrative [enthymemes] is that from opposites [*ek tōn enantiōn*]; for one should look to see if the opposite [predicate] is true of the opposite [subject], [thus] refuting the argument if it is not, confirming it if it is, for example [saying] that to be temperate is a good thing, for to lack self-

---

1–17. As the footnotes indicate, in those chapters they are not actually called topics, that term being reserved for common topics.

166. The subject of chap. 24.

167. *Parasēmainomenoi.* Chaps. 22–23 are thus a supplement, apparently added to the work at a late stage of its development. Cf. Düring 1966, 143.

168. The subject of chap. 25.

control is harmful. Or, as in the *Messianicus*,[169] "If the war is the cause of present evils, things should be set right by making peace." [Or,]

> For since it is unjust to fall into anger
> At those who have unwillingly done wrong,
> It is not appropriate for thanks to be owed
> If some one benefits another perforce.[170]

[Or,]

> But since, old man, false statements are persuasive
> Among mortals, you should believe the opposite too:
> That many truths turn out to be incredible to mortals.[171]

2. [Topic 2] Another is from [different] grammatical forms of the same word [*ek tōn homoiōn ptōseōn*]; for the same [predicate] should be true or not true, for example, [to say] that the just is not entirely good; for then what is done justly would be a good, but as it is, to be put to death justly is not desirable.

3. [Topic 3] Another is from correlatives [*ek tōn pros allēla*]; for if to have done honorably or justly is predicated of one of a pair, to have experienced [it honestly or justly] belongs to the other, and if [one person has the right] to order, [the other] also to act, for example, what Diomedon the tax farmer said about the taxes: "If it is not shameful for you to sell them, neither is it for me to buy."[172] And if something is honorably or justly predicated of one who experiences it, it is also of one who does it. But there is in this the possibility of false reasoning; for if some one has experienced something justly, he has justly experienced, but perhaps not from *you*. Thus, one ought separately to look at whether the sufferer deserves to suffer and whether the agent of the suffering is the right person to have acted, **[1379b]** then to use whichever

---

169. The speech of Alcidamas mentioned in 1.13.2.

170. Source unknown. The passage is in iambic trimeter and probably comes from some lost drama.

171. Euripides' *Thyestes*, fr. 396 ed. Nauck and Snell. The translation follows the text of Kassel.

172. Greek and Roman cities often sold the right to collect taxes to private individuals or groups who hoped to make a profit. Numerous abuses occurred; thus, some thought the procedure shameful.

argument fits; for sometimes there is disagreement in such cases, and nothing prevents [a response] like this in the *Alcmeon* of Theodectes: [Alphesiboa asks,]

> Did no one of mortals loathe your mother?

In reply, [Alcmeon] says,

> But one should examine the statement by taking it apart.

And when Alphesiboa asks how, he takes it up and says,

> They judged she should die, but not that I should kill her.[173]

Another example is in the trial of Demosthenes and those who killed Nicanor; for since the jury thought he had been justly killed, it seemed that they justly killed him. Also the case of the man murdered at Thebes, about whom [the defendant] demands a judgment as to whether he justly deserved to die, on the ground that it was not unjust to kill someone who died justly.[174]

4. [Topic 4] Another is from the more and less [*ek tou mallon kai hētton*],[175] for example, "If not even the gods know everything, human beings can hardly do so." For this is equivalent [to saying,] "If something is not the fact in a case where it would be more [expected], it is clear that it is not a fact where it would be less." Also, [the argument] that "a person who has beaten his father has also beaten his neighbors" follows from [the proposition that] if the lesser thing is true, the greater is also; for people strike their fathers less than their neighbors. Or [one can argue] this way: either

---

173. Theodectes is described by later writers as having been a student of Plato, Isocrates, and Aristotle. He became one of the best-known tragedians of the fourth century, as well as an orator and teacher of rhetoric. Alcmeon, like Orestes, murdered his mother, was driven mad, and eventually was purified; Alphesiboa is his wife.

174. Some editors move the last two sentences of this section back to follow the story of Diomedon; Kassel double-brackets them as a later edition by Aristotle to the text. Most agree that the Demosthenes mentioned here is not the famous orator, since his life is very well known and there is no other mention of his being involved in any such trial. Dionysius of Halicarnassus (*To Ammaeus* 1.12) unconvincingly sought to identify this trial with Demosthenes' defense of Ctesiphon in 330 B.C.

175. See 1.2.21.

"if something is not the fact in a case where it would be *more* [expected, etc.]" or "if in a case where it would be *less* [expected, etc.]," according to whichever there is need to show, whether that something is or is not the fact.[176] 5. Further, [there is a related form of argument] if [something is] neither more nor less. This is the source of the statement,

> Your father is pitiable for having lost his children;
> Is Oeneus not also then, for having lost a famous offspring?[177]

And [the argument] that if Theseus did no wrong [in abducting Helen], neither did Alexander [i.e., Paris, who also abducted her]; and if not the sons of Tyndareus [who abducted women], then not Alexander; and if Hector [did no wrong in killing] Patroclus, Alexander also [did no wrong in killing] Achilles. And if other professionals are not contemptible, neither are philosophers. And if generals are not contemptible because they are often put to death, neither are sophists.[178] And [the argument] that "if a private individual should care about your reputation, you should care about that of Greece."[179]

6. [Topic 5] Another is from looking at the time [*ek tou ton khronon skopein*],[180] for example, what Iphicrates said in the speech against Harmodius: "If, before accomplishing anything, I asked to be honored with a statue if I succeeded, you would have granted it. Will you not grant it [now] when I have succeeded? Do

176. This sentence has a number of textual problems, but the argument seems clear enough. Depending on what you want to prove, you can argue either that if B is more likely to be true of A than of C but is *not* true of A, then it is less likely to be true of C; or that if B is less likely to be true of C than of A but *is* true of C, then it is more likely to be true of A. See Grimaldi 1980–88, 1: 298–99.

177. The name Oeneus indicates this is from a play about his son Meleager, perhaps that by Antiphon.

178. The reference is probably to the execution of the defeated Athenian generals after the battle of Arginusae in 406 and to the execution of Antiphon the Sophist after the revolution of 411. But "often" is odd, and possibly the text is corrupt. Cope ([1877] 1970, 2: 249) conjectured "are defeated" for "are put to death."

179. "You," which is plural here, presumably refers to the Athenian citizens. Source unknown.

180. As the examples show, this topic is closely related to the more and the less, for it contrasts what was true in the past with what is more true in the present. This is a form of what is often called argument a fortiori (from the stronger).

not then make a promise in anticipation but refuse it in realization."[181] Another example: on the subject of [allowing] Philip to pass through Thebes into Attica **[1398a]** [the Macedonian ambassadors said] that if [the request was made] before [Philip] decided to help [the Thebans by moving] into Phocis, [the Thebans] would have promised [to let him pass through their territory into Attica]; it is strange, then, if they will not let him pass [now] because he let that opportunity go and trusted them.[182]

7. [Topic 6] Another is from [turning] what has been said against oneself upon the one who said it [*ek tōn eirēmenōn kath' hautou pros ton eiponta*], but the way of doing it differs [with the context]. For example, in the *Teucer* [of Sophocles]. . . .[183] And [there is] the argument Iphicrates used against Aristophon when he asked [the latter] if he would betray the fleet for money. After [Aristophon] denied it, [Iphicrates] said, "If you, being Aristophon, would not play the traitor, would I, Iphicrates?"[184] But the opponent should be one who seems more likely to have done wrong. Otherwise, it would seem ludicrous if some one were to say this in reply[, for example,] to an prosecution by Aristides,[185] but [it should be used] for discrediting the accuser; for the accuser always wants to be morally better than the defendant. This, then,

181. Iphicrates was a famous Athenian general of the early fourth century, repeatedly mentioned by Aristotle. A statue in his honor was voted in 390 B.C. but not erected, and twenty years later he brought successful action to implement the grant. Dionyius of Halicarnassus (*Lysias* 836d) thought the speech was written for Iphicrates by Lysias.

182. The first incident took place in 346 B.C., the second in 339. This is one of the latest datable references in the *Rhetoric;* see Appendix II.A. The Thebans refused permission, and the result was the definitive defeat of the Greeks, including Athens and Thebes, at Chaeronea in 338.

183. The example was either never filled in by Aristotle, or has been lost.

184. The occasion was probably allegations of treachery against Iphicrates during the Social War of 357–355 B.C. The basis of the argument is the contrasting reputation of the two speakers. We thus have a good example of an enthymeme whose specific topics are matters of *ēthos.* Note that an enthymeme, like a syllogism, can take the form *if . . . then.* If B is predicated of A and C is greater than A, then B can be predicated of C. The statement is, of course, only possibly true (thus rhetorical), not valid in formal logic.

185. The early fifth-century statesman Aristides was frequently taken as the type of the just man.

should be disproved. In general, it is out of place [*atopos*] when someone reproaches others for [failing to do] what he does not do—or would not do—himself.

8. [Topic 7] Another is from definition [*ex horismou*], for example: What is the divine? Is it not either a god or the work of a god? Still, whoever thinks it is the work of god must also think that gods exist.[186] And [another example is,] as Iphicrates [argued], that the best person is the most noble; for there was no noble quality in Harmodius and Aristogiton until they did something noble, while he himself was more like them [than his opponent was]: "At least, my deeds are more like those of Harmodius and Aristogiton than yours are."[187] And [another is,] as [said] in the *Alexander*,[188] that all would agree that those who are not well-behaved are not content with the enjoyment of one [woman's] body. And [another is] the reason Socrates gave for refusing to visit Archelaus; for he said *hybris* was just as much an inability on the part of those benefited to return a favor as [it was retaliation by] those harmed.[189] For all these [speakers], by making definitions and grasping the essence of a thing, draw syllogistic conclusions about the subject they are discussing.

9. [Topic 8] Another [*topos*] is from the varied meanings [of a word] [*ek tou posakhōs*], as discussed in the *Topics* on the meanings of *oxus*.[190]

186. An apparent reference to Socrates' argument in Plato, *Apology* 27b–e.

187. From the speech mentioned in 2.23.6 above. Iphicrates' opponent named Harmodius was apparently a descendant of the celebrated Athenian hero of the same name, who, together with his lover Aristogiton, killed Hipparchus, brother of the tyrant Hippias, in 514 B.C. Though this was really a private quarrel, they were later honored with statues in the marketplace as tyrannicides. As the earlier passage indicates, Iphicrates was claiming his right to a statue.

188. Apparently an epideictic speech about Paris by a sophist, possibly Polycrates, analogous to the encomia of Helen by Gorgias and Isocrates. Cf. 2.24.7, 2.24.9, and 3.14.3.

189. This statement is otherwise unknown. Archelaus was King of Macedon. Though he could lavish favors, Socrates thought ill of him; see Plato, *Gorgias* 470c–71d.

190. *Oxus* (sharp)—in music the opposite of *flat*, of a knife the opposite of *dull*. See *Topics* 1.15. *Oxus* is a conjecture of Thurot, accepted by Kassel and probably correct. The manuscripts read *orthōs* (rightly), but this does not occur in the *Topics*. Grimaldi, who keeps *orthōs*, translates "as has been mentioned in the topical discipline concerning the right use of a word."

10. [Topic 9] Another is from division [*ek diaereseōs*], for example, if [one says,] "All people do wrong for one of three reasons: either for this, or this, or this; now two of these are impossible, but even [the accusers] themselves do not assert the third."[191]

11. [Topic 10] Another is from induction [*ex epagōgēs*]; for example, in the case of the woman of Peparethus [it was argued] that women everywhere discern the truth about [who is the father of] children; **[1398b]** for when the orator Mantias at Athens was disputing [the parentage of] his son, the boy's mother declared the truth.[192] Similarly, when Ismenias and Stilbon were in a dispute at Thebes, the woman of Dodona identified the son of Ismenias; and for this reason Thettaliscus was recognized as Ismenias' son. And again, [another example is] from the *Law* [speech] of Theodectes[193] [to the effect that] if people do not entrust their horses to those who take poor care of others' horses nor [their own] ships to those who have overturned others' ships—if then this is similarly true in all cases—one should not employ for one's own safety those who have poorly guarded the safety of another. And [another example is] as Alcidamas [argued], that all honor the wise; at least, Parians honored Archilochus despite the nasty things he said [about them]; and Chians Homer, though he was not a citizen; and Mytilenaeans Sappho, although a woman; and Lacedaemonians, though least fond of literature, made Chilon a member of their council of elders; and Lampsacenes buried Anaxagoras, though a foreigner, and even now still honor him. And Athenians were prosperous while using the laws of Solon, and Lacedaemonians when [using] those of Lycurgus; and at Thebes, at the time the leaders became philosophers, the city prospered.[194]

12. [Topic 11] Another [*topos*] is from a [previous] judgment

191. The use of logical division in rhetoric is recommended in Plato's *Phaedrus* 265e–66a and is the method followed in Gorgias's *Helen;* see Appendix I.A.

192. Mantias was forced to recognize two illegitimate sons. The incident provides the background for Demosthenes' speeches *Against Boeotus,* but there is no reference here to that subsequent trial.

193. The fourth-century dramatist and orator mentioned in 2.23.13 and elsewhere.

194. Kassel double-brackets this sentence as a later addition by Aristotle. Other editors have thought that something to the effect that philosophers are the best rulers has been lost at the beginning. The "philosophers" at Thebes are presumably Epaminodas and Pelopidas in the years 371–361 B.C.

[*ek kriseōs*] about the same or a similar or opposite matter, especially if all always [make this judgment]—but if not, at least most people, or the wise (either all of them or most) or the good.[195] Or [another example is] if the judges themselves [have so decided] or those whom the judges approve or those whose judgment cannot be opposed, for example, those with legal authority to make it or whose judgment cannot be honorably opposed, for example, a father's or teacher's, as Autocles said against Mixidemides: "If it is right for the Dread Goddesses to stand trial in the Areopagus, should not Mixidemides?"[196] Or [another example is] as Sappho said, that it is bad to die; for the gods have so judged; for otherwise they would die. Or [another example is] as Aristippus [replied] to Plato, when the latter said something rather dogmatic, as he thought: "But our companion," he said, "would have said nothing of the sort," meaning Socrates. And at Delphi Agesipolis, after earlier consulting oracles at Olympia, asked the god if his opinion was the same as his father's, implying it would be shameful for him to say contradictory things.[197] **[1399a]** And as Isocrates wrote about Helen, that she was virtuous, since Theseus so judged, and about Alexander, whom the goddesses preferred to others, and about Evagoras, that he was virtuous, so Isocrates claims: for at any rate Conon, leaving all others aside, came to him [for help].[198]

13. [Topic 12] Another [*topos*] is from the parts [*ek tōn merōn*], as discussed in the *Topics*,[199] [for example,] What kind of motion is the soul? For it is this or that.[200] There is an example from the

---

195. This can be called argument from authority. The phraseology is reminiscent of the basis of dialectic in generally accepted opinions as described in *Topics* 1.1.

196. The Dread Goddesses are the Furies, who appear before Athena's court in Aeschylus' *Eumenides*. Autocles was active in military affairs in the 370s and 360s and, according to Demosthenes (*Against Phormio* 53), was prosecuted for some of his actions.

197. The god at Delphi was Apollo, son of Zeus, who was the god of Olympia.

198. Isocrates, *Helen* 18–22, 41–48; *Evagoras* 51–52.

199. *Topics* 2.4, beginning at 111a33. By *parts* is meant the species within a defined genus.

200. The kinds of motion defined in *Categories* 14 are generation, destruction, increase, diminution, alteration, and change of place. Aristotle regarded the soul as the vital principle in living things and thus inherently some kind of motion.

Socrates of Theodectes:[201] "Against what holy place has he pro-
faned? Which gods that the city recognizes has he not believed in?"

14. [Topic 13] Another is to exhort or dissuade and accuse or
defend and praise or blame on the basis of the consequence [*ek tou
akolouthountos*], since in most instances it happens that something
good and bad follow from the same [cause]. For example, being
envied is an evil result of being educated, but the wisdom [ac-
quired] is a good thing; therefore, [it may be argued] one should
not be educated; for one ought not to be envied. [Or] one should
then be educated; for one ought to be wise. This topic constitutes
the *Art* of Callippus, with the addition of the possible and other
things that have been mentioned.[202]

15. [Topic 14] Another [*topos* is employed] when there is need
to exhort or dissuade on two matters that are contrasted [*peri
duoin antikeimenoin*], and [one needs] to use the method mentioned in both; but there is the difference that in the previous case
any two things are contrasted, while here they are opposites. For
example, a priestess did not allow her son to engage in public
debate: "For," she said, "if you say what is just, the people will
hate you; but if what is unjust, the gods will." [She then continued:] "You should then engage in public debate; for if you speak
what is just, the gods will love you, if what is unjust, the people
will." This is the same as what is said about buying the marsh with
the salt.[203] This "twist"[204] occurs whenever good and evil follow
either of two opposites.

16. [Topic 15] Another [topic is employed] when [one's oppo-
nents] do not praise the same things openly as they do secretly [*ou
phanerōs kai aphanōs*], but to a great extent praise the just and
beautiful while privately they wish rather for what is to their advan-

201. Probably one of the *apologies* written by fourth-century authors, of which
those by Plato and Xenophon survive. If, as it seems, Aristotle is quoting literally,
use of the third person indicates that Theodectes' version took the imagined form of
a speech by some advocate.

202. Callippus was a student of Isocrates and author of a handbook. "The other
things" are presumably the impossible, past and future fact, and magnitude—as
described in 2.19.

203. Apparently a proverb, equal to "taking the bad with the good." Salt was
chiefly obtained from evaporating the seawater in marshes.

204. *Blaisōsis,* here referring to a retort to a dilemma.

tage. [The thing to do is] to try to draw the other conclusion from what they say; for this is the most effective topic in dealing with paradoxes.

17. [Topic 16] Another is from consequences by analogy [*ek tou analogon symbainein*]. For example, when they tried to force his son who was under age to perform public services because he was tall, Iphicrates said that if they deem large boys men, they should vote that small men are boys. **[1399b]** And Theodectes in the *Law* [speech said]:²⁰⁵ "Since you are making citizens of mercenary soldiers, for example Strabax and Charidemus, because of their merits, will you not make exiles of those among the mercenaries who have wrought irreparable damage?"

18. [Topic 17] Another is from [arguing] that if some result [*to symbainon t' auton*] is the same, the things from which it resulted are also. For example, Xenophanes²⁰⁶ said that those who say that the gods are born are as impious as those who say that they die; for in both cases, the result is that at some time the gods do not exist. And in general [this topic is a matter of] taking the result of each thing as always the same. [For example,] "You are going to make a judgment not about Isocrates, but about education: whether it is right to study philosophy."²⁰⁷ And that to give "earth and water" is to be a slave, and that to share in the "common peace" is to do what is commanded. One should take up whichever [side of the] argument is useful.²⁰⁸

19. [Topic 18] Another is from not always choosing the same

205. See 2.23.11.

206. Xenophanes of Colophon, sixth-century philosopher and poet who criticized conventional views of the gods.

207. Though the manuscripts read "Socrates," the quotation is an approximation of what Isocrates says in *Antidosis* 173–75.

208. That is, one can argue that these results do follow or that the specific action does not have the significance being given to it. Earth and water was demanded of the Greeks by the Persian king during the invasion of 480–479 B.C. as a symbol of acceptance of his domination; to offer it was thus thought to lead to slavery. The "common peace" is probably that forced on the Greek cities by Macedon after the battle of Chaeronea in 338. Ratification was not complete until 336, and this is often regarded as the latest datable reference in the *Rhetoric*. It is used by Rist (1989, 85–86) as part of his argument that Aristotle completed the *Rhetoric* after his return to Athens in 335. See Appendix II.A.

thing before and after [an event], but the reverse [*ek tou anapalin haireisthai*], for example, this enthymeme: "[It would be terrible] if when in exile we fought to come home, but having come home we shall go into exile in order not to fight."[209] Sometimes people have chosen to be at home at the cost of fighting, sometimes not to fight at the cost of not remaining at home.

20. [Topic 19] Another is to say that the purpose [*to hou heneka*] for which something might exist or might happen is the cause for which it does exist or has happened, for example, if someone gave somebody something so that he could cause him pain after he took it away. This is also the source of the following statement:

> God gives great good fortune to many, not out of good will,
> But so that the disasters people experience may be more obvious.[210]

And this from the *Meleager* of Antiphon:

> Not that they may kill the beast, but that
> They may be witnesses to Greece of the courage of Meleager.[211]

And from the *Ajax* of Theodectes, that Diomedes chose Odysseus not out of honor to him but in order that his companion might be inferior; for he could have done it for this reason.[212]

21. [Topic 20] Another that is common both to litigants and deliberative speakers is to look at what turns the mind in favor and what turns the mind against something [*ta protreponta kai apotreponta*] and for what reasons people both act and avoid action. For these are the factors that if present, impel action [but if not present, deter action]; for example, [consider] if [an action was] possible and easy and advantageous to a person or friends or harmful to enemies and, if punishable, [consider whether] the punishment is less than the reward of the action. People are urged on for these

209. Apparently an adaptation of Lysias 34.11 on the situation in Athens in 403 B.C. Cicero (*Topics* 55–56) calls an enthymeme an argument from contraries, a definition also found in some later rhetoricians and narrower than Aristotle's basic concept. But see Conley 1984.

210. A quotation from an unknown tragedy.

211. Cf. note on 2.23.5. The "beast" was a wild boar.

212. The situation is the night embassy described in *Iliad* 10.

reasons and dissuaded by their opposites, **[1400a]** and they use these same arguments in accusation and defense: they defend themselves by drawing on reasons that deter, and they prosecute by drawing on those that encourage. This *topos* is the whole *Art* of Pamphilus and Callippus.[213]

22. [Topic 21] Another is derived from things that are thought to have taken place but yet are implausible [*ek tōn apistōn*], [using the argument] that they would not seem true unless they were facts or close to being facts. And [one can argue] that they are all the more true [for that reason]; for people accept facts or probabilities as true; if, then, something were implausible and not probable, it would be true; for it is not because of probability and plausibility that it seems true [but because it is a fact].[214] For example, when Androcles of Pitthus was speaking against a law and said, "Laws need a law to correct them," there was general outcry against him. [He continued,] "And fishes need salt" (although it is neither probable nor credible that creatures born in the sea would need salt) "and pressed olives need oil" (though it is strange that things from which oil comes would need oil).[215]

23. [Topic 22] Another is refutative, a matter of looking at contradictions [*ta anomologoumena*] [in three separate ways]: once as applies only to the opponent (if something is contradicted by all dates, actions, and words),[216] for example: "And he says he loves

---

213. Perhaps the one technique most recommended in their handbooks, which were probably short works. In 2.23.14 Callippus' *Art* was said to discuss the *topos* of consequences, the possible, and other things; but these are closely related arguments.

214. Though Aristotle's example below is a piece of sophistry, this argument is an important one in religious preaching, where, e.g., the improbability of miraculous events becomes a reason for accepting them: they can only be the work of God, who, by definition, works in ways surpassing human reason. In a sentence often attributed to Tertullian (though not found in his works), "I believe because it is absurd."

215. Fishes, paradoxically, need salt, and pressed olives oil, to preserve them. Androcles was an Athenian demagogue of the late fifth century B.C.

216. Kassel double-brackets what is here in parenthesis, regarding it as a later addition by Aristotle to the text; other editors move it back before the previous clause.

you, but he took the oath with the Thirty";[217] once as applicable to
the speaker: "And he says I am litigious, but he cannot show that I
have brought any case to be judged in court"; and once as applicable to the speaker and the opponent: "And he has never lent any
money, but I have even ransomed many of you."

24. [Topic 23] Another, in reference to human beings or actions that have been prejudged or seem to have been, is to state
the cause of the false impression [*to legein tēn aitian tou para-
doxou*]; for there is some reason why it seems true. For example,
when a certain woman claimed that her son was the child of a
different mother, because she embraced him she was thought to be
involved with him as her lover; but when the reason was explained
[i.e., that he really was her son] she was freed from slander. Another example is in the *Ajax* of Theodectes: Odysseus tells Ajax
why he [Odysseus] does not seem braver than Ajax, although he
really is.

25. [Topic 24] Another is from the cause [*apo tou aitiou*] [and
effect]: if the cause exists, the effect does; if it does not, there is no
effect. The cause and that of which it is the cause go together, and
without cause there is nothing. For example, when Leodamas was
defending himself against Thrasybulus' charge that his name had
been inscribed [as a traitor] on a stele on the acropolis but had
been cut out in the time of the Thirty [Tyrants],[218] he said it was not
possible; for the Thirty would have trusted him more if his hatred
of the democracy had remained inscribed.

26. [Topic 25] Another is to see if there was or is a better
plan of a different sort [*ek beltion allōs*] from what is advised or is
being done or has been done; for it is evident that if this is so, it
has not been acted on; **[1400b]** for no one willingly and knowingly chooses the bad.[219] But this may be false reasoning; for it
often later becomes clear how things could have been better done
but earlier was unclear.

27. [Topic 26] Another, when something is about to be done

217. *You* (pl.) is the Athenian people; the Thirty are the Thirty Tyrants of 404 B.C.,
enemies of the democracy.

218. In 404 B.C.

219. The negative of this is a major argument in Demosthenes' speech *On the
Crown* in defense of his policy against Macedon: there was no better plan.

that is contrary to what has been done, is to look at them together [*hama skopein*]. For example, when the people of Elea asked Xenophanes if they should sacrifice and sing dirges to Leucothea or not, he advised them not to sing dirges if they regarded her as a god, and if as a human being not to sacrifice.[220]

28. [Topic 27] Another topic is to accuse or defend on the basis of mistakes that have been made [*ek tōn hamartēthentōn*]. For example, in the *Medea* of Carcinus[221] some accuse her on the ground that she has killed her children. At any rate, they are not to be seen; for Medea made the mistake of sending the children away. But she defends herself on the ground that [it is improbable she has killed them, because] she would have killed Jason [then as well], not [only] the children; for she would have made a mistake in not doing so if she had done the other thing. This topic and species of enthymeme is the whole art [of rhetoric] before Theodorus.[222]

29. [Topic 28] Another is from the meaning of a name [*apo tou onomatos*], for example as in Sophocles:

When [your mother] named you Sidero she clearly meant it.[223]

And [another example is] as people are accustomed to speak in praises of the gods,[224] and as Conon called Thrasybulus *thrasyboulon*[225] and as Herodicus said to Thrasymachus, "You are always

220. Leucothea (White Goddess) in Greek mythology was daughter of Cadmus, the legendary king of Thebes and originally named Ino. She was regarded as transformed into a sea goddess. Xenophanes is the sixth-century philosopher and poet. For the example to be appropriate the Eleans must earlier have either sacrificed to her or sung dirges.

221. Tragic poet of the early fourth century B.C.

222. Theodorus of Byzantium was a teacher of rhetoric and author of one or more handbooks around 400 B.C., mentioned by Plato in the survey of handbooks in *Phaedrus* 266c6. Probably, the point is that Theodorus extended rhetorical strategies beyond the limited understanding of argument from probability current in the fifth century.

223. *Sidērō* means Iron. Tyro, in the lost play by that name, is apparently addressing his cruel stepmother.

224. Perhaps an example has been lost here. The medieval commentator Stephanus suggests "Zeus is given his name as the cause of life (zōēs)."

225. "Bold in counsel."

thrasymakhos,"[226] and to Polus, "You are always a *polos,"*[227] and of Dracon the lawgiver that his laws were not those of a human being but of a *drakon;*[228] for they were harsh. And [another example is] as Hecuba in Euripides says of Aphrodite,

> And rightly the name of the goddess begins like *aphrosyne.*[229]

And [another is] as Chaeremon [said],

> Pentheus, named from his future unhappy fate.[230]

30. Refutative enthymemes are better liked [by audiences] than demonstrative ones because the refutative enthymeme is a bringing together of opposites in brief form, and when these are set side by side they are clearer to the hearer. In the case of all syllogistic argument, both refutative and demonstrative, those are most applauded that [hearers] foresee from the beginning, but not because they are superficial (at the same time, too, people are pleased with themselves when anticipating [the conclusion]), and [they like] those that they are slower to apprehend to the extent that they understand when these have been stated.

Chapter 24: Real and Apparent, or Fallacious, Enthymemes

■ The main function of this chapter is not to teach how to compose fallacious enthymemes, though Aristotle's wording at times seems to imply that, but to help a speaker recognize them when employed by others. Grimaldi appositely quotes (1980–88, 2: 337) Aristotle's remark in *Sophistic Refutations* (165a24–27): "It is the task of one who has knowledge about a thing to speak the truth about what he knows, and to be

226. "Bold in fight." Cf. the pun on the word *earnest* in Oscar Wilde's play, *The Importance of Being Ernest.*

227. "A colt."

228. "Snake," whence English *dragon.*

229. "Folly," but the words come from different roots. The quotation is from *Trojan Women* 990.

230. *Penthos,* or "sorrow."

able to expose the individual who makes false statements."
Some of the fallacies discussed here are also treated in *Sophistic Refutations,* which is an appendix to Aristotle's *Topics.*

1. But since it is possible for [a logical argument] to be a syllogism or for it not to be a [valid] syllogism but to appear to be one, necessarily [a rhetorical argument] also may be an enthymeme or not be one but appear to be one, inasmuch as an enthymeme is a sort of syllogism.[231]

[1401a] 2. [Fallacious Topic 1] There are *topoi* of apparent enthymemes, [of which] one is verbal [*para tēn lexin*], and one form of this resembles what occurs in dialectic when the final statement takes the form of a conclusion without constituting a [valid] syllogism ("since such and such [is true], necessarily also this and that follows"), and in the case of enthymemes [i.e., in rhetoric] a statement appears to be an enthymeme whenever it is spoken compactly and antithetically; for verbal style of this sort is the place where an enthymeme is at home, and such [a fallacy] seems to result from the shape of the expression.[232] For purposes of speaking in verbally [i.e., not logically valid] syllogistic form it is useful to enumerate the headings of several syllogisms; [for example] that [Evagoras] saved some, avenged others, and freed the Greeks.[233]

231. A syllogism may, on first hearing, seem to have major and minor premises from which a conclusion is drawn but be logically invalid. Similarly, the supporting reason in an enthymeme may seem to validate it on first hearing but not be logically valid; or the connection between an *if* clause and its apodosis may be specious.

232. The hearer accepts the verbal form as the equivalent of logical validity. This is especially easy to do when listening to a speech that continues rapidly and gives the audience no time to reflect, whereas a reader may pause and wonder at the validity of the argument. If a speaker, in compact antithetical form, proclaims, "You can trust me, for I have never deceived you," he has created an apparent enthymeme. As in this case, the *ēthos* of the speaker and the emotion of the audience can contribute to the acceptance of apparent enthymemes without further demonstrations.

233. Aristotle here draws on Isocrates' *Evagoras* (65–69), an epideictic speech honoring the king of Salamis in Cyprus; but he compresses Isocrates' argument into what he calls *kephalaia,* "headings" (actually conclusions), which then appear to support the proposition that Evagoras was brave, wise, and virtuous. Aristotle is not describing what Isocrates does but what a speaker could do with the material. By amplification of details, the audience's attention is drawn away from the logical weakness of the generalization, while at the same time a logical structure seems to be maintained that is emphasized by being stated in compact form.

Each of these statements has been demonstrated from other arguments, but when they are put together something else appears to result from them. The other form [of verbal fallacy] is by use of homonyms,[234] as saying that a mouse [*mys*] is a worthy creature from which comes the most honored of all festivals; for the [celebration of the Eleusinian] *Mys*teries is the most honored of all. Or [another example is] if someone delivered an encomium of the dog that included the Dog Star or [the god] Pan, because Pindar said [of Pan]

> O blessed one, whom the Olympians call dog
> Of the Great Goddess, taking every form[235]

or [if someone said that] because it is most dishonorable for there to be no "dog," thus clearly the dog is honored.[236] Or to say that Hermes is the "most sociable" [*koinōnikos*] of the gods; for he alone is called "Hermes the Sharer" [*koinos*].[237] And that *logos* is the best thing, because good men are worthy not of money but of *logos* ["esteem"]; for "worthy of *logos*" has more than one meaning.

3. [Fallacious Topic 2] Another is for the speaker to combine what is divided [*to diēirēmenon syntithenta*] or divide what is combined; for since what is not the same often seems to be the same, whichever is more useful should be done. This was Euthydemus' form of argument, for example, his claim to know there was a

234. Words that sound the same, but have different meanings, thus verbal equivocation. *Mystery* is not derived from *mys* (mouse), though they sound the same, but from the verb *myein* (to close the lips, keep secret).

235. Pindar, *Parthenia*, fr. 86, ed. Bowra. Pan was regarded as a doglike attendant on Cybele, mother goddess of all nature.

236. The metaphorical meaning of *dog* here is unclear, and the Greek could be translated "It is most dishonorable for no one to be a dog." Stephanus, the medieval Greek commentator, thought there was a reference to Diogenes the Cynic (Cynic = Dog). To call a person a dog in Greek was usually an insult, since dogs were thought shameless; but dog is occasionally used to mean watchman or attendant, as in the passage from Pindar, and something like that may have been in Aristotle's mind. Perhaps, "It is most dishonorable to have no attendant." Compare Alexander Pope's epigram inscribed on a dog collar: "I am His Highness' dog at Kew. Pray tell me, Sir, Whose dog are you?"

237. Hermes, among other things, was god of luck. If someone found something valuable, he exclaimed "Hermes *koinos*," meaning that he claimed a share of it.

trireme at the Peiraeus because he knew each of the terms.[238] And that knowing the letters, he "knew" the word; for the word is the same thing [as the letters]. And since twice as much of a thing induces illness, neither is a single portion healthful; for it would be odd if two goods equalled one evil. This is in refutation, but in demonstration thus: [a double portion is healthful;] for two goods do not equal one evil. The whole topic is contrary to logic. Again, [another example is] what Polycrates said in regard to Thrasybulus, that he deposed thirty tyrants; for he combines them.[239] Or [another example is] what is in the *Orestes* of Theodectes; for it is from division: "It is just," for this woman to die, "who has killed a husband" and for the son to avenge the father; so then these things have been [justly] done. **[1401b]** But perhaps when they are combined, it is no longer just. This would also be [a fallacy] by omission; for it ignores the [just] agent.

4. [Fallacious Topic 3] Another topic is constructing or demolishing an argument by exaggeration [*to deinōsei kataskeuazein*]. This occurs when one amplifies the action without showing that it was performed; for when [the accused] amplifies the charge, he causes it to appear that he has not committed the action, or when the accuser goes into a rage [he makes it appear] that [the defendant] has. There is then no enthymeme; for the hearer falsely reckons that he did it or did not, although this has not been shown.

5. [Fallacious Topic 4] Another is from a [nonnecessary] sign [*ek tou sēmeiou*]; for this, too, is nonsyllogistic, for example, if someone were to say, "Lovers benefit cities; for the love of Harmodius and Aristogeiton destroyed the tyrant Hipparchus."[240] Or [another example is] if someone were to say that Dionysius[241] is

---

238. He knew there was such a place as the Peiraeus and such a thing as a trireme, or warship; therefore, combining things that are really separate, he knew there was a trireme at the Peiraeus, the port of Athens. Euthydemus was a sophist, best known from Plato's dialogue named for him. A fuller version of this fallacy is discussed in *Sophistic Refutations* 177b12–13.

239. Thrasybulus was a leader in ending the rule of the Thirty Tyrants in 404 B.C. This was really one tyranny by thirty individuals. If an award is to be paid to one who ends a tyranny, should he get thirty times the fixed amount? (Cf. Quintilian 3.6.26). Polycrates was a sophist, active in the early fourth century.

240. See 2.23.8.

241. The "wicked" tyrant of Syracuse.

a thief; for this is certainly nonsyllogistic: not every wicked man is a thief, but every thief is wicked.

6. [Fallacious Topic 5] Another is through an accidental result [*dia to symbēbekos*]. For example, Polycrates says of mice that they aided [the Egyptians] by gnawing the bowstrings [of the invading Assyrians].[242] Or if someone were to say that to be invited to dinner is the greatest form of honor; for Achilles' wrath against the Achaeans at Tenedos resulted from not being invited. But he was angry because of being dishonored; and not being invited to dinner was an accidental result of this.

7. [Fallacious Topic 6] Another is in terms of what follows [from a fallacious assumption][*para to hepomenon*],[243] for example in the *Alexander*,[244] [the claim] that [Paris] was "high-minded"; for looking down on the society of the multitude he passed his time by himself on Mount Ida. [The argument is] that because the high-minded have this quality, [Paris,] too, should be thought high-minded.[245] And [another example is the allegation that] when someone is a dandy and "cruises" at night, he is sexually promiscuous; for that is the way such people act. Similarly, too, because beggars sing and dance in temple precincts and because exiles can live wherever they want, since these things are true of those seeming to be happy, such people might seem to be happy. But there is a difference in the circumstances [of the people mentioned and those who are really happy]. Thus, it, too, falls under [the fallacy of] omission [*eleipsis*].

8. [Fallacious Topic 7] Another is taking a noncause as a cause [*para to anaition*], for example, when something has happened at the same time or after [something else]; for people take what happens later as though it happened because of what preceded, and especially people involved in politics, for example, the way

---

242. The story is in Herodotus 2.141.

243. Or the fallacy of affirming the consequent and making it convertible with the subject.

244. The epideictic speech mentioned in 2.23.8.

245. I.e., Paris scorns the crowd. The high-minded scorn the crowd. Therefore, as a consequence, Paris is high-minded. But scorning the crowd is not convertible with being high-minded.

Demades [regarded] the policy of Demosthenes as the cause of all evils; for the war took place after it.[246]

9. [Fallacious Topic 8] Another is by omission of consideration of when and how [*para tēn elleipsin tou pote kai pōs*], for example, [the argument] that Alexander took Helen justly; for free choice [of a husband] had been given her by her father. [This is fallacious;] for presumably [the choice was] not for all time, only for the first time;[247] for the father's authority only lasts to that point. **[1402a]** Or [another example is] if someone were to say that it is hybris to beat those who are free; [this is fallacious;] for it is not always true, only when someone strikes the first blow.

10. [Fallacious Topic 9] Further, just as in eristics[248] an apparent syllogism occurs in confusing what is general and what is not general [*para to haplōs kai mē haplōs*] but some particular (for example, in dialectic that nonbeing exists, for what-is-not *is* what-is-not; and that the unknown is known, for it is known about the unknown that it is unknown), so also in rhetoric there is an apparent enthymeme in regard to what is not generally probable but probable in a particular case. The probability is not absolute, as Agathon, too, say:

> Probably one could say that this thing itself is probable:
> Many improbable things happen to mortals.[249]

For some things happen contrary to probability, so what is contrary to probability is also probable. If this is so, the improbable will be probable. But not generally so; as in eristics not adding the circumstances and reference and manner makes for deception,[250] so here [in rhetoric], because the probability is not general but qualified.

---

246. This is the only certain reference to the famous orator Demothenes in the *Rhetoric* and one of the latest historical references. "The war" is that between Athens (and allies) and Macedon, culminating in the defeat of the Greeks at Chaeronea in 338 B.C. Demades' statement could have been made any time thereafter.

247. The first time, she chose Menelaus of Sparta.

248. In sophistic argument.

249. On Agathon, see 2.29.13.

250. *Sykophantia,* on which see n. 41.

11. The *Art* of Corax is made up of this topic;[251] for example, if a weak man were charged with assault, he should be acquitted as not being a likely suspect for the charge; for it is not probable [that a weak man would attack another]. And if he is a likely suspect, for example, if he is strong, [he should also be acquitted]; for it is not likely [that he would start the fight] for the very reason that it was going to seem probable. And similarly in other cases; for necessarily, a person is either a likely suspect or not a likely suspect for a charge. Both alternatives seem probable, but one really is probable, the other so not generally, only in the circumstances mentioned.[252] And this is "to make the weaker seem the better cause."[253] Thus, people were rightly angry at the declaration of Protagoras;[254] for it is a lie and not true but a fallacious probability and a part of no art except rhetoric and eristic. This concludes discussion of real and apparent enthymemes.

251. Plato, *Phaedrus* 273a–b, attributes the following argument to Tisias. Corax and Tisias are the traditional fathers of the teaching of rhetoric as an art. They worked in Sicily in the second quarter of the fifth century.

252. The second possibility, that the strong man would have realized he would seem the probable aggressor, requires a specific knowledge of the circumstances and the character of the individual. He would have to be a canny person who foresaw the consequences of his action.

253. This is what sophists were accused of doing. Cf. esp. Aristophanes, *Clouds* 889–1104; it was also a charge against Socrates in his trial, cf. Plato, *Apology* 18b. Although to philosophers defense of the "weaker" cause seemed morally wrong, the willingness of the Greeks to give a hearing to it was basic to freedom of speech and to the advocacy of unpopular causes that might prove important to society. For a long time, many U.S. citizens would have regarded the claim of blacks to equality as "the weaker cause."

254. According to Diogenes Laertius (9.52), the opening sentence of Protagoras' now lost treatise *On the Gods* caused him to be expelled from Athens and his books burned. It read "Concerning the gods, I cannot know either that they exist or that they do not exist; for there is much to prevent one's knowing: the obscurity of the subject and the shortness of life." Presumably, he continued with arguments from probability for and against the existence of the gods, and it is this feature of the work that Aristotle criticizes. Another famous declaration opened his treatise *On Truth* (Sextus Empiricus 7.60): "Man is the measure of all things, of things that are insofar as they are, and of things that are not insofar as they are not." This continued with the argument that all truth is relative because perception and opinion exists only in relation to the individual. Here Protagoras would seem to be doing something closer to what Aristotle demands: determining probability on the basis of the particular circumstances.

Chapter 25: Lysis, *or Undoing an Opponent's Enthymemes*

1. The next point in the continuing discussion is to speak about refutation.[255] It is possible to refute either by stating an opposite syllogism or by bringing an objection [*enstasis*]. 2. Now, clearly, an opposite syllogism can be made frqm the same topics [as the opponents' but drawing the opposite conclusion]; for the syllogisms [of rhetoric] are derived from commonly held opinions [*endoxa*], and many opinions are opposed to each other. 3. Objections are brought as has been described in the *Topics*[256] [and] are of four sorts; for either they are derived from the original argument or from something similar or from the opposite or from what has been judged true. 4. By the original argument I mean, for example, if the enthymeme concerned love, claiming it was good; the objection [then] would be double: **[1402b]** for it could be generally claimed that all lack is bad [and love is a feeling of lacking something]; or, taking one kind, [one could claim] that there would be no talk of Caunian love if there were not also bad forms.[257] 5. Objection is brought by the opposite if, for example, the enthymeme was that "a good man benefits all his friends"; [and the objection is,] "But the wicked man does not harm [all his friends]." 6. [An objection is based] on something similar [to the original argument] if the enthymeme was that those who suffer always hate, [to which the objection is,] "But those who are benefited do not always love." 7. "Judgments" [*kriseis*] are those of well-known men, for example, if someone spoke the enthymeme that one should excuse those who are drunk, for their mistakes are made out of ignorance. The objection is that then Pittacus[258] didn't know what he was doing; for he legislated greater punishments if someone committed a misdeed when drunk.

---

255. *Lysis,* lit. "unloosing" or "undoing" the logical ties of a syllogism or enthymeme. *Enstasis* (lit. "stepping in") is used below to mean "objection" to a premise in the opponent's argument. In 3.17.13 the word for "refutation" in a speech is *elenkos.*

256. The treatise as a whole, not any particular passage.

257. "Caunian love" is incest, named from Caunus's passion for his sister in mythology.

258. Author of laws at Mytilene in the early sixth century B.C.

8. Since enthymemes are drawn from four sources and these four are probability [*eikos*], paradigm, *tekmērion* [or necessary sign], and *sēmeion* [or fallible sign][259] (enthymemes from probabilities are drawn from things that either are, or seem for the most part [to be], true; others come from example by induction of what is like, whether one thing or more, whenever a general statement is made and then supported by a particular instance; others are derived from a necessary and always existing sign [*tekmērion*]; others from signs [*sēmeia*] of what is generally or in part true or not) and since the probable is not always but for the most part true, it is clear that all these kinds of enthymemes can be refuted by bringing objections, but the refutation may be an apparent one, not always valid; 9. for the objector does not refute the probability but [shows] that [the conclusion in a particular case] is not necessary.[260] 10. As a further result, the defendant always has an advantage over the prosecutor because of this fallacy; for since the prosecutor demonstrates by probabilities and since it is not the same thing to show in refutation that an argument is not probable as to show it is not necessary, what is for the most part true is always open to objection; for otherwise it would not be *for the most part* and probable, but *always* and necessary. Yet when a refutation is made in this way, the judge thinks either that the thing is not probable or that it is not for him to decide, reasoning falsely as we said; [falsely,] because he should not only judge from necessary arguments but from probable ones, too; for this is to judge "in

259. See 1.2.14–18, where, however, paradigm (or example) is made coordinate with enthymeme rather than being one of its sources. But examples are used in making enthymemes and especially in refutation, where one example can refute a universal positive (e.g., U.S. presidents have not always lived in the White House; for George Washington never lived in the White House). Thus, the inclusion of paradigm here is appropriate.

260. *Tekmēria,* as necessarily valid signs (e.g., "She has milk, so she has had a child"), cannot really be refuted, as Aristotle grants in sec. 14 below. They can sometimes be attacked if the speaker can find some plausible exception that the audience will grant. The refutation is then only "apparent." E.g., "If a woman has had a child she has had sex with a man; but the Virgin Mary had a child without having sex with a man." The necessary sign, applicable to the natural world, is not refuted, since the example is supernatural; thus the conditions are different, and the woman is question is not the Virgin Mary.

accordance with the best understanding"[261] Therefore, it is not sufficient if one attacks an argument as "not necessary"; and one must refute it as "not probable." This will result if the objection is a more probable statement; 11. and that such is the case can be shown in two ways; either in terms of the time or the facts but most effectively if by both; **[1403a]** for if something is often true, it is more probable.[262]

12. Signs [*sēmeia*] and enthymemes that draw a conclusion through a sign are refutable, even if true, as was said in the first [lectures];[263] for that every sign[264] is nonsyllogistic is clear to us from the *Analytics*.[265] 13. The refutation of examples is the same as that of probabilities; for if we cite an example that does not accord [with the generalized] conclusion, the argument is refuted because it is not "necessary," even if something else is more often true or true in more cases. But if the larger number of instances is usually as the opponent says, one should contend that the present case is not similar or not in the same way or has some difference. 14. But *tekmēria* and enthymemes with infallible signs cannot be refuted as nonsyllogistic (this is clear to us from the *Analytics*), and what is left is to show that the alleged fact is not true. If it is evident that it is true and that there is an infallible sign of it, the argument is irrefutable from the start; for the whole demonstration is already evident.

Chapter 26: To Amplify, to Refute, and to Raise an Objection Are Not Topics

■ Since amplification is a feature common to all species of civic rhetoric (though most developed in epideictic as Aris-

261. For this phrase see note on 1.15.5.

262. Consideration of time can involve showing that at a particular time a particular action was not, is not, or will not be, probable and (to judge from the last clause) also that it is either probable as something that frequently was or is (and thus will be) done or improbable as rare.

263. In 1.2.18.

264. *Sēmeion*—not, of course, a *tekmērion*, which is an infallible sign.

265. *Prior Analytics* 2.27, as re erred to in 1.2.8.

totle noted in 1.9.38), it, like refutation and objection, might be thought to be a *topos*. To forestall that conclusion Aristotle appends this short chapter to his discussion of topics. Any of the topics can be amplified in a variety of ways, and amplification has no identifiable logical pattern of its own. There are some comments on amplification as an aspect of style in 3.6.7 and 3.12.4.

1. To amplify [*to auxein*] and to deprecate [*to meioun*] is not an element [*stoikheion*] of an enthymeme. (I call the same thing "element" and "topic"; for an element or a topic [is a heading] under which many enthymemes fall.)[266] To amplify and deprecate contribute to showing that something is great or small, just as also [to showing that something is] good or evil or just or unjust and anything else, 2. but all these things are the subjects of syllogisms and enthymemes,[267] so if each of them is not a topic of an enthymeme, neither is amplification and deprecation.
3. Nor are refutative enthymemes a distinct species; for clearly, one refutes by proving something or bringing an objection, but these are a demonstration in response to the adversary's position; for example, if one side shows that something has happened, the other [tries to show] that it has not, and if the first shows it has not, the second that it has. The result is that this is not the difference; for they both use the same [forms of argument] and bring in enthymemes to show that something is or is not true. 4. "Objection" [*enstasis*] is not an enthymeme either; but, as in the *Topics*,[268] it is a matter of stating an opinion from which it will be clear that the opponent's argument does not constitute a syllogism or that he has introduced something false.

---

266. Cf. 2.22.13.
267. That is, they are *idia* or *koina*. But *idia* have been called topics in 2.22.1 and 2.22.16, and *koina* seem to be so called in 3.19.2.
268. Perhaps *Topics* 1.10 is meant.

Transition to Book 3

Since there are in fact three things that should be systematically worked out in discussion of speech, 5. let us regard what has been said as enough about paradigms and maxims and enthymemes and in general about the thought [*dianoia*][269] and the sources of arguments and how we shall refute them. **[1403b]** It remains to go through the subject of style [*lexis*] and arrangement [*taxis*].

269. Or, in later terminology, *heuresis* (invention).

BOOK 3:
Delivery, Style, and Arrangement

■ Chapters 1–12 contain a discussion of *lexis*, chapters 13–19 of *taxis*. *Lexis* (Latin *elocutio*), refers to the "way of saying" something (in contrast to *logos*, "what is said") and is usually translated "style." In some passages Aristotle uses *lexis* in a broad sense of how thought is expressed in words, sentences, and a speech or work as a whole, but often he uses the term in the more restricted sense of "word choice, diction" (hence, English *lexical*). Translation needs to vary with context: "language," "choice of word," "expression," etc. Often it seems best to retain the Greek term and let the meaning emerge from the context. *Taxis* (Latin *dispositio*) means "arrangement" and refers to the "ordering" of the conventional parts of an oration, especially as seen in judicial speeches. On the time of composition of book 3, see Appendix II.A.

Chapter 1: Introduction

Chapter 1: Summary of Books 1–2; Some Remarks on Hypokrisis, *or Delivery; the Origins of Artistic Prose*

■ In chapter 1, the first two sections are a transition connecting what follows with Book 2, which itself ended with a short transition section. This repetition of transitions is awkward and probably results from joining two separate works together: the work in two books on *dianoia*, "thought" or "invention," and a work in one book on *lexis* and *taxis*. Perhaps Aristotle made this connection himself at a late stage in his revision of the whole, in which case the transition at the end of Book 2 indicated that further discussion of rhetoric continued on another papyrus scroll, which then began with a reminder that it is to be linked with the work on invention. Some scholars, however, have thought that the linkage was made—and possibly at least one of the transitions added—by Tyrannio or Andronicus when the works of Aristotle were edited and published in the first century B.C.; see Appendix II.B. A third beginning is then supplied in section 3, followed by some remarks on delivery, and the actual discussion of *lexis* does not begin until section 8.

1. Since there are three matters that need to be treated in discussion of speech—first, what will be the sources of the *pisteis*, second concerning the *lexis*, and third how the parts of a speech must be arranged—an account has been given of the *pisteis*, including the fact that they are drawn from three sources and what sort of things these are and why there are only these [three]. (All people are persuaded either because as judges they themselves are affected in some way or because they suppose the speakers have certain qualities or because something has been logically demonstrated.) An account has also been given of enthymemes and where they are to be found. (There are on the one hand species [*eidē*] of enthymemes and on the other hand there are topics.) 2. The next subject to discuss is *lexis;* for it is not enough to have a supply of things to say, but it is also necessary to say it in the right way, and this contributes much toward the speech seeming to have a certain quality.

HYPOKRISIS, OR DELIVERY

3. The first thing to be examined was naturally that which comes first by nature, the facts from which a speech has persuasive effect;

second is how to compose this in language [*lexis*]; and third is something that has the greatest force, but has not yet been taken in hand, the matter of the delivery [*hypokrisis*].[1] Even in regard to tragedy and rhapsody,[2] delivery was late in coming to be considered; for originally, the poets themselves acted their tragedies.[3] Clearly there is something like this in rhetoric, as in poetics. Some others have given attention to the latter, among them Glaucon of Teos.[4]. 4. It is a matter of how the voice should be used in expressing each emotion, sometimes loud and sometimes soft and [sometimes] intermediate, and how the pitch accents [*tonoi*] should be entoned, whether as acute, grave, or circumflex,[5] and what rhythms should be expressed in each case; for [those who study delivery] consider three things, and these are volume, change of pitch [*harmonia*], and rhythm. Those [performers who give careful attention to these] are generally the ones who win poetic contests; and just as actors are more important than poets now in the poetic contests, so it is in political contests because of the sad state of governments.[6]

5. An *Art* concerned with [the delivery of oratory] has not yet been composed, since even consideration of *lexis* was late in developing, and delivery seems a vulgar matter when rightly understood. [1404a] But since the whole business of rhetoric is with opinion, one should pay attention to delivery, not because it is right but because it is necessary, since true justice seeks nothing more in a speech than neither to offend nor to entertain; for to contend by means of the facts themselves is just, with the result that everything except demonstration is incidental; but, nevertheless, [delivery] has great power, as has been said, because of the

1. The prevailing meaning of *hypokrisis* in Greek is "acting" and the regular word for an actor is *hypokritēs*.

2. The recitation of epic poetry or dithyrambs.

3. Thus there was no need to consider the oral interpretation of a poem or play separately from the presentation of it by the author.

4. Probably the rhapsode mentioned in Plato's *Ion* 530 and quoted in *Poetics* 25.1461b1.

5. Every Greek word has an accent, either a rising tone (acute), falling tone (grave), or rising and falling (circumflex).

6. This point, repeated in the next section, seems to reflect the Platonic view (e.g., *Gorgias* 463a–b) that political oratory under democracy had become a form of flattery and that it offered entertainment to the mob.

corruption of the audience. 6. The subject of expression,[7] however, has some small necessary place in all teaching; for to speak in one way rather than another does make some difference in regard to clarity, though not a great difference; but all these things are forms of outward show and intended to affect the audience. As a result, nobody teaches geometry this way. 7. Whenever delivery comes to be considered[8] it will function in the same way as acting, and some have tried to say a little about it, for example, Thrasymachus in his [account of] emotional appeals.[9] Acting is a matter of natural talent and largely not reducible to artistic rule; but in so far as it involves how things are said [*lexis*], it has an artistic element. As a result, prizes go to those who are skilled at it, just as they do to orators on the basis of their delivery; for written speeches [when orally recited] have greater effect through expression [*lexis*] than through thought.[10]

8. The poets were naturally the first to set in motion [study of verbal expression]; for words are imitations,[11] and the voice, the most mimetic of all our parts, was there to start with. Thus, the verbal arts were established: rhapsody and acting and the others. 9. Since the poets, while speaking sweet nothings, seemed to acquire their reputation through their *lexis*, a poetic style came into existence [in prose as well], for example, that of Gorgias. Even now, the majority of the uneducated think such speakers speak most beautifully. This is not the case; but the *lexis* of prose differs from that of poetry. It is clear from what has happened [in other literary genres that the direction of development is away from the use of poetic diction]: for the makers of tragedies do not continue to use the same style, but just as they changed from tetrameters to

7. *Lexis,* here apparently including delivery.

8. As it apparently was by Aristotle's student Theophrastus; see Fortenbaugh 1985, 269–88.

9. The *Eleoi* of Thrasymachus of Chalcedon, referred to by Plato in *Phaedrus* 267c9.

10. There were oratorical contests, with prizes, at festivals in Greece. *Written speeches* here probably refers to works by sophists, written and then dramatically recited. The subject of oral and written style is further discussed in chap. 12.

11. This is consistent with some of Plato's *Cratylus* but not with Aristotle's own discussion of words in *On Interpretation* 1, where they are called "symbols" and "signs."

the iambic metre because it was most like ordinary speech, so also they have abandoned the use of words that are not conversational, with which they had at first ornamented their diction as the writers of hexameter poetry still do.[12] As a result, it is absurd to imitate those who themselves no longer use that style of speech. 10. Thus, it is clear that we need not go into detail about all matters concerned with *lexis,* only about what applies to the subject we are discussing. Concerning the other style there is a discussion in the *Poetics.*[13]

Chapters 2–12: *Lexis,* or Style

■ Chapters 2–4 are primarily concerned with *lexis* in the sense of diction, or choice of words, chapters 5–12 with the composition of words into sentences, which came to be known as *synthesis,* "putting together." Aristotle's discussion applies both to oral speech and to written prose.

Chapter 2: The Aretē, *or Virtue, of Good Prose Style; Word Choice and Metaphors*

■ This chapter begins with a definition of the virtue or excellence (*aretē*) of prose style and civic oratory as *clarity,* but with the accompanying requirement that a writer or speaker seek a mean between ordinary speech and poetic language as appropriate to the subject. In chapter 5, Aristotle will add a requirement of grammatical correctness and in subsequent chapters will discuss various forms of ornamentation. These

---

12. The turn to ordinary diction can be seen by comparing dialogue passages of Euripides, whose diction is often conversational, with those of Aeschylus, where the diction is sometimes bombastic; but the development was resisted by Aristophanes and probably others.

13. *Poetics* 20–22. Style in poetics is an aspect of imitation, in rhetoric of persuasion.

concepts were reformulated by his student Theophrastus in a treatise, now lost, *On Lexis,* as "correctness, clarity, propriety, and ornamentation" and appear in some form in most subsequent Greek and Roman treatments of rhetoric. See *Rhetoric for Herennius* 4.17; Cicero, *On the Orator* 3.37 and *Orator* 79; Quintilian 8.1–2; etc.

[1404b] 1. Let the matters just discussed be regarded as understood, and let the virtue of style [*lexeōs aretē*] be defined as "to be clear" (speech is a kind of sign, so if it does not make clear it will not perform its function)—and neither flat nor above the dignity of the subject, but appropriate [*prepon*].[14] The poetic style is hardly flat, but it is not appropriate for speech. 2. The use of nouns and verbs in their prevailing [*kyrios*][15] meaning makes for clarity; other kinds of words, as discussed in the *Poetics,*[16] make the style oramented rather than flat. To deviate [from prevailing usage] makes language seem more elevated; for people feel the same in regard to *lexis* as they do in regard to strangers compared with citizens. 3. As a result, one should make the language unfamiliar,[17] for people are admirers of what is far off, and what is marvelous is sweet. Many [kinds of words] accomplish this in verse and are appropriate there; for what is said [in poetry] about subjects and

14. Aristotle applies to word choice the concept of virtue as a mean between two extremes that is fundamental to his ethical philosophy. His emphasis on clarity as the most important requirement of good oratorical style is consistent with his stress on logical proof in the earlier books and his dislike of the style of sophists. For some possible implications see Consigny 1987. Artistic prose in Greek, though influenced by Gorgianic mannerism derived from poetry, was largely a matter of the purification of diction and regularization of syntax into an efficient, elegant tool of expression. The great models of Attic prose are Plato, Lysias, Isocrates, and Demosthenes.

15. *Kyrios* refers to the prevailing meaning in current usage and may also be translated "proper" in the sense found in dictionary definitions; it is not necessarily the scmantic, etymological, or essential meaning of the word. Modern literary critics, however, have called the concept into serious question, emphasizing the context as the determinant of meaning; cf. especially Richards 1936, 37–41.

16. *Poetics* 21–22.

17. The view of literary language as "defamiliarization" has been greatly extended in modern times by the Russian Formalist School, leading to Roman Jakobson's famous definition of poetry as "organized violence committed on ordinary speech"; see Erlich 1981, 219.

characters is more out of the ordinary, but in prose[18] much less so; for the subject matter is less remarkable, since even in poetry it would be rather inappropriate if a slave used fine language or if a man were too young for his words, or if the subject were too trivial, but in these cases, too, propriety is a matter of contraction or expansion. 4. As a result, authors should compose without being noticed and should seem to speak not artificially but naturally.[19] (The latter is persuasive, the former the opposite; for [if artifice is obvious] people become resentful, as at someone plotting against them, just as they are at those adulterating wines.) An example is the success of Theodorus' voice when contrasted with that of other actors; for his seems the voice of the actual character, but the others' those of somebody else.[20] 5. The "theft"[21] is well done if one composes by choosing words from ordinary language. Euripides does this and first showed the way.

Since speech is made up of nouns and verbs,[22] and the species of nouns are those examined in the *Poetics*, from among these one should use glosses[23] and double words and coinages rarely and in a limited number of situations. (We shall later[24] explain where; the reason has already been given: the usage departs from the appropriate in the direction of excess.) 6. A word in its prevailing and native meaning and metaphor[25] are alone useful in the *lexis* of

18. Lit. "in bare words"; Aristotle has no technical term for prose.

19. Perhaps the earliest statement in criticism that the greatest art is to disguise art.

20. The statement sounds as though Theodorus was still acting when Aristotle first wrote this passage; that would date it to the mid-350s B.C.; see Burkert 1975.

21. The concealment of the art involved in choosing words; see 3.2.10.

22. *Onomata*, "name words" (including adjectives) and *rhēmata*, "sayings, verbs, predicates," are the two major parts of speech recognized by Aristotle. In 3.5.2 he adds *syndesmoi*, "connectives." See also introduction to Appendix I.E. Full categorization of parts of speech is largely a development of the study of grammar in the third to the first century B.C.

23. Strange or rare words; see 3.3.2.

24. In chap. 3, 7.

25. *Metaphor* is itself a metaphor and literally means "carrying something from one place to another, transference." In *Poetics* 21.7 it is defined as "a movement [*epiphora*] of an alien [*allotrios*] name either from genus to species or from species to genus or from species to species or by analogy"; see Appendix I.E. On Aristotle's concept of the metaphor and the difference between its function in poetics

prose. A sign of this is that these are the only kinds of words everybody uses; for all people carry on their conversations with metaphors[26] and words in their native and prevailing meanings. Thus, it is clear that if one composes well, there will be an unfamiliar quality and it escapes notice and will be clear. This, we said, was the virtue of rhetorical language. 7. The kind of words useful to a sophist are homonyms[27] (by means of these he does his dirty work), to a poet synonyms. **[1405a]** By words that are both in their prevailing meaning and synonymous I mean, for example, *go* and *walk;* for when used in their prevailing sense, these are synonymous with each other.

Now what each kind of word is and how many species of metaphor there are and that metaphor has very great effect both in poetry and speeches has been said, as noted above, in the *Poetics*.[28] 8. In speech it is necessary to take special pains to the extent that speech has fewer resources than verse. Metaphor especially has clarity and sweetness and strangeness, and its use cannot be learned from someone else.[29] 9. One should speak both epithets and metaphors that are appropriate, and this will be from an analogy. If not, the expression seems inappropriate because opposites are most evident when side-by-side each other. But one should consider what suits an old man just as a scarlet cloak is right for a young one; for the same clothes are not right [for both]. 10. And if you wish to adorn, borrow the metaphor from something better in the same genus, if to denigrate, from something worse. I mean, for example, since they are opposites in the same genus, saying of a person who begs that he "prays" or that a person praying "begs," because both are forms of asking. That is composing in the way

---

and rhetoric, see Ricoeur 1977, 7–43. Ricoeur says (p. 20) that the Aristotelian idea of *allotrios* tends to assimilate three distinct ideas: *deviation* from ordinary usage *borrowing* from an original usage, and *substitution* for an absent word by an available ordinary word.

26. Ordinary language contains many metaphorical expression that have often lost their force, e.g., "It's raining cats and dogs," "The sun is smiling," etc.

27. By *homonym* Aristotle means a word that is "equivocal"; see 2.24.2, *Categories* 1.1, and *Sophistical Refutations* 1.7.

28. See Appendix I.E.

29. Cf. *Poetics* 22.17, where it is also said that an ability to use metaphor is a "sign of natural ability."

described, as also when Iphicrates called Callias a "begging priest" rather than a "torchbearer" and the latter replied that Iphicrates was not initiated into the Mysteries or he would not have called him a begging priest but a torchbearer;[30] for both are religious epithets, but one is honorable, one dishonorable. Then there are the "parasites of Dionysius," but the persons in question call themselves "artistes." These are both metaphors, the former one that sullies the profession, the latter the contrary. Pirates now call themselves "businessmen." Thus, one can say that a criminal "has made a mistake" or that someone making a mistake "has committed a crime" or that a thief either took or "plundered." A phrase like that of Euripides' Telephos, "lording the oar and landed in Mysia," is inappropriate [in prose], since *lording* is too elevated; there is no "theft" [if the metaphor is too flagrant].

11. There is a fault in the syllables if the indications of sound are unpleasant; for example, Dionysius the Brazen[31] in his *Elegies* calls poetry "Calliope's screech" because both are sounds; but the metaphor is bad because it implies meaningless sounds. 12. Further, in naming something that does not have a proper name of its own, metaphor should be used,[32] and [should] not be far-fetched but taken from things that are related and of similar species, so that it is clear the term is related; for example, in the popular riddle [*ainigma*], **[1405b]** "I saw a man gluing bronze on another with fire,"[33] the process has no [technical] name, but both are a kind of application; the application of the cupping instrument is thus called "gluing." From good riddling it is generally possible to derive appropriate metaphors; for metaphors are made like rid-

30. The incident probably took place about 390 B.C., when both served in a war between Athens and Sparta; see Xenophon, *Hellenica* 6.3.3. Callias was a heredity torchbearer in the Mysteries and apparently thought Iphicrates was just ignorant. Though a prominent Athenian general, he came from humble origins and had family connexions with the barbarous Thracians.

31. So called because he first proposed (early fifth century) the use of bronze rather than silver money at Athens.

32. This is known as *katakhrēsis* or *abusio*, but to regard it as metaphor is sometimes thought inconsistent with a rigorous "substitution" theory; cf. Genette 1982, 50–52.

33. The answer to the riddle is "cupping" or "bleeding," done by a physician with a hot bronze cup (in modern times a glass) that draws out blood as it cools.

dles; thus, clearly, [a metaphor from a good riddle] is an apt transference of words.

13. And the source of the metaphor should be something beautiful; verbal beauty, as Licymnius says,[34] is in the sound or in the sense, and ugliness the same; and thirdly there is what refutes the sophistic argument: for it is not as Bryson[35] said that nothing is in itself ugly, since it signifies the same thing if one word is used rather than another; for this is false; one word is more proper than another and more like the object signified and more adapted to making the thing appear "before the eyes."[36] Moreover, one word does not signify in the same way as another, so in this sense also we should posit one as more beautiful or more ugly than another; for both signify the beautiful or the ugly, but not solely as beauty or ugliness.[37] Or if they do, [it is] only in degree. These are the sources from which metaphors should be taken: from the beautiful either in sound or in effect or in visualization or in some other form of sense perception. It makes a difference whether the dawn is called "rosy-fingered"[38] or "purple-fingered." 14. In the use of epithets the transference is also sometimes from the bad or ugly, for example *mother-slayer,* sometimes from the better, for example *avenger of his father.*[39] When the winner in a mule race offered Simonides a paltry sum [for an ode in honor of the victory], he declined the commission as though annoyed at composing about "half-asses"; but when the winner paid enough, he wrote, "Hail, daughters of storm-footed mares!"[40] Nevertheless, they *were* daughters of asses. 15. The same effect can be achieved by diminution. A diminutive [*hypokorismos*] makes both bad and

34. The rhetorician mentioned in Plato's *Phaedrus* (267c2) as having written a discussion of beautiful words.

35. Sophist and mathematician, contemporary with Aristotle. The view here expressed was taken up later by the Stoics; see Cicero, *Letters to His Friends* 9.22.1.

36. To be discussed in 3.10–11.

37. Each word, though signifying one category of object and interchangeable in some contexts, carries its own connotations of beauty or virtue; cf. the difference between *vase, jar, pot,* and *jug.*

38. As frequently in the Homeric poems.

39. Either epithet could be applied to Orestes, as in Euripides, *Orestes* 1587–88.

40. Simonides of Ceos (c. 556–468 B.C.), fr. 10 ed. Page.

good less so, as Aristophanes does sarcastically in the *Babylo-nians*[41] when he substitutes *goldlet* for *gold, cloaklet* for *cloak, insultlet* for *insult,* and *diseaselet* [for *disease*]. But one should be careful and observe moderation in both [epithets and diminutives].

Chapter 3: Ta Psykhra, or Frigidities

■ Having discussed virtues of style, Aristotle now turns briefly to their opposites, the faults that come from violating the principles of clarity and appropriateness in choice of words and that make the language "frigid." Longinus follows the same approach in chapters 3–4 of *On Sublimity.* Frigidity, Aristotle says, may result from the use of ponderous compounds—often coined by the speaker—from unfamiliar words, from inappropriate epithets, and from farfetched metaphors.

1. Frigidities in [prose] *lexis* come about in four ways: [first] in double words,[42] as in Lycophron's phrase "the many-faced heaven of the great-summited earth" and "the narrow-passaged shore" and as Gorgias spoke of "beggar-mused flatterers, forsworn and right solemnly sworn" **[1406a]** and as in Alcidamas' expression "his soul full of anger and his face becoming fire-colored" and "end-fulfilling deemed he their zeal would be" and "end-fulfilling he made the persuasion of his words," and the foam of the sea was "copper-blue."[43] All these seem poetic because of the doubling.
2. This is one cause of frigidity, and another is the use of

---

41. Produced 426 B.C., now lost; fr. 90 ed. Kock.

42. Or compounds, which Aristotle thinks of as poetic. Greek, like German, forms compounds easily; and though the result is intelligible, it can also be pompous. Elaborate compounds were especially characteristic of the tragic style of Aeschylus and are ridiculed in Aristophanes' *Frogs* 830–94.

43. Lycophron and Alcidamas, like Gorgias, were sophists of the late fifth and early fourth century who used poetic language in prose.

glosses,[44] as when Lycophron called Xerxes "a *monster* man"[45] and Sciron "a *sinis* man"[46] and Alcidamas spoke of "[bringing no such] *toys* to poetry" and "the *wretchedlessness* of his nature" and one who was "*whetted* with the unmixed anger of his thought."

3. Third is use of epithets that are long or untimely or crowded.[47] In poetry it is appropriate to speak of "white milk,"[48] but in speech such things are not only rather unsuitable, but if used immoderately they convict [the writer of artificality] and make it clear that this is "poetry." Though there is some need to use them (for they change what is ordinary and make the *lexis* unfamiliar), nevertheless one should aim at the mean, for it does less harm than speaking carelessly; carelessness lacks merit, moderation lacks fault. As a result, Alcidamas' phrases seem frigid; for he uses epithets not as seasonings but as the main course, so frequent, extended, and conspicuous are they: for instance, not "sweat" but "wet sweat"; not "to the Isthmian games" but "to the convocation of the Isthmian games"; not "laws" but "the royal laws of cities"; not "in a race" but "in a racing impulse of the soul"; not "museion"[49] but adding "Nature's museion"[50]; and "sullen-visaged the thought of his soul"; and the artificer not of *favor* but of "pandemic favor," and "steward of the pleasure of the listeners," and hidden not by *boughs,* but "boughs of the wood," and not "he covered his body" but "he covered his body's shame," and "antimimicking was the desire of his soul" (this is at one and the same time both a compound and an epithet, so the result is poetry), and "so extravagant an excess of wickedness." Thus, by speaking poeti-

---

44. Lit., "tongues." The term *gloss* comes to be used chiefly of archaic or rare words, but Aristotle means anything that sounds strange and might puzzle an audience; cf. 3.10.2. Some of his examples are really strained metaphors. In *Poetics* 21.6 (see Appendix I.E) a gloss is defined as a word "other people use," thus words borrowed from another dialect or language.

45. *Pelōron* ("monster"), the reading of Parinius 1741, was a "gloss" (strange word) because archaic.

46. *Sinis* means "ravager"; both Sciron and Sinis were famous robbers.

47. By *epithet* (what is "added on") is meant a descriptive adjective or phrase.

48. Colloquial in the United States today, but Aristotle did not know about chocolate milk.

49. "Place, or haunt, of the Muses," Eng. museum.

50. The text is in doubt here.

cally in an inappropriate way [Alcidamas and other sophists] impart absurdity and frigidity, and also lack of clarity because of the verbiage, for when a speaker throws more words at someone who already understands, he destroys the clarity by the darkness. People coin double words when something has no name of its own and the word is easily formed, as is *pastime* [*to khronotribein*]. But if there is much of this, [the diction] becomes completely poetical. **[1406b]** Thus, *lexis* using double words is most useful to dithyrambic poets, for they are sensitive to sound,[51] but glosses to epic poets, for they are stately and self-assured.[52]

4. The fourth kind of frigidity occurs in metaphors; for there are inappropriate metaphors, some because they are laughable (comic poets, too, use metaphor), some because too lofty and tragic. And they are inappropriate if far-fetched, for example Gorgias's phrase about "pale and bloodless doings"[53] or "You have sown shamefully and have reaped badly." These are too poetic. And as Alcidamas calls philosophy "a fortress against the laws" and the *Odyssey* "a fair mirror of human life" and "bringing no such toys to poetry." All these are unpersuasive for the reasons given.[54] Yet Gorgias's exclamation to the swallow when she flew down and let go her droppings on him is in the best tragic manner: he said, "Shame on you, Philomela"; for if a bird did it there was no shame, but [it would have been] shameful for a maiden. He thus rebuked the bird well by calling it what it once had been rather than what it now was.[55]

---

51. A dithyramb was originally a hymn to Bacchus, thus somewhat wild and metrically varied; in the late fifth century it was a lyric vehicle for virtuoso performers, of whom Timotheus is the best known.

52. The manuscripts continue, ". . . metaphor to iambic poets, for they now use these, as has been said." But this was probably a marginal comment by some later reader, then copied into the text. The cross-reference is to the end of chap. 1.

53. On the basis of Demetrius *On Style* 116, Friedrich Solmsen (1979, 69) reconstructed Gorgias's original statement as "Trembling and wan are the writings, pale and bloodless the doings."

54. Some of the expressions Aristotle finds affected in Greek may be acceptable in English. The context of their use of course determines their suitability, but two thousand and more years of literature have dulled the ear for metaphor.

55. In Greek mythology Philomela (in some versions her sister Procne) was transformed into a swallow by the gods. On this passage see Rosenmeyer 1955.

Chapter 4: Eikōn, *or Simile*

■ An *eikōn* is a "likeness" (English *icon*). Though Aristotle views the simile as a characteristic poetic device, seen especially in the extended similes of epic poetry, simile is not discussed in the *Poetics*. In this chapter of the *Rhetoric* it is treated as an expanded form of the metaphor: a metaphor, that is, with an explicit comparison, whether provided by a verb, adjective, or adverb. Later rhetoricians often reverse this concept, taking a metaphor to be an abbreviated simile or regarding a simile as a figure, involving several words, while metaphor is a trope, the "turning" of the meaning of a single word. The distinction between tropes and figures is not explicit in Aristotle's work and is a development of his successors in the Hellenistic period. Aristotle has discussed *parabolē,* or comparison, as a topic of invention in 2.20.2–7; but neither there nor here does he relate it to simile, which he regards as a device of style; see McCall 1969.

1. A simile is also a metaphor; for there is little difference: when the poet says, "He rushed as a lion," it is a simile, but "The lion rushed" [with *lion* referring to a man] would be a metaphor; since both are brave, he used a metaphor [i.e., a simile] and spoke of Achilles as a lion.[56] 2. The simile is useful also in speech, but only occasionally; for it is poetic. [Similes] should be brought in like metaphors; for they *are* metaphors, differing in the form of expression. 3. Examples of similes are what Androtion said to Idreus, that he was "like puppies that have been chained"; for they jump to bite, and Idreus, freed from prison, was vicious.[57] And [another example

56. The simile comparing Achilles to a lion occurs in *Iliad* 20.164. "The lion rushed," meaning Achilles, does not occur in the Homeric poems; thus, Aristotle says *would be.* The Homeric poems and early Greek literature generally make very little use of metaphor but much of simile. Their personification of abstract forces or things represents a genuine view that these had life. Historically, at least in Greece, the use of metaphor seems to have developed out of the compression of simile, rather than the other way around, as Aristotle would have it; see Stanford 1936.

57. Androtion was a fourth-century Athenian politician, best known from Demosthenes' speech against him in 346 B.C.; Idreus succeeded Mausolus as king of Caria in 351.

is] the way Theodamus likened Archidamus to "a Euxenus that does not know geometry"; this is from analogy, for Euxenus will then be an Archidamus who knows geometry.[58] And [another example is] the one in the *Republic* of Plato, that those who strip the dead [on a battle field] are like curs that snap at stones but do not bite the throwers; and the one applied to the citizen body, that it is like a ship's captain who is strong but deaf; and the one about the verses of poets, that they are like youths without beauty (for when the latter have lost the bloom of youth and the former their meter, they do not seem the same).[59] **[1407a]** And [another example is] Pericles' simile for the Samians, that they are like children who accept the candy but keep crying, and his remark about the Boeotians, that they are like oaks, (for oaks are felled by oaks,[60] and the Boeotians by fighting each other). And [another example is] Demosthenes' about the citizen body, that it is like those sick on board ship.[61] And [another] the way Democritus likened orators to nannies who, after swallowing the pabulum, moisten the baby's lips with their spit. And [another is] the way Antisthenes compared skinny Cephisodotus to incense, because "He gives pleasure by wasting away." All these can be spoken both as similes and as metaphors, so whichever are approved when spoken as metaphors clearly will make similes too, and similes are metaphors needing[62] an explanatory word. 4. Metaphor from analogy should always have a correspondence between the two species of the same genus: thus, if the wine cup is the "shield" of Dionysus, the shield can fittingly be called the "cup" of Ares.[63] Speech, then, is composed from these things.[64]

58. I.e., they are equally stupid except that Euxenus knows some geometry.

59. The passages in the *Republic* are 5.469e, 6.488a, and 10.601b, respectively.

60. Perhaps from thrashing in a storm, perhaps from being cut down by oak-handled axes or oak wedges.

61. Probably not Demosthenes the famous orator, whom Aristotle seems to avoid quoting, presumably because of his hostility to Macedon; perhaps the fifth-century general of the same name.

62. When the metaphor would be obscure or too violent, it "needs" to be recast as a simile.

63. On metaphor from analogy see *Poetics* 21.11–14 in Appendix I.E, where the same example is given.

64. That is, from the different kinds of words discussed above; *kyria,* glosses, compounds, coined words, and metaphors, which include epithets and similes.

Chapter 5: To Hellenizein, *or Grammatical Correctness*

■ In chapters 5–12 attention turns to style as influenced by a variety of considerations of composition in the combination of words. The first of these considerations is what Aristotle calls "speaking Greek," by which he means observance of the rules of grammar and the conventions of idiom of the language; but much of what he says really relates more to clarity than to correctness. Perhaps the chapter is a survival of some earlier thoughts on clarity, placed here because it deals with composition of sentences rather than with choice of words. Although Protagoras and other sophists had made a start at the study of grammar, it was in Aristotle's time still a relatively undeveloped field of study. Systematic grammars of the Greek language did not appear until the second century B.C., when they reflect the research of Stoic philosophers.

1. The first principle [*arkhē*] of *lexis* is to speak [good] Greek [*to hellenizein*]. This is done in five ways,[65] 2. [of which the] first is in the [correct] use of connectives, when a speaker preserves the natural responsion between those that are prior and those that are posterior to each other, as some require. Thus, *ho men* and *ho ego* require [in a subsequent clause] *de* and *ho de* respectively.[66] The correlatives should occur while the first expression is still in the mind and not be widely separated, nor should another connective be substituted for the one needed; for it is rarely appropriate: "But I, when he spoke to me (for there came Cleon both begging and demanding), went, taking them along." In these words many connectives are thrown in, in place of what is expected; and if the interval is long, the result is unclear.[67]

65. Others could easily be added, and the chapter is one of the least successful sections of the *Rhetoric*.

66. As in English, "on the one hand" implies a following "on the other."

67. Though the sentence has a number of words that Aristotle would regard as connectives ("but," "when," "for," "both," "and") its faults come from the cumbersome syntax, not from separating connectives or failing to use the expected responsions. As the notes have indicated, Aristotle himself is capable of writing awkward sentences even worse than this one, with parentheses that may lead the

3. On the one hand, then, one merit is found in the use of connectives, a second, on the other hand, in calling things by their specific names and not by circumlocutions.[68] 4. Third is not to use amphibolies[69]—unless the opposite effect [obscurity] is being sought. People do this when they have nothing to say but are pretending to say something. Such are those [philosophers] who speak in poetry, Empedocles, for example. When there is much going around in a circle, it cheats the listeners and they feel the way many do about oracles: whenever the latter speak amphibolies most people nod in assent: "Croesus, by crossing the Halys [river], will destroy a great kingdom."[70] [1407b] Since there is generally less chance of a mistake, oracles speak of any matter in generalities. In the game of knucklebones one can win more often by calling odd or even than by specifying a particular number of counters, and the same is true about *what* will be in contrast to *when* it will happen, which is why soothsayers do not specify the time. All these things are alike, so they should be avoided except for the reason mentioned.

5. The fourth [rule is to observe] Protagoras' classification of the gender of nouns: masculine, feminine, and neuter. There should be correct grammatical agreement: "Having come and having spoken, she departed."[71] 6. Fifth is the correct naming of plural and singular: "Having come, they beat me." What is written should generally be easy to read and easy to speak—which is the

---

reader to forget the beginning of the sentence; but the *Rhetoric* is neither a speech nor a literary work. In his *published* dialogues his language was regarded as elegant and correct; see, e.g., Quintilian 10.1.83.

68. Though the point is probably clear without any illustrations, their absence is another sign of the sketchy nature of this chapter. Note that Aristotle's sentence illustrates the use of connectives he has just discussed.

69. An amphiboly (lit. what "shoots both ways") in dialectic is an equivocation based on a word or phrase with an ambiguous meaning, often creating a fallacious argument.

70. A famous and ambiguous response by the Delphic oracle to Croesus, king of Lydia. He interpreted it as encouragement, but the kingdom destroyed was his own.

71. In Greek, participles have distinct feminine forms. In the next example the participle is in the masculine plural to agree with *they*.

same thing. Use of many connectives[72] does not have this quality; nor do phrases not easily punctuated,[73] for example, the writings of Heraclitus. To punctuate the writings of Heraclitus is a difficult task because it is unclear what goes with what, whether with what follows or with what precedes. For example, in the beginning of his treatise he says, "Of the Logos that exists always ignorant are men." It is unclear whether *always* goes with what proceeds [or what follows]. 7. Further, the lack of correspondence creates a solecism (*to soloikizein*)[74] if you do not join words with what fits both: for example, if you are speaking of sound and color, seeing is not common to them, but perceiving is. And it is unclear if you do not first set forth what you are talking about when you are going to throw in much in the middle: for example, "I intended, after talking with that man about this and that and in this way, to go," instead of "I intended, after talking with that man, to go" and then "This and that transpired and in this way."

Chapter 6: Onkos, *or Expansiveness, and* Syntomia, *or Conciseness*

■ *Onkos* literally means "bulk, mass, swelling"; here it implies "elevation, dignity," though in other writers it is often a pejorative term. As Aristotle implies in section 7, *onkos* can be regarded as a stylistic form of *auxēsis,* amplification, of which some inventional aspects were discussed in 2.18.4, 2.19.26, and 2.26. Note the prescriptive tone of this chapter with its practical advice on how to amplify. As in the case of arguments in books 1–2, Aristotle is setting out "available" techniques. Although it appears several times in Demetrius'

72. *Polloi syndesmoi,* or *polysyndeton,* regarded by later rhetoricians as a figure of speech involving a surfeit of conjunctions, i.e., A and B and C, etc. rather than A, B, C, etc.

73. Classical Greek was generally written without punctuation and even without spacing between the words and thus had to be "punctuated" by the reader.

74. A mistake in usage; in later rhetorical theory contrasted to a "barbarism," or mistake in the form of a word.

treatise *On Style* (a work showing strong Aristotelian influence), *onkos* did not gain acceptance among later rhetoricians as a technical term.

1. The following things contribute to expansiveness [*onkos*] in *lexis:* to use a definition instead of a word, for example, not *circle* but "a plane figure equidistant from the center." For conciseness [*syntomia*], [one should make use of] the opposite: the word for the definition. 2. And if something is shameful or inappropriate, if the shame is in the definition, use the word, and if in the word, use the definition. 3. And make something clear by metaphor and epithets, while guarding against the poetic. 4. And make the singular plural, as poets do: though there is a single harbor, they say "to Achaean harbors," and "the tablet's many-leaved folds."[75] 5. And do not join [words with a single definite article] but use one with each: *tēs gynaikos tēs hēmeteras;* but for conciseness the opposite: *tēs hēmeteras gynaikos.*[76] 6. And speak [expansively] with a conjunction but if concisely, without a conjunction, yet not without grammatical connection: for example, "having gone and having conversed" compared with "having gone, I conversed." **[1408a]** 7. Antimachus'[77] technique of describing something on the basis of properties it does not have is also useful; he applies it to Teumessos [in the passage beginning], "There is a a windy little hill . . ." Amplification of this sort can go on indefinitely.[78] What it is not can be said of things good and bad, whichever is useful. This is the source of words the poets introduce such as *stringless* or *lyreless* music, for they apply privatives. This is popular when expressed in metaphors by analogy; for example, the trumpet is "lyreless music."

---

75. Of a tablet made up of only two pieces of thin wood, jointed together loosely.

76. Cope captures the difference in English by *that wife of ours* as contrasted with *our wife.*

77. Greek poet of about 400 B.C., author of an epic on the Theban cycle.

78. Cf. Christian amplification of the glory of God or Christ: without beginning or end, ineffable, unbegotten, etc.

Chapter 7: To Prepon, *or Appropriateness, Propriety*

■ The beginning of chapter 2 identified appropriateness of
style to subject as a necessary quality of good speaking or
writing. In this chapter Aristotle explains the concept more
fully.

1. The *lexis* will be appropriate if it expresses emotion and
character and is proportional to the subject matter. 2. Proportion
exists if there is neither discussion of weighty matters[79] in a casual
way nor shoddy things solemnly and if ornament is not attached to
a shoddy word. Otherwise, the result seems comedy, like the
[tragic] poetry Cleophon composes. Some of what he used to say is
like calling a fig "Madame." 3. Emotion is expressed if the style, in
the case of insolence (*hybris*), is that of an angry man; in the case
of impious and shameful things, if it is that of one who is indignant
and reluctant even to say the words; in the case of admirable
things, [if they are spoken] respectfully; but if [the things] are
pitiable, [if they are spoken] in a submissive manner; and similarly
in other cases. 4. The proper *lexis* also makes the matter credible:
the mind [of the listener] draws a false inference of the truth of
what a speaker says because they [in the audience] feel the same
about such things, so they think the facts to be so, even if they are
not as the speaker represents them; 5. and the hearer suffers along
with the pathetic speaker, even if what he says amounts to nothing.
As a result, many overwhelm their hearers by making noise.
    6. Proof from signs is expressive of character, because there is
an appropriate style for each genus and moral state. By *genus* I
mean things like age—boy, man, old man—or woman and man or
Spartan and Thessalian and by *moral state* [*hexis*] the principles by
which someone is the kind of person he is in life; 7. for lives do not
have the same character in accordance with [each and] every moral
state.[80] If, then, a person speaks words appropriate to his moral

---

79. Lit., those with "good *onkos.*"

80. Aristotle here employs terminology also seen in his later ethical writings, esp.
Nicomachean Ethics 2.1. *Hexis* is acquired moral principle that has become a permanent habit of character. Note its connection with education in the example given.

state, he will create a sense of character. A rustic and an educated person would not say the same thing nor [say it] in the same way. Listeners react also to expressions speechwriters[81] use to excess: "Who does not know?" "Everybody knows . . ." The listener agrees out of embarrassment in order to share in the [alleged] feelings of all others.

8. Opportune or inopportune usage is a factor common to all [three] species [of rhetoric]. **[1408b]** 9. There is a commonly used defense for every hyperbole: the speaker should preempt criticism;[82] for something seems true when the speaker does not conceal what he is doing. 10. Further, do not use all analogous effects [of sound and sense] together; for thus the hearer is tricked. I mean, for example, if the words are harsh, do not deliver them with a harsh voice and countenance. Otherwise, what you are doing is evident. But if sometimes one feature is present, sometimes not, you accomplish the same thing without being noticed. But if, as a result, gentle things are said harshly and harsh things gently, the result is unpersuasive.

11. Double words and frequent epithets and especially unfamiliar words suit one speaking passionately; for it is excusable that an angry person calls a wrong "heaven-high" or "monstrous." And [this can be done] when a speaker holds the audience in his control and causes them to be stirred either by praise or blame or hate or love, as Isocrates does at the end of the *Panegyricus:* "[How great the] fame and name . . ." and [earlier] "who endured . . . [to see the city made desolate"].[83] Those who are empassioned mouth such utterances, and audiences clearly accept them because they are in a similar mood. That is why [this emotional style] is suited to

---

81. Logographers, i.e., professional writers (like Lysias) of speeches for clients to deliver in the law courts.

82. The better manuscripts give *should add a censure;* but ancient rhetoricians (e.g., Quintilian 8.3.37) advised anticipation ("You may not want to believe what I am going to say, but. . . ."); some scribe may have wrongly inserted the single letter that makes the difference in meaning.

83. Reference to Isocrates' *Panegyricus* 186 and 96, respectively (c. 380 B.C.). But Aristotle perhaps misquoted from memory: manuscripts of the *Rhetoric* read *phēmē de kai gnōmē* (fame and reputation), whereas Isocrates' text has *phēmēn de kai mnēmēn* (fame and memory); rhyme (*homoeoteleuton*) contributes to the effect in both cases.

poetry, too, for poetry is inspired. It should be used as described—
or in mockery,[84] as Gorgias did and as in the *Phaedrus*.[85]

Chapter 8: Rhythm in Prose

■ A sense of rhythm begins to be evident in some Greek
prose of the late fifth century, but real feeling for it is first
seen in the writings of Plato, Isocrates, and Demosthenes in
the fourth. Demosthenes in particular (though ignored by
Aristotle) avoids a succession of short syllables. The reader
needs to keep in mind that Greek (and Latin) meter was
quantitative, based on long and short syllables, not on stress
accent.

1. The form of the language[86] should be neither metrical nor
unrhymical. The former is unpersuasive (for it seems to have been
shaped) and at the same time also diverts attention; for it causes
[the listener] to pay attention to when the same foot will come
again—as when children anticipate the call of heralds (in the law
courts): "Whom does the freedman choose as his sponsor?" [The
children call out] "Cleon!" 2. But what is unrhythmical is unlimited; and there should be a limit, but not by use of meter, for the
unlimited is unpleasant and unknowable.[87] And all things are limited by number. In the case of the form of language, number is
rhythm, of which meters are segments. 3. Thus, speech should
have rhythm but not meter; for the latter will be a poem. The
rhythm should not be exact; this will be achieved if it is [regular]
only up to a point.[88]

84. *Eirōneia;* see book 2, n. 22.

85. Cf. Gorgias's mockery of the swallow, cited above in 3.3.4; Plato, *Phaedrus*
231d, 241e.

86. *To schēma tēs lexeōs,* the term adopted by later rhetoricians for "figure of
speech," but here the language's metrical configuration.

87. A basic Aristotelian principle in metaphysics, physics, and other sciences; cf.
Metaphysics 2.4.999a27.

88. Prose rhythm, like other aspects of style, should be a mean between the
inartistic and the poetic.

4. Of rhythms, the heroic [dactylic hexameter] is solemn and not conversational and needs musical intonation;[89] the iambic by itself is the language of the many; thus, all people most often speak in iambics. But [formal speech] should be dignified and moving. The trochaic meter is rather too much of a comic dance, as is clear from trochaic tetrameters; for they are a tripping rhythm. **[1409a]** What remains is the *paian;* it came into use beginning with Thrasymachus, though at the time people did not recognize what it was. The paean is a third kind of rhythm, related to those under discussion; for it has the ratio of three to two [three short syllables and one long, the latter equal in time to two beats], whereas the others are one to one [the heroic, with one long syllable and two shorts] or two to one [iambic and trochaic, a long and a short or a short and a long, respectively]. And one-and-a-half [i.e., the proportion of three to two] is the mean ratio and this is what a paean is. 5. The other rhythms should be avoided for the reasons given and because they are [poetic] meters; and the paean should be adopted, for it alone of the rhythms mentioned is not a meter, and thus its presence most escapes notice. As it is, only the opening paean is in use, but it is necessary to distinguish the opening from the closing. 6. There are two species of paean opposite to each other, of which one [called a first paean] is suitable for an opening, as it is now used.[90] This is the one that begins with a long syllable and ends with three shorts: *Dālŏgĕnĕs eite Lukian* and *khrȳsĕŏkŏma Hekate pai Dios;* the other [called a fourth paean] is the opposite, where three shorts begin and a long ends: *mĕtă dĕ gān hŭdătă ōkĕŏnŏn ēphănĭsĕ nūx.* This makes an ending, for a short syllable [at the end] makes the expression seem cut short.[91] It should instead be cut off with a long syllable and be a clear termination, not through the action of a scribe or the

---

89. That is, it is chanted. In Aristotle's time rhapsodes no longer used a lyre.

90. Aristotle speaks as though the paean was frequently found in formal prose in the fourth century, but in fact it is rather rare. He does not consider the cretic (long–short–long) which has the same proportions and is the commonest ancient prose rhythm. The examples of paeans cited in the next sentence are from poetry, probably from Simonides of Ceos. Note that the third example consists of three paeans.

91. Some later rhetoricians, however, regard the last syllable of a sentence as automatically lengthened by position, as is the last syllable of a verse; cf. Cicero, *Orator* 217 and Quintilian's comment, 9.4.93.

presence of a marginal mark[92] but through the rhythm. 7. That *lexis* should, therefore, be rhythmical and not unrhythmical and what rhythms make it well rhythmed and what they are like has been said.

Chapter 9: Periodic Style

■ This chapter is somewhat difficult. One problem is the extent to which Aristotle thinks of a period as essentially a rhythmical unit; he says it has magnitude, is limited, and has number, he equates it with a line of verse in section 4, and the need for rhythm might be assumed from the previous chapter; but he does not here specifically speak of rhythms. See Fowler 1982, which denies that rhythm is involved, and, on the other side of the question, Adamik 1984. The most conspicuous features of a period and of its subdivision called a *kōlon* seem to be some syntactical completion (at least a complete phrase), unitary thought, and length that is a mean between "too short" and "too long," in order for the hearer to grasp the thought easily. Aristotle does not use the word *period* to mean one of the long complex sentences of Isocrates (or later Cicero) but quotes *parts* of Isocrates' complex sentences as good examples of periods. Thus, he would apparently view a long Isocratean sentence as made up of several periods.

1. The *lexis* [of formal speech and artistic prose] is necessarily either *strung-on*[93] and given unity by connection, like the preludes in dithyrambs, or *turned-down*[94] and like the antistrophes of the

---

92. *Paragraphē*. Though written punctuation was undeveloped, a mark was often made in the margin to indicate the change of speaker in a dramatic text.

93. Or "running" (*eiromenē*); strung together with connectives. Though this is seen in what is called *paratactic* sentence structure such as "We met, and we went for a walk, and we then had a drink," Aristotle is probably thinking of smaller units, as in polysyndeton; for otherwise it is not the opposite of his description of periodic style.

94. *Katestrammenē*, the periodic style.

ancient poets. 2. The strung-on style is the ancient one;[95] for in the past all used it, but now not many do. I call that strung-on which has no end in itself except in so far as the thought is completed. It is unpleasant because it is unlimited, for all wish to foresee the end.[96] Thus, as they complete the course [runners] pant and are exhausted; for they do not tire while the goal is in sight ahead. 3. This, then, is the strung-on style of *lexis,* but the turned-down style is that in periods. I call a period [*periodos*] an expression [*lexis*] having a beginning and end in itself and a magnitude easily taken in at a glance.[97] **[1409b]** This is pleasant and easily understood, pleasant because opposed to the unlimited and because the hearer always thinks he has hold of something, in that it is always limited by itself, whereas to have nothing to foresee or attain is unpleasant. And it is easily understood because easily retained in the mind. This is because utterance in periods has number, which is the most easily retained thing. Thus, all people remember verses better than prose;[98] for it has number by which it is measured. 4. And a period should also be complete in thought and not cut off, as it is in the iambic line:

Calydon [is] this land, of Pelops' soil . . .[99]

95. The manuscripts insert here the opening of Herodotus' *Histories:* "Of Herodotus of Thurii this is the account of the investigation." Kassel double-brackets the quotation as something added by Aristotle to the otherwise completed text. Though Herodotus' work in general is an example of the strung-on style, the opening sentence does not illustrate the use of connectives.

96. Compare what is said about unrhymical prose in the previous chapter.

97. Compare the concept of unity of plot in *Poetics* 7; but note that a period, unlike a plot, lacks a "middle." *Periodos,* from *peri* (around) and *hodos* (road), another of Aristotle's visual metaphors, suggests a circular motion; but, as the examples cited show, the technique is more one of antithesis and balance than circularity. Aristotle may not have originated the usage of *periodos* as a stylistic term; the Byzantine encyclopedia *Suda* attributes it to Thrasymachus. Note that an Aristotelian period is not a long sentence with subordinate clauses but a single clause or phrase, often within a longer sentence.

98. Lit. "what is heaped up, indescriminate."

99. Attributed by the manuscripts to Sophocles, but actually the first line of Euripides' *Meleager.* Aristotle thinks of a period, or its members, as equivalent to a line of verse; the line is metrically complete, but incomplete in thought because of the slight pause at the end. The next line, however, continues without grammatical break, making the geography clear: "Alas, across the straits facing pleasant plains, woe, woe!" (Demetrius, *On Style* 58).

Because of the line division it is possible to misunderstand the meaning, as though in this quotation Calydon were in the Peloponnesus.

5. A period is either divided into cola[100] or simple. *Lexis* in cola is completed and divided and easily uttered by the breath, not in its division but in the whole. A colon is one of the two parts of a period. I call a period simple when it has only one colon. 6. The cola and the periods should be neither stubby nor long. A short one often causes the hearer a bump; for when [his mind] is rushing toward what is to come and its measure, of which he has his own definition, if he is pulled up short by the speaker's pausing, he necessarily trips, as it were, at the abrupt close. Long ones cause him to be left behind, as do those walkers who go past the [expected] turning point; for they, too, leave behind their fellow strollers. Similarly, long periods turn into a *logos*[101] and are like a prelude. This is the source of the parody [of Hesiod, *Works and Days* 265–66] by Democritus of Chios, attacking Melanippides on the ground that he was composing preludes rather than antistrophes:

> A man does wrong to himself when he does it to another,
> And a long prelude is the worst thing for a composer.

Much the same applies to those who speak long cola, while those that are too short do not constitute a period. Thus, they drag the hearer headlong.

7. *Lexis* in cola is either divided or contrasted. It is divided in this example: "Often have I admired those organizing panegyric festivals and those instituting athletic contests." It is contrasted when in each colon opposite lies with opposite or the same is yoked with its opposites, **[1410a]** for example, "They helped both, both those who stayed and those who followed; to the latter they provided more than they had had at home and for the former they left enough behind." *Staying* and *following* are opposites, as are *enough* and *more*. [Another example is] "And so both to those

---

100. A colon (the visual image is that of the limbs of the body) is either a clause or a phrase that has some grammatical independence. A period may be made up of either one or two cola; as sec. 7 will explain, if there are two they may be parallel or contrasted.

101. *Logos* can mean anything from a word to a sentence to a speech but here seems roughly equivalent to "introductory remarks." Cf. its use to refer to the prooemium and narration in Gorgias's *Helen* 5 in Appendix I.A.

needing money and those wishing to enjoy it . . . ," where *enjoy* is opposed to acquisition. And again, [other examples are] "It happens often in these circumstances that the wise fail and the foolish succeed" [and] "Straightway they were thought worthy of meeds of valor and not much later they took command of the sea" [and] "To sail through the land, and to march through the sea, yoking the Hellespont and digging through Athos . . ." [and] "And though citizens by nature, by law deprived of their city . . ." [and] "Some of them miserably perished, and others were shamefully saved." And [another is] "Privately to use barbarian servants, and collectively to overlook the many who were enslaved . . ." [and] ". . . either while living to hold it or when dead to loose it."[102] And [another is] what someone said to Pitholaus and Lycophron[103] in the lawcourt: "When these men were at home, they sold you, but coming to you now, they have been bought." All these examples do what has been said. 8. Such a *lexis* is pleasing because opposites are most knowable and more knowable when put beside each other and because they are like a syllogism, for refutation [*elenkos*] is a bringing together of contraries.[104]

■ Up to this point in the chapter Aristotle has not used the word *antithesis* (some other translations paraphrastically insert it) even though some of the examples are clearly antithetical, but now he speaks of antithesis as the sort of thing he is discussing. For his readers it was hardly a technical term, since the meaning was clear from its two roots, as in *opposition*. It was, however, one of the characteristics of the prose style of Gorgias, though that sophist is not here mentioned; and Aristotle procedes to discuss other examples of what have come to be known as the Gorgianic figures. Note that Aristotle has no term for "figure of speech."

102. The quotations in this section are all from Isocrates' *Panegyricus* (1, 35, 41, 48, 72, 89, 105, 149, 181, and 186, respectively) but apparently from memory, since they are not very accurate. The most famous is the reference to Xerxes' invasion of Greece in 480 B.C., when he built a bridge of rafts across the Hellespont and dug a canal for his ships through the isthmus of Athos.

103. Assassins of Alexander of Pherai in 358 B.C. The text is uncertain, but the antithesis clear.

104. Cf. what is said about the refutative enthymeme in 2.23.30.

9. *Antithesis,* then, is one such thing, as is *parisōsis* if the cola are equal [in the number of syllables], and *paromoiōsis* if each colon has similar extremities [in sound]. This can occur either at the beginning or at the end [of the colon]. At the beginning it always takes the form of [similar] complete words,[105] but at the end it may consist of [the same] final syllables or [the same] grammatical form or the same word. At a beginning [of a colon] are found such things as Agron *gar elaben* argon *par'autou* and Doretoi *t'epelonto* pararretoi *t'epeesin,*[106] at an end *Oiēthes̄ an auton ou paidion* tetokenai, *all'auton paidion* gegonenai or *en plaistais de* phrontisi *kai en elakhistais* elpisin[107] and inflexion of the same word: (*Axios de stathēnai* khalkous, *oukh axios ōn* khalkou?)[108] and recurrence of the same word ("You spoke of him in life meanly and now you write of him meanly"). [One also finds] use of the same [concluding] syllable: "What would you have suffered so striking if you had seen the man shirking?" It is possible for one example to have all these features—for the same [colon] to be an antithesis and *parison* and *homoeoteleuton.*[109] **[1410b]** 10. The beginnings of periods have mostly been enumerated in the *Theodectea.*[110] There are also false antitheses, for example the one [the comic poet] Epicharmus wrote:

> Sometimes I was in their house, sometimes I was with them.

105. This resembles what is later known as the figure anaphora, but Aristotle's example (*Agron,* etc.) is a play on similar words rather than repetition of the same word: "*Land* they took, *unworked,* from him." It probably comes from a lost play of Aristophanes.

106. *Iliad* 9.526.

107. *Dōretoi* etc. = "Ready for *gifts* they were and ready for *persuasion* by words," from *Iliad* 9.526; *oiēthēs* etc. = "You would have thought him not to have *begotten* a child but himself to have *become* one"; *en plaistias* etc. = "in the greatest *cares* and the smallest *hopes.*" Sources of the last two examples are unknown.

108. "Worthy of being set up *in bronze* but not worth a coin *of bronze.*" Source unknown.

109. *Parison* is another name for *parisōsis* (sec. 9). *Homoioteleuton* is *paramoiōsis* at the end of cola.

110. Probably Aristotle's own lost survey of the rhetoric of Theodectes, who was repeatedly quoted in 2.23.

Chapter 10: Asteia, *or Urbanities, and* Pro Ommatōn
Poiein, *or Bringing-Before-the-Eyes, Visualization; with
Further Discussion of Metaphor*

■ *Astu* means "town," usually in the physical rather than the
political sense, the latter being *polis.* In contrast to the country, towns cultivate a certain elegance and grace; thus, *asteia,*
"things of the town," came to mean elegance of speech, wit,
good taste. Latin *urbanitas* (from *urbs,* "city") and thus English "urbanity," have similar meanings. Cf. also "polite"
from *polis* and "civil" from *civis* (citizen).

1. Since these things have been defined, there is need to say
what are the sources of urbanities [*asteia*] and well-liked expressions [*eudokimounta*].[111] Now it is possible to create them by natural talent or by practice, but to show what they are belongs to this
study. Let us say, then, what they are and let us enumerate them
thoroughly, and let the following be our first principle [*arkhē*].
2. To learn easily is naturally pleasant to all people,[112] and
words signify something, so whatever words create knowledge in
us are the pleasantest. Glosses are unintelligible, but we know
words in their prevailing meaning [*kyria*]. Metaphor most brings
about learning; for when he[113] calls old age "stubble," he creates
understanding and knowledge through the genus, since both old
age and stubble are [species of the genus of] things that have lost
their bloom. 3. Now the similes of the poets also do the same thing;
and thus, if they do it well, they seem urbane. (A simile is, as was
said earlier, a metaphor differing in how it is set out; thus, it is less

111. Dufour and Wartelle (1960–73) translates *asteia* as *bons mots. Eudokimounta*
are literally expressions that are "well thought of," hence "popular"; the audience is
pleased by them.
112. Cf. the first sentence of the *Metaphysics:* "All human beings by nature desire
to know." But note that in rhetoric Aristotle emphasizes that pleasure comes from
learning *easily;* cf. sec. 4. As in the case of enthymemes (2.22.3), demands on a
popular audience should be minimal.
113. Homer, in *Odyssey* 4.213.

pleasing because longer and because it does not say that this *is* that,[114] nor does [the listener's] mind seek to understand this.)

4. Those things are necessarily urbane, both in *lexis* and in enthymemes, which create quick learning in our minds. That is why superficial enthymemes are not popular [with audiences] (by *superficial* I mean those that are altogether clear and which there is no need to ponder), nor [are]those which, when stated, are unintelligible, but those [are popular] of which there is either immediate understanding when they are spoken, even if that was not previously existing, or the thought follows soon after; for [then] some kind of learning takes place, but in neither of the other cases. 5. In terms of the thought of what is said, such kinds of enthymemes are well liked; in terms of the *lexis*, [an expression is urbane] on the one hand because of shaped language,[115] if it is spoken with some contrast (for example, "regarding the *peace* shared by others as a *war* against their own interests,[116] where peace is opposed to war) 6. or on the other hand because of the words, if they have metaphor—and metaphor that is not strange[117] (for that would be difficult to perceive) nor superficial (for that causes nothing to be experienced). Furthermore, [urbanity is achieved] by means of bringing-before-the-eyes [*pro ommatōn poiein*, or visualization]; for things should be seen as being done rather than as in the future.[118] [To achieve urbanity in style] one should thus aim at three things: metaphor, antithesis, actualization [*energeia*].

---

114. Aristotle, unlike later classical rhetoricians, thus implies that metaphor is a form of predication, a major contention of Paul Ricoeur in *The Rule of Metaphor* (1977).

115. *Schēmata,* which becomes the word for "figures" of speech.

116. Isocrates, *Philippus* 73, s'ightly misquoted. The *Philippus* was published in 346 B.C. and quotation of it here and elsewhere seems to be the latest historical reference in book 3.

117. *Allotrios;* but according to *Poetics* 21.7 (see Appendix I.E), every metaphor is *allotrios* (alien).

118. What is meant is the use of the present tense to describe future action; but the use of the "historic" present to describe past action is commoner. Through the rest of the chapter Aristotle uses *bringing-before-the-eyes* as a technical term. He will define it at the beginning of chap. 11.

7. Of the four kinds of metaphor,[119] those by analogy are most well liked, **[1411a]** as when Pericles said that the young manhood killed in the war vanished from the city as though someone took the spring from the year.[120] And [another example of analogy is] Leptines' speaking about the Lacedaimonians, that he would not allow [the Athenians] to stand by while Greece was deprived of one of its "two eyes." And [another is that] when Chares was pressing to submit his financial account in the Olynthian war for approval,[121] Cephisodotos said he was trying to have his account approved while "strangling the state at the throat." And once, urging on the Athenians when they had secured supplies for a campaign to Euboea, he said they should march out "by the decree of Miltiades."[122] And Iphicrates, when the Athenians had made a truce with Epidaurus and the neighboring coast, complained that they had deprived themselves of "traveling expenses" for the war. And Peitholaos called the Paralus[123] "the bludgeon of the people" and Sestus "the baker's board of the Peiraeus."[124] And Pericles demanded the removal of Aegina, "the eyesore of the Piraeus." And Moerocles said he was no more wicked than ———(naming someone of the upper class); for that person was wicked "at thirty-three-and-a-third-percent interest," he himself "at ten." And Anaxandrides' iambic line about the daughters who were slow in marrying:

The maidens, I note, are in arrears in their marriages.

119. Genus to species, species to genus, species to species, or from analogy (proportional); cf. *Poetics* 21.7 in Appendix I.E.

120. In modern terminology a simile, but Aristotle has identified simile as a form of metaphor. Quoted in slightly different form in 1.7.34; see book 1, n. 147.

121. Probably about 347 B.C., when Aristotle left Athens, a relatively late reference for book 3.

122. The usual explanation is "without further planning and preparation," as Miltiades is supposed to have decreed at the time of the Persian invasion in 490 B.C. Some editors emend the sentence to read "to secure supplies for a campaign in Euboea after they arrived there," but this reflects the assumed meaning of the phrase. Demosthenes (*Against the Embassy* 303) uses "the decree of Miltiades" to mean an historical call to action against enemy threats.

123. The ceremonial ship of the Athenian state.

124. The city of Sestus had a strategic position on the trade route supplying grain from the Black Sea to the port of Athens. Except for Pericles, the Athenian politicians mentioned in this section were contemporaries of Aristotle, and he may have heard them speak.

And [another example is] the remark of Polyeuctes against the paralytic Speusippus, that he couldn't keep quiet though "bound by fate in a pillory of disease." And Cephisodotus used to call warships "colored millstones," and [Diogenes] the Cynic called fast-food shops, "the Attic common mess." Aeson, moreover, said they had "poured" the city into Sicily;[125] for this is a metaphor, and bringing-before-the-eyes. And [his phrase] "so that Greece cried aloud" is in a certain way metaphor, and a bringing-before-the-eyes. And [so is] the way Cephisodotus demanded that they not make the town meetings *syndromas*.[126] And Isocrates [provides another example] in regard to "those running together" in festivals.[127] And [consider] what is found in the Funeral Oration that "it was proper at the tomb" of those dying at Salamis for Greece "to cut her hair in mourning, since freedom was being buried with their valor."[128] If he had said it was proper to shed tears since their valor was being buried, it would be a metaphor and bringing-before-the-eyes, but the words "freedom with valor" provide an antithesis. **[1411b]** And when Iphicrates said, "My path of words is through the midst of Chares' actions," it was a metaphor by analogy, and "through the midst of" is bringing-before-the-eyes. And to say, "Call dangers to the aid of dangers" is bringing-before-the-eyes and metaphor. And [consider] Lycoleon speaking on behalf of Chabrias: "not ashamed of his suppliant attitude in that bronze statue"; it was a metaphor at the time it was spoken, but not at all times, but it was bringing-before-the-eyes,[129] for [then] when he was in danger, the statue [seemed to] supplicate, the lifeless for the living, the memorial of his deeds for the city–state. And [another example is] "in every way *practicing* lowly thinking";[130] for "to practice" is to increase something. And [another is]

---

125. In 414–413 B.C.

126. "The running together of a mob," a play on *synklētous* (duly called).

127. *Philippus* 12; see n. 116.

128. From Lysias 2.60; but the reference there is to the battle of Aegospotamos (405 B.C.), not to Salamis.

129. Lycoleon pointed at the bronze statue of the kneeling Chabrias visible from the court. The statue commemorated his ordering his troops to await the enemy on their knees.

130. Isocrates, *Panegyricus* 151.

that "God kindled the mind as a light in the soul"; for both make
something clear. [Another is] "For we do not settle wars, but post-
pone them"; both postponement and a peace of this sort are [a
species of] delaying. And [another is] to say that treaties are a
much better "trophy" than those won in wars;[131] for a trophy honors a moment and one success, while treaties apply to the whole
war; both are signs of a victory. And [another is] that cities give
"great financial account" in the censure of mankind; for a financial
account is a legal form of damages. Thus, that urbanities come
from metaphor by analogy and by bringing-before-the-eyes has
been explained.

Chapter 11: Continued Discussion of Bringing-Before-the-Eyes; Energeia, or Actualization; the Psychology of Metaphor and Its Similarity to Philosophy; Proverbs; Hyperbole.

■ This chapter completes Aristotle's discussion of devices of
style that defamiliarize language and explains why they do so.
The explanation is consistent with his cognitive psychology as
found in other works, including *Poetics* and *Nicomachean Ethics:* the hearer "sees" something in a different way and takes
pleasure in learning. Though Aristotle has no concept of "figures" of thought or speech, some of what he discusses here
corresponds to, but did not directly influence, the discussion
of figures in later rhetorical treatises. Note the emphasis on
the visual, which is characteristic of Aristotle. Paul Ricoeur
has called the beginning of this chapter "the most enigmatic
passage of the *Rhetoric*"; see Ricoeur 1977, 42 and his further
discussion, pp. 307–9.

1. But it is necessary to say what we mean by bringing-before-
the-eyes and what makes this occur. 2. I call those things "before the
eyes" that signify things engaged in an activity. For example, to say

131. Cf. Isocrates, *Panegyricus* 180.

that a good man is "foursquare"[132] is a metaphor, for both are complete; but it does not signify activity [*energeia*].[133] But the phrase "having his prime of life in full bloom"[134] is *energeia,* as is "you, like an *apheton*"[135] and "now then the Greeks darting forward on their feet."[136] *Darting* is actualization and metaphor; for he means "quickly." And [energeia is,] as Homer often uses it, making the lifeless living through the metaphor. 3. In all his work he gains his fame by creating activity, for example, in the following:

> Then to the plain rolled the ruthless stone[137]

and "the arrow flew" and [also of an arrow] "eager to fly" and [of spears] "They stood in the ground longing to take their fill of flesh," **[1412a]** and "The point sped eagerly through his breast."[138] In all of these something seems living through being actualized, for being "ruthless" and "longing" and the other examples constitute *energeia.* He applied these by using metaphor by analogy; for as the stone is to Sisyphus, so is the "shameless" one to the one "shamefully" treated.[139] 4. He does the same to lifeless things in his wellliked similes:

> Arched, foam-crested, some in front, but others upon others.[140]

He makes everything move and live, and *energeia* is motion.

132. Aristotle is probably thinking of the occurrence of the word in a poem by Simonides of Ceos (fr. 5).

133. The English cognate is *energy.* As a rhetorical term *energeia* may be translated "actualization" or "vivification." It is sometimes, but not always, "personification" and should be distinguished from *enargeia,* which means "clearness" or "distinctiveness." Cf. Eden 1986, 71–75.

134. Isocrates, *Philippus* 10; see n. 116.

135. "An animal allowed to range at will" (Isocrates, *Philippus* 127); see n. 116.

136. Euripides, *Iphigenia at Aulis* 80.

137. *Odyssey* 9.598.

138. The examples are from *Iliad* 13.587, 4.126, 9.574, and 15.541, respectively. Note that what seemed to Aristotle to be metaphors are personifications that were taken literally by the archaic mind.

139. In the Homeric passage *anaides* implies "ruthless, unfeeling"; but Aristotle takes it in its literal meaning of "shameless" and here substitutes *anaiskhynton,* "being shameless," as its equivalent.

140. *Iliad* 13.799, where it is part of a simile comparing battle to waves of the sea.

5. As was said earlier, metaphors should be transferred from things that are related but not obviously so, as in philosophy, too, it is characteristic of a well-directed mind to observe the likeness even in things very different. Thus, Archytas [the Pythagorean philosopher] said that an arbiter and an altar were the same thing; for one who has been wronged flies to both. Or [another example is] if someone said that an anchor and a rope hung from a hook are the same thing, for both are the same, but they differ in that one is hung from above and one from below. And to say that [the allotments of land in] cities "have been equalized"[141] is the same thing in widely differing cases: the equality is in the surface of land and the powers [assigned to each citizen].

6. Urbanities in most cases come through metaphor and from an added surprise;[142] for it becomes clearer [to the listener] that he learned something different from what he believed, and his mind seems to say, "How true, and I was wrong." The urbanity of epigrams derives from their not meaning what is [literally] said, for example that of Stesichorus that "the cicadas will sing to themselves from the ground."[143] Good riddles are pleasing for the same reason; for there is learning, and they are spoken in metaphor, as is what Theodorus calls *ta kaina legein*.[144] But this occurs when there is a paradox and not, as he says, in opposition to previous opinion; rather it is like the bogus word coinages in jests. Jibes involving change of a letter [i.e., puns] also have this effect, for they are deceptive. It occurs too in verses when they do not end as the listener expected: "He came on, having under his feet—blisters." The listener was expecting *sandals*. [To be effective,] the point should be clear as soon as the word is said. Changes of letter [as in a pun] make the speaker mean not what he says but what the word plays on, like the remark of Theo-

141. Perhaps a reference to Isocrates, *Philippus* 40; see n. 116.

142. This is sometimes now called "linguistic impertinence," which is then reduced to "pertinence" in the mind of the reader.

143. The metaphorical meaning is that the land will be devasted. Demetrius (*On Style* 99) attributes this to the tyrant Dionysius of Syracuse.

144. "Saying new things"; the rhetorical handbooks of Theodorus of Byzantium are mentioned also in 2.23.28 and by Plato (*Phaedrus* 266e6).

dorus[145] to Nikon the harpist, *Thrattei se*. He pretends to say, "It disturbs you" and deceives, for he means something different. Thus it is pleasing to the learner, **[1412b]** but if the latter does not understand that Nikon is a Thracian [barbarian], it will not seem urbane. And [consider] the remark *Boulei auton persai*.[146]

7. It is necessary for both examples to be said in the right way. Similarly also with urbanities, as in saying that the *arkē* [command] of the sea was not the *arkhē* [beginning] of misfortunes for the Athenians, for they benefited; or as Isocrates says,[147] that the *arkhē* [empire] was the *arkhē* [beginning] of misfortunes; for in both cases someone says what would not be expected, and its truth is recognized. To say that an *arkhē* is an *arkhē* is not very clever, but he means the words in different senses; and [in the first example the speaker] does not negate the *arkhē* he has spoken of but uses the word in a different sense.[148]

8. In all these cases, if a word is introduced appropriately, either as a homonym or a metaphor, it is done well. For example, [consider] "Mr. Baring is unbearable."[149] The homonym is negated, but appropriately if he is unpleasant. And [consider] "You should be no more strange than a stranger," or no more than you should be. Or again [consider]: "It is not necessary for the stranger always to be strange," for one word[150] is used in different senses. Similar is the admired line of Anaxandrides: "Good it is to die before doing anything worthy of death." That is the same as saying someone is worthy of dying when not worthy of dying or worthy of dying when not being worthy of death or not doing anything wor-

145. Perhaps the rhetorician mentioned above, more likely the actor mentioned in 3.2.4. The text (and thus translation and meaning of the pun) is not certain.

146. Lit. "You wish to destroy him." Unfortunately, Aristotle does not explain the two meanings. By analogy with the previous pun, *persai* is usually interpreted to allude to Persian women. There is perhaps a play on the two words in Aeschylus, *Persians* 178.

147. *Philippus* 61 and *On the Peace* 101.

148. Sometimes, as in the *boulei* quotation above, Aristotle does not offer adequate explanation; sometimes, as here, he seems to overexplain something. This reflects the origin of the text in his own notes, which have not been given a polished revision for publication.

149. Lit. "Anáschetus [as a personal name] is unbearable [*anaskhetós*]."

150. *Xenos* as an adjective = "strange," as a noun = "stranger."

thy of death. 9. The species of the *lexis* in these examples is the same, but in so far as they are spoken concisely and with a contrast, they are the better liked. The cause is that knowledge results more from contrast but is quicker in brief form. 10. There should always be application to the person addressed or [an awareness of] what is rightly said, provided what is said is true and not superficial. It is possible to have one quality [i.e., to be true] without the other [without teaching something in brief, striking form], for example, "One should die while still faultless." But that is not urbane. "A worthy man should marry a worthy woman." But that is not urbane [either]. But it *is,* if both [ideas] are present: "He is worthy to die when not worthy of dying." The more there is in the thought, the more it seems an instance of urbanity, for example, if the words are a metaphor and a metaphor of a certain sort and [if there is] antithesis and *parisosis,*[151] and if it has *energeia.*

11. As has been said above,[152] similes, which are well liked in some way, are also metaphors. They always involve two terms, as does metaphor from analogy. For example, we say the shield is the wine cup of Ares and his bow is a stringless lyre. **[1413a]** Thus, their meaning is not that of the single word, as would be the case if we said the bow is a lyre or the shield a cup. 12. People also make similes this way; for example, a flute-player [can be] compared to an ape[153] or a near-sighted man to a lamp sprinkled with water; for both [eyelids and flame] contract. 13. This is well done when there is metaphor; for it is possible to liken the shield to the cup of Ares and a ruin to the "rag" of a house and to say that Niceratus is a "Philoctetes bound by Pratys," a simile made by Thrasymachus after seeing Niceratus defeated by Pratys in a rhapsode contest, still dishevelled and dirty.[154] If poets do not do this well, they most fail with the public; and if they do it well, they are popular. I mean when they make terms correspond: "He has legs like stringy parsely" [or] "like Philammon boxing the punching ball." All such things are similes, and that similes are metaphors has been repeatedly said.

---

151. Defined at the beginning of chap. 9 as equality in the length of cola.
152. In 3.4.
153. While playing, the flute-player takes a stance that looks like an ape.
154. Like the hero Philoctetes in Sophocles' play.

14. Proverbs [*paroimiai*] are metaphors from species to species. For example, if someone brings home something, believing it is a good thing, and then suffers harm, it is "what the Carpathian says of the hare,"[155] for both experienced what has been described. So the sources and cause of *asteia* have been more or less stated.

15. Effective hyperboles[156] are also metaphors; for example, of a man with a black eye [one might say], "You would have thought him a basket of mulberries"; for his face is somewhat purple, but there is much exaggeration. And in *like* this or that there is hyperbole differing in the form of expression [*lexis*]: "like Philammon boxing the punching ball" (you would think him to be Philammon fighting a sack) "He has legs like stringy parsley" (you would think him to have parsley for legs, so stringy they are). Hyperboles are adolescent, for they exhibit vehemence.[157] (Therefore those in anger mostly speak them:

Not even if he gave me as much as the sand and the dust . . .
But I will not marry the daughter of Agamemmon, son of Atreus,
Not even if she rivals golden Aphrodite in beauty,
And Athene in workmanship.)[158]

[1413b] (The Attic orators especially use this.)[159] Thus, it is inappropriate for an older man to speak [in hyperbole].

Chapter 12: Oral and Written Style; Deliberative, Judicial, and Epideictic Style

■ Aristotle does not make the distinction of the different "characters" or levels of style (*genera dicendi* in Latin)—

155. The modern analogy is perhaps the Australian experience with the introduction of rabbits, which were first thought to be useful but proved devasting to crops.

156. The Greek term means "overshooting" (the mark).

157. The young overdo everything; cf. 2.12.14.

158. *Iliad* 9.385 and 388–89. Kassel double-brackets the parenthesis as a late addition by Aristotle.

159. This sentence is in the manuscripts but deleted by some editors. If it is genuine, Aristotle was probably not in Athens when he wrote it, placing it between 347 and 335 B.C. The orators "at Athens" are also referred to in 3.17.10.

grand, middle, and plain—that are a feature of later Greek and Latin rhetorical theory; but in this chapter he partly foreshadows that development by looking at style in an overall sense of what is appropriate for each of the three species of rhetoric as discussed in book 1, and he also considers the stylistic differences between written and oral compositions. Before the end of the fifth century B.C. most oratory was extempore and not published in written form; but sophists like Gorgias began the writing and publishing of epideictic speeches, and this was continued by Isocrates. In judicial oratory, speechwriters (*logographoi*)—of whom Antiphon is perhaps the earliest and Lysias the most famous—had made a profession for themselves in ghostwriting speeches for clients to memorize and deliver in court, and some of these speeches were published. By Aristotle's time, political orators, including Demosthenes, were publishing written, polished versions of speeches they had earlier delivered. Though writing had been introduced into Greece in the ninth century, "publication" long remained a matter of oral presentation. The period from the middle of the fifth to the middle of the fourth centuries B.C. has been called the time of a "literate revolution" in Greece, comparable to the changes brought in the fifteenth century by the introduction of printing and in the twentieth century by the computer, for reliance on writing greatly increased in this period and affected the perception of texts; see Havelock 1982 and Ong 1982. Important Greek texts dealing with the effect of writing include the end of Plato's *Phaedrus,* Plato's *Seventh Epistle* (341c–342a) and the essay by Alcidamas, *On Those Writing Written Speeches* (translation in Matson, Rollinson, and Sousa 1990, 37–42). Rhetoric gave increased attention to the study of written composition. The radical effects of greater reliance on writing can, however, be exaggerated; ancient society remained oral to a much greater degree than modern society, and the primary goal of the teaching of rhetoric was consistently an ability to speak in public:

1. One should not forget that a different *lexis* is appropriate for each genus [of rhetoric]. For the written and agonistic[160] [style] are not the same; nor are the demegoric [deliberative] and the dicanic [judicial], and it is necessary to know both. [Debate] consists in knowing how to speak good Greek; [writing] avoids the necessity of silence if one wishes to communicate to others [who are not present], which is the condition of those who do not know how to write. 2. Written style is most exact; the agonistic is very much a matter of delivery. Of the latter there are two species; for one form is ethical, the other emotional. Thus, actors are on the lookout for plays of these sorts, and the poets for these kinds of actors.[161] But poets who write for the reading public are [also] much liked, for example, Chaeremon (for he is as precise as a professional prose writer [*logographos*]) and, among the dithyrambic poets, Licymnius. On comparison, some written works seem thin when spoken, while some speeches of [successful] orators seem amateurish when examined in written form. The cause is that [their style] suits debate. Thus, things that are intended for delivery, when delivery is absent, seem silly, since they are not fulfilling their purpose. For example, *asyndeta*[162] and constant repetition are rightly criticized in writing but not in speaking, and the orators use them; for they lend themselves to oral delivery. 3. But [in speech] it is necessary to speak the same thought in different words; this, as it were, leads the way for the delivery: "He is the one cheating you; he is the one deceiving you; he is the one trying to betray you." This is the sort of thing Philemon the actor used to do in *Old Man's Madness*, [a comedy] by Anaxandrides, when reciting [the passage about] Rhadamanthus and Palamedes and in the *ego* passage in the prologue of *The Pious*. For if one does not act out these lines, it is a case of "the man carrying a beam."[163] Similarly with asyndeta: "I came, I encoun-

160. A speech in an actual debate (*agōn*).

161. Actors seek plays in which there is scope for the expression of character and emotion, and playwrights seek actors who can render their characters vividly.

162. Absence of connective words.

163. Probably a proverb descriptive of awkwardness: the man walks stiffly to keep the beam balanced. But perhaps the point is needless repetition. Diogenes Laertius (6.41) tells a story about Diogenes the Cynic being knocked by a beam. The man carrying it then called out "Look out!" Diogenes replied, "Why? Are you going to hit me again?" See Killeen 1971.

tered, I was begging." 4. For it is necessary to act this out and not to speak it as one talking in the same character and tone. Furthermore, asyndeta have a special characteristic; many things seem to be said at the same time; for the connective makes many things seem one, so that if it is taken away, clearly the opposite results: one thing will be many.[164] Asyndeton thus creates amplification [*auxēsis*]: "I came; I spoke; I besought" (these things seem many), "[but] he overlooked everything I said." **[1414a]** This is Homer's intention in the passage "Nereus, again, from Syme . . . Nereus, son of Aglaïa . . . Nereus who, as the handsomest man . . .";[165] for a man about whom many things are said must necessarily often be named. [Conversely, and wrongly,] people think that if someone is often named there must also be many things to say; thus [Homer] amplified [the importance of Nereus] (though mentioning him only in this passage) and by this fallacy made him memorable, though no account of him is given anywhere later in the poem.

5. The demegoric style[166] seems altogether like shadow-painting;[167] for the greater the crowd, the further the distance of view; thus, exactness is wasted work and the worse in both cases. Speaking in the law courts requires more exactness of detail,[168] and that before a single judge even more, for it is least of all a matter of rhetorical techniques; for what pertains to the subject and what is irrelevant is more easily observed [by a single judge], and controversy is gone, so the judgment is clear. As a result, the same orators are not successful in all these kinds of speeches. Where there is most need of performance, the least exactness is present. This occurs where the voice is important and especially a loud

---

164. As with metaphor, the listener learns something from asyndeton; see Blettner 1983.

165. *Iliad* 2.671–73. Aristotle has no hesitation in identifying the poet's "intent."

166. Cf. sec. 1 above.

167. Outline painting, without detail, intended to be seen at a distance and used for background scenery in the theater; cf. Plato, *Theatetus* 208e and *Parmenides* 165c.

168. As Cope ([1877] 1970) notes on this passage, Aristotle seems to confuse exactness of style with detailed treatment of argument. It is the latter that is important in a judicial situation, and especially before a single judge, as in a monarchy. The reader may wish to ponder how what is said here relates to the remarks in 1.1.10.

voice. The epideictic style is most like writing; for its objective is to be read. And the judicial style second[-most].

6. To make a further requirement of style that it should be pleasant and elevated[169] is superfluous. For why that, rather than chaste or liberal or any other virtue of character? The things discussed will make the style pleasant if the virtue of *lexis* has been rightly defined. For otherwise, what is the point of being clear and not flat, but appropriate?[170] For if it is luxuriant, it is not clear, nor if it is concise. But it is clear that the mean is suitable. And the things mentioned will make style pleasant, if they are well mingled: the conventional and the strange, and rhythm, and persuasiveness from propriety. This concludes the discussion of *lexis,* both in general about all of it and in particular about each genus. It remains to speak about arrangement.

Chapters 13–19; *Taxis,* or Arrangement

■ An effective speech follows a structural pattern; that is, it consists of parts, each performing some function, but joined together into an artistic unity; Plato had called for this in *Phaedrus* 246. How these parts are arranged differs somewhat with the conventions of public address in different societies, the occasion and the speaker's perception of the audience's knowledge of the subject and attitude, and the speaker's individual *ēthos* and style. Speeches in the Homeric poems already illustrate some of the structural patterns taught by later rhetoricians. The first teachers of rhetoric in the Greek world, Corax, Tisias, and their successors, seem to have recommended following a set order of parts in a judicial speech, beginning with an introduction to get the attention and good will of the audience, followed by a narration of the facts in the case, a statement of the speaker's position with reasons why the jury

169. Attributed by Quintilian (4.2.63) to Theodectes but perhaps originating with Isocrates.
170. The virtue of style as discussed in chap. 2.

should believe it, and a conclusion summarizing the argument; but some handbook writers of the fifth and fourth century exercised their originality in identifying additional parts in judicial speeches, which Aristotle scorns. He identifies only two necessary parts to a speech: statement, or proposition, and proof. Most rhetorical treatises, before and after Aristotle, discuss invention in terms of the conventional arrangement of parts of a judicial speech. In the *Rhetoric,* however, arrangement is ignored in the discussion of invention in books 1 and 2 and treated in book 3 almost as an afterthought: something expected in a discussion of rhetoric but of relatively little importance. The word *taxis* is common in military contexts and carries the connotation of the arrangement of troups for battle. Similarly, the speaker should marshal the available means of persuasion for debate.

Chapter 13: The Necessary Parts of a Speech

1. There are two parts to a speech; for it is necessary [first] to state the subject and [then] to demonstrate it. It is ineffective, after stating something, not to demonstrate and to demonstrate without a first statement; for one demonstrating, demonstrates *something,* and one making a preliminary statement says it first for the sake of demonstrating it. 2. Of these parts, the first is the statement [*prothesis*], the other the proof [*pistis*], just as if one made the distinction that one part is the problem, the other the demonstration.[171]

3. Currently [writers on rhetoric] make ridiculous divisions; for a *diēgēsis* [or narration of the facts of the case] surely belongs only to a judicial speech. How can there be the kind of *diēgēsis* they are talking about in epideictic or deliberative? Or how can there be replies to the opponent? Or an epilogue in demonstrative[172]

---

171. As, e.g., in geometry.

172. *Apodeiktikon.* Some manuscripts and editors read "epideictic," and in a sense this is what is referred to; but the point is that once something is "demonstrated,"

speeches? **[1414b]** *Prooimiom* [introduction] and *antiparabolē* [reply by comparison] and *epanodos* [recapitulation] sometimes occur in public speeches when there is debate on two sides of a question (for there is often both accusation and response), but not insofar as there is deliberation.[173] Moreover, an epilogue is not a requirement of every judicial speech—for example, if the speech is short or if the subject is easily remembered; for an epilogue results from shortening the length [of an argument].[174]

4. The necessary parts, then, are *prothesis* [statement of the proposition] and *pistis* [proof of the statement]. These are, therefore, the parts that really belong [in every speech]; and at the most, prooemium, *prothesis, pistis,* epilogue.[175] For replies to the opponent belong to the proofs; and reply by comparison is amplification of the same, so it is a part of the proofs. One who does this demonstrates something, but the prooemion does not, nor the epilogue; the latter reminds [the audience of what has been demonstrated]. 5. If one continues making such divisions as the followers of Theodorus make,[176] there will be a second *diēgēsis* and an *epidiēgēsis* [supplementary narration] and a *prodiēgēsis* [preliminary narration] and an *elenkos* [refutation] and *epexelenkos* [supplementary refutation], but one should attach a name only when speaking of a distinct species and difference; otherwise, the category becomes empty and laughable, like those Licymnius created in his *Art,* naming [parts] *epourosis* [wafting] and *apoplanēsis* [wandering] and *ozoi* [ramifications].[177]

---

there is no need to say more. Aristotle speaks in purely logical terms in this opening discussion, in opposition to the teaching of contemporary rhetoricians. In actual speeches, all these divisions can be found.

173. *Symboulē,* the coming to an agreement on the part of the council, which is the real objective of public debate.

174. It is a summary of what has been said.

175. Introduction, statement or proposition, proof, and summary conclusion.

176. The rhetorician mentioned in 2.23.28 and 3.11.6

177. On Licymnius' *Art* see also Plato, *Phaedrus* 267c. He may have applied the term to dithyrambs or epideictic rather than to judicial oratory.

Chapter 14: The Prooimion, or Introduction

■ *Oimos* literally means "stripe" or "layer" but metaphorically means the "course" or "strain" of a song. A *pro-oimion* is thus a "prelude" or introductory song. Transliterated into the Latin alphabet this becomes *prooemion* or *proemium,* sometimes shortened in English to *proem.* The Latin translation is *exordium,* in which the image is that of a warp set up on a loom before the web is started. Other analogous words are *prologue,* used originally of plays, and *preface,* from Latin *praefatio,* "what is said first." Among the works of Demosthenes is a collection of prooemia adaptable to a variety of judicial cases.

1. The prooemion is the beginning of a speech, what a prologue is in poetry and a *proaulion* in flute-playing; for all these are beginnings and, as it were, pathmakers for one who is continuing on. The *proaulion* is like the prooemion of epideictic speeches; for the flute-players, first playing whatever they play well, lead into the opening note of the theme, and this is the way to write in epideictic speeches: after saying whatever one wants, to introduce the keynote [or theme] and join the parts together, as all [epideictic writers] do. An example is the prooemion of Isocrates' *Helen,* where there is nothing in common between the eristics and [the subject of] Helen.[178] At the same time, even if [an epideictic writer] wanders from the topic,[179] it is appropriate for the whole speech not to be uniform.[180]

---

178. In the prooemion of the *Helen* Isocrates attacks philosophers who argue for the sake of argument (eristic) or sophists who speak on trivial subjects; in contrast, he says, Gorgias chose a fine subject in his *Encomium of Helen* but then composed an apology rather than a encomium. This leads into the body of the speech where Isocrates shows how Helen should be celebrated.

179. *Ektopisēi.* The sources of prooemia, like other material in a speech, are topics. As will be noted later in the chapter, some topics of prooemia are appropriate to the specific species of rhetoric (whether epideictic, judicial, or deliberative), and some are common to all speechmaking. Praise and blame, mentioned in the next sentence, have been identified in 1.3 and 1.9 as the characteristic topics of epideictic.

180. It could become monotonous. Aristotle recognizes that epideictic in practice is often display oratory, and unexpected variation is part of its charm.

EPIDEICTIC PROOEMIA

2. The prooemia of epideictic speeches are drawn from praise or blame. For example, in his *Olympic Discourse*[181] Gorgias praises those who founded national festivals: "You are worthy the admiration of many. O men of Greece . . ." Isocrates, on the other hand, blames them because they honored excellence of the body with gifts, but offered no prize to the wise.[182] 3. Another [source of epideictic prooemia is] from offering advice: for example, that one should praise the good, and thus the speaker praises Aristides;[183] or [should praise] such as are neither of good fame nor bad but are good while obscure, like Alexander the son of Priam.[184] [In these instances] the speaker offers advice. [1415a] 4. Another source [in epideictic] is borrowed from judicial prooemia; that is, from appeals to the audience, if the speech is about something paradoxical or difficult or already much discussed, in order to obtain pardon [for discussing it], as the verse of Choerilus:[185] "Now, when [the subjects of poetry] have all been treated. . . ." These, then, are the sources of the prooemia of epideictic speeches: from praise, from blame, from exhortation, from dissuasion, from appeal to the audience. The opening note must be either unrelated or related to [the subject of the] speech.

JUDICIAL PROOEMIA

5. As for the prooemia of judicial speeches, one should grasp that they have the same effect as the prologues of plays and the

181. A speech originally given at the Olympic games. According to Plutarch, *Moralia* 43.144b–c, the theme was concord among the Greeks.

182. *Panegyricus* 1.

183. See book 2, n. 185.

184. In 2.23.8, 2.24.7, and 2.24.9 Aristotle mentions a declamation about Alexander (better known as Paris). Given Paris's ambivalent reputation, the theme offered the kind of challenge that attracted the sophists. Paris was living in the country, unknown to the Trojans, when chosen as a judge in the beauty contest of the goddesses.

185. Fifth-century epic poet, complaining of the limited subjects left for treatment to poets of his time.

prooemia of epic poems. ([Introductions] in dithyrambs are like [prooemia] in epideictic speeches, for example: "Through you and your gifts and then spoils. . . .")[186] 6. In [judicial] speeches and in epic there is a sample of the argument in order that [the audience] may know what the speech is about and [their] thought not be left hanging. The unlimited leads astray;[187] he who gives, as it were, the beginning into the hand [of the hearer] allows him, by holding on, to follow the speech. This is the reason for [the first line of the *Iliad*,] "Sing, Goddess, the wrath . . ." [and the first line of the *Odyssey*,] "Speak to me, Muse, of the man . . ." [and]

> Bring to me another theme, how from the land of Asia
> There came to Europe a great war.[188]

And the tragedians make the subject of the play clear—if not right away as Euripides does, at least somewhere in the prologue, as Sophocles does too: "My father was Polybus . . ."[189] and the comedians similarly.

The most necessary and specific function of the prooemion is this: to make clear what is the "end" [*telos*] for which the speech [is being given]. As a result, if the subject is clear or short, there is no need of a prooemion. 7. The other kinds that are used are *remedies*[190] and [are] common [to all species of rhetoric]. These are derived from the speaker and the hearer and the subject and the opponent:[191] from the speaker and the opponent [are derived] whatever refutes or creates a prejudicious attack [*diabolē*].[192] But

---

186. Attributed to the late-fifth-century dithyrambic poet, Timotheus (fr. 18 Page).

187. As in the case of unrhythmical prose in 3.8, Aristotle seeks a sense of "limit."

188. From the prooemion of an epic poem on the Persian wars by Choerilus of Samus (fr. la Kinkel); see n. 185.

189. *Oedipus the King* 774—not, indeed, from the prologue of the play, but from the prologue of a long speech by Oedipus. Kassel double-brackets the quotation as a late addition by Aristotle.

190. *Iatreumata.* They are intended to correct possibly negative assumptions of the audience.

191. These are the topics of prooemia as identified in many Greek and Roman rhetorical treatises, e.g., *Rhetoric for Herennius* 1.8.

192. *Diabolē*, which recurs frequently in this chapter and the next, regularly means "slander, prejudice" and is so rendered throughout this passage by most translators. The cognate verb *diaballō*, however, which also occurs in the passage, means

these are not done in the same way; in the defendant's speech replies to attack come first, in the prosecution's [they come] in the epilogue. The reason is not unclear; for the defendant, when he is going to introduce himself, has to remove whatever hinders his case, and thus must first counteract the attack. But the attacker ought to put his attack in the epilogue in order that [the audience] may better remember it.

Remarks aimed at the audience derive from an effort to make them well disposed[193] and sometimes to make them attentive or the opposite; for it is not always useful to make them attentive, which is why many speakers try to induce laughter. All sorts of things will lead the audience to receptivity if the speaker wants, including his seeming to be a reasonable person.[194] They pay more attention to these people. [1415b] And they are attentive to great things, things that concern themselves, marvels, and pleasures. As a result, one should imply that the speech is concerned with such things. If they are not attentive, it is because the subject is unimportant, means nothing to them personally, [or] is distressing. 8. But one should not forget that all such things are outside the real argument: they are addressed to a hearer who is morally weak and giving ear to what is extrinsic to the subject, since if he were not such a person, there would be no need of a prooemion except for setting out the "headings" of the argument in order that the "body" [of the speech] may have a "head."[195] 9. Furthermore, making the audience attentive is a feature common to all parts of a speech, if there is need of it [at all]; for these remedies are sought

---

"attack"; and Aristotle's discussion does not draw a sharp distinction between attacks that may be justified and those that are slanderous.

193. The manuscripts continue "and to make them mad," but this is probably an addition by a later student.

194. Aristotle regards the "remedial" functions of the prooemion as two: to make the audience well disposed (*eunous*) and attentive (*prosektikos*). He then speaks of receptivity (*eumatheia*), apparently regarding it as much the same as attentiveness. Other Greek and Latin rhetorical works (e.g., *Rhetoric for Herennius* 1.7) usually speak of three functions: to make the audience receptive or teachable (Lat. *docilis*), well disposed (*benivolus*), and attentive (*attentus*). Aristotle's denigrating tone here is a reaction to the rules he found in handbooks or the teaching of Isocrates.

195. The Greeks characteristically thought of the head as a beginning; moderns tend to speak of things "coming to a head" at the end.

everywhere, not just when beginning. Thus, it is ridiculous to amass them at the beginning, where all listeners are most paying attention. As a result, whenever there is an opportunity, one should say [things like] "And give me your attention, for nothing [that I say] pertains more to me than [it does] to you" and "I shall tell you something strange, the like of which you have never heard" or "[something] so marvelous." To do this is, as Prodicus[196] said, "to throw in some of the fifty-drachma lecture when the hearers nod." 10. But it is clear that this is not addressed to the hearer in his proper capacity as hearer; for all [who do it] are attacking others or absolving themselves in their prooemia.

[Some examples are] "Lord, I shall not speak as one [who has come] in haste. . . ." [and] "Why this proem? . . ."[197] And [those do it] who have or seem to have a bad case; [in such situations] it is better to spend words on anything other than the subject. That is why slaves do not answer questions, but go around in a circle and "prooemi-ize" [when accused of something].

11. The sources of creating good will have been mentioned and [so have] each of the other similar [states of mind].[198] But since it is well said,

Grant me to find among the Phaiacians friendship or compassion,[199]

these are the two things one should aim at. In epideictic, however, one should make the hearer think he shares the praise, either himself or his family or his way of life or at least something of the sort; for what Socrates says in the funeral oration[200] is true, that it is not difficult to praise Athenians in Athens, but among the Spartans [is another matter].[201]

---

196. Fifth-century sophist, best known from his role in Plato's *Protagoras*.

197. From Sophocles, *Antigone* 223 and Euripides, *Iphigenia Among the Taurians* 1162, respectively. The quotations apparently are intended to illustrate what follows. They are double-bracketed again by Kassel as late additions by Aristotle.

198. See 2.1.7, 2.4, and 2.8.

199. *Odyssey* 7.327.

200. Plato, *Menexenus* 235d.

201. The modern equivalent is "trying to sell refrigerators to Eskimos."

DELIBERATIVE PROOEMIA

The prooemia of deliberative rhetoric are copied from those of judicial, but in the nature of the case there is very little need for them. Moreover, they are concerned with what the audience [already] knows, and the subject needs no prooemion except because of the speaker or the opponents[202] or if the advice given is not of the significance they suppose, but either more or less. Then it is necessary to attack or absolve and to amplify or minimize. It is for this that a prooemion is needed or for ornament, since the speech seems carelessly done if it does not have one. **[1416a]** An example of the latter is Gorgias' encomium to the Eleans: without preliminary sparring or warm-up[203] he begins abruptly, "Elis, happy city."

Chapter 15: Ways of Meeting a Prejudicial Attack; the Question at Issue

■ The subject is a logical continuation of the discussion of meeting attacks in the prooemion, but these strategies may occur anywhere in a speech. Much of what Aristotle discusses in this chapter was later absorbed into *stasis* theory, the technique of determining the question at issue in a trial—whether it was one of fact, law, quality of the act, or jurisdiction of the court—with many subdivisions and variations. This subject was first organized systematically by Hermagoras of Temnos in the second century B.C. and supplies the major theoretical basis for inventional theory in the *Rhetoric for Herennius* and rhetorical writings of Cicero, Quintilian, Hermogenes, and later authorities; see Kennedy 1963, 303–19. Aristotle touches on the subject in 1.13.9–10 and again here and in 3.17.1, but does not seem to have realized the

202. When the speaker needs to explain why he rises to speak or what his opponents' hidden motives are.

203. The metaphors are from boxing. Epideictic was often thought of as analogous to an athletic contest; cf. the quotation from Isocrates' *Panegyricus* earlier in this chapter.

fundamental rhetorical importance of determining the question at issue. His failure to treat stasis as a part of invention and to create technical terminology to describe it is probably one reason why the *Rhetoric* was rather little studied in later antiquity and the Byzantine period.

1. One source of counteracting a prejudicial attack[204] is the use of arguments that might refute an unpleasant suspicion. It makes no difference whether someone has [actually] expressed the suspicion or not, so this is of general applicability. 2. Another topic[205] is to make a denial in regard to what is at issue: either that it is not true or not harmful or not to this person or not so much as claimed or not unjust or not very or not disgraceful or that it is not important. The question at issue [*amphisbētēsis*] concerns things like this, as in the reply of Iphicrates to Nausicrates,[206] for he admitted that he had done what the other claimed and that it caused harm but not that he had committed a crime. Or one may balance one thing against another when a wrong has been done, [saying that] though it was harmful, it was honorable [or that] though it caused pain, it was advantageous, or something of this sort.

3. Another topic: that [the act in question] is a mistake or bad luck or necessity, as Sophocles said he was not trembling for the reason his accuser said—in order to seem old—but out of necessity; for it was not of his own volition that he was eighty years old.[207] And it is possible to offer a different reason: that one did

204. *Diabolē;* see n. 192.

205. The evidence for the text here and in sec. 3 varies between *topos* (topic) and *tropos* (way). Though Aristotle might have used either, *topos* seems confirmed by its appearance in sec. 9 in all manuscripts and is preferable throughout in that Aristotle is talking about "sources" of arguments and thus "places" where arguments can be found. These are, however, specific topics—the *idia* of 1.2.21 or the *koina* of 2.19, not the *topoi* of 2.23.

206. Iphicrates is the Athenian general who has often been mentioned; Nausicrates (called Naucrates by Roman writers) was a student of Isocrates. Quintilian says (3.6.3) that some attributed the first formulation of stasis theory to him. Possibly this is a misunderstanding of Aristotle's example.

207. Perhaps Sophocles the dramatist, when accused by his son of mental incompetence as described in an anonymous *Life* prefixed to some manuscripts, otherwise perhaps the fifth-century general of the same name whose trial Aristotle mentions in 1.14.3 and 3.18.6.

not intend harm but some other objective and not what the accuser alleged but [that] the accidental result was harmful: "It would be just for you to hate me, if I had acted in order to bring this about."

4. Another [topic is recrimination], if the accuser has been involved [in the action or something similar], either now or in the past, either himself or one of those near him. 5. Another [is] if there are others with similar characteristics but [the opponents] agree they are not liable to the charge; for example, if a person who is fastidious about his appearance is [to be judged] an adulterer, then so-and-so must be. 6. Another [is] if the opponent or someone else has attacked others [in the past] or if, without arraignment, others have been under suspicion as the speaker now is and have been shown not guilty. 7. Another [topic] comes from counterattacking the accuser; for it will be strange if his words are believable when he himself is unbelievable. 8. Another [topic can be used] if there has been a previous decision, as in Euripides' reply to Hygiainon in an *antidosis* trial when accused of impiety because he had written a line recommending perjury: "My tongue swore, but my mind was unsworn."[208] He said [Hygiainon] was wrong to bring trials into the law courts that belonged in the Dionysiac contest; for he had given or would give an account of the words there if anyone wanted to bring a complaint.[209] 9. Another is to use [the nature of] slander[210] as a basis of attack, considering what a bad thing it is, and this because it alters legal judgments and

---

208. Euripides, *Hippolytus* 612. The *antidosis* procedure, best known from Isocrates' speech by that title, demanded an exchange of property and was employed when one person claimed that another was better able financially to bear the cost of some assigned state service. The result of the trial is unknown. Hygiainon was trying to show that Euripides' oath (presumably about the amount of his financial resources) could not be trusted, since he seemed to recommend perjury in a play. The line was notorious but was appropriate for Hippolytus in context.

209. The trilogy of which the *Hipppolytus* was a part had been given first prize by the judges in the dramatic contest of 428 B.C. and Euripides was claiming a charge of impiety should be brought before those judges. This is an example of what comes to be known as stasis of transference or jurisdiction, the claim that the charge is brought before the wrong court.

210. Here *diabolē* clearly means slander. Aristotle has in mind developing the commonplace of its dangers to society.

does not rely on the fact. To speak of *symbola*[211] is a topic[212] common to both sides; **[1416b]** for example, in the *Teucer* [of Sophocles] Odysseus claims Teucer is a relative of Priam, for his mother Hesione was [Priam's] sister, but Teucer says that his father Telamon was Priam's enemy and that he had not betrayed the spies. 10. Another [topic], for the accuser, is to find fault with some big thing briefly after praising some little thing at length or, after setting forth many good things [about the opponent], to find fault with the one thing that bears on the case.[213] Such [speakers] are most artful and most unjust; for they seek to harm by saying good things, mingling them with the bad. [A topic] common to accuser and defendant [occurs] when the same thing can have been done for many reasons: the accuser should attribute an evil motive, pointing to the worse interpretation, the defendant the better [motive]. For example, when Diomedes picked Odysseus [as a companion on an expedition in *Iliad* 10.242–46] one [speaker] might say that he regarded him as the best man, another [that] no, [he regarded him] as worthless, chosen because he alone would not be a rival.[214] Let this be enough about prejudicial attack.

Chapter 16: The Diēgēsis, *or Narration, and the Use of Narrative*

■ *Diēgēsis* literally means "a leading through" the facts. It has become usual to distinguish *narration* as a part of a speech from *narrative,* meaning any account of a course of

---

211. Often physical evidence, or "tokens," but here a "probable sign": the assumption of family loyalty as contrasted with evidence from actions. Teucer was accused of treachery to the Greeks.

212. *Topos* here occurs in both major manuscript traditions (P and F), though some editors delete it.

213. As Antony does in regard to Brutus in his funeral oration for Caesar in Shakespeare's play: that Brutus is "an honorable man" is repeatedly stated, but he is "ambitious."

214. As in the *Ajax* of Theodectes; see 2.23.20.

events; but Greek *diēgēsis* and Latin *narratio* are used of both. As in the previous chapter, Aristotle begins with epideictic, then considers narrative in judicial speeches and some qualities of all good narrative, with a note on narrative in deliberative oratory at the end.

EPIDEICTIC NARRATIVE

1. *Diēgēsis* in epideictic speeches is not continuous[215] but part-by-part, for one should go through the actions that constitute the argument [*logos*]. The argument is composed partly from what is nonartistic, since the speaker is in no way the cause of the [narrated] actions, and partly from art, which is a matter of showing either that the action took place, if it seems unbelievable, or that it was of a certain kind or important or all these things. 2. For this reason, sometimes everything should not be narrated continuously, because this kind of demonstration is hard to remember. From some actions a man is shown to be brave, from others wise or just. A speech so arranged is simpler; the other approach[216] is intricate and not plain. 3. Well-known actions should only be recalled [not described in detail]. Thus, many [epideictic speeches] have no need of narrative, for example, if you wish to praise Achilles; for all know his actions. But it *is* necessary to make use of these. On the other hand, if you are praising Critias, you should [narrate his good actions], for not many know them. . . .[217]

---

215. As it usually is in judicial oratory. The reader should remember that Aristotle regards epideictic as praise or blame of one or more persons. To demonstrate the qualities of the subject the orator will need to narrate actions, such as valor in war; but these narrative passages will be scattered through the speech as needed in support of the claims made.

216. Grouping the narrative of the subject's life into a single section, which the audience is expected to remember later as moral qualities are discussed.

217. Critias was one of the Thirty Tyrants in Athens in 404 B.C. Something seems to have been lost in the text at this point; in what follows Aristotle is discussing narrative in judicial speeches. The manuscripts fill the gap by repeating 1.9.33–37. See book 1, n. 176.

JUDICIAL NARRATIVE

4. But nowadays they[218] ridiculously say that the narration [in a judicial speech] should be rapid. Yet, as the man said to the baker when asked whether he should knead the dough hard or soft, "What? Can't it be done *right?*" Similarly here, one should not narrate at length, just as one should not speak prooemia at length, nor proofs [*pisteis*]; for speaking well is not a matter of rapidity or conciseness but moderation, and that means saying just as much as will make the thing clear or as much as will make [the audience] suppose that something has happened or that harm has been done or injustice **[1417a]** or that the facts are as important as you want. 5. [As] the opposing speaker, [you] should do the opposite: seize an opportunity in the narration to mention whatever bears on your own virtue (for example, "By stressing justice I kept admonishing him not to abandon his children") or bears on the opponent's wickedness ("But he answered me that whatever he may be, there will be other children," which is what Herodotus[219] says the Egyptian rebels replied [when begged by Psammetichus not to desert their wives and children]) or what is pleasing to the judges.

6. The defendant's narration can be shorter; for what is in doubt is whether something happened or whether it was harmful or unjust or not important, so one should not waste time on what is agreed unless something contributes to the defense, for example, if [it is agreed that] something has been done but not that it was unjust.[220] 7. Further, actions should be spoken of in the past tenses except for what brings in either pity or indignation when it is dramatized. The account [*apologos*] of [what was told to] Alcinous is an example, in that it has been compressed into sixty verses for Penelope,[221] and [other examples are] the way Phaÿllus told the epic cycle and the prologuc of the *Oeneus*.[222]

218. The writers of handbooks and, perhaps, the followers of Isocrates.

219. *Histories* 2.30.

220. In the terminology of later rhetoricians, if the stasis is not fact but quality.

221. The story told to Alcinous includes Odysseus' dramatic narration of his adventures, with much direct discourse, and stretches through *Odyssey* 9–12. In *Odyssey* 23.264–84, 23.310–43 (not quite sixty verses) Odysseus gives Penelope a summary of his adventures.

222. Nothing is known of Phaÿllus; the *Oeneus* was a tragedy by Euripides.

8. The narration ought to be indicative of character [*ēthikēn*]. This will be so if we know what makes character [*ēthos*]. One way, certainly, is to make deliberate choice [*proairesis*] clear: what the character is on the basis of what sort of deliberate choice [has been made]. And choice is what it is because of the end aimed at. Mathematical works do not have moral character because they do not show deliberate choice (for they do not have a [moral] purpose), but the Socratic dialogues do (for they speak of such things). 9. Other ethical indications are attributes of each character, for example, that someone walks away while talking; for this makes his arrogance and rudeness of character clear. And do not speak from calculation, as they do nowadays, but from moral principle: [not] "I desired it" and "For I chose this" [but] "Even if I gain nothing, it is better so." The first [two examples] are the words of a prudent man, the last of a good one; for the quality of a prudent man consists in pursuing his own advantage, that of a good man in pursuing the honorable. If [what you say] seems incredible, add the cause, as Sophocles does. An example is the passage from the *Antigone,* arguing that there is more obligation to a brother than to husband or children, for the latter can be replaced if they die,

> But when mother and father have gone to Hades
> There is no brother who can be born again.²²³

If you do not have a reason to give, say that you are not unaware that what you say may seem incredible but [that] you are naturally this sort of [virtuous] person and [that] people never do believe [that] anyone willingly does anything except for some advantage. 10. Further, speak from the emotions, narrating both the results [of emotion] and things the audience knows and what are special characteristics of the speaker or the opponent: "And he went off, scowling at me." **[1417b]** And as Aeschines says of Cratylus, that he was hissing and violently shaking his hands; for these things are persuasive since they are indications [*symbola*] that the audience

---

223. Sophocles, *Antigone* 911–12, with minor textual difference. The argument has been difficult for some modern critics, but Aristotle's citation is strong evidence that it is genuine, and there are other testimonia as well.

knows, pointing to the character of those they do not know. Many such things are to be found in Homer:

Thus she spoke, and the old nurse covered her face with her hands.[224]

For those who begin to cry place their hands over their eyes. And at the beginning you should introduce yourself as a person of a certain character—and your opponent as well—but do it inconspicuously. That this is easy can be seen from messengers [in tragedy]; for we know nothing of what they are going to say, but we get some inkling of it [from their attitude]. Narrative should occur in many places and sometimes not at the beginning.

DELIBERATIVE NARRATIVE

11. Narrative is least common in deliberative oratory, because no one narrates future events. But if there is narrative, it is of events in the past, in order that by being reminded of those things the audience will take better counsel about what is to come (either criticizing or praising).[225] But then the speaker does not perform the function of an adviser.[226] If something [in a narrative] is unbelievable, promise to tell the cause of it immediately and to refer [judgment] to somebody, as Iocasta in the *Oedipus* of Carcinus is always promising when someone is trying to find out about her son.[227] And [similarly] Haemon in Sophocles.[228]

Chapter 17: The Pistis or Proof, as Part of an Oration

■ This somewhat rambling chapter begins with discussion of proofs in judicial oratory, turns to epideictic and deliberative

224. *Odyssey* 19.361.

225. Double-bracketed by Kassel as one of Aristotle's late additions.

226. A deliberative speaker by definition advises about the future rather than praising or blaming the past.

227. On the text here see MacKay 1953.

228. *Antigone* 683–723. The passage does not well illustrate Aristotle's point— though Haemon does eventually give a reason (701–3) for his loyalty to his father, which Aristotle may have thought an unlikely attitude.

speeches and the differences among the species, returns to epideictic, comments on refutation, and ends with further remarks on the presentation of character.

1. Proofs should be demonstrative [*apodeiktika*].[229] Since four points may be open to dispute [*amphisbētēsis*],[230] there is need to provide a demonstration bearing on what is disputed: for example, if the issue disputed in a trial involves a denial that something was done, there is special need to provide a demonstration that it was, and if [the act is admitted by both parties but one alleges] that it did no harm, [the other needs to show] that it did; and if [it is denied] that it was important or [claimed] that it was done justly, similarly. And if the dispute is about whether something has been done [by one of the parties], 2. do not forget that it is necessary on this issue alone for one or the other to be a liar; for ignorance is not an excuse, as it might be if the dispute were about justice.[231] So in this case one should use [the topic of the opponent's wickedness] but not in others.

3. In epideictic speeches there will be much amplification about what is good and advantageous [in the actions of the subject being praised]; for the facts need to be taken on trust, and speakers rarely introduce evidence of them, only if any are incredible or if someone else is held responsible.[232]

4. In deliberative speeches one may debate whether the events predicted [by a previous speaker] will occur or, if they do, whether the policy recommended is unjust or disadvantageous or unimpor-

229. Here the term seems to mean "logically valid," or at least "persuasive."

230. Aristotle here again anticipates some categories of later stasis theory; his four questions are fact, harm, importance, and justice, of which the last three become subdivisions of stasis of quality in later theory.

231. In *Nicomachean Ethics* 5.10.1135b30 Aristotle somewhat qualifies this: if a speaker denies an action that he has performed because he has genuinely forgotten it, he is not necessarily wicked. But generally, when one person claims something was done and another denies it, one is lying.

232. In epideictic, the main body of the speech, corresponding to the proof in judicial oratory, consists largely of a discussion of the actions and qualities of the person or persons being praised, amplified by vivid description, comparisons, or other rhetorical techniques; but occasionally the facts may be controversial and require argument to justify attibution to the subject.

tant. One should also look to see if any incidental details are falsified; for these are sure signs[233] that he also falsifies things more to the point. **[1418a]** 5. Paradigms [i.e., examples] are most appropriate to deliberative oratory, enthymemes more suited to judicial. The former is concerned with the future, so it is necessary to draw examples from the past; the latter is concerned with what are or are not the facts, which are more open to demonstration and a logically necessary conclusion; for the past has a necessity about it. 6. But the enthymemes should be mixed in and not spoken continuously; otherwise, they get in each other's way. (There is a limit to how much an audience can take, [as in the line]

Oh friend, since you have spoken as much as a wise man would[234]—

as much as not *such things as.*) 7. And do not seek enthymemes about everything; otherwise you do what some of the philosophers do whose syllogisms draw better known and more plausible conclusions than their premises. 8. And when you would create pathos, do not speak in enthymemes; for the enthymeme either knocks out the pathos or is spoken in vain. (Simultaneous movements knock out each other and either fade away or make each other weak.) Nor should you seek an enthymeme when the speech is being "ethical"; for logical demonstration has neither *ēthos* nor moral purpose.[235] 9. Maxims [*gnōmai*] should be used both in a narration and in a proof; for they are "ethical": "I *have* given [the money], though knowing one should not trust."[236] Or [they should be used]

---

233. *Tekmēria.* But this hardly meets the standards of *tekmēria* as discussed in 1.2.16.

234. *Odyssey* 4.204.

235. The rejection of enthymemes as too coolly rational in arousing emotion or portraying character (modified in sec. 12) is evidence against the view that Aristotle's discussion of *pathos* and *ēthos* in book 2 is intended to supply premises for enthymemes even if the restriction is limited to the *pistis* or a speech, as Wisse (1989, 24–25) allows. Logical demonstration may use premises relating to character or emotion, as in the case of a demonstration of the wickedness of the opponent but in doing so provides rational explanation rather than arouses the emotional reaction of the jury. Cf. 3.17.2.

236. The situation is that of a man who has deposited money with another though knowing the common saying, "Don't trust others."

if the context is emotional: "Though wronged, I have no regret;
the profit belongs to him, the justice [of the act] to me."[237]

10. Speaking in a deliberative assembly is more difficult than in
a law court, as one would expect, since it is concerned with the
future, the other with the past, which is known already, "even to
prophets," as Epimenides the Cretan said (he used not to prophesy
about the future but about things in the past that were unclear);
and the law is a hypothesis in judicial cases: having a starting point,
it is easier for one to find proof.[238] And [deliberative oratory] does
not have many opportunities for "diatribes," for example, against
the opponent or about oneself, or to create pathos.[239] Least of all
[species of rhetoric can deliberative do this], unless one digresses.
Therefore, one should do this [only] when at a loss for something
to say, as the orators at Athens do, including Isocrates;[240] for even
when giving advice, he uses invective, for example, against the
Lacedaimonians in the *Panegyricus* and against Chares in the
Symmachicus.[241]

11. In epideictic one should interweave the speech with praise,
as Isocrates does; for he is always bringing in somebody [to praise].
What Gorgias used to say—that he was never at a loss for words—
is similar: if he is talking about Achilles, he praises [his father]

237. Despite what Aristotle says, this seems to qualify as an enthymeme since a
reason is given.

238. In a trial the prosecutor proposes to the court the assumption that the defendant is guilty of violating specific provisions in the law and then seeks to show that
the facts of the case support the assumption.

239. *Diatribē* basically means "spending time" on some subject; from the example
one can see how it has come to mean "personal attack" in English. To illustrate
Aristotle's point, compare the general absence of personal invective against his
Athenian opponents in Demosthenes' deliberative speeches with his extended invec-
tives in judicial speeches such as *On the Crown*. In the Hellenistic philosophical
schools a diatribe was an informal, personal speech, sometimes rather like a ser-
mon, addressed by a teacher to his students, often in response to questions.

240. See note on 3.11.15. Isocrates died in 338 B.C., but was apparently still alive
when Aristotle wrote this passage.

241. The *Symmachicus* is commonly known as *On the Peace;* cf. sec. 27. Note that
Aristotle regards the *Panegyricus* as a deliberative speech, since it urges the union
of the Greeks under Athenian leadership. As a festival oration and because of its
extensive praise of Athens, it could be classified as epideictic. It was published as a
pamphlet rather than actually spoken.

Peleus, then [his grandfather] Aeacus, then the god [Aeacus' father, Zeus]; similarly, [if he is praising] courage, that does this and that or has certain qualifies [that can be amplified]. 12. If one has logical arguments, one should speak both "ethically" and logically; if you do not have enthymemes, speak "ethically." And to seem virtuous suits a good person more than an exact argument does.

[1418b] 13. Refutative enthymemes are better liked [by audiences] than demonstrative ones, because what makes a refutation is more clearly syllogistic; for inconsistencies are clearer when placed side-by-side. 14. Refutations of the opponent are not a separate species but belong to proofs.[242] Some [refutations] disprove by objection [to a premise], some by [a counter]syllogism.[243] In both deliberation and in court the opening speaker should [usually] state his own premises first, then should meet those [expected] of his opponent by disproving and tearing them to pieces before he can make them. But if the opposition has many points to make, put the refutations first, as Callistratus did in the Messenian assembly; for first removing the objections they were going to voice, he then spoke his own case.[244] 15. But if you speak second you should reply first to the opposing speech, refuting and offering opposed syllogisms, especially if what was said seems to have met with approval. Just as the mind is not receptive toward a person who has been previously criticized, in the same way it is not [receptive] toward a speech if the opponent seems to have spoken well. One should thus make room in the hearer's mind for the speech one is going to give, and this will happen if you take away [the impression that has been left]. Thus, after fighting against everything or the most important things or the popular things or the easily refutable things, one should then make one's own persuasive points:

---

242. Cf. 2.26.3. Thus, Aristotle does not regard the refutation as a distinct part of an oration, as did the followers of Theodorus; cf. 3.13.5.

243. Cf. 2.25.1.

244. On an embassy to the Messenians in 362 B.C. (see Nepos, *Epaminondas* 6), Callistratus began by reasons why they should not ally with Thebes before introducing arguments why they should join with Athens. When an orator confronts a hostile audience it is often most effective to face immediately the arguments or prejudices in their minds. Cicero's speech *For Cluentius* is a large-scale example.

> First shall I be a defender of the goddesses,
> And shall show she does not speak justly.
> For I do not think that Hera. . . .[245]

In these lines [Hecuba] seizes first on [Helen's] most foolish argument. So much for *pisteis*.[246]

16. In regard to *ēthos*,[247] since there are sometimes things to be said about oneself that are invidious or prolix or contradictory, and about another that are abusive or boorish, it is best to attribute them to another person, as Isocrates does in the *Philippus* and in the *Antidosis*[248] and as Archilochus does in censure; for he introduces the father speaking of his daughter in an iambic poem: "Nothing is unexpected nor declared impossible on oath"[249] and [introduces] Charon the carpenter in [another] iambic work, which begins "Nothing to me the [wealth] of Gyges." And as Sophocles does, making Haemon speak to his father about Antigone on the basis of what others say.[250] 17. Sometimes it is advisable to change enthymemes into maxims; for example: "Sensible men should seek reconciliation when successful; for thus they get the greater advantage." As an enthymeme this would be "If it is necessary to seek reconciliations whenever such changes are most profitable and most advantageous, then it is necessary to seek changes when one is successful."[251]

245. Euripides, *Trojan Women* 969–1032, where Hecuba begins her reply to Helen by defending the action of the goddess involved in the judgment of Paris. *She* is Helen.

246. The next sentence shows that *pisteis* here are limited to logical arguments.

247. The introduction of a section on *ēthos* here may reflect the fact that Greek judicial orations sometimes included an "ethical digression," i.e., a passage elaborating on the character of the speaker or the opponent, at the end of the proof and before the epilogue; see May 1988, 28–29. Hermagoras, followed by some other rhetoricians, included the digression (*ekbasis*) as a regular feature of a judicial speech; see Cicero, *On Invention* 1.97.

248. *Phillippus* 4–7 and *Antidosis* 132–39, 141–49 attribute flattering remarks to Isocrates' friends.

249. Archilochus, sixth-century-b.c. poet, when disappointed in his love for Neobule, attributed opprobrious remarks about her to her father in a passage beginning with this line.

250. *Antigone* 688–700.

251. In syllogistic form, if A = B when B = C, then A, since B = C. The maxim

Chapter 18: Erotēsis, or Interrogation

■ In Athenian judicial procedure indictment resulted from a preliminary hearing before one of the archons, or magistrates, at which some prima facie evidence of a wrong was presented and witnesses offered testimony. Though rather little is known about how a hearing was conducted, it is likely that the defendant could interrogate the witnesses and try to show that there was no merit in the charge. The evidence of the witnesses was taken down in writing and then read out by a court secretary if a trial took place. Interrogation was also used in auditing officials on the completion of a term in office. Though the prosecution and defense in trials often discuss the evidence of witnesses, there was no cross-examination of them there in the modern sense. The principals in the trial could, however, ask questions directly of each other and demand an answer, which is principally what Aristotle here discusses; examples can be found in Plato's *Apology* (24c–27d), Lysias' speech *Against Eratosthenes* (12.25), and elsewhere, but rhetorical questions, not expecting an answer, are far more frequent. Chapter 5 of Anaximenes' *Rhetoric to Alexander* discusses investigational oratory (*exetasis*) and has some similarity to Aristotle's chapter on interrogation (*erotēsis*) but does not consider the possibility of replies. *Erotēsis* did not become a distinct part of an oration nor is investigation a species of oratory in the standard teaching of Greek and Roman rhetoricians. See Carawan 1983.

1. As for interrogation, it is most opportune when an opponent has said one thing and [when] if the right question is asked, an absurdity results. **[1419a]** For example, Pericles questioned Lampon about the holy rites of the Savior Goddess. When he replied that it was not permitted for an uninitiated person to hear about them, Pericles asked if he knew them himself. Since he admitted he did, [the next question was,] "And how, since you are uniniti-

---

cited here, however, fulfills the requirements of an enthymeme as given in 2.21.2, since it already has a supporting reason.

ated?" 2. A second situation is when something is self-evident and it is clear to the questioner that the opponent will grant another point. Receiving the expected answer to this, he should not asked about what is self-evident but should state the conclusion to which it points, as Socrates did when Meletus denied that Socrates believed in the gods; he asked if *daimones* ["spirits," in which Meletus admitted Socrates believed] were not either children of gods or something divine, and when Meletus said "They are," Socrates asked, [drawing the conclusion,] "Does anybody think there are children of gods but not gods?"[252] 3. Another situation is when [the speaker] intends to show that [the opponent] is contradicting himself or saying something paradoxical. 4. And a fourth when it is not possible to answer the question except sophistically; for if he answers that it is and isn't or "Some yes, some no" or "In a way, but in another way not," [the audience] calls out that he is at a loss [for a good answer]. Otherwise, do not attempt interrogation; for if the opponent resists, you seem to be defeated; for it is not possible to ask a series of question because of the [mental] weakness of the audience. (For the same reason one should condense enthymemes as much as possible.)[253]

5. Amphibolies[254] need to be answered by examining them logically and in some detail,[255] supplying a resolution of seeming contradictions directly in the answer before [the opponent] asks a follow-up question or draws a conclusion; for it is not difficult to see to what the train of argument may lead. Let how to do this and how to make replies be evident from the *Topics*.[256] 6. If a conclusion takes the form of a question, explain the reason for the conclusion: for example, when Sophocles[257] was asked by Pisander if he

---

252. Plato, *Apology* 27d. Aristotle's citation is evidence that some of the contents of Plato's *Apology* have a basis in what Socrates actually said.

253. Cf. 1.2.13, where it is said that an audience cannot follow an extended argument.

254. See n. 69. Here an amphiboly is an ambiguous statement, or question that cannot be answered in the terms asked. A notorious modern instance is "Have you stopped beating your wife yet?"

255. This seems inconsistent with what has just been said in sec. 4.

256. Book 8.

257. Orator involved in the oligarchic revolution of 411 b.c., not the dramatist.

had approved establishing the government of the Four Hundred, as the others on the committee to draft legislation did, he admitted it. "But why? Did these measures not seem to you to be wicked?" "Yes," he said; "but there were no better alternatives!" And [reply] as the Spartan replied, when rendering an account of his term as ephor and being asked if the others on the board had not justly been put to death: the examiner asked, "Did not you take the same measures as they?" He admitted it. "Therefore would it not be just to put you also to death?" "Not at all," he replied, "for they took bribes to do these things; I did not, but acted in accordance with my own judgment." Thus, one should not ask any further question after drawing a conclusion nor couch the conclusion as a question, **[1419b]** unless the balance of truth is in one's favor.[258]

7. As for humor, since it seems to have some use in debate and Gorgias rightly said that one should spoil the opponents' seriousness with laughter and their laughter with seriousness, the different forms of humor have been discussed in the *Poetics*,[259] of which some are appropriate for a gentleman to use and some not. Each speaker will take up what suits him. Mockery[260] is more gentlemanly than buffoonery; for the mocker makes a joke for his own amusement, the buffoon for the amusement of others.

Chapter 19: The Epilogos, *or Conclusion of a Speech*

■ *Epilogos* simply means *logos*, "speech," that is added on (*epi*). The Latin is *peroratio*.

1. The epilogue is made up of four things: disposing the hearer favorably toward the speaker and unfavorably toward the opponent; amplifying and minimizing; moving the hearer into emotional reactions [*pathē*]; and [giving] a reminder [of the chief points made in the speech]. After he has shown himself to be truthful and his

258. The examiner would have been better advised to state the conclusion, "You, too, would justly be put to death," and left it at that.

259. In the lost second book.

260. *Eirōneia;* see book 2, n. 22.

opponent false, the natural thing is [for a speaker] to praise and blame and drive the point home.[261] One should aim at showing one or the other of two things: either that the speaker is a good man in terms of the issues or that he is good generally; or either that the opponent is a bad man in terms of the issues or that he is bad generally. The topics [*topoi*] from which such characterizations are derived have been discussed.[262] 2. After this, in natural order, is the amplification or diminution [of the importance] of what has already been shown [in the proof]; for what has been done should be agreed upon before talking about its importance. Similarly, the growth of bodies comes from the preexistent.[263] The topics which should be used for amplification and diminution have previously been laid out.[264] 3. After this, when the nature and importance [of the facts] are clear, lead the hearer into emotional reactions. These are pity and indignation and anger and hatred and envy and emulation and strife. Their topics have also been mentioned earlier.[265] What remains, then, is to remind the audience of what has been said earlier. 4. This may be fittingly done in the way that [writers of rhetorical handbooks] wrongly speak of [it] in discussing prooemia. They require that points be made several times in order to be easily learned. In the prooemion it is right to identify the subject, in order that the question to be judged not escape notice; but in the epilogue one should speak in recapitulation of what has been shown.

The starting point [of the recapitulation] is [for the speaker] to claim that he has performed what he promised, 5. so there should be mention of what these things are and why. The discussion is [sometimes] derived from comparison with the case of the opponent. Compare what both have said on the same subject, if not throughout: "But he says this about that, while I say this and for these reasons." Or use mockery [*eirōneia*]: "He says this, I that.

---

261. This again seems to reflect the use of an "ethical digression"; see n. 247.

262. In 1.9.

263. Aristotle views politics, poetry, rhetoric, etc. as developing analogously with biological organisms; their matter and form have potential to be actualized.

264. Presumably in 2.19, though to call them topics here confuses the distinction otherwise maintained between that term and *koina*.

265. In 2.2–11; but neither *topic* nor any other rhetorical term is used of the propositions set out there.

And what would he have done if he had shown this but not that?"[266] **[1420a]** Or use interrogation:[267] "What has not been shown?" or "What did he show?" Either do this by comparison or in the natural order as the statements were made, first one's own and again, if you want, **[1420b]** the opponent's claim separately. 6. Asyndeton is appropriate for the end of the discourse, since this is an *epilogos,* not a *logos:* "I have spoken; you have listened, you have [the facts], you judge."[268]

266. If he had really proved all of his contention rather than whatever he did succeed in showing.

267. Here meaning rhetorical question.

268. Cf. the end of Lysias, *Against Eratosthenes* (12.100): "You have listened, you have seen, you have suffered, you have [the facts]. You be the judge."

Appendix I:
Supplementary Texts

A. Gorgias' *Encomium of Helen*

■ Gorgias was born in Leontini in Sicily about 480 B.C., visited Athens in 427 and probably on several other occasions, and died in Thessaly as a very old man sometime after 380. He and his student Polus appear as characters in Plato's *Gorgias,* and Aristotle (*Rhetoric* 3.1.9) cites him as the example of the "poetical" style of earlier Greek prose. The translation below seeks to imitate features of this style, including antitheses, assonance, a fondness for parallel phrases or clauses with an equal number of syllables (called *parisōsis* or *parison* by Aristotle in *Rhetoric* 3.9.9), and word play (*paronomasia*), of which the use of *homoeoteleuton* (rhyming syllables) is the most conspicuous. The date of composition of the *Helen* cannot be firmly identified; probably Gorgias gave the speech repeatedly, sometimes in slightly different forms; and written copies were in circulation as models for imitation by others. The speech illustrates his mannerisms of style, techniques of amplification, and also the logical method of dividing a question and seeking proof by refuting the alternative possibilities of blame. Gorgias taught by example, delivering and writing speeches for others to imitate, and did not lecture on, or publish, theoretical works, as Aristotle notes in *Sophistical Refutations* (183b38). Isocrates was in some sense a follower of Gorgias and also composed an *Encomium of Helen*. It praises Gorgias for his choice of a worthy subject, but criticizes him for offering a defense, rather than praise, of Helen. Gorgias has thus, in Isocrates view, confused the species of rhetoric. His speech is epideictic in the sense that it does not seek an actual judgment by a court; but it takes the literary form of a judicial speech. An earlier version of this translation was published in Sprague 1972; the translation below has been revised and takes account of improvements in the text as edited by Donadi (1983).

[Prooemion] 1. Fairest ornament [*kosmos*] to a city is a goodly army and to a body beauty and to a soul wisdom and to an action virtue and to speech truth, but their opposites are unbefitting. Man and woman and speech and deed and city and object should be honored with praise if praiseworthy, but on the unworthy blame should be laid; for it is equal error and ignorance to blame the praiseworthy and to praise the blameworthy. 2. It is the function of a single speaker both to prove the needful rightly and to disprove the wrongly spoken. Thus, I shall refute those who rebuke Helen, a woman about whom there is univocal and unanimous testimony among those who have believed the poets and whose ill-omened name has become a memorial of disasters.[1] I wish, by giving some logic to language, to free the accused of blame and to show that her critics are lying and to demonstrate the truth and to put an end to ignorance.

[Narration] 3. Now that by nature and birth the woman who is the subject of this speech was preeminent among preeminent men and women, this is not unclear, not even to a few; for it is clear that Leda was her mother, while as a father she had in fact a god, though allegedly a mortal, the latter Tyndareus, the former Zeus;[2] and of these the one seemed her father because he was, and the other was disproved because he was only said to be; and one was the greatest of men, the other lord of all. 4. Born from such parents, she pos-

---

1. Cf. Aeschylus, *Agamemnon* 689, a play on Helen's name: "Hell to ships, hell to men, hell to the city." Gorgias ignores the more favorable treatments of Helen in Stesichorus' *Palinode,* Herodotus' *Histories* (esp. 2.113–20), and Euripides' *Helen*.

2. Leda was thought to have conceived Helen when Zeus came to her in the form of a swan; cf., e.g., Yeats's poem "Leda."

sessed godlike beauty, which getting and not forgetting she pre-
served. On many did she work the greatest passions of love, and by
her one body she brought together many bodies of men greatly
minded for great deeds.[3] Some had the greatness of wealth, some
the glory of ancient noblesse, some the vigor of personal prowess,
some the power of acquired knowledge. And all came because of a
passion that loved conquest and a love of honor that was uncon-
quered. 5. Who he was and why and how he sailed away taking
Helen as his love, I shall not say; for to tell the knowing what they
know is believable but not enjoyable.[4] Having now exceeded the
time alloted for my introduction [*logos*],[5] I shall proceed to my
intended speech [*logos*] and shall propose the causes for which
Helen's voyage to Troy is likely [*eikos*] to have taken place.

[Proposition] 6. For [either] by fate's will and gods' wishes and
necessity's decrees she did what she did or by force reduced or by
words seduced or by love induced.

[Proof] Now if for the first reason [fate, the gods, etc.], the responsible one should rightly be held responsible: it is impossible to
prevent a god's predetermination by human premeditation, since
by nature the stronger force is not prevented by the weaker, but
the weaker is ruled and driven by the stronger; the stronger leads,
the weaker follows. But god is stronger than man in force and in
wisdom and in other ways. If, therefore, by fate and god the cause
had been decreed, Helen must of all disgrace be freed.[6]

7. But if she was seized by force and illegally assaulted and
unjustly insulted, it is clear that the assailant as insulter did the
wrong and the assailed as insulted suffered wrongly. It is right for
the barbarian who laid barbarous hands on her by word and law
and deed to meet with blame in word, disenfranchisement in law,
and punishment in deed, while she who was seized and deprived of

---

3. Helen's many suitors swore to defend the rights of the one who gained her hand.
This was Menelaus. When Helen was seduced, stolen, or raped by Paris, her former
suitors went off to Troy to recover her in the war described in the *Iliad*.

4. The unnamed person is Alexander or Paris, son of Priam, king of Troy.

5. On this use of *logos,* cf. *Rhetoric* 3.9.5.

6. Helen, thus, is not to be blamed if she was promised to Paris by Aphrodite as a
result of his judging that goddess more beautiful than Hera and Athene in the
celebrated beauty contest on Mount Ida.

her country and bereft of her friends, how should she not be pitied rather than pilloried? He did dread deeds; she suffered them. Her it is just to pity, him to hate.

8. But if speech [*logos*] persuaded her and deceived her soul, not even to this is it difficult to make answer and to banish blame, as follows. [First reason] Speech is a powerful lord that with the smallest and most invisible body accomplished most godlike works. It can banish fear and remove grief and instill pleasure and enhance pity. I shall show how this is so. 9. It is necessary for it to seem so as well in the opinion of my hearers. All poetry I regard and name as speech having meter.[7] On those who hear it come fearful shuddering and tearful pity and grievous longing, as the soul, through words, experiences some experience of its own at others' good fortune and ill fortune. But listen as I turn from one argument to another.

10. [Second reason] Divine sweetness transmitted through words is inductive of pleasure, reductive of pain. Thus, by entering into the opinion of the soul the force of incantation is wont to beguile and persuade and alter it by witchcraft, and the two arts of witchcraft and magic are errors of the soul and deceivers of opinion. 11. How many speakers on how many subjects have persuaded others and continue to persuade by molding false speech? If everyone, on every subject, had memory of the past and knowledge of the present and foresight of the future, speech would not do what it does; but as things are, it is easy neither to remember the past nor to consider the present nor to predict the future; so that on most subjects most people take opinion as counselor to the soul. But opinion, being slippery and insecure, casts those relying on it into slippery and insecure fortune. 12. What is there to prevent the conclusion that Helen, too, when still young, was carried off by speech just as if constrained by force? Her mind was swept away by persuasion, and persuasion has the same power as necessity, although it may bring shame; for speech, by persuading the soul that it persuaded, constrained her both to obey what was said and to approve what was done. The persuader, as user of force, did wrong; the persuaded, forced by speech, is unreasonably blamed.

13. [Third reason] To understand that persuasion, joining with speech, is wont to stamp the soul as it wishes, one must study, first,

7. A view rejected by Aristotle, *Poetics* 1.10–12.

the words of astronomers who, substituting opinion for opinion, removing one and instilling another, make incredible and unclear things appear true to the eyes of opinion;[8] second, forceful speeches in public debate, where one side of the argument pleases a large crowd and persuades by being written with art even though not spoken with truth; third, the verbal wrangling of philosophers in which, too, a swiftness of thought is exhibited, making confidence in opinion easily changed. 14. The power of speech has the same effect on the condition of the soul as the application of drugs [*pharmaka*] to the state of bodies; for just as different drugs dispell different fluids from the body, and some bring an end to disease but others end life, so also some speeches cause pain, some pleasure, some fear; some instill courage, some drug and bewitch the soul with a kind of evil persuasion.

15. Thus, it has been explained that if she was persuaded by speech she did no wrong but was unfortunate. I shall now go on to the fourth cause in a fourth argument [*logos*]. If it was love that did these things it will not be difficult to escape the charge of error that is alleged: for [first reason] we see not what we wish but what each of us has experienced: through sight the soul is stamped in diverse ways. 16. [Second reason] Whenever men at war, enemy against enemy, buckle up in the armaments of bronze and iron, whether in defense or offense, when their sight beholds the scene, it is alarmed and causes alarm in the soul, so that often they flee in terror from future danger as though it were present. [Third reason] Obedience to law is strongly brought home by fear derived from sight which, coming upon people, has made them desire both what is judged seemly by law and thought good by the mind, 17. but as soon as they have seen terrible sights they have abandoned the thought of the moment. Thus, discipline is extinguished and fear drives out the concept. And [fourth reason] many fall victim to imaginary diseases and dreadful pains and hard-to-cure mental aberrations; thus does sight engrave on the mind images of things seen. And many terrors are left unmentioned [in my speech], but those that are omitted are very like things that have been said. 18. Moreover [fifth reason], whenever pictures of many colors and figures create a perfect image of a single figure and form, they

8. E.g., by demonstrating that the world is round.

delight the sight. How much does the production of statues and the workmanship of artifacts furnish pleasurable sight to the eyes! Thus is it natural for the sight sometimes to grieve, sometimes to delight. Much love and desire for many objects is created in many minds. 19. If, then, the eye of Helen, pleased by the body of Alexander, gave to her soul an eagerness and response in love, what wonder? If love, a god, prevails over the divine power of the gods,[9] how could a lesser one be able to reject and refuse it? But if love is a human disease and an ignorance of the soul, it should not be blamed as a mistake but regarded as a misfortune. For she [Helen] went [with Paris] caught by the nets around her soul, not by the wishes of her mind, and by the necessity of love, not by the devices of art.

[Epilogue] 20. How, then, can blame be thought just? Whether she did what she did by falling in love or persuaded by speech or seized by violence or forced by divine necessity, she is completely acquitted. By speech I have removed disgrace from a woman. I have abided by the principle I posed at the start of my speech: I have tried to refute the injustice of defamation and the ignorance of allegation. I wished to write a speech that would be Helen's celebration and my own recreation.[10]

B. Art as an Intellectual Virtue, from Aristotle, *Nicomachean Ethics* 6.4

■ [In *Nicomachean Ethics* 6.3 Aristotle says that the soul possessess truth through five intellectual processes: *epistēmē,* or scientific knowledge; *tekhnē,* or art; *phronēsis,* or practical wisdom; *sophia,* or philosophical wisdom; and *nous,* or intuitive reason. His discussion of *tekhnē* is as follows.]

[1140a] 6.4.1. Included among what is capable of being other

9. Zeus and other gods often fall in love in Greek mythology.

10. The word here translated "recreation" (in order to rhyme with "celebration") is *paignion*, "sport, play." Thus, at the end Gorgias plays at undercutting a serious purpose in the speech.

than it is are both what is made and what is done, 2. but making [*poiēsis*] and doing [*praxis*] are different (on these matters too we rely on the exoteric discourses);[11] so, too, a reasoned habit of mind [*hexis*] in doing is different from a reasoned habit of mind in making. As a result, neither is [logically] contained within the other; for neither is doing [to be identified with] making nor is making [to be identified with] doing. 3. Since architecture [for example] is an art [*tekhnē*] and essentially a reasoned habit of mind in making and since there is no art that is not a reasoned habit of mind in making nor any such habit that is not an art, art would be the same thing as a reasoned habit of mind in making. 4. All art is concerned with coming into being and contriving and seeing how something may come to be among things that are capable of being and not being and of which the first principle [*arkhē*] is in the maker but not in what is made; for there is no art of things that exist or come into being by necessity, nor of things that exist by nature; for these things have their first principle in themselves. 5. But since making and doing are different, art is necessarily a matter of making but not of doing. And in a way, chance [*tykhē*] and art are concerned with the same things, as Agathon says: "Art loves chance and chance art." 6. Art is, then, has been said, a reasoned habit of mind in making, and artlessness the opposite: a habit of making with false reasoning, [in both cases] concerning things that can be other than they are.

C. An Introduction to Dialectic, from Aristotle, *Topics* 1.1–3

■ Aristotle does not provide a formal definition of dialectic, but in the following passage distinguishes it from other kinds of reasoning and discusses its uses.

[**100a18**] [Chapter 1] The purpose of this treatise is to find a method from which we shall be able to syllogize about every pro-

---

11. Meaning either Aristotle's earlier, published writings addressed to a general readership (as opposed to his lectures to students of philosophy) or, as Aulus Gellius (20.5.2) thought, debates held in Aristotle's school.

posed problem on the basis of generally accepted opinions [*en-doxa*] and while upholding an argument ourselves say nothing self-contradictory. First, then, there should be a statement of what a syllogism is and what are its different kinds, in order that the dialectical syllogism may be grasped; for that is what we are seeking in the treatise at hand.

Now syllogism is a statement [*logos*] in which, certain things having been posited, something other than the posited necessarily results through what is posited. *Apodeixis* [logically valid demonstration] occurs whenever the syllogism is drawn from things that are true and primary or from things that are of the sort as to have taken the first principle [*arkhē*] of knowledge of them from what is primary and true; but a syllogism is dialectical when drawn from generally accepted opinions. **[100b18]** Things are true and primary when they are persuasive through themselves, not through other things; for in the case of scientific principles there is no need to seek the answer to *why,* but each of the first principles is persuasive in and by itself.[12] Generally accepted opinions [*endoxa*], on the other hand, are those that seem right to all people or most people or the wise—and in the latter case all the wise or most of them or those best known and generally accepted [as authorities] [*endoxoi*]. Syllogism is eristical [or contentious] when derived from what appear to be generally accepted opinions but are not and when it appears [but is not logically] derived from generally accepted or apparently generally accepted opinions; for every opinion that appears to be generally accepted is not generally accepted; for none of the apparently accepted opinions has an altogether obvious manifestation, as results in the case of the first principles of eristic argument, where immediately and for the most part the nature of the falsehood is obvious to those with even a small capacity of comprehension. **[101a]** Therefore, let the former kind of syllogism that has been termed eristical also be called *syllogism,* and the other not syllogism but *eristical syllogism,* since it appears to syllogize but does not syllogize.

Furthermore, in addition to all the syllogisms that have been

---

12. *Apodeixis* begins with what are called a priori propositions, such as the axioms of geometry, or from propositions proved in some other science, as physics uses propositions from mathematics.

mentioned there are *paralogisms* drawn from premises concerned with specific sciences, as in fact occurs in geometry and subjects related to it; for this form seems to differ from the syllogisms that have been mentioned. One who draws a faulty [geometrical] diagram does not syllogize from what is true and primary nor from generally accepted opinions. He does not fall within the definition; for he does not take [as premises of his argument] what seems so to all nor to the majority nor to the wise (and among the latter all or most or the most authoritative) but makes the syllogism from assumptions peculiar to the science but not true; for he makes a *paralogism* by drawing semicircles wrongly or by extending lines in a way they should not be extended.

Let the species of syllogisms, then, to take them in outline, be as has been said. Speaking in general about all the matters discussed and those to be discussed later, let us make definitions [only] to this degree [of precision], because we do not propose to offer an exact account of any of them but want to give an account to the extent of an outline, thinking it quite sufficient in accordance with the method we have set to be able to recognize each of them in some way.

[Chapter 2] What would [logically] follow the matters discussed is [now] to say for how many and what [purposes] the study [of dialectic] should be useful. It is useful for three purposes: for mental training, for [serious] conversation, and for the sciences along philosophical lines. That it is useful for mental training is obvious in itself; for by having a method we shall be able more easily to undertake discussion of any proposed question.[13] [It is useful] for conversation because after enumerating the opinions of the many we shall engage in discussion with others on the basis of their own beliefs rather than that of others, restating whatever they

---

13. Aristotle is here thinking of the dialectical exercises or disputations that were a common feature of ancient philosophical schools (and continued to be practiced in some form until the early modern period). Two students were set against each other to debate a question. One stated a proposition (e.g., "I say that pleasure is the only good" or "I say that monarchy is the best form of government"). The other, by asking a series of questions that can be answered *yes* or *no,* sought to refute the proposition.

seem to be saying to us when it is not well said.[14] [The study is useful] for the sciences along philosophical lines because if we are able to raise difficulties on both sides of the issue, we shall more easily see in each case what is true and what false. Further, [it is useful] in regard to what things are primary in each science; for it is impossible to say anything about them on the basis of the specific first principles of each proposed science, since the principles are primary in all cases,[15] [101b] and it is necessary to discuss them on the basis of generally accepted opinions in each case. This is specific and most proper to dialectic; for since it is investigative [exetastikē], it leads the way to the first principles of all methods.

[Chapter 3] We shall possess the method completely when we are in the same situation as in rhetoric and medicine and such faculties [dynameis]: that is, [able] to accomplish what we choose from the available means;[16] for neither will the one with rhetorical skill persuade by every means nor will the doctor heal, but if none of the available means is neglected we shall say that he has knowledge adequately.

■ The *Topics* then continues with discussion of propositions and problems, an account of the four "predicables" (definition, property, genus, and accident), and definitions of the ten "categories" (essence, quantity, quality, relation, place, time, position, state, activity, and passivity).

14. This refers to any serious discussion among individuals on almost any kind of issue in a private or informal setting but not to public debate in the assembly or law courts. In the public forum dialectic becomes rhetoric, as understood by Aristotle; and there ethical and pathetical means of persuasion are invoked, as well as logical argument.

15. No science (mathematics, physics, metaphysics) can prove its own first principles; they have to be taken from somewhere else, either from what is proved in another science or (Aristotle's point here) from assumptions accepted generally or by the wise. Thus, in the beginning of his *Physics* Aristotle raises the question whether there is one, or are several, first principles of physics and considers the opinions of earlier Greek thinkers on this subject in search of some agreed-upon starting point.

16. Cf. *Rhetoric* 1.2.1.

D. Cicero's Description of Aristotle's *Synagōgē Tekhnōn*

■ Aristotle compiled a summary of the rhetorical precepts of earlier Greek authors in a treatise now lost. Probably, he did so at the time he first undertook to teach rhetoric, and the approach is similar to his preliminary collection of the opinions of others in all areas of his research. Cicero and other later writers refer to this treatise. Cicero wrote *On Invention* when he was very young, between 91 and 89 B.C.; and although he tries to sound authoritative, he is probably only repeating the lectures of his (unidentified) Greek teacher; probably he had not actually read Aristotle's *Synagōgē* himself. Nor was the text of the *Rhetoric* available to him at that time. When he wrote *Brutus* in 46 B.C., he had some knowledge of the *Rhetoric* and perhaps had read the *Synagōgē,* though he may not report it accurately.

[*On Invention* 2.6] Aristotle sought out and brought together in one place the ancient writers of the art, starting with the first inventor, Tisias, and wrote a clear account, naming the authors, of the precepts of each, which he examined with great care and set out carefully in an annotated form; and he so surpassed the inventors of the subject in attractiveness and brevity of speaking that no one learns their precepts from their own books, but all who want to know what they taught turn to him as to a much more useful explicator. 7. Thus, he himself has made available for us both his own teaching and that of those before him, so that we learn about others and about him through him.

[*Brutus* 46–48] Aristotle speaks as follows. When tyrannies were abolished in Sicily and private property, after a long interval of time, was being recovered in the lawcourts, then for the first time, since that people was shrewd and born for controversy, the Sicilians Corax and Tisias compiled an *Art* and precepts [of rhetoric];[17] for before that, no one was accustomed to speak by method and

17. The date was about 467 B.C. Aristotle's emphasis on the Sicilian origins of rhetoric may have been an effort to disprove the Athenian chauvinism of Isocrates and others. It is not clear that Aristotle specifically associated the beginnings of rhetoric with democracy; but from our point of view the two are inseparable.

art, though many did carefully and in an orderly way,[18] and disputations about remarkable things had been written and prepared by Protagoras, what are now called *loci communes*. [Aristotle says] Gorgias did the same when he wrote praises and blames of separate things, because he judged that the most appropriate duty of an orator was to be able to amplify a subject and to attack it by invective. Antiphon of Rhamnus is said [by Aristotle] to have written some things similar to this. Thucydides, a learned author, wrote that he heard Antiphon speak in his own defense and that no one ever pleaded better in a capital case.[19] Lysias [according to Aristotle] at first was accustomed to teach the art; then, because Theodorus was subtler in art but drier in speech, he abandoned [teaching] the art and began to compose orations for others, which they used in the law courts. Similarly, Isocrates at first denied that there was an art of speaking[20] but was accustomed to write speeches for others; but when he himself was often brought into court because he was alleged to have broken a law that forbade anyone from being unjustly convicted, he stopped writing speeches for others and transferred his activities to compiling *arts*.[21]

▪ Further information on what may have been found in the *Synagōgē* was collected (in Greek) by Radermacher (1951).

E. Word Choice and Metaphor, from Aristotle, *Poetics*, Chapter 21

▪ Chapters 20–22 of the *Poetics* discuss *lexis,* with special attention to poetic diction. In chapter 20 Aristotle surveys

18. As seen even in the speeches in the Homeric poems.

19. Thucydides 8.68. This is probably Cicero's addition.

20. If this is true, it probably shows the influence of Socrates.

21. Cicero has perhaps misunderstood Aristotle; there is some evidence that Isocrates may have composed a handbook and more evidence that he lectured on rhetoric, but his major activity was composing orations, not arts.

what he calls the "parts" of *lexis,* which are element (or intelligible sound), syllable, connective, noun, verb, conjunction (or article?), inflection, and proposition (*logos*). He then continues with the following account of the species of words, of which metaphor is one.

[1456b20] [Chapter 21] 1. The species [*eidē*] of name[22] are, on the one hand simple (and by *simple* I mean not composed of signifying elements, for example *earth*), and on the other double, 2. and of the latter one form is made up of a signifier and nonsignifier (though not [separately] signifying and nonsignifying in the [composite] word) and the other of [two] signifiers.[23] 3. There would also be triple and quadruple and multiple compounds [like] *Hermo-kaïko-xanthos.* **[1457b]**

4. Every name is either *kyrion*[24] or *glotta*[25] or metaphor or ornament or coined or lengthened or abbreviated or altered. 5. I call *kyrion* what everybody uses and *glotta* what other people use;[26] 6. so it is apparent that both a *glotta* and a *kyrion* can be the same, but not to the same people. *Sigynon* [for "spear"] is *kyrion* among the Cyprians but a *glotta* to us.

7. Metaphor is the movement [*epiphora*] of an alien [*allotrios*] name from either genus to species or from species to genus or from species to species or by analogy.[27] 8. I call from genus to species, for example, "My ship stands here"; for to be at anchor is [a species] of standing. 9. [I call] from species to genus, "Yea, Odysseus did ten thousand noble deeds"; for "ten thousand" [*myria*] is [a species of] much [*poly*], used here for "many." 10. [I call] from

---

22. *Onoma,* "noun"—but including what we call adjectives; and according to *On Interpretation* 3.16b20–21 a verb (*rhēma*) is, by itself, also a "name" or "noun." In fact, *onoma* could be translated "word" throughout the passage.

23. E.g., *unearthly* (nonsignifying plus signifying) and *earthborn* (two signifying elements); but each has only a single signification.

24. The "prevailing" or "proper" meaning of the word; cf. *Rhetoric* 3.2.2.

25. "Strange, foreign"; see also *Rhetoric* 3.3.2 and n. 44.

26. E.g., speakers of another dialect or language or time.

27. For detailed examination of this passage, see the discussions by Ricoeur (1977, esp. 9–43) and Levin (1982).

species to species, for example, "drawing off his life with bronze" and "cutting with tireless bronze"; for here "to draw off" means to "to cut" and "to cut" means "to draw off."[28] 11. I call it analogy when the second thing is related to the first as the fourth is to the third; for [a poet] will say the fourth for the second or the second for the fourth. 12. And sometimes they add something to which it relates in place of what it [usually] refers to. I mean, for example, the cup is related to Dionysus as the shield to Ares.[29] [The poet] will then say that the cup is the shield of Dionysus and the shield the cup of Ares. 13. Or since old age is to life as evening is to day, then he will call evening the old age of day or, like Empedocles, call old age the evening of life or "life's gloaming." 14. In some cases there is no corresponding term within the analogy, but none the less a likeness will be expressed; for example, scattering seed is sowing, but in the case of the sun the [dispersion of] light has no name [in Greek].[30] Nevertheless, this has the same relation to the sun as scattering has to seed, so it is expressed as "sowing divine fire."

15. It is possible to use this turn[31] of metaphor in another way, too, by applying the alien term while denying one of its attributes; for example, if someone were to say not that the shield is Ares' cup but [that it is] a "wineless" cup.

■ The chapter continues with brief discussion of the other categories of names and an attempt to identify the grammatical gender of nouns on the basis of their final letters. Chapter 22 then begins with a statement similar to that in *Rhetoric* 3.2.1: "The virtue [*aretē*] of *lexis* is to be clear and not flat."

28. In the first case *bronze* is apparently a spear, in the second a cupping vessel; cf. *Rhetoric* 3.2.12.

29. These are the "iconographic" symbols of the god of wine and the war god in literature or art.

30. In English it is *beaming*.

31. *Tropos*, which later became the general term for "tropes," including metaphor.

F. The Concept of the Enthymeme as Understood in the Modern Period

■ Aristotle's statement in *Rhetoric* 1.2.13 that an enthymeme is "drawn from few premises and often less than those of the primary syllogism" became in postclassical times the authority for defining an enthymeme as a syllogism in which one or more propositions are not expressed. A good example of this view is found in *La Logique ou l'art de penser,* better known as "The Port Royal Logic" and one of the most influential textbooks of the early modern period. Largely the work of Antoine Arnauld, it was first published in 1664. The selection here translated is from Arnauld 1858, part 3, chapter 14. Another important, and more detailed, account of the Aristotelian enthymeme in terms of traditional logic is found in Hamilton [1866] 1969, 3: 386–94.

It has already been said that an enthymeme is a syllogism, perfect in the mind but imperfect in the expression, because one there suppresses some one of the propositions as too clear and too well known and as being easily supplied by the mind of those to whom one speaks. This manner of argument is so well known in speeches and writings that it is rare, on the contrary, that one expresses there all the propositions, because there is ordinarily one clear enough to be assumed and because the nature of the human mind prefers that one leave something to it to be supplied rather than believing that it needs to be instructed completely.

Thus, this suppression flatters the vanity of those to whom one speaks by leaving something to their intelligence and, in abridging the statement, makes it stronger and more lively. It is certainly so, for example, in this verse from the *Medea* of Ovid, which contains a very elegant enthymeme:

> I was able to save you; do you then ask if I could slay you?

One could make a formal argument of this as follows: "He who can save can slay; but I was able to save you; therefore I would be able to slay you." All the grace is gone. The reason is that just as it is one of the principal beauties of a statement to be full of meaning and to give an opportunity to the mind to form a thought more extended than the expression, so, on the contrary, it is one of the greatest defects to be empty of meaning and to close off some few thoughts, which is almost inevitable in philosophical syllogisms; for when the mind moves more rapidly than the tongue and one proposition suffices to cause two to be conceived, expression of the second becomes useless, since it contains no new meaning. This is what makes these [philosophical] types of arguments so rare in ordinary life; because, even without reflecting on it, one avoids that which causes boredom, and one contents oneself with what is absolutely necessary to make oneself understood.

Enthymemes are thus the ordinary way in which men express their reasoning, while suppressing the proposition they judge to be easily supplied; and this proposition is often the major premise, often the minor, and sometimes the conclusion; in the latter case it is not properly called an enthymeme, since all the argument is, in a way, contained in the two first propositions.

It also sometimes happens that one combines the two propositions of the enthymeme into a single proposition, which Aristotle calls, in this case, a *sentence enthymématique* and of which he gives this example [*Rhetoric* 2.21.6]: "Being a mortal, do not cherish immortal anger." The full argument would be, "He who is mortal ought not to keep immortal hatred; but you are mortal; let your hatred than not be immortal."

Appendix II: Supplementary Essays

A. THE COMPOSITION OF THE *RHETORIC*

How and when the text of the *Rhetoric* developed into the form that we now read has been discussed by scholars without reaching complete agreement. Though most would perhaps admit that different parts of the work were originally written at different times, some would insist that the whole was rather thoroughly revised, presumably at a late date in Aristotle's career, and that it represents a unified view of its subject,[1] while others are more impressed by inconsistencies between different parts.[2] It can, of course, be argued that however it was composed, Aristotle left the treatise in substantially the form in which we have it and that it represents his thinking at one point in time, that it was read as a unity by students from ancient to modern times without serious difficulties, and that what is important is not how it evolved but how it can be understood as a theory of rhetoric. But this view does require the conscientious reader to exercise considerable ingenuity in interpreting some passages to mean something different from what they literally say. To a greater extent than most works of Aristotle, the *Rhetoric* shows signs of haste, for example, in the haphazard way the chapters on pathos and ethos in Book 2 are integrated into the whole, in the inconsistent use of the term *topos,*

1. E. g., Grimaldi 1975.
2. E. g., Solmsen 1929 and Rist 1989.

and in the absence of examples in some passages in contrast to their abundance elsewhere.

Differences in approach to the *Rhetoric* seem to reflect different assumptions and different objectives on the part of readers. Some believe that it should be possible to make objective and true statements about politics, ethics, and rhetoric in the way that scientists seek to make objective and true statements about the physical world (though whether even the latter is possible is now sometimes called into doubt). Such a view is variously known as *logocentrism* or *foundationalism.* In dealing with a text these readers seek the intent of the author, and in the case of Aristotle they regard the author as one who at all times knew exactly what he was doing and expressed his full intent. Others feel that the nature of human language introduces a factor that is always centrifugal, escaping the author's control and that meaning arises from context and from the reader. They welcome differences as opening an opportunity for ongoing dialogue. Aristotle's own view lay somewhere between these schools. Unlike Plato, he did not believe that there was such as thing as abstract truth about human values; but he also thought that progress could be made toward some consensus about the good life on the basis of probable argument through dialectic. In this sense, Aristotelianism is an open philosophical system, always subject to revision.

To a greater extent than his predecessors, Aristotle thought that knowledge grows and develops over time, that philosophy and scholarship is a collegial process in which assumptions are continually reexamined, and that there are numerous avenues that have not yet been opened up.[3] His students, Theophrastus in particular, carried on this work; and we continue to do so today. As Abraham Edel (1982) has emphasized, Aristotelian thought is a network of interreacting ideas, constantly in development. There is a method common to all parts; and there are certain common assumptions, of which one of the most important is the concept of potentiality/ actuality. Aristotle defines rhetoric as a potentiality (*dynamis,* 1.2.1); his treatise represents an attempt to visualize it when actualized in its fullest form, but he would doubtless agree that there is more in rhetoric (and in any other discipline) than is met with in his

3. See, e.g., *Sophistical Refutations* 34 and *Rhetoric* 3.1.

philosophy. It is an interesting mental exercise to try to enter into the evolution of his own thought. As pointed out in the Introduction, if one does so, it is possible to see in the text a kind of debate in Aristotle's mind between a more philosophical and a more pragmatic view of rhetoric (a continuation of what is found in Platonic dialogues) and possible also to enter into this debate in making one's own judgments about the nature, functions, and morality of rhetoric.

The outside dates for the development of the *Rhetoric* are from about 360 to about 334 B.C. In 360 Aristotle was a student in Plato's Academy and living in Athens, where rhetoric in its many forms enjoyed perhaps the greatest prestige and influence in its history. Plato's hostility to it could have whetted Aristotle's attempt to understand it better, an attempt probably made around 360 in the lost dialogue *Gryllus* and continued in his early teaching of rhetoric in the 350s. In 335, after an absence of twelve years, he returned to the hotbed of debate in Athens, having lived meanwhile in the courts of kings in Assos and Macedon and having reflected deeply on many aspects of life and society. There is no reasonable doubt that the *Rhetoric,* along with the *Poetics* and the *Constitution of the Athenians,* is one of his most Athenian works, primarily addressed to Athenians; for only in Athens did rhetoric fully function in the way he describes, and it is from Athenian rhetoric that he draws the largest number of his practical illustrations. That he hoped eventually to return to Athens is probable, given its leadership in Greek intellectual life; and that the possibility of returning bulked large in his mind at least by 338, when Philip defeated the Athenians at Chaeronea, is also likely. That he hoped to have some practical influence on life in Athens and elsewhere seems clear from the passion evident throughout the *Nicomachean Ethics.* Although his revisions of the *Rhetoric* were never complete, the evidence supports the view that he worked on the treatise between 340 and 335 in anticipation of his return to Athens and the opening of a school there. The most compelling evidence is furnished by the historical allusions, of which the latest are to events in that period.

Dionysius of Halicarnassus, writing in the late first century B.C., devotes his *First Letter to Ammaeus* to answering an unnamed Peripatetic philosopher who had claimed that Demosthenes learned the art of rhetoric from Aristotle. Dionysius assumes that the Peripatetic meant that Demosthenes was familiar with the *Rhetoric* (whether by reading it or by hearing it delivered as a series of lectures is not said); and he also regards the treatise in three books as we have it as a single work, written all at one time. Living in Rome, Dionysius probably used the edition published by Andronicus, noted in section B below. Dionysius argues that the Peripatetic was mistaken (because when the *Rhetoric* was written, Demosthenes was already at the height of his career) and that the converse is true: Aristotle wrote the treatise on the basis of a comparative study of the works of Demosthenes and other orators. His evidence for the date of composition falls into two groups. The first are the cross-references in the *Rhetoric* to the *Topics, Analytics,* and *Methodics,* which he takes as showing that Aristotle had earlier written a number of his most substantial works and was therefore well along in his career. He does not consider the possibility that cross-references could have been added at a later date to otherwise completed passages. Second, Dionysius seeks to show on the basis of historical references in the treatise that it was written after all of Demosthenes' great public speeches of the period of the Olynthian War in 349–348 B.C., after Philip's breaking his alliance with Athens in 340–340 and even after *On the Crown,* delivered in 330. The latter argument, however, is unconvincing in that it requires an unsubstantiated identification of the trial of "Demosthenes and those who killed Nicanor" (2.23.3) with Demosthenes' defense of Ctesiphon in *On the Crown.*

It is probably prudent to separate attempts at dating books 1–2 from the dating of book 3, since these may have originally been separate works. The list of the writings in Diogenes Laertius, along with various other oddities, contains (5.24) an *Art of Rhetoric* in two books and a treatise *On Lexis,* also in two books (style plus arrangement?). Perhaps more compelling, Books 1–2 not only do not anticipate but seem to forestall any consideration of style until the final transitional passage in 2.26.3. Possibly, Aristotle, in his final set of revisions, decided to link two works together to make a single treatise; possibly the linkage was made by the grammarian Tyrannio or by Andronicus of Rhodes.

In books 1–2 the latest historical references seem to be to the embassy from Artaxerxes (2.20.3) and the trial of Philocrates

(2.3.13) in 343, the death of Diopeithes in 342 or 341 (2.8.11), Philip's envoy to Thebes in 339 (2.23.6), Demades' comment about Demosthenes' policy (2.24.8, any time after 338), and finally the Common Peace (2.23.18, probably that imposed by Macedon on Greece in 336). It is worth noting that reference to events after 340 all occur in chapters 23–24 of Book 2—the discussion of topics, a section of the work that Aristotle introduces with the verb *parasēmainō* (2.22.17), indicating that it is a kind of supplement. This suggests that Aristotle may have integrated these chapters into the *Rhetoric* about 336 or 335. One implication is that the concept of the *topos* as applied to rhetoric is a relatively late addition to the treatise. In 1.2.21–22 Aristotle makes a sharp distinction between *idia* and *topoi* and throughout books 1 and 2 continues to talk about *idia;* but in what may be a late addition in 1.15.19 he refers to the *idia* as *topoi,* and in 1.2.22 and 1.6.1 as *stoikheia,* which in 2.22.13 and 2.26.1 he says are the same as topics. From this we might conclude that Aristotle eventually came to the view, shared by most later rhetoricians, that what he had earlier called *idia* or *stoikheia* are a kind of topic, differing from common topics in being specific to a particular body of knowledge.

A general hypothesis of the composition of books 1–2 might start with what Rist (1989, 85–86, 136–44) calls the "early core" of the treatise, 1.5–15, with numerous references to historical events before 350 and some philosophical concepts that Aristotle later abandoned. Some revision was subsequently given to these chapters, including perhaps the insertion of chapter 8 with its cross-reference to the *Politics.* The "early core" seems to require 1.3–4, or something like them, to define the species of rhetoric and introduce the discussion of deliberative oratory. The discussions of pathos in 2.2–11 and of ethos in 2.12–17 apparently originated in a separate context and have been imperfectly integrated into the *Rhetoric* at a relatively late stage by occasional references to the needs of a speaker and a transition in 2.18; the beginning of 2.20 sounds as though it originally followed 1.5–15. As noted in the Introduction, the otherwise unneeded statement in 2.14.4 about the maturity of the mind at the age of forty-nine *could* be taken as a wry reference to the past that Aristotle was that age when he wrote the passage, thus around 335 B.C. The concluding chapters of book 2 (18–26) are the adaptation of Aristotle's dialectic to rhetoric, a product of the period 340–335 B.C. With this must go 1.2, the definition of rhetoric and its parts, which organizes the whole revision.

The dating of 1.1 is the most problematic. It seems difficult to associate it with a revision of the work that added 2.2–17, since it rejects concern with the matters discussed there. Although it is the most Platonic part of the work, it is difficult to connect it with Aristotle's earliest teaching of rhetoric if our sources are correct that that was of a general, practical sort.[4] Possibly it should be thought of as an introduction to rhetoric for his associates in the Academy at the time he was teaching a more general course to others. Possibly it resulted from his teaching of rhetoric to Alexander as an extension of instruction in dialectic and part of a general course in philosophy. He may have let it stand in the final version for his return to Athens because he liked this linkage, possibly because he liked the challenge to traditional teaching and thought it worthwhile for students in his new school to meet an extreme view of philosophical rhetoric at the outset, knowing that this would be modified as study continued.

Even if book 3 was originally a separate work, its development seems to have been roughly parallel to that of books 1–2. Burkert (1975) pointed out that the reference to Theodorus in 3.2.4 sounds as though he was alive when it was written, putting it probably in the 350s. That would mean that some of the material may go back to Aristotle's early teaching of rhetoric—logically enough if that teaching was indeed of a popular sort. This may include some of the discussion of diction in 3.2–12 and Aristotle's version of a traditional rhetorical handbook in 3.13–19, but some of the discussion has certainly been added later or revised. The latest historical references seem to be to the *Philippus* of Isocrates (e.g., 3.10.7, 3.11.2, etc.), published in 346 B.C., and other references to Isocrates in 3.17.10–11 could be taken to imply that he was still alive, putting them before his death in 338. Again, teaching Alexander may have drawn Aristotle's attention back to the matter of style. Two references to "Attic" or "Athenian" orators (3.11.16 and

4. The chief sources are Cicero, *On the Orator* 3.141, *Orator* 46; Philodemus, *On Rhetoric* 2:50–51 Sudhaus; Quintilian 3.1.14; Diogenes Laertius 5.3. See Chroust 1964.

3.17.10) may imply that Aristotle was not in Athens when he wrote these passages, putting them before 335. The final revision of book 3 refers to, and somewhat expands, the discussion of metaphor in the *Poetics,* and Aristotle's interest in Athenian drama and in making a reply to Plato's view of imitation, though possibly awakened by teaching Alexander, seems better associated with a hoped-for return to Athens. It may well be that he arrived with the two works completed and that he inaugurated his school there with lectures on these two subjects of special interest to an Athenian audience. The text of the *Rhetoric* suggests that some revision was made hastily, perhaps in preparation for his return. We cannot be certain that in teaching rhetoric Aristotle read out the treatise we have; even if he did so he is likely to have expanded and commented on its contents as he went along or to have omitted some parts; and one hopes he reponded to questions from the audience.

B. THE HISTORY OF THE TEXT AFTER ARISTOTLE

The geographer Strabo (13.1.54), an often-well-informed writer of the late first century B.C., and the historian–philosopher Plutarch (*Sulla* 26.1–2), writing a hundred years later, are the major sources for the early history of the text of the works of Aristotle. They are in general agreement and probably drew on the same source. The tale they tell has not always been believed, but in the case of the *Rhetoric* it is consistent with the very limited knowledge of the treatise shown by Greek and Latin writers from the late fourth to middle of the first centuries B.C. The story goes as follows.

After Aristotle's death his library became the property of his most famous student, Theophrastus, who had succeeded him as head of the Peripatetic School. (Theophrastus wrote on several aspects of rhetoric; and though these works have not survived, they seem often to have been an extension of Aristotle's thinking. "Topics," "enthymemes," delivery, and style were all treated by him, his treatise *On Lexis* being especially influential. In this work he seems to have reformulated Aristotle's discussion of the virtue of style in terms of diction and composition under four major headings: correctness, clarity, ornamentation, and propriety.[5] After Theophrastus' death (about 285 B.C.), some of Aristotle's still unpublished manuscripts probably remained in the Peripatetic School in Athens, and copies of some were probably made for research libraries, of which the most important was the great Library at Alexandria in Egypt; but there is no clear indication that the *Rhetoric* was among these books.) Aristotle's library was inherited from Theophrastus by the philosopher Neleus and taken to Scepsis in Asia Minor, where it fell into the hands of people who were not scholars. To prevent the books from being seized by agents for the library at Pergamum, these owners hid them and then forgot about them. Thus, the Peripatetics after Theophrastus did not have the original works of Aristotle, or at least not all of them. Subsequently, perhaps about 100 B.C., Aristotle's library, now in a damaged condition, was sold by the heirs of those who had hidden it to Apellicon of Teos, living in Athens. After Apellicon's death it was seized by the Roman general Sulla and sent to Rome, around 83 B.C. There the grammarian Tyrannio "arranged" the works and furnished copies to Andronicus of Rhodes, who "published" them and drew up lists of the works.

It has often been assumed that some editing was done by Tyrannio and Andronicus, and one possibility is the combining of books 1–2 of the *Rhetoric* with book 3, including some of the transitional passages. The reference to Aristotle's *Lexis* in Demetrius (*On Style* 116) may imply that he regarded it as a separate work; and, as noted in section A above, Diogenes Laertius (5.24), writing much later, lists an *Art of Rhetoric* in two books, not three, as well as a work *On Lexis* in two books. Possibly, two traditions existed, one containing all three books, one containing only books 1 and 2. The version known to Quintilian (2.17.14) had three books.

When Cicero wrote *On Invention* as a very young man and before the arrival of the library of Apellicon in Rome, he knew that Aristotle had written on the subject, describes the work as providing aids and ornaments to the art (1.7), and attributes to Aristotle the view that the duty (*officium*) of the orator was exercised in three *genera:* demonstrative, deliberative, and judicial.

5. See, esp., Cicero, *Orator* 79.

That, of course, is not quite what Aristotle says in 1.3, but it does indicate that the division of rhetoric into three species was traditionally, and rightly, associated with Aristotle. This may well represent an oral tradition that goes back to Aristotle's own students in the fourth century rather than a knowledge of the text in the intervening centuries.

Even if the *Rhetoric* were available to scholars between 300 and 100 B.C., new developments in rhetorical theory had rendered it obsolete as a school text. Hermagoras of Temnos, in the middle of the second century, had worked out stasis theory, a systematic way to determine the central question at issue in a speech. Aristotle shows some awareness of such matters in 1.13.9–10 and 3.15, 17 but failed to present a systematic theory, which by Cicero's time was the foundation of the study of rhetorical invention, and continued so throughout the Byzantine period. In the study of style, the Stoics had developed the theory of tropes and figures of speech, concepts unknown to Aristotle; and these two were major concerns of later rhetoricians. Aristotle's topical theory did remain a subject of interest, though modified by subsequent writers including Cicero, Quintilian, and Boethius.

When Cicero wrote *On the Orator* in 55 B.C., he clearly had some knowledge of the *Rhetoric,* probably from the edition of Tyrannio and Andronicus; and the discussion of invention in *On the Orator* 2.114–306 is considerably more Aristotelian than what is found in *On Invention* or in the other early Latin treatise, *Rhetoric for Herennius.* Cicero refers to the *Rhetoric* repeatedly and even makes his character Antonius claim to have read it in Athens in the late second century B.C. (2.160). Aristotelian influences include the role of logical proof, presentation of character, and emotional appeal (2.115), described later in *Orator* 69 as the three *officia* of the orator—to prove, to delight, and to move—and then associated with the three kinds of style: plain, middle, and grand. This represents an important and long influential restatement and extension of Aristotle's basic concepts in *Rhetoric* 1.2.

The Aristotelian works were reedited and extensively studied in later antiquity, beginning with Alexander of Aphrodisias around A.D. 200; but the *Rhetoric* was given very little attention. In the new organization of the corpus it was assigned to the *Organon,* following the *Topics* and preceding the *Poetics.* By implication, rhetoric was to be regarded as a logical tool, not as a practical or productive art. There are only occasional references to the treatise in writers of the Roman empire or early Middle Ages, but it did survive intact because of its Aristotelian authorship. Our earliest— and often best—manuscript is *Parisinus* 1741, written in the tenth century. It is a compilation of rhetorical treatises by Menander, Dionysius of Halicarnassus, and others, plus the *Rhetoric* and *Poetics;* there are two, rather short Greek commentaries on the *Rhetoric* written in the twelfth century, one attributed to a certain Stephanus, one anonymous.[6] The work was also known to Arabic scholars of Greek philosophy; and in the thirteenth century Hermannus Alemannus in Spain made a Latin translation of an Arabic commentary attributed to al-Farabi. Two Latin translations of the Greek text were then produced, introducing the *Rhetoric* to the Western Middle Ages. The first of these, the Old Translation, was perhaps the work of Bartholomew of Massina; and the second was by William of Moerbeke, urged on by Thomas Aquinas. Giles of Rome then wrote a Latin commentary; but (as this commentary indicates) what interested readers of the time was not the rhetorical theory (for which they kept to the Ciceronian tradition) but its political and moral teachings.[7]

In the fifteenth century George of Trebizond brought Aristotle's theory to the attention of Italian humanists and prepared a new Latin translation, which was the first printed version of the *Rhetoric* (about 1477). The complete Greek text was not printed with early editions of Aristotle's philosophical works and first appeared in 1508 in the Venice edition of the collected *Rhetores graeci,* published by Aldus Manutius. Thereafter, new editions of the Greek text began to appear, and new translations were made.[8] The first English version, a kind of outline summary, was the work of the political philosopher Thomas Hobbes, printed in London in 1637. Although the *Rhetoric* was much read in the later Renaissance and although important scholarship on the text and the fine commentary of E. M. Cope appeared in the nineteenth century, real appreciation of the significance of the treatise is a phenome-

6. Texts in Rabe 1896; on Byzantine study of the *Rhetoric* see Conley 1990b.

7. On western medieval study of the *Rhetoric,* see Murphy 1974, 89–101.

8. See Brandes 1989.

non of twentieth-century interest in speech communication and critical theory.

The division of the original *Rhetoric* into two or three books can be attributed to Aristotle himself, and presumably reflects the convenient length of a papyrus scroll in his time. The division into numbered chapters was first made by George of Trebizond in the fifteenth century as a convenience for teachers and readers and is generally logical, though some discussions are divided into separate chapters when the Greek suggests they should be read as continuous. The division of chapters into numbered sections originated in the Bipontine Edition of J. T. Buhle (Zweibrucken, 1793) and is often erratic. The standard way to refer to specific passages in the Greek text is by use of page, column, and line numbers in the 1831 Berlin edition of the complete works of Aristotle as edited by Immanuel Bekker.

C. THE STRENGTHS AND LIMITATIONS OF THE *RHETORIC*

The great strength of the *Rhetoric* of Aristotle derives from its clear recognition (in contrast to the views of Plato) that rhetoric is a technique or tool applicable to any subject and from the universality and utility of its basic, systematically organized, concepts. It provides a method for looking at rhetoric as a human phenomenon, for learning how to use it, and also for a system of criticism, in that the features of speech that Aristotle describes can be used not only to construct a speech, but to evaluate any form of discourse. The most important of the concepts that Aristotle uses as frameworks for his discussion are, first, the identification of three (and only three) *pisteis,* or forms of persuasion deriving from the factors in any speech situation: presentation of the trustworthy character of the speaker, the logical argument set out in the text, and the emotional effect created by the text on the audience or reader. Second is the distinction of three (and only three) species of rhetoric—judicial, deliberative, and epideictic—based on whether the audience is a *judge* in the sense of being able to take specific action as a result of being persuaded to do so and on a characteristic "time" and "end" assigned to each.

There are other important principles as well. In rhetoric the speaker or writer deals with probabilities—what could have or can happen based on what happens for the most part in such situations—not on certainties. Forms of persuasion are either *nonartistic* (evidence the speaker uses but does not—or should not—invent) and *artistic* (arguments constructed from the evidence, situation, and character of those involved). Arguments are either inductive (drawing a particular conclusion from parallel instances with an implied universal conclusion, which Aristotle calls *paradigm,* or example) or deductive (drawing a specific conclusion from a more general premise by an implied syllogistic argument). To distinguish a formal logical argument from the form it takes in popular discourse, Aristotle calls the latter *enthymeme.* The materials of enthymemes come from the premises of other disciplines, especially politics and ethics; but their formal structure draws on *topics,* strategies of argument useful in dealing with any subject. The work is strong in its emphasis on the importance of logical validity. There are also valuable concepts in the discussion of style, especially the demand for clarity, the understanding of the effect of different kinds of language and sentence structure, and the explication of the role of metaphor. The work is also of interest in that it summarizes many of the political and moral assumptions of contemporary Greek society and preserves many quotations from writers or speakers that we would not otherwise have.

Aristotle worked from rhetoric as he observed it in Greece; but, as in all of his philosophy, he sought to discover what was universally true, and to a considerable extent he was successful. His system of rhetoric can, and has been, used to describe the phenomenon of speech in cultures as diverse from the Greeks as the ancient Hebrew, the Chinese, and primitive societies around the world; and it can be used to describe many features of modern communication.

The treatise nevertheless has limitations and needs to be expanded or revised to provide a complete, general rhetoric. With only occasional exceptions, its focus is on public address or civic discourse and is somewhat conditioned by the circumstances and conventions of these forms in Greece. Epideictic, in particular, needs to be looked at in a variety of ways not recognized by Aristotle. Though his theory of *ēthos* is striking, it limits consideration of the effect of character to what is conveyed by the words of a speech and fails to recognize the great role of the authority of a speaker as already perceived by an audience. Many speakers—especially great religious leaders—have been able to proclaim a message with personal authority without providing logical proof of it. There are more rhetorics than are met in Aristotle's philosophy. The discussion of both *ēthos* and *pathos* is not very well articulated into the uses of rhetoric and generally lacks needed illustration. The discussion of logical argument is better in this respect but fails to provide a method for determining the question at issue in a debate, which was later supplied by stasis theory; and Aristotle's failure to give his treatise a full, final revision has left a number of inconsistencies, including inconsistent use of such key terms as *pistis* and *topos*. Great emphasis is put on understanding the enthymeme as the key to logical persuasion; but its theoretical importance is probably exaggerated, since its syllogistic qualities are very slippery, and Aristotle's precepts can be reduced to a recommendation that a speaker give a reason (or apparent reason) for what is asserted. Nor does Aristotle take a strong stand against the common Greek preference for circumstantial evidence over the direct evidence of documents and witnesses.

It is probably also a weakness that Aristotle treats the matter of style as secondary to content and that he draws no connection between the use of examples as logical devices and the use of the simile; nor does he connect amplification of subject matter with stylistic amplification. Rhetoricians in the seventeenth century began to rewrite their systems beginning with the nature of language and its various uses, and any modern theory of rhetoric should be based more squarely on a theory of the nature and uses of language. Aristotle's approach was, however, adopted by most ancient rhetoricians; and the result is that invention and style became separate processes: thoughts, already worked out and arranged, are then deliberately cast into words. But language, including metaphor, is already there in the thought; and this becomes especially important in the examination of the rhetoric of a literary work. Although Aristotle is the father of the study of metaphor, modern research has revealed complexities far beyond what he considers. He also seems to make too sharp a distinction between rhetoric (controlled by the speaker's intentionality) and poetics (in which the creative artist plays more the role of a facilitator or agent of expression of something beyond himself) and gives a higher status to dialectic than rhetoric, probably because he regarded it as dealing with universals rather than particulars; whereas rhetoric, as the more all-inclusive phenomenon, is probably better regarded as the archdiscipline of which dialectic and poetics are smaller, more limited parts.

Finally, Aristotle thinks of rhetoric as an aspect of politics. His political, ethical, and rhetorical treatises, taken together, seek the means to secure the good life and human happiness. Elsewhere (esp. in *Nicomachean Ethics*) he speaks passionately on this subject. It is perhaps a weakness of the *Rhetoric* that it fails to articulate this goal fully. The modern reader thus needs to reflect more than Aristotle explicitly does on the role of rhetoric in society, (necessary and legitimate but also potentially dangerous), on the public expression of values, and on the relationship between discourse and social and political change. But the *Rhetoric,* especially if read in conjunction with the *Gorgias* and *Phaedrus* of Plato, the *Antidosis* and other speeches of Isocrates, and Aristotle's own political and ethical writings, provides a powerful entry into the still continuing debate about the peculiar and ambivalent phenomenon, characteristic of life itself, that since Plato's time has been called rhetoric.

Glossary

All syllables and letters should be pronounced. The original pitch accent on Greek nouns occurred on one of the last three syllables of a word but can only be determined for a particular noun or adjective by consulting a dictionary. It is acceptable to pronounce Greek terms in accordance with Latin rules of stress accent. Thus, the next-to-last syllable is stressed if it contains a long vowel, a diphthong, or a short vowel followed by either two consonants or a double consonant (*x* or *z*); otherwise, stress goes on the third syllable from the end. Systems of transliteration vary. In the following list, *y* represents Greek upsilon, roughly equivalent to *u* as in French *lune; ē* represents eta, pronounced as long *a* in English, *ō* is omega, or long *o; nk* represents an original gamma kappa (*gk*), which was, however, nasalized. Latin writers used the letter *c* to represent Greek kappa (*k* in the words below) and Latin spelling continues to be used by some scholars today; thus *arkhē* or *arche, kōlon* or *colon,* and so on. The definite article in Greek is, in the singular, *ho* (masculine), *hē* (feminine), *to* (neuter); in the plural, *hoi, hai, ta.* In the following list the gender is indicated by *m., f.,* or *n.*

amphisbētēsis, pl. *amphisbētēseis* (f): the question at issue, what is being debated (1.13.10, 3.17.1).
antistrophos, pl. *antistrophoi* (m.): counterpart, correlative (1.1.1).
antithesis, pl. *antithesis* (f): contrast or opposition of words, phrases, or ideas (3.9.9, 3.10.7, 3.11.10).

apodeixis, pl. *apodeixeis* (f): logical demonstration (1.1.11).

apologia, pl. *apologiai* (f): a speech in self-defense (1.3.3, 1.10).

aretē pl. *aretai* (f.): excellence, moral virtue (1.6.6–10, 1.9.4); the virtue of style (3.2.1).

arkhē, pl. *arkhai* (f.): beginning, starting point, first principle (1.2.21, 1.7.12). The word has a variety of other meanings (see 3.11.7).

asyndeton, pl. *asyndeta* (n.): asyndeton, absence of connectives (3.6.6, 3.12.2, 3.19.6). For its opposite, now called *polysyndeton,* Aristotle uses *polloi syndesmoi* (3.5.6).

atekhnos pistis, pl. *atekhnoi pisteis* (f.): nonartistic proof or proofs, used but not invented by a speaker (1.2.2), by later writers often called *extrinsic.* Those discussed in 1.15 are laws, witnesses, contracts, evidence of slaves, and oaths. In 3.16.1 the facts in an epideictic speech are called *atekhnon.*

auxēsis (f.) or *to auxein* or *to auxētikon* (n.): amplification or intensification of a statement to heighten its effect; characteristic of epideictic oratory (1.9.38–39, 3.6.7, 3.12.4) but used in all species (2.18.4); not to be regarded as a topic of enthymemes (2.26.1–2). Its opposite is *to meioun* (deprecation).

blaisōsis (f.): a twist, given to refute the enthymeme of an opponent by showing that two opposite conclusions can follow from the premises (2.18.15).

diabolē, pl. *diabolai* (f.): prejudicial attack or slander in a speech (3.15).

diairesis, pl. *diaireseis* (f.): division of an argument into logical headings (2.23.10).

dialektikē (f.) dialectic, the art of logical argument on general issues of a political or ethical nature; practiced as an exercise for students of philosophy in the form of question-and-answer dialogue (1.1).

dianoia (f.): thought; used in 1.26.3 to mean rhetorical invention.

diatribē, pl. *diatribai* (f.): dwelling on a subject; usually personal invective, often in digressions (3.17.10).

diēgēsis, pl. *diēgēseis* (f.): the narration or narrative passages in a speech (3.16).

(to) dikaion, pl. *(ta) dikaia* (n.): what is just, the subject of judicial oratory (1.3.5, 1.13).

dikanikos (*logos*), pl. *dikanikoi* (m.); *dikanikon* (*genos* or *eidos*), pl. *dikanika* (n.): judicial speech, as in a court of law (1.3.1–6, 1.10–15).

dikastēs, pl. *dikastai* (m.); a member of a jury (1.3.2).

dikē, pl. *dikai* (f.): justice; also, a trial relating to alleged violation of someone's rights (1.13.3).

dynamis, pl. *dynameis* (f.): potentiality, ability, or faculty of doing or becoming something. All arts, including rhetoric, are *dynameis* (1.2.1). In Aristotelian philosophy regularly contrasted with *energeia* (actuality, realization).

eidos, pl. *eidē* (n.): form; species in contrast with *genos,* genus; in 1.2.22 used to mean *specific* topics in contrast to *common* topics.

eikōn, pl. *eikones* (f.): simile (3.4).

eikos, pl. *eikota* (n.): probability (1.2.15, 2.24.10–11, 2.25.8–11).

eiromenē: see *lexis eiromenē.*

eirōneia (f.): dissimulation, mockery (2.2.24).

ekklēsiastēs, pl. *ekklēsiastai* (m.): a member of a public assembly (1.3.2).

elenkos, pl. *elenkoi* (m.): refutation (3.17.13–15).

energeia (f.): actualization, realization, representing inanimate things as animate (3.11.2). (Confused by some later writers with *enargeia,* which means "clarity" or "vividness" but does not occur in the *Rhetoric.*)

enkōmion, pl. *enkōmia* (n.): praise of the deeds of a person; a form of epideictic (1.9.33).

enstasis, pl. *enstaseis* (f.): objection to a premise in an opponent's argument (2.25.1–7, 2.26.3).

entekhnos pistis, pl. *entekhnoi pisteis* (f.): artistic or intrinsic means of persuasion, derived from the presentation of the character of the speaker as trustworthy, moving the emotions of the audience, and the use of logical argument (1.2.3, 2.1).

enthymēma, pl. *enthymēmata* (n.): enthymeme; a rhetorical syllogism, i.e., a statement with a supporting reason introduced by *for, because,* or *since* or an *if . . . then* statement. In contrast to a logical syllogism, the premises and conclusion are ordinarily probable, not necessarily logically valid. A premise may be omitted if it will be easily assumed by the audience. See 1.2.8–22, 2.22.

epagōgē, pl. *epagōgai* (f.): induction (1.2.8).

epainos, pl. *epainoi* (m.): praise, the positive form of epideictic (1.3.3, 1.9.33).

epideiktikos (*logos*), pl. *epideitikoi* (m.); *epideiktikē* (*lexis*), pl. *epideiktikai* (f.); *epideitikon* (*genos* or *eidos*), pl. *epideiktika* (n.): epideictic speech, demonstrative rhetoric, the oratory of praise or blame (1.3.1–6, 1.9, 3.12).

epieikeia (f.): fair-mindedness (1.2.4); (*to*) *epieikes* (n.): fairness (1.13.13, 1.15.6).

epilogos, pl. *epilogoi* (m.): epilogue, peroration, the conclusion of a speech (3.19).

epistēmē, pl. *epistēmai* (f.): knowledge; in Aristotle's other works often scientific knowledge, in contrast to *tekhnē,* or art; in the *Rhetoric* used of a discipline—such as politics or ethics—that has a systematic body of thought (1.1.1).

epitheton, pl. *epitheta* (n.): epithet (3.2.14, 3.3.3).

erotēsis, pl. *erotēseis* (f.): interrogation, a question by a speaker to an opponent (3.18).

ēthos, pl. *ēthē* (n.): character, usually the moral character of a person, either the speaker or the listener (1.2.3–4, 1.8.6, 1.9.1, 2.1.1–7, 2.12–17).

(*ta*) *eudokimounta* (n.): expressions that are well liked with audiences (3.10.1, 3.10.7).

glotta, pl. *glottai* (f.)(in non-Attic Greek also *glossa, -ai*): a gloss; a strange, obsolete, or foreign word, causing frigidity in style (3.3.2, 3.10.2).

gnōmē, pl. *gnōmai* (f.): a maxim (Latin *sententia*), a general statement relating to life (2.21, 3.17.9).

(*to*) *hellenizein* (n.): speaking good grammatical Greek (3.5).

homoioteleuton, pl. *homoioteleuta* (n.): *paromoisis,* or rhyme at the end of cola (3.9.9).

hyperbolē, pl. *hyperbolai* (f.): hyperbole, exaggerated metaphor (3.11.15).

hypokrisis (f.): acting, delivery in oratory (3.1.3–7).

idiai (*protaseis, pisteis*) (f.); *idion,* pl. *idia* (n.): specific (propositions or proofs); the special topics of such disciplines as politics and ethics in contrast with common topics (1.2.21–22).

(*to*) *kalon,* pl. (*ta*) *kala* (n.): what is fine, good to look upon, honorable, or noble, as praised in epideictic (1.3.5, 1.9).

katēgoria, pl. *katēgoriai* (f.): accusation or prosecution (1.3.3, 1.10).

koinai pisteis (f.): logical means of persuasion common to all three species of rhetoric: paradigm, maxim, and enthymeme (2.20–22).

koinoi topoi: see *topos.*

(to) koinon, pl. *(ta) koina (n.):* subjects for argument common to all three species of rhetoric: the possible and the impossible, past and future fact, degree of magnitude (1.3.7–9, 1.7, 1.14, 2.19).

kōlon, pl. *kōla* (n.): colon, one of the two parts of a period (3.9.5).

krisis, pl. *kriseis* (f.): judgment, as made by an assembly or jury (1.1.4, 2.1.2).

kritēs, pl. *kritai* (m.): a judge, often meaning a member of a jury but also a member of a deliberative assembly (1.3.2).

kyrios, pl. *kyrioi* (m.); *kyria,* pl. *kyriai* (f.); *kyrion,* pl. *kyria* (n.): in grammar, the prevailing or proper meaning of a word (3.2.2); in other contexts the word has a variety of other meanings (e.g., "authoritative" in 1.8.2).

lexis, pl. *lexeis* (f.): how something is said, style, often word choice, sometimes composition of sentences or speeches (3.1–12).

lexis agōnistikē (f.): the style of a speech spoken in actual debate (3.12.1).

lexis eiromenē (f.): the "strung-on" or running, style of composition, in contrast to the periodic style (3.9.1).

lexis graphikē (f.): the written style (3.12.1).

lexis katestrammenē (f.): the "turned-down," or periodic, style of composition (3.9).

logographos, plural *logographoi* (m.): a prose writer (2.11.7, 3.12.2); a speech writer (3.7.7).

logos, pl. *logoi* (m.): word, sentence, rational argument, speech, tale, esteem, etc.

lysis, pl. *lyseis* (f.): refutation of an argument by "undoing" its logic, showing that a premise is not valid or that a different conclusion can follow (2.25).

metaphora, pl. *metaphorai* (f.): metaphor (3.2, 3.10, 3.11); the movement or transfer of an alien name from genus to spe-

cies, species to genus, species to species, or by analogy
(*Poetics* 21.7–15 in Appendix I.E).

nomos, pl. *nomoi* (m.): law (1.4.12, 1.15.3–12). Law is either
gegrammenos (written) or *koinos* (common to the tradition
of all). (See 1.10.3, 1.13.2.)

onkos (m.): expansiveness in style (3.6).

paian, pl. *paiones* (m.): a metrical foot consisting of one long and
three short or three short and one long syllables, regarded
by Aristotle as the most appropriate rhythm in prose
(3.8.5–6).

parabolē, pl. *parabolai* (f.): comparison, a form of example
(2.20.2–4).

paradeigma, pl. *paradeigmata* (n.): paradigm, inductive argument
from example (1.2.8–10, 2.20).

parison, plural *parisa* (n.), or *parisōsis*, pl. *parisōseis* (f.): an equal
number of syllables in each of two *cola* (3.9.9).

paromoiōsis, pl. *paromoiōseis* (f.): similarity in sound at the beginning or ending of cola (3.9.9).

pathos, pl. *pathē* (n.): emotion, a temporary state of feeling awakened by circumstances; in the *Rhetoric* especially the emotions of members of an audience as moved by a speaker
(1.2.5, 2.1–11).

periodos, pl. *periodoi* (f.): an expression having a beginning and
end in itself and consisting or one or two cola (3.9).

pistis, pl. *pisteis* (f.): proof, means of persuasion. The categories
of *pistis* discussed in the *Rhetoric* are artistic (*entekhnikē*)
and nonartistic (*atekhnikē*) and among the artistic those
based on the presentation of the character of the speaker,
on arousing the emotions of the audience, and on logical
demonstration. (See esp. 1.2; but in 3.17.15 and probably in
1.1.3 *pistis* means logical argument in contrast to character
presentation or emotional appeal).

(to) prepon (n.): the appropriate, propriety as a quality of style
(3.2.1, 3.7).

proairesis (f.): deliberate choice or moral purpose, a decision
made on the basis of character (1.1.14, 1.8.6, 3.16.8).

prooimion, pl. *prooimia* (n.): the proem, exordium, or introduction of a speech (3.14).

pro ommatōn poein (n.): bringing-before-the-eyes, visualization (3.10–11).

protasis, pl. *protaseis* (f.): a proposition or premise of an argument (1.3.7).

prothesis, pl. *protheseis* (f.): the statement of a case at the beginning of a speech (3.13.2).

psogos, pl. *psogoi* (m.): blame, the negative form of epideictic (1.3.3).

(ta) psychra (n.): frigidities of style (3.3).

rhētōr, pl. *rhētores* (m.): a speaker (1.1.14).

rhētorikē (*tekhnē*) (f.): the ability, in each particular case, to see the available means of persuasion (1.2.1).

rhythmos, p. *rhythmoi* (m.): recurring proportion in the quantity (long or short) of syllables giving a sense of limit to language, esp. at the beginnings and endings of sentences and clauses (3.8).

(to) saphes (n.): clarity, the *aretē* of style (3.2.1).

sēmeion, pl. *sēmeia* (n.): sign, a probable or necessary indication that something is so (1.2.14–18).

semnos (m.), *semnē* (f.), *semnon* (n.): stately or solemn in style (3.3.3–4).

soloikizein: to make a mistake in word usage (3.5.7).

sophistēs, pl. *sophistai* (m.): sophist, a person who engages in specious argument (1.1.14).

stoikheion, pl. *stoikheia* (n.): element, identified with topics in 2.22.13 and 2.26.1.

syllogismos, pl. *syllogismoi* (m.): syllogism, a deductive argument consisting of a major premise, a minor premise, and a conclusion (1.2.8).

symbouleutikos (*logos*) (m.), pl. *symbouleutikoi; symbouleutikon* (*genos* or *eidos*) (n.): deliberative speech, as before a public assembly (1.3.1–6, 1.4–8).

(to) sympheron, pl. *(ta) sympheronta* (n.): what is advantageous or beneficial to a speaker or audience, the subject of deliberative oratory (1.3.5, 1.6.1).

taxis (f.): arrangement, esp. of the parts of a speech in conventional order (3.13–19).

tekmērion, pl. *tekmēria* (n.): a necessarily valid sign (1.2.16–18).

tekhnē, pl. *tekhnai* (f.): art, a reasoned habit of mind in making something (*Nicomachean Ethics* 6.4.3 in Appendix I.B).

theoros, pl. *theoroi* (m.): a spectator; one who listens to a speech but is not asked to take a specific action, as in the case of epideictic (1.3.2).

topos, pl. *topoi* (m.): topic; a mental "place" where an argument can be found or the argument itself; in 1.2.21, a form or strategy of argument usable in demonstrating propositions on any subject, to be distinguished from an *idion,* which is a proposition specific to some body of knowledge (twenty-eight such *topoi* are described in 2.23); but in 1.15.19 *idia* are referred to as (specific) topics. See also note on 3.15.2.

Bibliography

Modern Editions of the Greek Text of the *Rhetoric*

Dufour, Médéric, and André Wartelle. 1960–73. *Aristote, "Rhétorique"*
    With French translation. 3 vols. Paris: Les Belles Lettres.
Kassel, Rudolf. 1976. *Aristotelis "Ars Rhetorica"*. Berlin: De Gruyter.
Ross, W. David. 1959. *Aristotelis "Ars Rhetorica"*. Oxford: Clarendon.

Translations of the *Rhetoric*

Cooper, Lane, trans. [1932] 1960. *The Rhetoric of Aristotle*. New York:
    Appleton-Century-Crofts.
Freese, John H., trans. 1926. *Aristotle, "The 'Art' of Rhetoric"*. With
    Greek text. Cambridge: Loeb Classical Library. Harvard Univer-
    sity Press.
Roberts, W. Rhys, trans. 1924. *Rhetorica = The Works of Aristotle*.
    Vol.11. Oxford: Clarendon. Rpt. 1954 in *Aristotle, "Rhetoric" and
    "Poetics"*. trans. W. Rhys Roberts and Ingram Bywater. New York:
    Modern Library. Also rpt., with corrections, 1984 in *The Works of
    Aristotle*. ed. Jonathan Barnes, 2.2 152–2269. Princeton: Princeton
    University Press.

Books and Articles Referred to in the Notes, with Additional Works Useful for Study of the *Rhetoric*

Adamik, Tomás. 1984. "Aristotle's Theory of the Period." *Philologus* 128: 184–201.

Arnauld, Antoine. 1858. *La Logique, ou l'art de penser.* Paris: Jules Delalain.

Arnhart, Larry. 1981. *Aristotle on Political Reasoning.* DeKalb: Northern Illinois University Press.

Barnes, Jonathan, Malcolm Schofield, and Richard Sorabji, eds. 1979. *Articles on Aristotle: Psychology and Aesthetics.* London: Duckworth.

Benoit, W. L. 1980. "Aristotle's Example: The Rhetorical Induction," *Quarterly Journal of Speech* 66:182–92.

Blettner, Elizabeth. 1983. "One Made Many and Many Made One: The Role of Asyndeton in Aristotle's *Rhetoric.*" *Philosophy and Rhetoric* 16:49–54.

Brandes, Paul D. 1989. *A History of Aristotle's "Rhetoric".* Metuchen, N.J.: Scarecrow.

Burkert, Walter. 1975. "Aristoteles im Theater: Zur Datierung des 3. Buch der *Rhetorik* und der *Poetik.*" *Museum Helveticum* 32.67–72.

Carawan, E. M. 1983. "*Erotēsis:* Interrogation in the Courts of Fourth-Century Athens." *Greek, Roman, and Byzantine Studies* 24:209–26.

Chroust, Anton-Hermann. 1964. "Aristotle's Earliest Course of Lectures on Rhetoric." *L'Antiquité Classique* 33.58–72. Rpt. in Erickson 1974:22–36.

Conley, Thomas. 1982. "*Pathē* and *Pisteis:* Aristotle, *Rhet.* II 2–11." *Hermes* 110:300–315.

———. 1984. "The Enthymeme in Pespective." *Quarterly Journal of Speech* 70:168–87.

———. 1990a. *Rhetoric in the European Tradition.* New York: Longman.

———. 1990b. "Aristotle's *Rhetoric* in Byzantium." *Rhetorica* 8:29–44.

Consigny, Scott. 1987. "Transparency and Displacement: Aristotle's Concept of Rhetorical Clarity." *Rhetoric Society Quarterly* 17:413–19.

Cope, Edward M. [1867] 1970. *An Introduction to Aristotle's "Rhetoric".* Reprint. Hildesheim: Olms.

———. [1877] 1970. *The "Rhetoric" of Aristotle, with a Commentary.* 3 vols. Ed. J. E. Sandys. Reprint. Hildesheim: Olms.

Corbett, Edward P. J. 1990. *Classical Rhetoric for the Modern Student.* 3d. ed. New York: Oxford University Press.

Donadi, Francesco. 1983. *Gorgiae Leontini in Helenam laudatio*. Rome: Bretschneider.

Douglas, Alan E. 1955. "The Aristotelian *Synagōgē Technōn* After Cicero, *Brutus,* 46–48." *Latomus* 14:536–39.

Dover, Kenneth J. 1974. *Greek Popular Morality in the Time of Plato and Aristotle*. Berkeley: University of California Press.

———. 1978. *Greek Homosexuality*. Cambridge: Harvard University Press.

Düring, Ingmar. 1957. *Aristotle in the Ancient Biographical Tradition* Göteborg: Göteborg University.

———. 1966. *Aristoteles: Darstellung und Interpretation seinen Denken*. Heidelberg: Carl Winter Verlag.

Edel, Abraham. 1982. *Aristotle and His Philosophy*. Chapel Hill: University of North Carolina Press.

Eden, Kathy. 1986. *Poetic and Legal Fiction in the Aristotelian Tradition*. Princeton: Princeton University Press.

Eggs, Ekkhard. 1984. *Die "Rhetorik" des Aristoteles: Ein Beitrag zur Theorie der Alltagsargumentation und zur Syntax von Komplexen Sätzen*. Frankfurt: Lang.

Enos, Richard Lee, ed. 1982. "The Most Significant Passage in Aristotle's *Rhetoric:* Five Nominations," *Rhetoric Society Quarterly* 12:2–20.

Erickson, Keith, ed. 1974. *Aristotle: The Classical Heritage of Rhetoric*. Metuchen, N.J.: Scarecrow.

———. 1975. *Aristotle's "Rhetoric": Five Centuries of Philological Research*. Metuchen, N.J.: Scarecrow.

Erlich, Victor. 1981. *Russian Formalism: History–Doctrine*. New Haven: Yale University Press.

Fortenbaugh, William W. 1970. "Aristotle's *Rhetoric on Emotion*." *Archiv für Geschichte der Philosophie* 52:40–70. Rpt. in Erickson 1974: 205–34, and in Barnes et al. 1979:133–53.

———. 1975. *Aristotle on Emotion: A Contribution to Philosophical Psychology, Rhetoric, Poetics, Politics, and Ethics*. New York: Barnes & Noble.

———. 1985. "Theophrastus on Delivery." *Rutgers University Studies* 2:269–88.

———. 1986. "Aristotle's Platonic Attitude Toward Delivery." *Philosophy and Rhetoric* 19:242–54.

Fowler, R. L. 1982. "Aristotle on the Period." *Classical Quarterly* 32:89–99.

Fuhrmann, Manfred. 1960. *Das Systematische Lehrbuch*. Göttingen: Vandenhoeck & Ruprecht.

Gabin, Rosalind J. 1987. "Aristotle and the New Rhetoric: Grimaldi and Valesio." *Philosophy and Rhetoric* 20:170–82.

Gaines, Robert N. 1986. "Aristotle's Rhetorical Rhetoric." *Philosophy and Rhetoric* 19:194–200.

Garver, Eugene. 1986. "Aristotle's *Rhetoric* as a Work of Philosophy." *Philosophy and Rhetoric* 19:1–22.

———. 1988. "Aristotle's *Rhetoric* on Unintentially Hitting the Principles of the Sciences." *Rhetorica* 6:381–93.

Genette, Gérard. 1982. *Figures of Literary Discourse*. Trans. Alan Sheridan. New York: Columbia University Press.

Green, Lawrence D. 1990. "Aristotelian Rhetoric, Dialectic, and the Traditions of *Antistrophos*." *Rhetorica* 8:5–27.

Grimaldi, William M. A. 1975. *Studies in the Philosophy of Aristotle's "Rhetoric"*. Wiesbaden: Steiner.

———. 1980–88. *Aristotle, "Rhetoric": A Commentary*. 2 vols. New York Fordham University Press.

Hamilton, William. [1866] 1969. *Lectures on Logic*. Reprint. Stuttgart: Frommann Verlag.

Hauser, Gerald A. 1968. "The Example in Aristotle's *Rhetoric:* Bifurcation or Contradiction?"*Philosophy and Rhetoric* 1:78–90.

———. 1985. "Aristotle's Example Revisited." *Philosophy and Rhetoric* 18:171–79.

Havelock, Eric A. 1982. *The Literate Revolution in Greece and Its Cultural Consequences*. Princeton: Princeton University Press.

Heidegger, Martin. 1962. *Being and Time*. Trans. John Macquarries and Edward Robinson. New York: Harper & Row.

Hellwig, Antje. 1973. *Untersuchungen zur Theorie der Beredsamkeit bei Platon und Aristoteles*. Göttingen: Vandenhoeck & Ruprecht.

Hill, Forbes. 1981. "The Amorality of Aristotle's *Rhetoric*," *Greek, Roman, and Byzantine Studies* 22:133–47.

Johnstone, C. L. 1980. "An Aristotelian Trilogy: Ethics, Rhetoric, and the Search for Moral Truth." *Philosophy and Rhetoric* 13:1–24.

Kassel, Rudolf. 1971. *Der Text der Aristotelischen "Rhetorik"*. Berlin: De Gruyter.

Kennedy, George A. 1963. *The Art of Persuasion in Greece*. Princeton: Princeton University Press.

———. 1980. *Classical Rhetoric and Its Christian and Secular Tradition from Ancient to Modern Times*. Chapel Hill: University of North Carolina Press.

———, ed. 1989. *The Cambridge History of Literary Criticism*. Vol. 1: *Classical Criticism*. Cambridge: Cambridge University Press.

Killeen, J. F. 1971. "Aristotle, *Rhet.* 1413a." *Classical Philology* 76:186–87.

Kinneavy, James. 1987. "William Grimaldi—Reinterpreting Aristotle" *Philosophy and Rhetoric* 20:183–200.

Leighton, Stephen R. 1982. "Aristotle and the Emotions." *Phronesis* 27:144–74.

Levin, Samuel R. 1982. "Aristotle's Theory of Metaphor." *Philosophy and Rhetoric* 15:24–46.

Lienhard, Joseph T. 1966. "A Note on the Meaning of *Pistis* in Aristotle's *Rhetoric.*" *American Journal of Philology* 87:446–54.

Lord, Carnes. 1981. "The Intention of Aristotle's *Rhetoric.*" *Hermes* 109:326–39.

———. 1986. "On the Early History of the Aristotelian Corpus." *American Journal of Philology* 107:137–61.

Lossau, Manfred. 1974. "Der Aristotelische *Gryllos* antilogisch." *Philologus* 11:12–21.

McCall, Marsh. 1969. *Ancient Rhetorical Theories of Simile and Metaphor.* Cambridge: Harvard University Press.

MacKay, L. A. 1953. "Aristotle, *Rhetoric,* III, 16, 11 (1417b12–20)." *American Journal of Philology* 74:281–86.

Matson, Patricia P., Philip Rollinson, and Marion Sousa, eds. 1990. *Readings from Classical Rhetoric.* Edwardsville: Southern Illinois University Press.

May, James A. 1988. *Trials of Character: The Eloquence of Ciceronian Ethos.* Chapel Hill: University of North Carolina Press.

Merlan, Philip. 1954. "Isocrates, Aristotle, and Alexander the Great." *Historia* 3:68–69.

Miller, Carolyn R. 1987. "Aristotle's 'Special Topics' in Rhetorical Practice and Methodology." *Rhetoric Society Quarterly* 17:61–70.

Mills, Michael J. 1985. "*Phthonos* and Its Related *Pathē* in Plato and Aristotle." *Phronesis* 30:1–12.

Mirhady, David. 1991. "Non-Technical *Pisteis* in Aristotle and Anaximenes." *American Journal of Philology* 112:5–28.

Murphy, James J. 1974. *Rhetoric in the Middle Ages.* Berkeley: University of California Press.

Natali, Carlo. 1989. "*Paradeigma:* The Problems of Human Acting and the Use of Examples in Some Greek Authors of the Fourth Century B.C." *Rhetoric Society Quarterly* 19:141–52.

Nikolaides, A. G. 1982. "Aristotle's Treatment of the Concept of *Proatēs.*" *Hermes* 110:414–22.

Nussbaum, Martha C. 1986. *The Fragility of Goodness.* Cambridge: Cambridge University Press.

Ober, Josiah. 1989. *Mass and Elite in Democratic Athens: Rhetoric, Ideology, and the Power of the People.* Princeton: Princeton University Press.

Ong, Walter J. 1982. *Orality and Literacy: The Technologizing of the Word.* New York: Methuen.

Palmer, Georgiana P. 1934. *The Topoi of Aristotle's "Rhetoric" as Exemplified in the Orators.* Chicago: University of Chicago.

Pearson, Lionel. 1962. *Popular Ethics in Ancient Greece.* Stanford: Stanford University Press.

Pease, A. S. 1926. "Things Without Honor." *Classical Philology* 21:27–42.

Perelman, Chaim, and L. Obrechts-Tyteca. 1969. *The New Rhetoric: A Treatise on Argumentation.* Trans. John Wilkinson and Purcell Weaver. Notre Dame: University of Notre Dame Press.

Rabe, Hugo., ed. 1896. *Commentaria in Aristotelem Graeca.* Vol. 15. Berlin: Reimer.

Radermacher, Ludwig. 1951. *Artium scriptores.* Vienna: Oesterreichische Akademie der Wissenschaften.

Radt, Stefan L. 1979. "Zu Aristoteles *Rhetorik.*" *Mnemosyne* 32:284–306.

Richards, I. A. 1936. *Philosophy of Rhetoric.* Oxford: Oxford University Press.

Ricoeur, Paul. 1977. *The Rule of Metaphor.* Trans. Robert Czerny, Kathleen McLaughlin, and John Costello. Toronto: University of Toronto Press.

Rist, John M. 1989. *The Mind of Aristotle: A Study in Philosophical Growth.* Toronto: University of Toronto Press.

Rorty, A. O. 1984. "Aristotle on the Metaphysical Status of *Pathē.*" *Review of Metaphysics* 37:521–46.

Rosenmeyer, Thomas G. 1955. "Gorgias, Aeschylus, and *Apatē.*" *American Journal of Philology* 76:225–60.

Ryan, Eugene E. 1984. *Aristotle's Theory of Rhetorical Argumentation.* Montreal: Bellarmin.

Schiappa, Edward. 1990. "Did Plato Coin *Rhētorikē?*" *American Journal of Philology* 111:457–70.

Schröder, Joachim. 1985. "Ar. *Rhet.* A2. 1356a35–b10, 1357a22–b1." *Hermes* 113:172–82.

Solmsen, Friedrich. 1929. *Die Entwicklung der Aristotelischen Logik und Rhetorik.* Berlin: Weidmann.

———. 1938. "Aristotle and Cicero on the Orator's Playing Upon the Feelings." *Classical Philology* 33:390–404.

———. 1941. "The Aristotelian Tradition in Ancient Rhetoric." *American Journal of Philology* 62:35–50 and 169–90. Rpt. in Erickson 1974:278–309.

————. 1979. Review of Kassel, *Aristoteles "Ars rhetorica". Classical Philology* 74:68–72.

Sprague, Rosamond Kent, ed. 1972. *The Older Sophists.* Columbia: University of South Carolina Press.

Sprute, Jürgen. 1982. *Die Enthymemtheorie der aristotelischen Rhetorik.* Göttingen: Vandenhoeck & Ruprecht.

Stanford, William B. 1936. *Greek Metaphor.* Oxford: Blackwell.

Thür, Gerhard. 1977. *Beweisführung vor den Schwurgerichthöfen Athens.* Vienna: Oesterreichische Akademie der Wissenschaften.

Toulmin, Stephen. 1958. *Uses of Argument.* Cambridge: Cambridge University Press.

Wartelle, André. 1981. *Lexique de la "Rhétorique" d'Aristote.* Paris: Les Belles Lettres.

Wieland, Wolfgang. 1968. "Aristoteles als Rhetoriker und die Exoterischen Schriften." *Hermes* 86:323–46.

Wikramanayake, George H. 1961. "A Note on the *Pisteis* in Aristotle's *Rhetoric." American Journal of Philology* 82:193–96.

Wisse, Jakob. 1989. *Ethos and Pathos from Aristotle to Cicero.* Amsterdam: Hakkert.

Wooten, Cecil W. 1973. "The Ambassador's Speech: A Particularly Hellenistic Genre of Oratory." *Quarterly Journal of Speech* 59:209–12.

Index

Achilles, 49, 65, 126, 133, 188, 189, 193, 208, 229, 269, 275
Acting, 154, 218–19, 222, 255
Advantageous or beneficial, the, 49, 63, 66, 74, 78, 90, 91, 110–11, 115, 166, 167, 271
Aenesidemus, 101
Aeschines, 271
Aeschylus, 159, 251n, 284n
Aeson, 247
Aesop, 179–80
Agathon, 175–76, 209, 289
Agesipolis, 197
Alcibiades, 170
Alcidamas, 103, 196, 226–28, 254
Alexander of Aphrodisias, 307
Alexander of Troy, 65, 193, 195, 197, 208, 209, 261, 285, 288
Alexander the Great, 6, 31, 304–5
Amasis, 154
Amphiarius, 165
Amplification, 85–87, 118, 173–74; 178, 213–14, 233–34, 256, 281. *See also* Magnitude
Analogy, 199, 246, 296
Anaxagoras, 196
Anaxandrides, 246, 251, 255
Androcion, 229
Androcles of Pitthus, 201
Andronicus of Rhodes, 217, 302, 306

Anger, 90, 104, 121, 124–30
Antimachus, 234
Antiphon of Rhamnus, 193n, 254, 294
Antiphon the Poet, 129, 148–49, 193n, 200
Antisthenes, 230
Antithesis, 242–43, 252, 313
Appelicon of Teos, 306
Appropriateness, *See* Propriety
Archelaus, 195
Archilochus of Paros, 277
Archytas the Pythagorean, 250
Areopagus, 30, 197
Ares, 230, 252, 296
Argument, 9, 39–47, 50–51, 172–215, 310. *See also* Probability, argument from
Aristeides the Just, 194, 261
Aristippus, 197
Aristocracy, 75–77
Aristophanes, 135n, 210n, 226
Aristophon, 194
Aristotle
  Analytics, 33n, 40, 42, 44, 213, 302
  Categories, 71n, 197n
  Constitution of the Athenians, 55n, 106n, 301
  esoteric works, 4
  Eudemian Ethics, 61n, 84n, 92n
  exoteric works, 5, 289

Note: For Greek terms, see Glossary, pp. 313–20. For more detailed indices of the *Rhetoric,* see Kassel 1976, 199–259, and Wartelle 1981.